TOWARD

A GEOPOLITICS OF HOPE

TOWARD
A GEOPOLITICS OF HOPE

WILLIAM H. THORNTON

SONGOK HAN THORNTON

Los Angeles | London | New Delhi
Singapore | Washington DC | Melbourne

First published in 2012 by

SAGE Publications India Pvt Ltd
B1/I-1 Mohan Cooperative Industrial Area
Mathura Road, New Delhi 110 044, India
www.sagepub.in

SAGE Publications Inc
2455 Teller Road
Thousand Oaks, California 91320, USA

SAGE Publications Ltd
1 Oliver's Yard, 55 City Road
London EC1Y 1SP, United Kingdom

SAGE Publications Asia-Pacific Pte Ltd
3 Church Street
#10-04 Samsung Hub
Singapore 049483

Published by Vivek Mehra for SAGE Publications India Pvt Ltd, typeset in 10/13pt Palatino Linotype by Star Compugraphics Private Limited, Delhi.

Library of Congress Cataloging-in-Publication Data

Thornton, William H., 1950–
    Toward a geopolitics of hope/William H. Thornton, Songok Han Thornton.
        p. cm.
    Includes bibliographical references and iondex.
1. Geopolitics—History—21st century.   2. Balance of power—History—21st century.   I. Thornton, Songok Han.   II. Title.

| JC319.T525 | 327.101—dc23 | 2012 | 2012017741 |

ISBN: 978-81-321-0944-0 (HB)

The SAGE Team: Rudra Narayan, Dhurjjati Sarma, and Vijay Sah

For Mom and Hans

Thank you for choosing a SAGE product!
If you have any comment, observation or feedback,
I would like to personally hear from you.

Please write to me at **contactceo@sagepub.in**

Vivek Mehra, Managing Director and CEO, SAGE India.

Bulk Sales

SAGE India offers special discounts
for purchase of books in bulk.
We also make available special imprints
and excerpts from our books on demand.

For orders and enquiries, write to us at

Marketing Department
SAGE Publications India Pvt Ltd
B1/I-1, Mohan Cooperative Industrial Area
Mathura Road, Post Bag 7
New Delhi 110044, India

E-mail us at **marketing@sagepub.in**

Subscribe to our mailing list
Write to **marketing@sagepub.in**

This book is also available as an e-book.

CONTENTS

LIST OF ABBREVIATIONS

ABFSU	All Burma Federation of Student Unions
ABSDF	All Burma Students' Democratic Front
AFSPA	Armed Forces (Special Powers) Act
AIPAC	American Israel Public Affairs Committee
APEC	Asia-Pacific Economic Cooperation
ASBM	Anti-Ship Ballistic Missiles
ASEAN	Association of Southeast Asian Nations
BG	Bilderberg Group
BJP	Bharatiya Janata Party
BSP	Bahujan Samaj Party
BSPP	Burma Socialist Programme Party
BRIC	Brazil, Russia, India, and China
CCP	Chinese Communist Party
CECC	Congressional-Executive Commission on China
CFR	Council on Foreign Relations
CIA	Central Intelligence Agency
CIC	China Investment Cooperation
CIS	Commonwealth of Independent States
CLS	Critical Legal Studies (Movement)
CMAS	Chasi Mulia Adivasi Sangh
CPI(M)	Communist Party of India (Marxist)
CRC	Convention on the Rights of the Child
CTBT	Comprehensive Test Ban Treaty
DPP	Democratic Progressive Party
DRC	Democratic Republic of the Congo
EATO	Euro-Atlantic Treaty Organization

FAR	Rwandan Armed Forces
FDI	Foreign Direct Investment
FER	Foreign Exchange Reserves
FSB	Federal Security Service
GAIL	Gas Authority of India Limited
GCC	Gulf Cooperation Council
GE	General Electric
GNP	Gross National Product
GPA	Global Political Agreement
ILGI	Informal Local Governance Institutions
IMF	International Monetary Fund
IOC	International Olympic Committee
KIA	Kachin Independence Army
KNU	Karen National Union
LDF	Left Democratic Front
LSE	London School of Economics
MCA	Millennium Challenge Account
MCC	Maoist Communist Centre
MENA	Middle East and North Africa
MFN	Most Favored Nation
MITI	Ministry of International Trade and Industry
NAM	Non-Aligned Movement
NEDB	National Economic Development Board
NGO	Non-Governmental Organization
NLD	National League for Democracy
NPT	Non-Proliferation Treaty
NREGS	National Rural Employment Guarantee Scheme
NSG	Nuclear Suppliers Group
NTC	National Transitional Council
OSCE	Organization for Security and Cooperation in Europe
PAP	People's Action Party
PLA	People's Liberation Army
PPP	Purchasing Power Parity
PR	Public Relations
PRC	People's Republic of China
PSPC	Poststructural and Postcolonial Theory
PWG	People's War Group
R2P	Responsibility to Protect
RBI	Reserve Bank of India
RDF	Rapid Deployment Force
RIL	Reliance Industries Limited

ROC	Russian Orthodox Church
RPF	Rwandan Patriotic Front
SAARC	South Asian Association for Regional Co-operation
SADC	Southern African Development Community
SAP	Structural Adjustment Programs
SCO	Shanghai Cooperation Organization
SEZ	Special Economic Zone
SLORC	State Law and Order Restoration Council
SOE	State-Owned Enterprises
SPDC	State Peace and Development Council
SWF	Sovereign Wealth Fund
TAR	Tibet Autonomous Region
TC	Trilateral Commission
TCC	Transnational Capitalist Class
TNC	Transnational Corporation
TVE	Township and Village Enterprise
UMNO	United Malays National Organisation
UNOCAL	Union Oil Company of California
UPA	United Progressive Alliance
VHP	Vishwa Hindu Parishad

ACKNOWLEDGMENT

The authors wish to thank the *Journal of Developing Societies and World Affairs: The Journal of International Issues* for allowing us to use parts of articles previously published with them.

INTRODUCTION

SECOND WORLD REDUX
The Case for Moral Realism

A HOUSE DIVIDED

It has been a quarter of a century since Paul Kennedy posted his prophetic warning of America's military overstretch and impending economic slide.[1] He got the timing wrong, but was more than vindicated by the Bush-era meltdown of America's global standing. That sea change now reaches to the West in general, and carries profound ideological implications. The Western democratic experiment of the last two centuries looks far more tentative and parochial than it did in the late 1980s. "Globalization" turns out to be anything but the steadfast ally of democratization it purports to be. It is, in fact, the greatest gift to a new breed of authoritarian capitalists.

The case of China alone is enough to dispel the notion that capitalism and democracy are two sides of the same globalist coin. This neoliberal shibboleth was disputed long before by the proponents of so-called Asian values, but that hardly mattered so long as these repressive "values" were safely sequestered in the sphere of Asian exceptionalism. Now, however, they are being packaged for global export. What had been taken as a passing illiberal phase, closely resembling the undemocratic character of early Western capitalism, is starting to look like a permanent feature of

---

[1] Paul Kennedy, *The Rise and Fall of the Great Powers: Economic Change and Military Conflict from 1500 to 2000* (Hammersmith, UK: Fontana Press, 1988), 666 and 679.

21st century development. As Slavoj Žižek puts it, the China model may be less a reminder of our past than a portent of our future.[2]

This is the dark side of the phenomenal "reOrientization"—to slightly revise Andre Gunder Frank's term[3]—that is turning globalization on its head ideologically.[4] Authoritarian capitalism is already on full and unabashed display in the Beijing Consensus, or what we term Sino-globalization.[5] Though capitalism is very much on the march globally, democracy is on the wane. A new authoritarian order is taking shape, this time within, rather than against, the capitalist world order. Post–Cold War triumphalism was obviously premature in the funeral it staged for the Second World, defined in terms of its autocracy rather than its erstwhile communism.

A failure to appreciate the scope and significance of today's intra-capitalist schism allows Western leaders to imagine that they are still at the helm of globalization, slowly but surely steering a recalcitrant "East" in their direction. Meanwhile, much of the developing world is moving in the opposite direction—toward the Asianism that Frank predicted, but more specifically toward a highly reactionary strain of Asian values. The capitalist character of these values lulls Western globalists into indifference regarding the draconian politics of the new Second World. For many in high places, it is still inconceivable that global capitalism could be a house divided.

Thus, President Obama, during his first trip to China, took a position that astonished his more liberal supporters, but was sure to please his hosts. To the consternation of rights activists throughout the world, he followed the lead of his Secretary of State, Hillary Clinton, in calling for extraordinary "patience" on the human rights front. Instead of pressing China to mend its ways, this administration was asking democracy and human rights

---

[2] Slavoj Žižek, "China's Valley of Tears: Is Authoritarian Capitalism the Future?" *In These Times* (December 3, 2007), http://www.inthesetimes.com/main/print/3425/

[3] See Andre Gunder Frank, *ReOrient: Global Economy in the Asian Age* (Berkeley: University of California Press, 1998).

[4] In this respect it is more meaningful to speak of an ideological chasm between the Global "East and West" than the "North and South," since the moral injunction of the Global South (most famously voiced in dependency theory) is not incompatible with the North's concept of justice. The North–South gap is therefore one of practice rather than principle. By contrast, our figurative (rather than strictly geographic) "East–West" dichotomy connotes a deep contest of cultural norms that closely resembles Leon Trotsky's allusion to the divide between the Asian knout and the "liberal" capitalism of the West. The unresolved contradictions of Western liberalism allowed for neoliberalism's fateful accord with Dengism, Putinism and the newly capitalized Second World.

[5] See William H. Thornton, "Sino-Globalization: Politics of the CCP/TNC Symbiosis," *New Political Science: A Journal of Politics & Culture* 29, no. 2 (June 2007): 211–35.

advocates to shelve their concerns indefinitely.[6] Apparently Obama felt he had little leverage with America's major creditor in the midst of a protracted recession. Whatever the reason for his diffidence, this was not the defiantly "liberal" president that the world had expected.

Even more than the Beijing Olympics had, this visit signaled a changing of the guard in world affairs. At the very least, it suggested the parity of China and America in terms of global clout. Even President Bill Clinton had managed to get some human rights concessions in return for his execrable "about face" on China. The rights community well remembers that the famous dissident, Wang Dan, was released just prior to Clinton's arrival. Obama did not even press for such gratuities. His one urgent request was that China revalue its currency, unpegging it from the falling US dollar. Beijing not only refused, but went on the offensive by having its chief banking regulator, Liu Mingkang, blast America for fueling global speculation by holding interest rates so low.[7] Needless to say, there would be no discussion of human rights reform, much less general political reform.

Nor is present scholarship very attentive to these issues. An entire academic industry has been developed to explain away the plainly fascistic nature of the new authoritarian capitalism. For years there was talk of village-level democratization in China. When that idea proved farcical, true believers turned with equal avidity to new apologetic devices, ranging from so-called e-democracy to the idea of "intra-Party democracy."[8] That term is often applied to the Chinese Communist Party (CCP), much as the term "managed democracy" is applied with a straight face to Putin's United Russia Party. In both cases, the crux of the issue is an uncanny confusion of party factionalism with democratic pluralism.

The West quite literally "buys" this democratic hokum, investing billions in regimes that are dedicated to the extirpation of Western political ideals. Part of the reason, of course, is the lure of mega-profits, but there is also the false assumption that robust capitalism—which for neoliberals means unregulated capitalism—is by definition, a prelude to progressive politics. Given this hermetic paradigm, no amount of contrary evidence could dislodge the idea that democracy is waiting right around the corner

---

[6] In response, the Chinese toughened their stance. Dissidents were detained, and Obama's vaunted "town hall" meeting with Chinese students was all but blacked out. See Jonathan Weisman, Andrew Browne, and Jason Dean, "Obama Hits a Wall on His Visit to China," *The Wall Street Journal* (November 19, 2009), http://online.wsj.com/article/SB125857743503654225.html

[7] *Ibid.*

[8] For example, Cheng Li, "The Chinese Communist Party: Recruiting and Controlling the New Elites," *Journal of Current Chinese Affairs*, 38, no. 3 (2009): 25 (13–33).

wherever corporate profits beckon. Putting the halo of political liberalism over capitalism as such begs the question of what political system—be it Yeltsin's or even Putin's—could possibly *not* be judged proto-democratic. Still more outrageous is the idea that party factionalism is inherently democratic. By this standard, even the Soviet Union under Stalin or China under Mao would qualify, so long as Trotsky or Lin Biao were on hand to provide an intra-party challenge.

By these preposterous standards, President Hu Jintao and the upcoming fifth generation of CCP leaders can be taken as a democratic vanguard, simply because they lack the party unity that Deng could muster. Chinese advisors like Susan Shirk, for fear of a hardline reaction, have urged Washington to avoid any direct confrontation with nominal "reformists" like Hu and Premier Wen Jiabao.[9] This diffidence is now planted so deeply in the marrow of US–China policy that it scarcely matters if a Democrat or Republican occupies the Oval Office. Unqualified "engagement" with the CCP and its ilk is ingrained in the bipartisan Washington Consensus.

The price of such appeasement is already sorely felt in human rights terms, and is going to be equally costly in security terms as well. Right and might can no longer be segregated in the hackneyed manner of economic modernism and geopolitical realism. The moral realism we posit puts the ethical factor at the center of world affairs, though not to the exclusion of effective power politics. Every human rights abuse that we fail to protest will be a battle lost in a new kind of Cold War, where values will increasingly define conflicts and alliances, not to mention our own geopolitical resolve. Resource competition will exacerbate this coming "war of the worlds," but it is extremely unlikely that democratic nations will choose war, or even the threat of war, as a way to resolve resource conflicts between themselves. That is not the case where democratic and authoritarian nations are locked in similar conflicts of interest. In coming years, the ultimate arbiter of war and peace is going to be political values.

One must concur with Robert Kagan when he says that "the old competition between liberalism and autocracy has reemerged, with the world's great powers increasingly lining up according to the nature of their regimes."[10]

---

[9] Reformist hopes are now more vested in Wen than Hu, as Hu has tended to side with conservative commissars like Li Changchun, PR chief of the CCP, and Liu Yunshan, director of the Propaganda Department. Both have faulted Wen for advocating "universal values" that suggest the need for political liberalization. See Willy Lam, "Rivalry Grows Between China's Top Leaders," *Asia Sentinel* (August 30, 2010), http://www.asiasentinel. com/index.php?option=com_content&task=view&id=2668&Itemid=171

[10] Robert Kagan, *The Return of History and the End of Dreams* (New York: Alfred A. Knopf, 2008), 4. Kagan's position could be described as a moral realism of the Right,

What Kagan completely ignores, however, is the present ideological crisis within the "liberal" camp itself, whereby (neo) liberal economics erodes the material and spiritual foundations of political liberalism, including what Amartya Sen has termed "development as freedom."[11] Kagan's powerful critique of the new authoritarianism is compromised by his silence concerning the odious nature of the new global capitalism. It is arguable that many of today's autocracies are even more "capitalistic" than Western countries that fuse capitalism and democracy, diluting both.

It turns out that globalist economism and democracy are anything but the natural allies that neoliberals posit.[12] Azar Gat understands their seeming alliance as a double contingency: the accident of their coexistence in American history, plus the accident of America's phenomenal influence since World War II.[13] We take this point one step farther by suggesting that the closer compatibility is between globalism and some forms of authoritarianism, however covert. This not only works against formative democracies, but tends to erode established ones as well. The economic elite that Leslie Sklair calls the transnational capitalist class (TCC)[14] finds ways to buy political power. That purchase can be effected through outright vote buying, as in Thailand, or indirectly through the labyrinth of campaign finance, as in the US. Either way, as Carl Boggs warns, the result is a rise of corporate power and a decline of the public sphere.[15]

Meanwhile, an even larger external threat looms on the horizon. Gat is right to reserve his greatest concern for authoritarianisms that combine the dynamics of global capitalism with open anti-democratism. A whole army of Anna Politkovskayas could not fend off the nightmare of Russia's Putinism or China's CCPism. It follows that authoritarian capitalism, not Muslim terrorism, is the foremost security threat of our times.[16]

---

whereas ours is of the Left. Our points of overlap are nonetheless substantial, as will be obvious if one compares them with the amoral realism of a Kissinger. For a 21st century update of such pure-power realism, see Leslie H. Gelb, *Power Rules: How Common Sense Can Rescue American Foreign Policy* (New York: HarperCollins, 2009).

[11] Amartya Sen, *Development as Freedom* (New York: Alfred A. Knopf, 1999).

[12] The core assumption of globalism, as John Ralston Saul construes it, is the perception "that civilization should be seen through economics, and economics alone." See John Ralston Saul, *The Collapse of Globalism and the Reinvention of the World* (Woodstock and New York: The Overlook Press, 2005), 35.

[13] Azar Gat, "The Return of Authoritarian Great Powers," *Foreign Affairs* 86, no. 4 (July/August 2007): 64 (59–69).

[14] Leslie Sklair, *The Transnational Capitalist Class* (Oxford, UK: Blackwell Publishers, 2001).

[15] Carl Boggs, *The End of Politics: Corporate Power and the Decline of the Public Sphere* (New York: Guilford Press, 2000), *passim*.

[16] See Gat, *op. cit.*, 59.

What is harder to accept is Gat's residual optimism regarding America's future developmental influence. A far more pessimistic assessment was provided by Parag Khanna's *Second World*,[17] which foresaw a US decline relative to an ascendant China and Europe. Half of that thesis is now obsolete, just three years after its publication.

With the EU insolvent and in danger of total dissolution, and with the US mired in a chronic economic slide, the China model seems to shine even brighter, while the erstwhile Washington Consensus has given way to a broad and revanchist post-Americanism.[18] Far from being a global magnet, the American model is increasingly taken as a blueprint for how *not* to develop.

The prime mover behind this anti-American recoil is not just the geopolitical balancing act that realists had expected after the Cold War. No less it is a moral reflex, born of revulsion at Washington's "unipolar" mode of globalism after the Cold War. Developing countries were pressured to accept a "one size fits all" structural adjustment that included the removal of controls on capital flows. Again and again this led to disaster, yet the new orthodoxy was not adjusted in view of these test results. If the most infamous case in point was the unnecessary trauma of Washington's "rescue" operation after the 1997–98 Asian Crash, the prototype was the virtual seizure of the Mexican economy by the International Monetary Fund (IMF) in 1982.

The glory years of neoliberal globalization were years of stagnation for most of the Third World. That of course made these blighted economies all the more dependent upon IMF assistance. After so much deceit and so many shattered hopes—the latest chapter, one might say, in the saga of Eduardo Galeano's *Open Veins of Latin America*, but on a global scale—one can scarcely blame the Third World for being suspicious of anything that smacks of US corporate interests.

Even within the IMF, there was grudging recognition of the fact that the neoliberal system was dysfunctional. However, instead of changing the system, IMF "reforms" simply called for a more gradual implementation of neoliberal goals. This resulted in an irrational schism between gradualists (who did, at least, have regrets over the damage neoliberalism was causing) and "big bang" purists who wanted to solve the problem of Third World recalcitrance by accelerating the process and using the resulting shock

---

[17] Parag Khanna, *The Second World: Empires and Influence in the New Global Order* (New York: Random House, 2008).

[18] See Walden Bello, "The Post-Washington Dissensus," *Transnational Institute* (September 17, 2007), http://www.tni-org/detail_page.phtml?act_id=17336

effect to crush all resistance. Neither group was ready to give an inch on ultimate globalist objectives.[19]

Unless America and the West in general can escape this neoliberal taint,[20] the developing world will be inclined to embrace the Beijing Consensus or some other authoritarian model on the rebound. That reverse-effect gathered so much force through the Bush years that by 2008 the whole edifice of globalization was on borrowed time, both morally and financially. Those two aspects were inseparable, for America's illusion of economic well-being rested on its borrowing capacity, which in turn rested on its willingness to ignore the dictatorial repression of its major creditor, China.

Globalization, in short, has depended on a quid pro quo whereby the West sold out its most basic principles for borrowed affluence. Given the economic as well as ethical and ecological unsustainability of this system, all that was needed to bring it down was the right global tremor, which was

---

[19] Jeffrey M. Chwieroth, *Capital Ideas: The IMF and the Rise of Financial Liberalization* (Princeton, NJ: Princeton University Press, 2010), 2.

[20] See David Harvey, "The Crisis of the Consolidation of Class Power," *Counterpunch* (March 13/15, 2009), http://www.counterpunch.org/harvey03132009.html

Despite its initial New Deal simulation, the Obama administration did a fine job of resuscitating the financial heart of neoliberalism. See Paul Krugman, "The Market Mystique," *The New York Times* (March 27, 2009), http://www.nytimes.com/2009/03/27/opinion/27krugman.html and Joseph E. Stiglitz, "Obama's Ersatz Capitalism," *The New York Times*, http://www.nytimes.com/2009/04/01/opinion/ 01stiglitz.html

To appreciate the scope of Obama's neoliberal ties, consider the globalist affiliations of some of his original advisers:

- Treasury Secretary, Timothy Geithner—Bilderberg Group (BG), Trilateral Commission (TC)
- Secretary of State, Hillary Rodham Clinton—BG, Council on Foreign Relations (CFR), married to TC member Bill Clinton
- Ambassador to the UN, Susan Rice—TC
- National Security Advisor, Gen. James L. Jones—BG, TC, CFR
- Department National Security Advisor, Thomas Donilon—CFR, TC
- Special State Department Envoy, Henry Kissinger—BG, TC, CFR
- Chairman of the Economic Recovery Committee, Paul Volcker—BG, TC, CFR
- Director of National Security, Adm. Dennis C. Blair—BG, TC, CFR
- Secretary of Defense, Robert Gates—BG, TC, CFR
- Department Secretary of State, James Steinberg—BG, TC, CFR
- State Department Special Envoy, Richard M. Haass—BG, TC, CFR (President)
- Presidential Advisor, Alan Greenspan—BG, TC, CFR
- State Department Special Envoy, the late Richard C. Holbrooke—BG, TC, CFR

See Roberto Jelash, "Review: The Obama Deception by Alex Jones," *Infonews.com* (March 16, 2009), http://www.infowars.com/review-the-obama-deception-by-alex-jones/

amply supplied by the 2008 financial crisis. Suddenly, worldwide demand for copies of *Das Kapital* could hardly be met by publishers.[21]

The ethical poverty of global capitalism was suggested by Slavoj Žižek's observation that ex-communist apparatchiks were much better able to adapt to the sordid realities of actually existing capitalism than could most anti-communist idealists.[22] The latter—much like Francis Fukuyama on the American side—were handicapped by their conception of capitalism as a democratic wonderland. Thanks to the Great Recession of 2008, the truth was out, even if the major players were in denial. The myth of a benign and universally appealing globalization has gone the way of Wilson's "war to end all wars."

That, however, was only half of the 2008 shock effect. Another rude awakening was in store for market fundamentalists who thought that "great game" geopolitics had been permanently retired by the geoeconomic gospel of corporate deregulation and unfettered global finance. As late as the summer of 2008, these true believers held firm to their notion that the only thing between them and global hegemony was Osama bin Laden and his ilk. Then came the second of 2008's double-barreled blasts. The Russian invasion of Georgia in August 2008 was in some ways more shocking to globalists than 9/11, for this was the work of a fellow G8 member.

RUSSIA AND THE NEW COLD WAR

Many world leaders got this news while attending the opening ceremonies of the Beijing Olympics. Comparisons would be made to Prague Spring, or even to Hitler's attack on the Sudetenland. However, as Charles King notes, the best comparison is to Russia's invasion of the Crimean Peninsula and the subsequent Crimean War of 1853–56. It was here that Russia broke definitively with the West, setting a pattern of militarist rancor and ultimate defeat that would be repeated up through the Cold War. What distinguishes the Georgia case from this pattern, King observes, is that today "there are plenty of other countries, from China and Venezuela to Iran and Syria, that share Russia's view of the global order."[23]

---

[21] One of its German publishers reported sales in the thousands in 2008, as compared with about 100 the year before. See Leo Panitch, "Thoroughly Modern Marx," *Foreign Policy* (May/June 2009), http://www.foreignpolicy.com/story/cms.php?story_id=4856

[22] See Slavoj Žižek, "Post-Wall," *London Review of Books* 31, no. 22 (November 19, 2009): 10.

[23] Charles King, "The Five-Day War: Managing Moscow After the Georgia Crisis," *Foreign Affairs* 86, no. 6 (November/December 2008): 3 (2–11).

For those who missed the earlier danger signals, Georgia served warning that a new era had dawned in East–West relations, and that Russia was effectively "turning East."[24] Already Russia and China claim to be "strategic partners," and a host of lesser powers are leaning in the same direction. That is not to say that Moscow is cutting its ties with the West per se. It is simply locking out the ideological tradition that has viewed capitalism and democracy as liberal soul mates. Georgia was a belated wake-up call for those who had somehow slept through the Chechen nightmare and the litany of Putinist rants of recent years.

Even this awakening, however, did not translate into much corrective action. Ironically, it was Russia's allies in the Shanghai Cooperation Organization (SCO) who signaled their disapproval of the invasion in terms that might give Moscow second thoughts about a repeat performance.[25] That too shows how much the global balance of power has shifted since the Cold War. For all its complaints about North Atlantic Treaty Organization (NATO) expansion, Russia's greatest anxiety has also started to "turn East." Brighter analysts in Moscow surely know that they have much more to fear from Beijing than from Washington or NATO. The 2008 invasion was, in fact, a confirmation of how little fear Moscow has of NATO.

With the First World in manifest retreat, Russia not only went on the offensive in Georgia but threw down the glove to NATO in classic Cold War language. This was all the more shocking because President Dmitry Medvedev had been greeted early in 2008 as the great corporate hope of the West. Now he seemed bent on confirming the prediction of Andrei Illarionov, Putin's former chief economic advisor, that he would overcompensate by becoming more a Putinist than Putin.[26] Medvedev summed up the new Kremlinism in one sentence: "We're not afraid of anything, [including] the prospect of a Cold War."[27]

---

[24] On this "Eastward" turn, see William H. Thornton and Songok Han Thornton, "Russia Turns East: Putinism and the Making of the New Second World," *Journal of Developing Societies* 24, no. 4 (October–December 2008): 439–63.

[25] That disapproval, in turn, sparked Russian resentment and no doubt was a factor in Moscow's subsequent cooling of its relations with Beijing. Russia's brutal sinking of a Chinese cargo vessel in Russian waters in February 2009 would have been unthinkable just a year before. But what is most significant about this sinking is how both sides understood the need to shelve the incident as fast as possible. It would not become the Sino-Russian equivalent of the Hainan Incident which, with far less provocation, rocked Sino-American relations early in 2001.

[26] Arkady Ostrovsky, "Swaggering on," *The Economist* (November 19, 2008), http://www.economist.com/ PrinterFriendly.cfm?story_id=12494494

[27] Adrian Blomfield and Damien McElroy, "Russia 'Ready for new Cold War' over Georgia," *Telegraph* (August 27, 2008), http: //www.telegraph.co.uk/news/worldnews/Europe/Georgia/2629981/Russia-ready-for-new-Cold-War-over-Georgia.html

The big question is how the West can and should react. So far, its response has left no doubt that broad support for democratic "color revolutions" is over. An odd assortment of Right-wing realists and old school Leftists has joined hands in granting Russia a "sphere of influence" that includes Georgia.[28] Meanwhile neoliberals and cosmopolitans—clearly joined by President Obama at the London G-20 Summit of April 2009—cling to the tattered hope that Russia can be brought in from the cold through the right mix of commercial and organizational elixirs. These latter-day dreamers of a new world order are loath to admit that in many places where Europe would expect to hold cultural sway, including Hungary and even Belarus, globalism has abandoned any pretense of having democratic and humanitarian priorities. Those bedrock Western values were supposed to ensure political development after the Cold War. Francis Fukuyama set this mold by declaring "history" (no pun intended) a thing of the past. Henceforth, outside the Islamic world, only (neo)liberal democracy would count as a viable political end.[29]

Unfortunately, "history" turned out to be very much a thing of the future. Russia under Putin was resource-rich enough to jettison democracy and human rights. Loose and abundant credit from Western banks sent an unequivocal signal to the Kremlin that what really counted for the hypocritical West was the economic bottom line. So long as profits flowed West, Russia had no reason to fear commercial censure. Meanwhile, the Kremlin could gain domestic and Third World stature by not acting the part of a pliant member of the jaded new world order.

(Neo)liberal institutionalists like Anne-Marie Slaughter—drawing on the liberal–functionalist faith in natural cooperation between states—insist that in today's world "the measure of power is connectedness."[30] However, it is precisely Moscow's ability to spurn globalist cooperation when it so chooses that validates its global credentials. Russia does connect, but on its own "sultanistic" terms, to borrow Max Weber's word for

---

[28] Michael Walzer, "Spheres of Influence," *Dissent* (September 15, 2008), http://www.dissentmagazine.org/online.php?id=143. Likewise some on the far Left are ready to consign nearly the whole South China Sea to China's "sphere of influence." See, for example, Justin Raimondo, "China: The Next Big Enemy? The Domestic Politics of the New Sinophobia," *Antiwar.com* (March 11, 2009), http://antiwar.com/horton/?articleid=14384

[29] Francis Fukuyama, *The End of History and the Last Man* (New York: The Free Press, 1992), 211.

[30] See Anne-Marie Slaughter, "America's Edge: Power in the Networked Century," *Foreign Affairs*, 88, no. 1 (January/February 2009): 94 (94–113).

authoritarian regimes that specialize in patronage and cronyism.[31] Although the Kremlin no longer has a universal ideology to impart to the world, as the Soviets possessed in communism, it has the next best thing: the distinction of being the most spiteful "anti" member of an increasingly anti-American Second World. One explanation for this belligerence is that it is little more than a restoration after a brief and very un-Russian detour.

Vladimer Papava (a former Georgian minister of the economy and member of parliament) argues that the Cold War never ended, but was merely "frozen" during the Gorbachev and Yeltsin years.[32] To the extent that he is right, the new Cold War merely takes geopolitics out of cold storage. Whether Western policies of the 1990s sparked Cold War II or simply failed to finalize Cold War I, grievous mistakes were made, and Moscow has a legitimate axe to grind with the West. The neoliberal "shock therapy" that was imposed on Russia in the name of neoliberal "reform" made many ordinary Russians feel they were living in occupied territory. The country suffered a five-year drop in life expectancy between 1991 and 1994, and by 2008 that figure had fallen to 60 years for Russian men, as opposed to 67 in 1985.[33] This was happening even as Russia was doing well in aggregate growth terms and even better in regional power politics. Flush with oil and natural gas revenues, the nation bounced back onto the geopolitical stage, yet continued to suffer population losses on a wartime scale.[34]

GDP growth helped to camouflage the deterioration of general living conditions. With the Russian population imploding and the military shrinking, the Georgia offensive can be seen as a case of geopolitical false advertising. On closer inspection, the war reveals glaring weaknesses in military tactics, equipment, communications, and intelligence.[35] And this is just the tip of the iceberg. At the annual Defense Ministry Conference in November 2008, a document was quietly released which revealed a plan to cut the Russian officer corps from 355,000 to 150,000 and to close 80 percent of the military's

---

[31] See Leon Aron, "21st-Century Sultanate," *The American: A Magazine of Ideas* (November 14, 2008), http://www.american.com/archive/2008/november-december-magazine/21st-century-sultanate

[32] Vladimer Papava, "The End of the Frozen Cold War? A Comment," *Caucasian Review of International Affairs*, 3, no. 1 (Winter 2009): 98–102.

[33] Judy Dempsey, "Study Looks at Mortality in Post-Soviet Era," *The New York Times* (January 16, 2009), http://www.nytimes.com/2009/01/16/world/europe/16europe.html

[34] Nicholas Eberstadt, "Drunken Nation: Russia's Depopulation Bomb," *World Affairs* (Spring 2009), http://www.worldaffairsjournal.org/2009%20-%20Spring/full-Eberstadt.html

[35] Fred Weir, "In Georgia, Russia Saw its Army's Shortcomings," *The Christian Science Monitor* (October 10, 2008), http://www.csmonitor.com/2008/1010/p01s01-woeu.html

educational institutions. This amounts to the dismantlement of the imperial conscript military that is a basic prerequisite for Putinism.

Perhaps to save face, President Medvedev now talks of plans for a fully restored mega-military. This is hard to imagine in view of the country's economic plight, plus the fact that demographic shrinkage has cut the conscript pool in half.[36] In any case, the previously announced military downsizing offers insight into the real opinions of Moscow's strategic planners. Beneath its inflammatory rhetoric, the Kremlin does not actually consider NATO much of a threat. Such talk is at once a diplomatic bargaining chip and a way of diverting attention from Russia's internal woes.

A more exigent concern, at the time of the "color revolutions," was regional democratization, but even that worry has abated recently, especially after the victory of the pro-Russian Viktor Yanukovych in Ukraine's presidential election of February 2010. Events in Belarus and Hungary leave no doubt that this reversal is a regional trend. The most pressing problem facing Moscow is internal rather than external. Its own social and economic decay heightens its sense of vulnerability, making it more suspicious of the West than at any time since the Cold War. This wariness is more a product of economic and cultural anxiety than of military insecurity.

The dam finally broke in 2008, as oil prices plummeted from nearly $150 per barrel to about $40. That made it increasingly difficult for Russia to play its chosen role as the region's apex hegemon. With a plunging ruble and corporate debt at around $500 billion, $50 billion of which was Gazprom's alone, Putinism was marching on thin ice. At the risk of alienating its European clients, Moscow felt compelled to squeeze Ukraine to accept higher gas prices late in 2008. The West saw this as another Putinist power play, but it was also a sign of profound economic trauma. Ukraine held its ground, prompting Moscow's gas shutdown on January 1, 2009.

While part of Russia's dilemma can be blamed on global price fluctuations, another big factor has been the diversion of capital from upkeep and development to the purchase of private companies, not to mention outright graft. This is homegrown crony capitalism. Long before the energy crash, Russia was sinking under the weight of its own corruption and mismanagement. Tellingly, its stock market plunge of 70 percent in 2008 started before the full US crash.[37]

The West, however, cannot afford to let this ailing behemoth go down. That would not only raise the specter of clandestine nuclear sales, but

---

[36] Alexander Golts, "U.S. Not a Threat After All," *The Moscow Times* (November 18, 2008), http://www.themoscowtimes.com/articles/detal.php?ID=372453&print=Y

[37] "Putin, Pipe Down on Ukraine," *The Christian Science Monitor* (January 8, 2009), http://www.csmonitor.com/2009/0108/p08s01-comv.html

would leave an inviting power vacuum in Central Asia and Siberia for China to exploit. Much like prewar Germany at the time of Munich, Russia feels compelled to take foreign policy risks that the West is not prepared to counter. Its very weakness thus translates into a paradoxical strength. The brinkmanship it exhibited in Georgia could be a harbinger of worse things to come if the West does not get its geopolitical act together. That not only means reconstructing a solid intra-European consensus and a renewed Atlanticism, but also forging a global concert of democracies that would encourage rising powers like India and Brazil to follow a liberal rather than a Sino-globalist or Putinist development path.

Perhaps the greatest challenge will be getting Western leaders weaned on the notion of universal capitalist harmony to accept the fact that some capitalist powers are not their natural-born allies. But neither are they natural-born enemies. Despite its Putinist detour, Russia is a swing state that could still be brought in from the cold. This time, however, Russians must be offered something better than the neoliberal cronyism that Bill Clinton brokered with Boris Yeltsin. Until December 2011, which saw the biggest anti-Kremlin demonstrations since the Soviet fall, Russia's two communist parties were the only real threats to Putinism. Meanwhile, Western globalists rushed to strike deals with Putin and his understudy, Medvedev. This collusion between neoliberal and authoritarian capitalisms is globalism's defining act. And, like the Hitler–Stalin pact that it so resembles, this globalist accord will not last long.

A NEW GEOPOLITICAL ERA

It was all too obvious after 2008 that the big winner of current globalization was less likely to be the Washington consensus than its Beijing counterpart. Although China has been boosted by Western capital and technology, it has delivered a stunning blow to conventional wisdom concerning the developmental politics of capitalism. It has not needed a trace of political liberalism to outperform the West in terms of standard growth measures. Indeed, its chief developmental asset seems to be its freedom from that kind of freedom. What Deng Xiaoping called "socialism with Chinese characteristics" was, in fact, privatization with very familiar capitalist characteristics. One of those "Chinese" components, as David Harvey notes, has been undisguised market manipulation,[38] and we may add, an

---

[38] David Harvey, *A Brief History of Neoliberalism* (Oxford, UK: Oxford University Press, 2005), 122.

equally undisguised disregard for ecological sustainability and the welfare of ordinary workers.

That indifference to natural and human welfare is no small part of China's attraction for transnational corporations (TNCs). The corporate dream of union-less factories and freedom from effective environmental regulations (there is no lack of unenforced regulations) has been the supreme gift of the CCP to foreign investors. Western firms love this utterly "un-Western" business climate, and corporate-minded globalists dismiss the East–West value-clash at issue here. American politicians likewise tend to "see no evil," not only because of their deep TNC ties, but also because China does a fine job of misrepresenting itself. We know Beijing means well because it keeps saying so.

This putative softness is appreciated all the more because it stands in stark contrast to the surrounding political climate. President Hu Jintao's pledge of a "peaceful rise" was never much of a crowd pleaser, and also met inner circle resistance. A window on this sentiment was provided by the Asian Cup soccer matches of August 2004, where Japanese players were treated like virtual war criminals. The international community excuses the government for not condemning such behavior on the assumption that it has no choice, depending as it does on exuberant nationalism for its post-communist legitimacy.[39] However, given the CCP's iron grip on the news media, public attitudes are more the product than the producer of government policies.

The main reason for Washington's "see no evil" vantage is no mystery: China is not only corporate America's cheap-labor dreamland—with Wal-Mart alone importing around $18 billion in goods from China annually[40]—but also the US treasury's major creditor. Already the US owes the People's Republic of China (PRC) about $1.5 trillion, or approximately $6,000 per US citizen. Only China has the foreign reserves to service such gargantuan credit needs.[41] The threat is in the air that Beijing might stop buying treasury bonds, and in January and February 2009, it underscored that menace by selling more than it purchased.[42] Call this a soft-power reminder that debtors should not be too critical of creditors.

---

[39] See Minxin Pei, "Beijing's Closed Politics Hinders 'New Diplomacy'," *Financial Times* (September 12, 2004), http://www.carnegieendowment.org/publications/index. cfm?fa=view&id=15836&prog=zch

[40] Fareed Zakaria, *The Post-American World* (New York: Norton, 2008), 91.

[41] John F. Cooper, "China's Clout Grow as U.S. Economy Weakens," *Japan Times* (January 28, 2009), http://wearch.janantimes.co.jp/print/eo20090128a2.html

[42] Keith Bradsher, "China Slows Purchases of U.S. and Other Bonds," *The New York Times* (April 13, 2009), http://www.nytimes.com/2009/04/13/business/global/ 13yuan.html

Clearly, this was an inconvenient time for Washington to begin questioning China's "smile diplomacy" or assailing its human rights record, which the Obama administration was not inclined to do anyway. Nonetheless the tide was turning against the US–China financial symbiosis. Beijing was much aggrieved by the US Federal Reserve's "quantitative easing," which sank the value of the dollar and hence the treasury bonds that China bought en masse. Already China was shifting from treasuries and other US government bonds to hard commodities like iron, oil, and copper. In the first half of 2010, it spent $31 billion on these assets and only $23 billion on US debt instruments.[43] That November the Fed dealt the death blow to the globalist quid pro quo by purchasing $600 billion in government bonds. "QE2," as the tactic was called, may have saved the US stock market, but it spelled an open currency war with China.

This economic rift, which Niall Ferguson sees as the end of "Chimerica,"[44] compounds the muffled political conflict that haunts the current globalist system. The legitimacy of globalism has depended upon keeping this conflict mute. Like Putin, Hu and Wen are hardliners who double as buffers against even more extreme nationalists, or so the story goes. The simple truth is that Washington has found it convenient to protect the globalist status quo by casting these autocrats as "moderates."[45] Détente, after all, worked for the West in its contest with the Soviets. In that case, the gross inefficiencies of the communist Second World were the West's best ally. Some Chinese scholars, like Minxin Pei and Gordon Chang, believe this is still the case with China. It should be noted, however, that Pei has been saying this for two decades. Perhaps he will eventually be proved right, but meanwhile the economic engine of capitalism hums along in China and much of the recycled Second World. Indeed, it may work even better without the political inefficiencies that are the bane of democratic processes.

It is time to recognize that the economic dynamism of the new Second World is not a fleeting phenomenon. The capitalist world is splitting into

---

[43] Leslie P. Norton, "China's Sure Bet," *Barron's* (November 6, 2010), http://online. barrons.com/article/ SB50001424052970203281504575590290564950892.html#articleTabs_panel_article%3D1

[44] Niall Ferguson, "'Chimerica' is Headed for Divorce," *Niall Ferguson.com* (August 31, 2009), http://www.niallferguson.com/site/FERG/Templates/ArticleItem. aspx?pageid=210

[45] This is especially true of Wen, who has been cast as an agent of intra-party reform. Even Elizabeth Economy, whose insights have often been more discerning, takes Wen's own word for his liberal commitments. See Elizabeth Economy, "Lessons for China in Peace Prize," *Council on Foreign Relations* (October 8, 2010), http: www.cfr.org/publication/23122/lessons_for_china_in_peace_prize.html

politically antithetical camps, and no amount of soft diplomacy will close this gap. The fact that these rival capitalisms trade with each other will not prevent dangerous geopolitical friction between them, coupled with grating moral conflict. Most Western leaders and pundits are but dimly aware of what this means. Only a few churlish iconoclasts like Robert Kagan, mostly ensconced on the non-globalist Right, are ready to squarely confront the dark implications of this spreading global divide. The problem is that the Right, with its fruitful concentration on the new authoritarianism, completely misses the capitalist dynamic behind it. Conversely, the Left focuses so intently on the defects of Western capitalism that it usually fails to recognize the even more grotesque defects of Sino-globalization in the sphere of income inequality, not to mention democracy and human rights.

What, then, is to be done? It might be better to ask what should be categorically avoided. We must retire the pugnacious Atlanticism that Samuel Huntington prescribed as the solution to today's "civilizational clash."[46] That kind of cultural hermeticism contributed much to the "us versus them" syndrome of the Bush administration. The most lethal clash we face, dwarfing the danger of jihadic Islamism, is the growing contest of rival capitalisms.

The supercharged authoritarianism that the West now confronts cannot be defeated by either Kennanesque containment or Clintonesque engagement. What is sorely needed is moral realism, which combines the liberal Left's critique of unregulated capitalism with the Right's (usually very selective) critique of authoritarianism. Both are urgently required, if the democratic West is to recover its sense of moral direction. Its present geopolitical inertia is first and foremost a product of the moral vertigo we call globalization. Before the Georgia invasion, Kagan asked what Europe and America would do if Russia decided to "play hardball" in either Ukraine or Georgia. He correctly guessed that they would do very little, Europe being too "postmodern" and America being mired in costly and needless wars. Such a crisis, he speculated, would usher in a new geopolitical era[47] — and so it has.

Now, lacking even a credible promise of economic "trickle down," the neoliberal world order has no choice but to preserve its power by forceful means. This applies as much to domestic as to foreign affairs. The post-Crash restoration of Wall Street power began under Bush with the emergency

---

[46] See Samuel P. Huntington, *The Clash of Civilizations and the Remaking of the World Order* (New York: Simon and Schuster, 1996), 312.

[47] Robert Kagan, *The Return of History and the End of Dreams* (New York: Alfred A Knopf, 2008), 24.

measures rammed through by Treasury Secretary Henry Paulson. The job was finished under Obama, with an equally neoliberal Timothy Geithner playing the Paulson role. Thus, the American financial establishment was saved, even as its authority eroded worldwide. The big question is what will take its place on the world stage. The China model is staking its claim to that power vacuum, and if a potent third way is not made available as an egalitarian alternative, the Washington Consensus will give way to the Beijing Consensus or its authoritarian equivalent.

MORAL REALISM: IDEALISM FOR A "NORMAL" WORLD

Even after the Georgia debacle, it is common on the liberal Left as well as the neoliberal Right to dismiss the idea of a new Cold War as a reactionary flight of imagination.[48] This denial is possible because, for all their bluster, the Russians do not yet come across as the global players they yearn to be. Meanwhile, until very recently, the Chinese have paid heed to Sun Tzu by declaring that military solutions are not part of their international agenda (Taiwan, Tibet, and most of the South China Sea being regarded as strictly internal affairs).

That passive pose is belied by a ballooning military budget that is already the second largest in the world.[49] The heir apparent to Hu's presidency, Xi Jinping, is known to have deep military ties,[50] and there can be no doubt that the military's voice in foreign affairs will be much greater now that the Chinese economy can afford to pick up the bill. This transformation is already obvious in hotspots like Sudan, Zimbabwe, and Burma, where China's policies go far beyond commercial motives in their anti-Western animus. Clearly, Beijing makes the support of authoritarian regimes an end in itself, as does Moscow in its "Near Abroad."

---

[48] The more extreme and categorically anti-American Left, however, is prone to accept the new Cold War as a long-awaited turning of the tide against US hegemony. See, for example, Seumas Milne, "Why the US Fears Cuba," *The Guardian* (July 31, 2003), http://www.guardian.co.uk/politics/2003/jul/31/cuba. world/print

[49] Officially China raised its defense spending by 18 percent in 2008, bringing its total defense budget to $51 billion, but the Pentagon considers the real budget to be much greater. See Edward Wong, "China Sees Separatist Threats," *The New York Times* (January 21, 2009), http://www.nytimes.com/2009/01/21/ world/asia/21china.html

[50] Edward Wong, "China Grooming Deft Politician as Next Leader," *The New York Times* (January 23, 2011), http://www.nytimes.com/2011/01/24/world/asia/24leader.html

Despite differences in style, these alter-capitalist powers share the same hostile view of the democratic West. Russia's operating assumption, churned out daily by the Kremlinized media, has been that Cold War II is already in full swing.[51] Putinist invective portrays the encroachment of NATO as a serious geopolitical provocation, whereas the West regards it as a mark of democratic progress. That gap cannot be bridged by the rhetorical "reset" that Obama offered and Medvedev gladly accepted, on his own terms. A better indicator of Medvedev's leaning was his announcement of plans for "a large-scale rearming" in 2010.[52] Meanwhile there is every indication that Obama is reviving the Clintonian corporatism that seeded Russia's animosities in the 1990s.

One who well understands this East–West standoff is Edward Lucas, who deplores the Western denial of Russia's renewed threat: "one of the most peculiar features of the Putin years has been the number of Western commentators who are so keen to protest about the 'demonization' of Russia and so unwilling to criticize what is happening there."[53] At first, Lucas was widely dismissed as a Strangelovean Russophobe, but after the Georgia crisis many former skeptics began to see him as prescient,[54] and in the Baltics the Estonian-speaking Lucas is regarded as an intellectual hero. Of course, his message is not so well received within decision-making circles of the EU. There the mood has been better captured by Joschka Fisher, Germany's ex-foreign minister and vice chancellor, who advocates a "strategic partnership" with Russia, including its full membership in NATO. This he calls, with no comic intent, "an answer to the Russian challenge."[55]

The West must meet that challenge, but not by treating Russia, China, and other authoritarian regimes as unqualified enemies. The last thing we need is a return to the kind of Cold War hostility that favored victory at all costs, including the sacrifice of the moral priorities that the West was supposedly defending. Coupled with the "authoritarian transition" model of

---

[51] Michael Idov, "Cooling Down the New Cold War," *The New Republic* (December 9, 2008), http://www.tnr.com/politics/story.html?id=a6ddceef-c50d-4b27-bbd1-1b2b65b53aa6

[52] Clifford J. Levy, "Russia is Planning a 'Large-Scale Rearming'," *The New York Times* (March 18, 2009), http://www.nytimes.com/2009/03/18/world/europe/18medvedev.html

[53] Edward Lucas, *The Cold War: Putin's Russia and the Threat to the West* (revised and updated edition). (New York: Palgrave Macmillan, 2009), 214.

[54] Christian Caryl, "The Russians are Coming?" *The New York Review of Books*, 56, no. 2 (February 12, 2009), http://www.nybooks.com/articles/22277

[55] Joschka Fisher, "An Answer to the Russian Challenge," *The Moscow Times* (January 14, 2009), http://www.themoscowtimes.com/articles/detail.php?ID=373546&print=Y

Third World development, the amoral tactics that America put in play were a black mark on the so-called "free world." Far from speeding the defeat of communism, such nominal "realism" prolonged the Cold War by yielding the moral high ground of egalitarian fairness to the Second World.

The First World cannot afford to repeat that blunder as a new kind of Cold War takes shape. We call, therefore, for *moral* realism as both a strategic and humanitarian imperative. Our concern for human rights must extend to the kind of distributive justice that any Rawlsian liberal would demand. The idea is to inject rights and democracy promotion (meaning social democracy, not just election-day theatrics) into the heart of US foreign policy.

This task begins roughly where our last work left off. In *Development Without Freedom* we followed Amartya Sen by wedding democracy and development.[56] Sen delivered a compelling case against Singapore-style Asian values, which for several decades have amounted to development as repression.[57] Unfortunately, he all but ignored the most grievous threat to freedom in the 1990s: the social and political inroads of neoliberal globalization. Far from stoking democratization, as utopian globalists predicted, globalization on these terms seeded a new wave of Asian authoritarianism. That in turn helped to spawn the distinctly anti-liberal mode of globalization that now stands ready to bite the hand that fed it.

The most glaring case in point, Sino-globalization, has been so successful in raw GDP terms that the system itself is becoming a major export commodity. Third World countries that have been grossly exploited by Western development schemes are looking with rapt interest at this China model, with its blend of illiberal politics and capitalist restructuration. Regimes that never felt comfortable with talk of democratic reform are relieved that this brand of globalization rewards the coercive "stability" that is their specialty. This, in fact, was the forte of all the "Asian miracle" regimes during their "takeoff" periods. China only differs in its more overt and intractable authoritarian convictions. Its present SCO alliance with an increasingly authoritarian Russia recycles the Second World cohesion of the early Cold War and challenges the shotgun marriage of democracy and "free market" globalization that has been the trademark of neoliberal development theory (as opposed to its very undemocratic practice).

---

[56] Songok Han Thornton and William H. Thornton, *Development Without Freedom: The Politics of Asian Globalization* (Aldershot, UK: Ashgate, 2008).

[57] Sen, *op. cit.*, 149–50. Ten years ago Sen's "Development as Freedom" thesis seemed to afford an alternative vision of Asia's political future. In stark contrast to the standard Asian values model, which at most put a democratic veneer over corporate statism, Sen pointed the way toward an Asian Renaissance that held profound implications for the whole developing world.

Globalization, in short, is shedding its liberal cloak. Sino-globalization is unique in that it makes no pretense about its authoritarian values. While there is hope that India could offer an alternative set of Asian values and the prototype for a global third way, the China model is so far stealing the show. To the extent that this trend continues, the democratic wing of development will be expelled, closing the book on the Asian Renaissance that many envisioned after the 1997 Asian Crash. It was then that development theory came to a stark crossroads: either democratization would have to be upgraded to a first-priority issue, on a par with economic growth, or consigned to the ash heap of failed utopian dreams. At that fateful moment, Western as well as Asian globalization turned its back on everything that did not spell maximum profits. In effect it sold itself to the highest bidder, which in China meant the CCP and its cronies. The quantitative success of the China model has paved the way for the signal revolution of our times: the rise of a capitalist Second World.

In retrospect, Sen's "freedom" model amounts to a map of the road not taken. Once the market was accepted as the necessary and sufficient definition of development—its prime mover as well as its prime measure—it was only a short hop to the acceptance of democratic rollback as a price worth paying for progress. Massive infusions of global capital came to the rescue of some of the worst regimes in Asia, putting domestic reform out of reach. In country after country, the lights went out on "People Power"—sometimes by way of a single crushing blow, as at Tiananmen, but more often, as in Korea, by way of the Western-style consumerism that took hold in the 1990s.[58] Either way, "globalization" gave priority to corporate interests at the expense of People Power.

It is no accident that the high tide of neoliberal globalization in the 1990s and 2000s exactly coincided with the decline of "third wave" democratization.[59] Nor is it any accident that the areas where democracy has continued to make moderate gains, such as Latin America, are regions where neoliberal dogma has been most contested.[60] The most astounding case of democratic

---

[58] Songok Han Thornton, "The 'Miracle' Revisited: The De-Radicalization of Korean Political Culture," *New Political Science* 27, no. 2 (June 2005): 176 (161–76).

[59] Official notice of this decline was effectively issued by Thomas Carothers in 2002. See Thomas Carothers, "The End of the Transition Paradigm," *Journal of Democracy* 13, no. 1 (January 2002): 5–21.

[60] A good example of this third way resistance is the thought and practice of the Brazilian minister of strategic affairs, Roberto Mangabeira Unger, who rejects the determinist element in traditional Marxism but all the more embraces its liberatory project. Having drawn this distinction on the socialist side, Unger is certainly not going to be seduced by neoliberalism's equally deterministic notion of universal capitalism.

resistance, however, has exploded out of the Arab World, as treated in Chapter 8. Here, globalist development has been scant and usually abortive, even when it did not trigger a radical Islamist reaction.

The big surprise is that democratic values have been warmly embraced by the resurgent "Arab Street." Globalist theory could never have predicted this, for economic development was supposed to precede political development. That is why globalists have been so receptive to "East Asian" or "Singapore" models of development, and even to the Beijing model that flatly eschews democracy. Now, however, this encomium for so-called Asian values is put on the defensive. Indeed, the Arab Spring of 2011 brought the whole globalist house of cards tumbling down. From a neo-liberal perspective as well as a "civilization clash" vantage, the democratic thrust of the Arab revolts defies belief.

Like it or not, this insurgent Arab democratism forces us to face some hard facts concerning First World globalism. Far from being an agent of substantive democracy, in the Fukuyama mold, globalization has become the nemesis of liberal political development. In that sense, the anti-democratic impact of the new Second World can easily be exaggerated. Authoritarian capitalism cannot be blamed for suppressing what Washington-directed globalization had already destroyed. To revitalize democratization as a global force—what could be called "People Power without borders"—a radically different mode of globalization will have to be fostered, along with a matching power politics. We call this moral realism, but what it amounts to is a geopolitics of hope.

His very Latin blend of Rousseau and Marx affords a political romanticism that would never submit to any dogmatic straitjacket, be it of the Left or Right. It is worth noting that this very "neo" Marxism is making its mark in North America as well—for example, in the Critical Legal Studies movement (CLS).

1

AFTER THE AMERICAN CENTURY
The De-Westernization
of Globalization

POWER SHIFT

Few Americans could have imagined that the end of the Cold War was something they should fear. Like the British a century before, they thought they were on the verge of conquering history itself. Both had it just backwards. Arnold Toynbee recounted how history took Britain by the throat in 1914,[1] and the same could be said for America in the present century. By fall 2008, in the throes of two protracted wars and a failing economy, it was obvious that US power was on the wane. This of course was going to create an enormous geopolitical vacuum. Since no Western nation shows any sign of filling this void, there can be little doubt that the coming "post-American" age is also a post-Western one.

This all came about so fast that its broad ramifications have scarcely registered in the West, and least of all in the US. As late as the 1990s there was renewed confidence in America's global primacy. However, this optimism came in two very antithetical forms. While neoliberalism viewed America as the leading edge of a globalization process that would lift all ships and ensure world peace, neoconservatism, as embodied in the

---

[1] See quotation in Lawrence L. LeShan, *The Psychology of War: Comprehending its Mystique and its Madness* (New York: Helios Press, 2002), 34.

New American Century project, saw the world in zero-sum terms that would lock the country into permanent global struggle. Strategic preemption (strike them before they can strike you) was the neocon answer to the new world disorder.

Under Ronald Reagan and the first President Bush, the neocons had been kept in line, and the Clinton administration disowned them completely. That all changed after September 11, 2001. Suddenly this eccentric dream of empire became US foreign policy. The second President Bush personified the paranoia and revanchism that gripped the country after 9/11. For him, Cheney, Rumsfeld and most ranking neocons, world affairs was reducible to an endless war of "us versus them." The notorious "Bush Doctrine" effectively declared the whole world eligible for possible preemptive strikes, while terror tactics like extraordinary rendition and water board-ing—cheered on by the justice department's legal counsel John Yoo—set Washington beyond the reach of international norms.

If the rationale for these actions was the need to fight fire with fire and terror with terror, their blatant ineffectiveness suggests that their main point was more symbolic than strategic. Domestically this crowned the execu-tive power that had been growing for decades,[2] while in terms of foreign relations it amounted to a rabidly unipolar statement. The Iraq invasion told Europe and the entire world that globalization on Washington's terms would not be a multilateral enterprise. The Bush administration surely knew that it was not just attacking Saddam Hussein, that alleged procurer of weapons of mass destruction. More fundamentally the invasion was a graphic testament to Washington's global resolve. To friends and foes alike it declared that "we can do as we please."

That might be true for the moment, but not without dire consequences. For all its bluster, the Bush administration presided over an America in rapid decline. To invoke Toynbee once more: civilizations are more likely to die from suicide than murder, and the same can be said for world pow-ers. Accordingly, it was not so much 9/11 itself as this petulant executive response that wounded America's global stature. Confusing geopolitical power with "shock and awe" coercion, the Bush team proved incapable of understanding the most basic dynamics of world leadership. The president's advisors seemed never to have read Hans Morgenthau on balance of power realism or Joseph Nye on soft power. America's growing pugnacity was

---

[2] Garry Wills—who plays the role of Madison to Yoo's Hamilton in today's executive power debate—traces the power shift to the politics of the atomic bomb. See Garry Wills, *Bomb Power: The Modern Presidency and the National Security State* (New York: The Penguin Press, 2010); John Yoo, *The History of Executive Power from George Washington to George W. Bush* (New York: Kaplan Publishing, 2010).

in fact the answer to Osama bin Laden's prayers, but even more so it was a gift to rising geopolitical competitors such as China.

Spurning the goodwill that the world lavished on America after 9/11, when even the normally anti-American *Le Monde* hastened to say that "we are all Americans,"[3] the White House made it clear that it would conduct its "war on terrorism" without the assistance or even the advice of America's best allies. Oddly, however, a great deal of effort would be spent in courting the anti-Islamist support of Russia and China, thus licensing their brutality in Chechnya and Xinjiang. The New World Order that Bush I inaugurated was effectively dismantled by Bush II. His eight years in office, punctuated by the longest and deepest economic collapse since the Great Depression, will be remembered as the time when history took America by the throat.

When the sun finally set on the British Empire, America was there to fill the geopolitical void. The "American Century" thus saved the primacy of the West in general. This time, however, the West will get no reprieve. Barack Obama has had to deal not only with national decline but also with the almost Spenglerian decline of the West. Declinism was so much in the air in the midst of the 2008 presidential race that politicians could no longer evade the issue. While on the campaign trail, Obama made a point of being photographed carrying a copy of Fareed Zakaria's *The Post-American World*. Palinite critics took umbrage at the title, but the book actually had an upbeat intention. Zakaria holds out hope for a much transformed yet still salient US role, with Washington cast as something of a Bismarckian power broker.[4]

The root of this optimism is an unwavering faith in global capitalism as a force for the general good. The most basic tenet of neoliberal globalism is that commercial interaction greases the gears of international affairs, all but banishing serious conflicts between capitalist powers. The minor frictions that remain can be readily resolved through institutional channels such as the G8, Davos, the Trilateral Commission, the Bilderberg Group, etc. This basically Clintonian faith returned to power with Obama, though he hedged his bets by acting the part of Bush III in Afghanistan.

Where China is concerned, Obama could follow both Clinton and Bush without risk of schizophrenia, for their China policies were almost identical. That is because they both subscribed to the commercial orthodoxy that

---

[3] Jean-Marie Colombani, "Nous sommes tous Américains," *Le Monde* (September 13, 2001), reprinted in the May 23, 2007 edition of *Le Monde*, http://www.lemonde.fr/opinions/article/2007/05/23/nous-sommestous americains_913706_3232.html

[4] Fareed Zakaria, *The Post-American World* (New York: W. W. Norton & Company, 2008), 233.

precludes any "realist," balance-of-power strategy toward China. From this "liberal institutionalist" perspective there is nothing to lose and much to gain by seating the world's most contrarian powers in the top tiers of the global system. Zakaria assures us that American ideals will remain "overwhelmingly dominant" in the new multilateral world order.[5] Obama clearly agrees, and therefore from the day of his inauguration he set about sidestepping the whole tradition of geopolitical realism. Not since Woodrow Wilson has power politics been yoked to such naïve idealism as Obama brought to the Oval Office.

Many found something refreshing about a diplomacy based on friendly persuasion, and the Norwegians went so far as to give the new president a Nobel Peace Prize in advance of any accomplishments whatsoever. However, a vexing question arose: if America could so easily bend global organizations toward its chosen ends, what would prevent China, Russia, and other authoritarian powers from doing the same thing, as they already had in the case of the UN Security Council?[6] John Mearsheimer notes that while Cold War bipolarity was dangerous yet manageable, a similar stability cannot be expected in the fractured world we are entering. Anyone who thinks a sweeping multipolarity is a guarantee of world peace should recall the years before 1815, 1918, and 1945.[7]

It should be obvious that unrestrained capitalism, which is Obama's real god, is just as likely to magnify conflicts of interest as to lessen them. Our new great game has no anti-capitalist players. That, however, does not reduce nationalistic competition over resources and market domain. Already intense competition for raw materials is raising the likelihood of resource wars. Niall Ferguson reminds us that the heavy economic integration of capitalist powers like Britain and Germany in the early 20th century

---

[5] Fareed Zakaria, "The Future of American Power: How America Can Survive the Rise of the Rest," *Foreign Affairs* (May/June 2008), http://www.foreignaffairs.org/2008/0501facoment87303/fareed-zakaria/the-future-of-american-power.html

[6] It must be asked if some new institutions might be better equipped to protect democratic freedoms. Despite its tainted association with John McCain's presidential platform, Kagan's proposed League of Democracies is worth a second look as a balancing agent against regressive organizations like the SCO. Even Association of Southeast Asian Nations (ASEAN), under the guise of its "no politics" rule, is falling more and more under China's spell. Medvedev's proposal for a post-NATO and post-OSCE (Organization for Security and Cooperation in Europe) Eurasia, epitomized by a newly minted Euro-Atlantic Treaty Organization (EATO), would do for Eurasia what ASEAN has done for Southeast Asia—to claim a victory for peaceful cooperation by muting all non-commercial concerns, such as human rights.

[7] John J. Mearsheimer, *The Tragedy of Great Power Politics* (New York: W. W. Norton, 2001), 356.

did nothing to prevent World War I. And there is no more reason to believe that the analogous economic bond between the US and China, which Ferguson dubs "Chimerica," will be any more effective when it comes to conflict abatement.[8]

Today's globalist idealism tends to imagine the emerging world order as a vastly expanded EU. While European nations can still have grating conflicts of interest, their cultural cohesion helps to keep these disputes under a parliamentary roof. Nothing of the kind is possible on a global scale. Problems are enormously exacerbated when resource competition or economic friction cuts across civilizational boundaries. This is what Samuel Huntington had in mind when he propounded his famous clash of civilizations thesis. Anyone who thinks that power relations in today's world are on a harmonious track should take a careful look at the outcome of the Copenhagen Climate Conference of December 2009. Knowing full well the catastrophic consequences of business as usual, world leaders did exactly what the darkest Hobbesian pessimist would expect them to do: nothing at all.

Forgetting the lessons of World War I, the neoliberals who took charge after the Cold War have had an almost religious faith in the power of market forces to pacify world affairs. They not only have overlooked non-market forces like radical Islamism, but have missed the even greater danger lurking within the capitalist system itself. The rise of authoritarian capitalism registers with them as a profit-making opportunity rather than a geopolitical or human rights minefield. Thus the West/East power shift of recent years has been largely funded by the West.[9] The result is a new

---

[8] Niall Ferguson, "'Chimerica' is Headed for Divorce," *Newsweek* (August 31, 2009), http://www.newsweek.com/id/212143/output/print

[9] A graphic illustration of how corporatism trumps geopolitics and other vital interests is the case of US-linked multinationals doing business with Iran. Despite the Iran Sanctions Act of 1996 and Washington's constant efforts to discourage investment with Iran, companies like Shell and Honeywell continued doing massive business there. Halliburton, Vice President Cheney's former company, exited its Iran operations under a storm of criticism only in 2007. Shell announced the end of its gasoline sales to Iran only in March 2010. Meanwhile the federal government itself has in the last decade awarded over $107 billion in contracts, grants and other benefits to corporations active in Iran. This includes $15 billion in payments to companies that, in complete defiance of American sanctions law, have assisted Iran's development of its oil and gas reserves. See Jo Becker and Ron Nixon, "U.S. Enriches Companies Defying its Policy on Iran," *The New York Times* (March 6, 2010), http://www.nytimes.com/2010/03/07/world/middleeast/ 07sanctions.html and "Profiting from Iran, and the U.S.," *The New York Times* (March 6, 2010), http://www.nytimes.com/interactive/2010/03/06/world/iran-sanctions.html and "Shell Stops Selling Gasoline to Iran," *The New York Times* (March 10, 2010), http://www. nytimes.com/aponline/2010/ 03/10/business/AP-EU-Netherlands-Shell-Iran.html

form of globalization that circumvents not just US leadership but the whole Western project of liberal democratization.

It would be unfair and inaccurate, however, to pin the blame for this democratic crisis solely on new members of the capitalist club. Globalization's reactionary turn was well underway before the globalist project was hijacked by non-Western powers. Washington had consistently endorsed policies that pillaged Third World resources and subverted local democratic reform. People Power withered on this vine, and Third World democracy was not the only loser. This democratic retreat ultimately erodes the foundation for Washington's leadership throughout the developing world. It offers no solvent for the tight bond that is forming between Third World authoritarianism and the resurgent Second World.

Thus America is already paying a high price for the neoliberal Ponzi scheme that we call globalization. The decline of neoliberal globalism can be traced to the 1997–98 Asian Crash, when a Washington-directed IMF helped to turn a mere recession into a prolonged depression. In an effort to distance itself from blatantly defective Asian capitalism, Western leaders turned against former puppets like Suharto, who were now labeled "crony capitalists." It took another decade for a sizable number of Americans to realize how much the charge of cronyism applied to their own political and economic elites. The Great Recession of 2008–09 exposed the reverse dependency that was fast developing around the world. Instead of Asia looking to the West for a bailout, Washington now looked East, and not just for temporary emergency assistance. A full paradigm shift was in the making.[10]

Even on a moral plane the old assumptions were defunct. Given the lack of transparency and accountability that the American crash revealed, it was no longer possible for Wall Street financiers to claim the moral high ground over their Asian counterparts. Nonetheless, acting as if nothing had fundamentally changed, President Obama devoted his first year in office to restoring Wall Street business as usual.[11] It was obvious, however, that Washington had lost its grip on the broader processes of globalization.

---

[10] See Noam Scheiber, "Sachs Appeal," *The New Republic* (August 12, 2009), http://www.tnr.com/ story_print.html?id=0894daOb-0375-421a-9f6d-0d8b1b2bd41d

[11] In line with Roger D. Hodge's *The Mendacity of Hope*, Johann Hari holds that Obama set us all up for another global crash by refusing to reregulate the banks or stop even their riskiest practices.... Obama was brought to power by the 'donations'—actually investments—of Goldman Sachs, JP Morgan Chase, Citigroup, IBM, Morgan Stanley, General Electric, and others. So it is not unsurprising that his Presidency has largely served their interests. See Johann Hari, "The Real Reason Obama has Let us All Down," *The Independent* (October 26, 2010), http://www.independent.co.uk/opinion/commentators/johann-hari/johann-hari-the-real-reason-obama-has-let-us-all-down-2116272.html

The winner by default was Sino-globalization, which had the advantage of being a relative dark horse.

Despite his huge personal popularity, President Obama went to the April 2009 G20 Summit as an underdog so far as his recovery plan was concerned. The reason was simple: for all his advertised difference from President Bush, he also went as the de facto defender of neoliberalism, whereas European and Asian leaders favored other models of globalization.[12] For Europeans, steeped in a softer brand of capitalism, the needed economic corrective would not require the surrender of political freedoms. Neither America nor Asia had such a social democratic tradition to draw upon. One fell back on a neoliberal market fix while the other leaned all the more toward the authoritarianism of so-called Asian values.

On the surface Asia's reactionary turn is nothing new. Pro-capitalist autocrats like Marcos, Suharto, Park Chung Hee, and Lee Kuan Yew were an integral part of America's Cold War system. That, however, is precisely where the difference lies. The new authoritarians are forging their own systems. Indeed, through the mechanism of sovereign wealth funds (SWFs), they are beginning to swallow up substantial sections of the Western system that once ingested them. That Great Reversal is the hallmark of the "Chimerican" juncture that Ferguson excoriates. Already America's major creditor, China is now shopping at fire sale prices for the best financial and technological assets on the US market.

It was in this spirit that President Hu Jintao came to Washington on his second state visit of January 2011. Since his first visit in 2006, China's economic clout and bargaining power have mushroomed, while America's power has plummeted.[13] At a very private state dinner (not the "Grand State Dinner" staged for press corps photo ops), a select group of bankers, generals, and politicos from both sides feasted on the most important "Chimerican" deal since Nixon and Kissinger went to Beijing in 1972. In effect, the US treasury would be forgiven for profligate monetary policies that reduced the value of Chinese-owned securities, in return for China's unprecedented access to a veritable cornucopia of vital technological transfers—many with formerly high security defense applications—from companies like Boeing and GE.[14]

---

[12] Chris ti Parsons, "Obama at G-20 Summit: Popular President, Unpopular Plan," *Los Angeles Times* (March 30, 2009), http://articles.latimes.com/2009/mar/30/world/fg-g20-obama30

[13] "On Hu's Second Visit, a Tale of Two Economies," *MSNBC.COM* (January 20, 2011), http://www.msnbc.msn.com/id/41181121/ns/business-world_business/

[14] These concerns were compellingly voiced by the investment strategist Jeb Handweger. See Jeb Handweger, "Gold and Silver Investors Should Be Following China's Moves into U.S. Financials," *iStockAnalyst* (January 26, 2011), http://www.istockanalyst.com/article/viewarticle/articleid/4837937

Obama, however, did not initiate this sellout. It was in full swing under Bush, and Clinton before him (simply substitute the name McDonnell Douglas for Boeing).[15] The Great Recession of 2008 marked its climax rather than its origin. A prime consideration in Washington's decision to rescue the mortgage giants Fannie Mae and Freddie Mac was the fact that China had an investment in them amounting to 10 percent of its GDP.[16] Likewise, on the eve of the crash, China Citic Bank was already negotiating heavy investment in Wall Street icons such as Bear Stearns, Citigroup, Morgan Stanley, and Merrill Lynch. At any other time such financial incursions might have set off alarm bells, but in the midst of an unprecedented credit crunch this move was welcomed as a timely capital injection. Ferguson sees these SWF penetrations as more than simple business transactions between West and East. No less they represent a mammoth transfer of power.[17]

THE DE-WESTERNIZATION OF GLOBALIZATION

Few Western globalists have fully awakened to the fact that their Cold War alliance with Asian authoritarianism is obsolete. It is time to revisit East–West relations from a 21st century vantage. Commonly we think of the Cold War as an ideological contest that had its ground zero in Europe. However, the Cold War's most decisive battles were economic and most were fought without headlines or much awareness of their geopolitical impact. It is fair to say that the Cold War was won accidently and it should be noted that this outcome took most supposed experts by surprise.

The exigencies of Cold War geopolitics encouraged a no-questions-asked symbiosis between Asian and Western capitalisms. Already the one was more export-driven and the other more consumption-driven, such that the two systems fed on each other's excesses. At least there was a real quid pro quo, with Asian cheap labor bartered in exchange for Western technology and

---

[15] A 16-count indictment was brought against McDonnell Douglas for its part in this treasonous sellout. Charges against one of its chief executives, Robert Hitt, were dismissed due to a statute of limitations, since the crime had taken place in 1994. He was promptly hired by Boeing. See "McDonnell Douglas, China Firm Indicted," *Los Angeles Times* (October 20, 1999), http://articles.sfgate.com/1999-10-20/news/ 17703752_1_mcdonnell-douglas-trunkliner-program-manufacturing-tools/2

[16] See "China Eyes Fannie Mae, Freddie Mac Bailout," *National Public Radio* (September 7, 2008), http://www.npr.org/templates/story/story.php?storyId=94369826

[17] Niall Ferguson, "An Ottoman Warning for Indebted America," *Financial Times* (January 1, 2008), http://www.ft.com/cms/s/0/6667a18a-b888-11dc-893b-0000779fd2ac.html

security services. It may have seemed like the perfect geoeconomic marriage, but the seeds of later discord were already planted in the very success of the Asian "miracle." As Rim nations acquired their own high tech, one of the West's main comparative advantages evaporated.

So too, the end of the Cold War reduced the security needs that were the major engine of American hegemony. At its moment of seeming triumph, Washington found itself playing with a much weaker geopolitical hand. In fact this transformation had quietly begun a decade before on the Cold War's Eastern front. Once China adopted capitalism, the economic side of the Cold War in the Far East effectively ended. This was hardly the case politically, however, for an enduring conflict between democratic and authoritarian systems not only persists but is growing in intensity as non-liberal globalisms begin to go their own way, no longer willing to submit to neoliberal dictates.

This disjunction between Asian and Western capitalism has a déjà vu quality, for even in the 1980s Rim allies were beginning to look more like cutthroat competitors than geoeconomic shield mates. The Plaza Accord of 1985 took some of the pressure off a growing trade imbalance, but a deep structural rift remained. In a vain attempt to compete on these terms, America began to "Asianize" its own production through wage stagnation, de-unionization, and environmental laxity. These were basic ingredients of the "Reagan revolution," and they provided the foundation for emerging neoliberalism.

A ray of hope broke through as Japan, Asia's "lead goose," seemed in turn to be Westernizing. But higher wages and tougher environmental standards would soon put Japan at an all-too-Western impasse. To the extent that its mode of production was "de-Asianized," Japan started to lose its comparative advantage relative to the new Asian tigers. They embarked on a second "Asian miracle," adding another layer of disadvantage to America's trade dilemma. That fact went largely unnoticed, however, during the glory years of the US "New Economy." It was still possible in the exuberant 1990s to believe that IT creativity could recharge American production, sparing leading sectors of the US economy the atrophy that rust belt industries had suffered long before.

As that hope began to fade, the promise of a new "American Century" was put on hold. American exceptionalism, and by extension Western exceptionalism, then rested on the last-ditch proposition that liberal democratic culture constitutes the real brick and mortar of development. This is the subtext of Samuel Huntington's later Atlanticism, and in a less xenophobic way it is also an element in Amartya Sen's "development as freedom" thesis. Despite their double-digit growth and pliant work forces, Asia's miracle economies are seen as ultimately doomed unless they add political reform to their modernizing agenda. From this perspective the Asian Crash of 1997–98 could almost be taken as a blessing. For a fleeting moment it pushed Rim nations toward greater democracy and transparency.

Unfortunately that political reformism came wrapped in a globalist agenda that included deregulation and a host of other neoliberal "reforms." It soon became obvious that these "structural adjustments" had more to do with corporatism and the free flow of capital than with democratic development and accountability. As Asian elites regained their economic footing, it was easy for them to avail themselves of Western modes of production without the incubus of political reform. The Asian and Russian crashes had amply exposed what comes from neoliberalization. The pernicious impact of IMF policies on crisis-stricken nations had become so obvious, and so protracted, that the liberatory claims of globalist institutions lost all credibility.

Globalization on these terms was obviously geared toward corporate advantage by way of cheap labor, tax abatement, the suspension of workers' rights, deregulation of capital flows, and unrestricted access to local markets. Thus "IMFism" became a dirty word in much of the developing world.[18] If globalization is not such a dirty word, that is because it is no longer just another name for Westernization, much less Americanization. The First World is in denial as to how un-Western globalization is becoming. Much of Asia and the global South are ready to explore other globalist avenues, such as the China model, which combines capitalism with highly coercive mechanisms of planning and social control.

Until recently this statist agenda rarely bothered foreign investors. They were pleased to utilize authoritarian regimes as their comprador agents and tools of enforcement. China has been their tool of choice, but others such as Indonesia, Vietnam, Malaysia, Thailand, and the Philippines are worthy competitors. In all of these graft is part-and-parcel of the capitalist system. Singapore, by contrast, makes a fairly credible claim of maintaining "good governance" and the "rule of law" commercially. However, this highly advertised exception is limited, on its political side, to what empowers the ruling People's Action Party (PAP). While the IMF, the World Bank, and the WTO have effectively defined stability as support for transnational

---

[18] For many Newly Industrialized Countries (NICs), the turning point came with the 1997 Asian Crash, which revealed Washington's real priorities. When Thailand's prime minister, Thaksin Shinawatra, paid back his country's IMF loan long before its scheduled deadline, he was not just saying "no" to America's meddling in his affairs. No less he was rejecting a style of globalization that Asian oligarchs found constrictive.

capital, Asia's rising powers are more politically astute. For them economics is always subordinate to politics.

That is not to whitewash the political machinations of Western powers. It is easy to criticize Beijing for the support it showers on authoritarian regimes worldwide, but it should not be forgotten that America and the West do not hesitate to do the same thing where oil is at stake, and in countless cases Washington has gone the extra mile by actively undermining democratic governments that happen to resist US corporate interests. One of the most infamous cases in point was Washington's role in subverting Chile's democratic government in the early 1970s. Augusto Pinochet's US approved coup provided an early test of Milton Friedman's "Chicago school" development model, a precursor of neoliberalism. This showcase of "free market" reform took Chile's unemployment rate from 4.3 percent in 1973 to 22 percent in 1983, while real wages tumbled by 40 percent. Whereas 20 percent of the Chilean population lived in poverty in 1970, that figure had doubled by 1990.[19]

Nor was this a uniquely Latin American fiasco. Australia in the 1980s carried out "free market" experiments that resulted in a reduction of national income by over 5 percent a year till the end of the decade.[20] How, one may ask, could such a defective model be democratically accepted where these facts were widely known? The answer is that the popularity of neoliberal globalization, like the more openly authoritarian development models of Asia, has depended largely on factual suppression. The nature of this blackout certainly varies in the East and West, but its end result is similar. On both sides it can best be understood by what it inhibits or flatly prohibits. Whether subtly, as in the West, or overtly, as in China, globalism dismantles the whole ethos of democracy.

Asian systems of repression have been tacitly encouraged by the corporate West. It is no exaggeration to say that Western capital laid the foundation for a new, super-charged Second World. Of course it was never intended that the China model would take capitalism and go its own way. The paradox is that this reactionary Second World has not only broken free, but has streamlined capitalism by dumping the liberal baggage that puts the Western model at a huge disadvantage. Sensing this weakness, as registered in lost profit opportunities, First World leaders have scrambled to de-liberalize the West as well.

---

[19] Gregory Palat, "Miracle Cure, but the Medicine was Bright Red," *The Guardian* (November 22, 1998), http://www.guardian.co.uk/Columnists/Column/0,5673,324875,00.html

[20] Noam Chomsky, *Year 501: The Conquest Continues* (Cambridge, MA: South End Press, 1993), Chapter Two: The Contours of World Order, http:// cyberspacei.com/jesusi/authors/chomsky/year/y501_002.htm

Hence globalization was never a purely Western process. From the very beginning it was a product of East–West cross-fertilization. The Asian values prescription for de-unionization and environmental laxity was imported by way of the TINAesque notion that there was no choice. This neoliberal mantra was substituted for any form of democratic deliberation regarding the ends and means of globalization. For the better part of a generation, neoliberalism enjoyed a lucrative partnership with Asian values capitalism, and there was mutual influence at all stages. The globalism that the West exported to the developing world after the Cold War had already been "Asianized," so to speak.

Far from encouraging democratic reform, this East–West hybrid promoted the most reactionary social elements. Washington's actions helped to seed the authoritarian reversal that pulverized the People Power movements of the 1980s. Only briefly had American influence been supportive of real democratization. For a fleeting moment, Washington was willing to test the utility of People Power as a boon to US interests. Thus the two Kims of Korea and Corazon Aquino of the Philippines came to power with Washington's blessing, albeit with tight strings attached. Then the tide turned, just as it had in the case of Japan's "reverse course" four decades before. Once again America took a decisive stand against democracy.

Nowhere, however, has it taken that stand more baldly than in China after Tiananmen. These were the glory years of globalist thought and practice, when Western investors brushed human rights aside and embraced China as the paragon of pure economism. The IMF's carpetbagger policies after the Asian Crash had taught Rim nations an indelible lesson in economic sovereignty: the need to avoid future bailouts by fortifying their foreign exchange reserves. In this sense China has simply been a good student of Washington Consensus tutelage. It took this lesson without having to pay the tuition fee of IMF structural adjustment.

As other Rim nations one by one paid off their IMF loans and joined the globalist club, they could get on with the usual business of suppressing political opposition. Indeed, foreign capital has tended to favor those countries which did exactly that. Globally funded authoritarianism provided a prophylactic against unionization, living wages, workers' rights, environmental protection, social welfare costs, and the instability that attends democratic reform. Especially after 9/11, Washington was thankful for strong central governments like Thaksin's in Thailand. In the name of "anti-terrorism" Thaksin launched a pogrom on religious minorities, much as China has done in Tibet and Xinjiang. That too is an integral part of the China model.

People Power came under siege throughout Asia, but nowhere more banefully than in the PRC. With its $100 billion in foreign reserves, China came through the Asian financial crisis with flying colors, and hence avoided the second wind that People Power got from the Crash in stricken countries. Flaunting its "stability," China soaked up the capital that fled neighboring economies, thereby prolonging the Crisis by obstructing capital "flowback." By 2005 China's reserves weighed in at $1 trillion, and soon would reach $1.8 trillion, by far the biggest in the world.[21] Meanwhile, its heavy investment in US treasury bonds underwrote America's burgeoning debt.

The easy credit that afforded kept US interest rates low, which fueled household debt and a housing bubble that was the mirror opposite of the excess savings problem in China, Japan, and the Persian Gulf states. Debt-financed consumption pushed the U.S. current account deficit from 1.7 percent of GDP in 1997 to 6.5 percent ten years later.[22] The bubble finally burst in 2008, putting the whole global system in jeopardy. Though China's export economy also suffered, its geopolitical status was enormously enhanced by America's shameless dependence on Chinese credit. On balance, China's geoeconomic status would be a major victor of the recession. Hugo Chávez of Venezuela trumpeted that China had already replaced the United States as the world's indispensable nation.[23] The irony is that many American investors hope Chávez is right, insofar as a buoyant Chinese economy could energize global demand and prevent a world depression.[24]

THE DYNAMICS OF SECOND WORLD GLOBALIZATION

China's global rise is now so taken for granted that scholars tend to treat it as the natural order of things. Where stress is laid on social and economic "stability," it is Western liberalism that is starting to look out of step with the times. Western democratism (meaning the whole spectrum of liberal values and institutions, not just the act of holding pro forma elections, which even

---

[21] John Detury, "Will America's Pain be China's Gain?," *Korea Times* (October 26, 2008), http://www.koreatimes.co.kr/www/news/opinion/2008/12/160_33285.html

[22] Sherle R. Schwenninger, "Redoing Globalization," *The Nation* (December 23, 2008), http://www.thenation.com/doc/20090112/schwenninger/print

[23] Joseph S. Nye, "Barack Obama and American Power," *Project Syndicate* (November 2008), http://www.project-syndicate.org/print_commentary/nye63/English

[24] See "Suddenly Vulnerable," *The Economist* (December 11, 2008), http://www.economist.com/opinion/PrinterFriendly.cfm?story_id=12773135

Singapore accepts) is increasingly regarded as a developmental impediment. China simply takes the extra step of dispensing altogether with the democratic ball and chain. This has not dented the Chinese growth record or the corporate approval rating for PRC policies (other than copyright infringement, of course). Among rising Asian powers, only India has completely defied this trend, and until recently its corporate approval rating has been abysmal. While the most reactionary Asian values get a corporate seal of approval, any form of "People Power" is viewed with suspicion.

There is nothing new about this, however. Even Japan, the prototype for East Asian development, was locked in an illiberal mold after its "reverse course" of 1947. Meanwhile America's other Cold War allies erected even more tawdry "democratic" façades: Korea under Park, Taiwan under the Chiangs, the Philippines under Marcos, Indonesia under Suharto, Malaysia under Mahathir, Singapore under Lee Kuan Yew, and Thailand under an array of military-approved autocrats. It was only in the sunset years of the Cold War that this dismal pattern met effective resistance, most notably from the "People Power" that shook the Philippines in the 1980s. At that point the pan-Asian call for substantive democracy was starting to look like a teleology that even China could not escape. It was so pervasive, so "in the air," that one Chinese expert thought he had located the source of it all in Chinese pop culture.[25]

All Rim countries found ways to extinguish People Power after the crash, but China did so with such draconian gusto that the West was forced to react one way or the other. To "engage" China under such grim circumstances would require a very different development model than the classic vision of democratic globalism set forth by Francis Fukuyama in *The End of History*. If Tiananmen was a turning point for China itself—or rather was the obliteration of a possible turning point—it also marked the dead end of the short idealist phase of neoliberal development. It was a radically amoral globalism that came to the aid of the CCP in its hour of greatest need. That timely rescue enabled the architects of the June 1989 crackdown to repair their wounded legitimacy on purely material grounds.

The idea that unfettered capitalism will weaken authoritarian governments was the signal myth of post-Cold War foreign affairs. Though no

---

[25] See Orville Schell, *Discos and Democracy: China in the Throes of Reform* (New York: Knopf Doubleday, 1989). The current Chinese government seems to agree, at least where the pop artist Ai Weiwei is concerned. It razed his studio and bans all mention of him in the media. See Ron Gluckman, "The Art of Social Advocacy," *The Wall Street Journal* (January 25, 2011), http://online.wsj.com/article/SB10001424052748704624504576097932 2998562592.html

present Chinese leader holds the emperor-like power of Deng Xiaoping,[26] James Mann cogently argues that today's CCP is collectively stronger than it was in 1989, when for weeks it dared not act in the face of mounting resistance at Tiananmen. The regime stood by watching and fretting as the protests reached an almost revolutionary crescendo.[27] We know from Zhao Ziyang's posthumous book, *Prisoner of the State*,[28] that the CCP inner circle was deeply divided over how to handle the unrest of that fateful spring.

For a precious moment there was hope that China would add some form of democratization to its other modernization efforts, but Tiananmen snuffed out that dream once and for all. The big question at that point was how the international community would respond to China's dictatorial recidivism. Now more than ever the CCP needed stupendous economic growth to justify itself. Its very survival hinged on its ability to attract vast amounts of foreign investment and technological assistance. It would get all that, courtesy of Washington-directed globalization.

In the West as well as the East, a quiet developmental revolution was in progress. Political idealism would no longer be part of development planning. The "de-moralized" globalization that resulted culminated in the ratification of China's permanent MFN (most favoured nation) status in 2000. One of America's last viable instruments for pro-democratic action was thus dismantled.[29] Neoliberals who cheered the end of annual MFN assessments insisted, of course, that economically engaged dictatorships would soon accept democratic reform, just as the military dictatorships of Korea and Taiwan finally did. By the same logic Russia had been granted permanent MFN in 1992, and for years Boris Yeltsin was set up as the poster boy of neoliberal development. He had, after all, kept the communists at bay and the investment bankers happy, even as ordinary Russians seethed.

---

[26] James Mann, "China's Repression of Dissent Hasn't Changed Since 1989," *The New Republic*, originally from *TNRtv* lecture (April 6, 2009), http://blogs.tnr/blogs/the_plank/archive/2009/06/04/tnrty-what-s-really-changed-since-tianamen.aspx

[27] "Legacy of Tiananmen Crackdown Lingers over China's Politics," *The Online News Hour* (June 4, 2009), http://www.pbs.org/newhour/bb/asia/jan-june09/tiananmen2 06-04.html

[28] Zhao Ziyang, *Prisoner of the State: The Secret Journal of Zhao Ziyang*, ed. Bao Pu, Renee Chiang, and Adi Ignatius (New York: Simon & Schuster, 2009).

[29] Though Congress had often threatened to put real teeth into MFN provisions, their actual effect had been minimal. As former China ambassador James Lilley put it, the Chinese had long since learned that "MFN is a bullet which we put in the gun and never fire." Lilley quoted in Robert Garson, *The United States and China Since 1949: A Troubled Affair* (London: Pinter, 1994), 216. A toothless remnant of that earlier oversight mandate is found in the annual report of the Congressional-Executive Commission on China (CECC). See Gary Feuerberg, "Pattern of Harsh Prison Sentences Emerging in China," *Epoch Times* (August 10, 2010), http://www.theepochtimes.com/n2/content/view/40704/

It was against this globalist backdrop, which shelved not only human rights but the entire human factor in development, that Amartya Sen issued his seminal thesis that democratic freedom and human capabilities form the very axis of healthy development. Casual readers of Sen's *Development as Freedom* might assume he was basically defining development as Westernization, but he denies any such equation. His subtext, here and in other works like *The Argumentative Indian*, is an alternative set of Asian values which is conducive to democratic development at all stages.

Hence there is nothing inherently "Western" about democratization. It was simply a historical accident that Western countries reached this stage of political development first. In the aftermath of the 1997–98 Asian Crash, Senism seemed to point the way for Asia's future. The so-called Asian values that bred the region's infamous "crony capitalism" had failed both economically and politically. People Power seemed to be getting a second wind, and there was talk of a coming Asian Renaissance, complete with robust democratization and a more equitable distribution of income.

Soon, however, it began to dawn on Rim nations that there was an economic price to be paid for these reforms. They would be very costly in the short run, and few Asian leaders had the interest or vision to consider the longer run. Once again the old priorities were slipped back into operation. What expedited this reversal was the shimmering example of China, which had come through the crash almost unscathed. China's uncanny growth seems to testify that "development without freedom," as we term it,[30] is the surest and fastest path to success in the coming century.

Now the whole developing world is taking note of this policy option. What is not so widely recognized is the extent to which the success of the China model has been underwritten by Western investors. Capitalism abhors instability, and there is a broad but seldom-stated understanding among investors that substantive democratization is something to avoid. So it was that Deng Xiaoping, who never wavered in his dictatorial resolve, was always highly regarded by the Western investment community.

The China model would seem to offer an easy remedy for the instability that plagues much of Asia. After Tiananmen, Dengism laid Hu Yaobang's progressivism to rest and even stripped away the more moderate *glasnost* of Zhao Ziyang's still-authoritarian modernism.[31] It soon became obvious that the post-Tiananmen China model could better attract and manage capital

---

[30] See Songok Han Thornton and William H. Thornton, *Development without Freedom: The Politics of Asian Globalization* (Aldershot, UK: Ashgate, 2008).

[31] Jonathan Mirsky, "China's Dictators at Work: The Secret Story," *The New York Review of Books* 56, no. 11 (July 2, 2009), http://www.nybooks.com/articles/22801

than the democratic competition elsewhere in Asia. Now, under the shadow of the 2008 crash, the West is up against the most daunting adversary it has faced since World War II. The Soviet Union was an economic minnow by comparison, and the civilizational nemesis that America confronted on September 11, 2001, where the polar opposition was between Western capitalism and Muslim anti-capitalism, was just a warm-up exercise for the coming clash of rival capitalisms.

We must ask if Europe and America will stand together in this global contest, or will Europe stay on the geopolitical sidelines it has occupied since 1990, earning it the less virtuous place in Robert Kagan's Mars and Venus analogy. The last real Western solidarity was seen during the 1990–91 Gulf War. That fleeting new world order now seems almost as distant as the Berlin Wall. Parag Khanna's *The Second World* effectively gives it the last rites. Not only does Khanna draw a fateful line between China and America, but also between Europe and America. The result is a tripartite division of world power consisting of the EU, China and a flagging but still potent US.

Now, with the Euro crumbling and the very existence of the EU thrown in doubt, the sole victor of globalization's restructuration process is China. In two short years that part of Khanna's thesis has been reduced to rubble. He did get some things right, however. One was the importance of the less developed "tipping states" that he dubbed the "Second World."[32] Given its imperial overstretch and mounting economic woes, America is at risk of sliding into the downwardly mobile ranks of those global non-achievers. We agree with Khanna about China's growing clout, but must reject his implied geopolitical seesaw whereby this rising power all but requires a sinking US.

George Friedman, in *The Next 100 Years*,[33] posits a very different global future. Noting that the US only became *the* superpower in 1991, and reminding us that the tenure of world powers has usually spanned centuries, he doubts that America's total power is shrinking. In our view that is overshooting the mark. Such a blanket reaffirmation of US paramountcy requires that we completely discount the threat posed by authoritarian nations in general and China in particular. In fact, China's international power is stupendous, and getting more so.[34] Friedman can dismiss this

---

[32] Parag Khanna, *The Second World: Empires and Influence in the New Global Order* (New York: Random House, 2008), x.

[33] George Friedman, *The New 100 Years: A Forecast for the 21st Century* (New York: Doubleday, 2009).

[34] See Zhang Yongxing, "China's International Influence at All-Time Peak: Singapore Expert," *China View* (August 27, 2009), http://news.xinhuanet.com/english/2009-08/27/content_11952622.htm

conspicuous fact because in his view China's demographics are going to weigh it down. With over a billion Chinese to feed, and with most living in utter destitution, internal security will have to be the almost singular task of the Chinese military.[35]

These are crucial points to bear in mind, but they do not support the comfortable conclusion that Friedman reaches. In Ma Jian's novel, *Beijing Coma*, the protagonist was gravely injured at Tiananmen and came out of a long coma to find that China had forgotten the ideals he had been ready to die for. Like him, it is time for us to wake up to the hard reality that the CCP could well be here to stay. It is proving remarkably adept at managing the country's upper as well as underclasses. The undertow effect that Friedman believes *should* be there is simply missing, at least for now.

Our own position falls between the Zakaria/Khanna conception of a post-American world and the Friedman/Albright faith in America's utter indispensability. Like Friedman we hold that America's global role is vital and need not be in decline. Yet, with Toynbee, we bear in mind that nations and civilizations alike are capable of self-destruction, and America's brand of globalism is nothing less than suicidal. US world leadership cannot be secured by either neoliberal economism or the shock and awe militarism favored by neoconservative hawks. If Washington is to lead, it must be by the strength of example and the moral force of its generosity and fair dealings with Third World nations.

A NEW KIND OF COLD WAR

The question is what to do about Second World nations. There is a wide semantic gap between Khanna's "worldly" terminology and ours. His "Second World" is mostly composed of nations in economic limbo or collapse, whereas ours includes a congeries of highly successful capitalist authoritarianisms. The case of China alone is enough to inspire a strident Asian triumphalism, typified by the West-bashing Kishore Mahbubani, Singapore's former ambassador to the UN. Like his mentor, Lee Kuan Yew, Mahbubani is not bothered by the fact that the disempowerment of the West could deal a lethal blow to democratization, human rights, and the whole complex of progressive causes that trace to the Western Enlightenment.[36]

---

[35] George Eaton, "Q&A: George Friedman," *New Statesman* (August 27, 2009), http://www.newststes.com/international-politics/2009/08/united-states-power-chma

[36] One reason Western scholars may be slow to register the full implications of Mahbubani's Asianism is that they too, under the rubric of postmodernism, have spent years lambasting the Enlightenment ethos. For a bracing corrective to this

He declines to mention the reactionary thrust of Singapore-style development, which China takes to the highest level.

One silver lining on this East–West values clash is the impetus it could give for renewed Western solidarity. Charles de Gaulle once predicted that Europe would wait in vain for a statesman to integrate it, but instead "will be united by the Chinese."[37] The same can be said of a broken Atlantic alliance. Eventually Europe will realize that its fate is again linked with America's in a struggle that could be every bit as portentous as the old Cold War. Unfortunately "Old Europe" is in denial. France has even been willing to discuss Russia's proposal for a security pact that would effectively retire NATO.[38]

Other EU nations were shocked in October 2010 when Germany's Merkel and France's Sarkozy met with Russia's Medvedev in a tripartite summit aimed at establishing an EU–Russia Political and Security Committee. Merkel had previously joined Washington in opposing similar efforts by Germany's ex-Chancellor Schröder, France's Chirac, and Russia's Putin.[39] Now, she and many others were having second thoughts, as was Russia. On both sides China was coming to be seen as reason enough for Eurasian solidarity.[40] *The China Threat*, a new book by the Russian conservative Oleg Glazunov, supports the contention of analysts like Pavel Felgenhauer that Russia needs a major Rapid Deployment Force (RDF) on its Eastern front. Similar warnings from orientalists inside the Russian Academy of Sciences leave no doubt why President Medvedev stunned the defense world by accepting NATO's plan for a pan-European anti-missile shield.[41]

This geostrategic convergence is already in full swing. The question is on whose terms. Does it come as a Trojan horse, not so much signifying the political Westernization of Russia as the Asianization of Europe? An ancillary

---

anti-Enlightenment bias, see Susan Neiman, *Evil in Modern Thought: An Alternative History of Philosophy* (Princeton, NJ: Princeton University Press, 2002).

[37] Charles de Gaulle quoted in Nick Witney, "The Death of NATO," *The Moscow Times* (December 2, 2008), http://www.themoscowtimes.com/articles/detail.php?ID=372823&print=Y

[38] "U.S. Calls Russia's Pact Anti-NATO," *The Moscow Times* (December 5, 2008), http://www.themoscowtimes.com/articles/detail.php?ID=372913&print=Y

[39] Judy Dempsey, "Russia Wants to Formalize Relation with E.U.," *The New York Times* (October 17, 2010), http://www.nytimes.com/2010/10/18/world/europe/18iht-germany.html

[40] Robert Marquand, "Facing a Rising China, Russia Looks to Boost Europe Ties," *The Christian Science Monitor* (October 18, 2010), http://www.csmonitor.com/layout/set/print/content/view/print/332908

[41] Albert L. Weeks, "Why Russia is Warming to the West," *The Christian Science Monitor* (December 15, 2010), http://www.csmonitor.com/layout/set/print/content/view/print/350102

question is whether this rapprochement with Russia will necessarily be a blow to Atlanticism. What, that is, will America's place be in the new Eurasianism? It is surely no accident that Sarkozy at this moment has proposed bringing France back into NATO after 40 years of Gaullist isolation. Unfortunately, the terms he attaches to this reentry would further weaken Atlanticism by downgrading America's role in European security. That would send the wrong message to the Second World. Cutting America out of the loop would supplant Atlanticism with an ill-timed Eurasianism that condones Russia's misconduct at home and abroad. Judged by its actions rather than words, Russia is clearly not "turning West." Ten months after its Georgian invasion, it was again conducting war games near Georgia's border.[42]

Must Europeans choose between Moscow and Washington? Europe's ecstatic reception of Obama's presidential victory, coupled with Obama's "reset" policy toward Russia, suggests otherwise. But this leaves the question hanging as to how Europe will respond to an increasingly Sino-centric Second World. China's $2 billion in foreign exchange reserves is fast being converted into militarist capital and diplomatic bully tactics, as when China demanded that EU governments boycott the Nobel Peace Prize award for the Chinese dissident Liu Xiaobo.[43] Even a geopolitically inert Europe is starting to get nervous after being told by a Chinese vice foreign minister that countries attending the awards ceremony at Oslo would "have to bear the consequences."[44] In this context it is not good news that China is making huge investments in Europe and buying large blocks of government bonds issued by the EU's most indebted members. Doubtless these moves are designed to forge the same kind of financial dependency on Europe's part that already exists in America.[45]

Similar concerns are prompting China's Asian neighbors to take renewed interest in the US as a balancing force on the Rim. This time, however, they are asking themselves if a nearly bankrupt America is up to the task.[46]

---

[42] Sarah Marcus, "Russia's Maneuvers in Caucasus Highlight Volatility of Regions," *The Washington Post* (June 28, 2009), http://www.washingtonpost.com/wp-dyn/content/article/2009/06/27/AR2009062702303.html

[43] See Roger C. Altman, "The Great Crash, 2008: A Geopolitical Setback for the West," *Foreign Affairs* 88, no. 1 (January/February 2009), 3 (2–14); "China Blusters On," *The New York Times* (November 5, 2010), http://www.nytimes.com/2010/11/06/opinion/06sat3.html

[44] *Ibid.*, "China Blusters On."

[45] Wieland Wagner, "China Expands its Influence in Europe," *Spiegel Online* (December 14, 2010), http://www.spiegel.de/international/world/0,1518,druck-734323,00.html

[46] Mark Landler, Jin Yardley, and Michael Wines, "China's Fast Rise Leads Neighbors to Join Forces," *The New York Times* (October 30, 2010), http://www.nytimes.com/2010/10/31/world/asia/31china.html

Fortunately Beijing also has some very pronounced vulnerabilities.[47] It is estimated that China must maintain an annual growth rate of 8 percent just to stave off a social and political cataclysm. Production plummeted during the 2008 recession, with 10,000 factory closings in the Pearl River Delta alone.[48] By early 2009 millions of jobs had been lost, including over 20 million once held by migrant workers.[49] While there were signs of recovery by mid-2009, the recession gave us a glimpse of how dependent China is on an unsustainable growth rate.

That does not mean the CCP will collapse in the event of a long and deep recession. However, lacking the legitimacy that comes with high growth, it will have to make policy adjustments that do not bode well for civil international relations. The key word here is Taiwan, since the world accepts the Chinese claim to Tibet and Xinjiang as purely internal affairs. Taiwan, by contrast, has huge geopolitical if not diplomatic status, and is linked to the democratic West in its (highly exaggerated) political development. Strained as the argument may be in empirical terms, many regard Taiwan as living proof that there is no necessary incompatibility between Chinese culture and multiparty politics.[50] Naturally this is a message that the CCP would like to delete, whether by way of economic pressure, military threat, or even invasion. Placating Beijing will not alter its resolve in the matter. The common assumption that full internationalization will inspire Chinese compromise and liberalization has it just backwards. Beijing takes this red carpet as an opportunity to cast the international order in its own image.

To the shock of some who expected the Olympics to open China up, the government included a massive human rights crackdown in its pre-Olympics preparations, and has clamped down even harder since then. This surely is not surprising to marathon China critics like Minxin Pei. In *China's Trapped Transition* he documents the government's mafia-like machinations, which have had disastrous effects on workplace safety, education, public health, the environment, and a host of other nightmares.[51] This degree

---

[47] See Robert Dujarric and Andy Zelleke, "The American Century isn't Over," *The Christian Science Monitor* (January 7, 2009), http://www.csmonitor.com/2009/0107/p09s02-coop.html

[48] John Lee, "How China Bought its Graduates' Loyalty," *The Guardian* (December 8, 2008), http://www.guardian.co.uk/commentisfree/2008/dec/08/china-graduates-credit-crunch

[49] Michael Wines, "China's Leader Says He Is 'Worried' Over U.S. Treasuries," *The New York Times* (March 14, 2009), http://www.nytimes.com/2009/03/14/business/worldbusiness/14china.html

[50] See Edward Friedman, "China: A Threat to or Threatened by Democracy?" *Dissent* (Winter 2009), http://dissentmagazine.org/article/?article=1318

[51] Minxin Pei, *China's Trapped Transition: The Limits of Developmental Autocracy* (Cambridge, MA: Harvard University Press, 2006), 169–76.

of corruption was still rare in the 1980s, but grew rapidly in the globalist 1990s.[52] Like Gordon Chang, Pei is usually regarded as a China pessimist,[53] but in fact they are both closet optimists, for thinking that oppression cannot persist is a very uplifting thought.

There are some grounds for optimism in the thousands of local protests, mostly rural, that Beijing is powerless to prevent. One estimate puts these demonstrations at more than 230,000 in 2009 alone.[54] Why, then, does the regime do so little to mollify the rural majority? One reason is that it is not at liberty to push through reforms that could alienate nouveau riche urbanites. Thailand's Thaksin lost his urban–bourgeois following and ultimately his political career when he was perceived as being too generous to the rural poor. So, the CCP faces a parlous dilemma: anything it does to ameliorate the rural crisis could alienate the urban elites, and could also embolden the rural malcontents themselves. The party's natural impulse is to beat them down. But meanwhile it is at risk from exposure of the fact that nearly all its vaunted institutional reforms—a somewhat stronger legislature, some experiments in rural self-government, a slight loosening of controls over civil society, etc.—were implemented in the 1980s, long before the globalist take-off of the next decade.[55]

Beijing's priorities were fully exposed in the aftermath of the 2008 earthquake in Sichuan. The worst destruction by far was to public schools that had obviously been shoddily constructed by corrupt builders. Twenty of these schools collapsed while surrounding buildings stood firm. Characteristically, the government refused to investigate the matter, yet arrested many who demanded answers. The artist Ai Weiwei was savagely beaten when he spoke on behalf of protesters facing trials.[56]

Why, in view of such glaring injustice and maldevelopment, does Sino-globalization hold so much attraction for the developing world? First and foremost, there is the formidable power of disinformation. China's remarkably successful media and internet oversight, along with its global public relations blitz, equips it to control its bad news better than an open society like India ever could. The fractious Indian dissident Arundhati Roy

---

[52] *Ibid.*, 159.

[53] See Minxin Pei, "Think Again: Asia's Rise," *Foreign Policy* (June 22, 2009), www.foreignpolicy.com/articles/2009/06/22/think_again_asia's_rise

[54] Perry Link, "Waiting for WikiLeaks: Beijing's Seven Secrets," *The New York Review of Books* (August 19, 2010), http://www.nybooks.com/blogs/nyrblog/2010/aug/19/waiting-wikileaks-beijings-seven-secrets/

[55] Pei, *China's Trapped Transition*, *op. cit.*, 11.

[56] Ron Gluckman, "The Art of Social Advocacy," *The Wall Street Journal* (January 25, 2011), http://online.wsj.com/article/SB10001424052748704624504576097932998562592.html

is often threatened with arrest, but is still able to voice her grievances full blast.[57] Some Chinese dissidents, such as the refractory Ai and the amiable Liu Xiaobo, can readily broadcast their messages around the world, but not inside China itself. By contrast, Roy takes her message directly to the people, drawing huge crowds in small villages and cities alike.[58] She makes sure, for example, that the atavistic injustice of India's Public Safety Act gets much more exposure than do China's equivalent but far more actively employed "security" laws. India's increasing use of this act may well be inspired by China's example, which is the gold standard for having it both ways: simultaneously reaping the profits of globalization and repression.

This reactionary globalism—the crux of the China model—is a dream come true for hard-liners in developing countries. For them the model's human rightlessness and gaping income disparity register as its prime virtues. It is little wonder, then, that Second and Third World elites get along so well. Try as they will, America and the First World cannot compete with China and the Second World when it comes to the twin arts of venality and brutality. The only lasting bond that is going to be possible between the First and Third Worlds is a post-globalist one, which is to say a democratic and egalitarian one.

Winston Churchill once said that America will eventually do the right thing, after exhausting all the other possibilities. The good news is that Washington has reached that dead end in its dealings with the developing world. It is now manifestly in Washington's interest to promote real democracy abroad, just as it is categorically in Beijing's interest to undermine democracy and human rights wherever possible. This is going to be the fundamental dividing line of world affairs in the 21st century. There is no question which side of that divide China will be on, but Russia, as Chapter 2 will show, is still a potential swing state that could be brought in from the cold.

---

[57] See Murtaza Shibli, "Arundhati Roy and Kashmir's Struggle for Justice," *The Guardian* (October 28, 2010), http://www.guardian.co.uk/commentisfree/2010/oct/28/kashmir-arundhati-roy-india and Leo Mirani, "Arundhati Roy has Stirred up a Debate, not about Kashmir, but about Herself," *The Guardian* (October 31, 2010), http://www.guardian.co.uk/commentisfree/2010/oct/31/arundhati-roy-kashmir-controversy

[58] Ian Jack, "Arundhati Roy: India's Bold and Brilliant Daughter," *The Guardian* (January 29, 2011), http://www.guardian.co.uk/theguardian/2011/jan/29/arundhati-roy-interview-india-activism-novel

2

RUSSIA TURNS EAST
Putinism and the Making
of Kremlin Capitalism

KREMLIN CAPITALISM

In both its timing and its social impact, Russia's neoliberal encounter of the 1990s had much in common with India. Rapid economic "reform" misfired in both cases, giving rise to a "worst of both" marriage of modern and traditional populism. While Indians had recourse to fascistic "Hindutva," Russians reverted to an equally reactionary fusion of Orthodox religion and rabid anti-liberalism. This anti-Western recoil has become synonymous with the name Vladimir Putin. The irony is that Putin's rise to power was a virtual gift from the West. Here, as in India, Western globalism has cultivated the worst indigenous forces at the expense of the democratic values it claims to foster.

Russians had hoped for broad economic regeneration after their historic turn toward the West. Instead, Washington-directed privatization froze investment, squandered capital, and pillaged collective assets,[1] as when the government's share of Gazprom, valued at $119 billion, was sold for

---

[1] Joseph E. Stiglitz, *Globalization and its Discontents* (New York: W. W. Norton, 2002), 144.

$20 million.[2] With a 41 percent drop in output from 1990 to 1997, the loss in GDP was even greater than in World War II.[3] Insult was added to injury as Moscow suffered an abject fall from great power status. Increasingly Russians looked back on Soviet Kremlinism with nostalgia, such that the communist Gennady Zyuganov captured nearly a third of the votes in the 2000 presidential election. Most Russians, however, did not want a rollback that abandoned the promised land of capitalism. With Putin they got the best of both: Kremlin capitalism.

To be sure, the difference between Putin and Zyuganov goes far beyond economics. Putin does not just return Russia to its pre-capitalist mold. No small part of his appeal owes to the fact that in some respects he rolls the clock back to a pre-communist ethos. Russians not only associate communism with long food lines and empty store shelves, but with the vacuity of a failed secular theology. Much like India's Vajpayee, Putin shrouds an economic revolution in a religious cloak. One of the few parts of his KGB indoctrination that he repudiates is its guardianship of official atheism.[4] As did Bush on the American side, Putin offers himself as God's political emissary. This may explain Bush's claim to have looked Putin in the eye and gotten "a sense of his soul."[5]

Unfortunately, Putin's religiosity extends no farther than the Russian Orthodox Church (ROC). The late Church Patriarch Alexi II grandly returned the favor, working in tandem with Putin to legitimize his Kremlinism. The first post-Soviet law restricting Protestant worship was enacted under Yeltsin in 1997, but was scarcely enforced. It was Putin who turned the ROC's antipathies into state policies, unleashing the FSB (Federal Security Service) and other clandestine agencies on competing Christian denominations. Non-Orthodox believers are now treated as heretics and as criminals if they dare congregate without a license. This Church–State reciprocity has solid public support,[6] and increasingly extends to the sphere of foreign policy. The ROC, now under Patriarch Kirill I, not only militates

---

[2] John P. Willerton, Jr., "The Presidency: From Yeltsin to Putin," in *Developments in Russian Politics*, ed. Stephen White, Alex Pravda, and Zvi Qitelman (Hampshire, UK: Palgrave, 2001), 36 (21–41).

[3] Stiglitz, *op. cit.*, 143–44.

[4] Michael Binyon, "Russian Roulette," *New Humanist* 123, no. 2 (March/April 2008), http://newhumanist.org.uk/1729

[5] By contrast, John McCain says that he looked into Putin's soul "and saw three letters: KGB." See Ken Fireman, "McCain Would Evict Medvedev from G-8, Push Russia on Democracy," *Bloomberg.com* (May 6, 2008), http://www.bloomberg.com/apps/news?pid=20601087&sid=a2Toncy6GkjI&refer=home#

[6] A 2008 poll indicated that 71 percent of the population embraces Russian Orthodoxy, up from 59 percent in 2003. See Clifford J. Levy, "At Expense of All Others, Putin Picks

against the secular principles of the Russian Constitution, but pushes for foreign policies that would expand the sway of the Church throughout the "near abroad" or wherever ROCs happen to live.[7] The almost perfect match between ROC interests and Putin's personal preferences goes far to explain how Putin came to be one of the most popular leaders in Russian history, with an 80 percent approval rating at the end of his eight years as president.

Nothing more epitomizes Putin's KGB mentality than the zero-sum terms he applies to all politics, domestic and foreign.[8] His clenched-fist diplomacy set the stage for renewed geopolitical confrontation with America as soon as Russia had the means to afford it. Did American and NATO actions precipitate this renewed KGBism? No doubt they accelerated it. However, when Stephen Cohen charges that "the cold war ended in Moscow, but not in Washington,"[9] he overlooks the fact that today's provocation would have been little more than an annoyance in 1989.[10] One event, late in that year, suffices to prove this point: when reactionaries loyal to the executed dictator Nicolae Ceausescu tried to restore authoritarian rule in Rumania, US Secretary of State James Baker expressed Washington's willingness to back a Soviet military intervention on the side of democracy.[11] There can be no doubt that as of that moment the Cold War was over on *both* sides, at least at the presidential level.

The problem was that Russia's anti-Western factions were implacable, and growing fast. At first this hardly mattered, since Russia was in no economic condition to directly challenge the emerging new world order. It was not long, however, before an all-too-familiar Kremlinism reasserted

---

a Church," *The New York Times* (April 24, 2008), http://www.nytimes.com/2008/04/24/world/europe/24church.html

[7] Robert C. Blitt, "Russia's 'Orthodox' Foreign Policy: The Growing Influence of the Russian Orthodox Church in Shaping Russian Policies Abroad," paper presented at a conference on Religion in the Public Square, in Budapest, Hungary, June 4–5, 2010.

[8] This was less obvious in the early Putin years. Thus Dmitri Trenin found it easy to argue that Putin was averse to Eurasianist anti-Westernism. We agree with Trenin that Putin was not ideologically fixated on a "turn East" agenda, but he took very little convincing in the face of the subsequent color revolutions, and his tendency has been to vastly overrate the threat of Western encroachment in the "near abroad" relative to the far greater China threat. See Dimitri Trenin, *The End of Eurasia: Russia on the Border Between Geopolitics and Globalization* (Moscow: Carnegie Moscow Center, 2001).

[9] Stephen F. Cohen, "The New American Cold War," *The Nation* (July 10, 2006), http://www.thenation.com/doc/20060710/cohen

[10] Concerning this provocation, see Pierre Hassner, "Russia's Transition to Autocracy," *Journal of Democracy* 9, no. 2 (April 2008): 13 (5–15).

[11] Steve Sesser, "Are Invasions Sometimes OK?" *The New York Times* (January 17, 1990), http://www.nytimes.com/2008/05/11/opinion/11opclassic.html

itself in the "near abroad."[12] Even Mikhail Gorbachev sent tanks into Vilnius, Lithuania, while world attention was frozen on Kuwait.[13] By spring 1992 Russia was playing a crafty divide and conquer game in the war between Armenia and Azerbaijan. Turkey's increasing support of Azerbaijan forced Armenia to purchase Moscow's backing at the price of Russian hegemony.

By that July, in the name of peacekeeping, Russian forces were invading Georgia to enforce a cease-fire that effectively granted South Ossetia its independence. The process was soon repeated in Abkhazia, where Moscow insidiously played both sides of the fence, offering military assistance to Georgia in return for the kind of deal Armenia had accepted. President Eduard Shevardnadze flatly refused, and by October 1993 Abkhazia had de facto autonomy.[14] There was little reaction from Washington, due largely to its post-historical ("end of history") faith in instant-mix democratization. Cohen has it just backwards. Believing the East–West contest of the Cold War had been "won," not just suspended, Western leaders could not foresee a renewed global contest or regional great game. Hence the conflagration in the Caucasus was seen as a fleeting anachronism.

Today, with Russia's literal occupation of South Ossetia and Abkhazia, that illusion has been vaporized. By supporting these insurgencies, Moscow denied Georgia the same sovereignty rights that it swore by in its own brutal suppression of Chechen independence. To defend such policies, Andrei P. Tsygankov must resort to the jaded argument that Russia's aggression in the Caucasus is motivated by a legitimate quest for security and stability.[15] Hitler used much the same argument as he annexed Czechoslovakia, and some will of course apologize for Putin's domestic crackdown on liberal democracy by arguing that he had no choice.

Granted, communism was as much a means of order as a mode of production. The Soviet system had so programmatically destroyed competing means of social restraint that the sudden removal of the state's authoritarian oversight was bound to throw society into chaos. In the absence of civil institutions to co-support a democratic culture, the "shock therapy" of

---

[12] This zone, which is subsumed politically by the Commonwealth of Independent States (CIS), encompasses most of the ex-Soviet sphere.

[13] See Peter Hitchens, "Moscow Hangover," *The American Conservative* (July 16, 2008), http://www.Amconmag.com/2008/2008_06_16/article.html

[14] Svante E. Cornell, *Georgia After the Rose Revolution: Geopolitical Predicament and Implications for U.S. Policy* (Carlisle, Panama: Strategic Studies Institute, 2007), 19–20.

[15] Andrei P. Tsygankov, "If not by Tanks, then by Banks? The Role of Soft Power in Putin's Foreign Policy," *Europe-Asia Studies* 58, no. 7 (November 2006): 1080–81 (1079–1099).

globalization made a bad situation far worse. It can be argued that by the end of the decade, the choice was between anarchy and some form of radical statism. It follows that if Putinism had not filled this vacuum, something equally heinous would have.[16] Before Putin there was General Alexander Lebed, whose motto was "First we act, then we explain." In the 1996 presidential race against Zyuganov, Yeltsin used Lebed, whom he introduced as his heir apparent, to sate the public's yearning for a strongman. The problem was that Lebed was not just strong but grossly impolitic. By comparison, the early Putin came across as a consummate diplomat. The general was sacked after the election, and later he conveniently died in a helicopter crash. As Alec Rasizade puts it, Russia would have to look for a new "Bonaparte."[17]

A NEW SECOND WORLD

The global ramifications of Putin's Bonapartism can hardly be overstated. While America and Europe weigh in as the avatars of liberal capitalism, and China as the unrivaled poster child for authoritarian capitalism,[18] Russia is emerging as the 21st century "decider." As the crucial Eurasian swing state, its decision to support or isolate China will largely determine the fate of a rehabilitated Second World. Early globalists took it as a foregone conclusion that Russia would swing toward the West. This confidence rested on the glib assumption that liberal democracy was a natural by-product of globalization. Even after Tiananmen and the subsequent TNC/CCP symbiosis that fuels Sino-globalization,[19] the fact has not sunk in that capitalism can be

---

[16] See Songok Han Thornton and William H. Thornton, *Development Without Freedom: The Politics of Asian Globalization* (Hampshire, UK: Ashgate, 2008), 183.

[17] Alec Rasizade, "Putin's Mission in the Russian Thermidor," *World Affairs: The Journal of International Issues* 11, no. 4 (Winter 2007), 151 (142–76). Had Putin not been there to play this part, others could easily have done so. Moscow's former mayor, Yuri M. Luzhkov, who funneled hundreds of millions into pro-Moscow insurrection in Georgia and Ukraine, could have taken Putin's place in a flash. See Clifford J. Levy, "Russians React to Article on Moscow Mayor's Ventures," *The New York Times* (October 27, 2008), http://www.nytimes.com/2008/10/27/world/europe/27reax.html

[18] A strong case can be made that the entrepreneurial capitalism that emerged in the Chinese countryside during the 1980s went into eclipse in the 1990s, such that much of China has been becoming less "capitalistic" in the Western sense of the word. See Yasheng Huang, *Capitalism with Chinese Characteristics: Entrepreneurship and the State* (Cambridge, UK: Cambridge University Press, 2008).

[19] See William H. Thornton, "Sino-Globalization: Politics of the CCP/TNC Symbiosis," *New Political Science: A Journal of Politics & Culture* 29, no. 2 (June 2007): 211–35.

rabidly authoritarian, and not just in the short run. As Robert Kagan notes, Putin has had good reason to look on China as a role model.[20]

Faith in globalization's democratic teleology has proved as fallacious and costly as the domino theory once was. Western leaders tend to forget that freedom does not unfold from any deterministic formula, least of all one that has a dollar sign in front of it. Huge amounts of Western aid and investment were pumped into Russia in the early 1990s, only to be squandered, stolen, or simply reinvested abroad for private profit. Russian banks invested about $450 million domestically as opposed to around $15.5 billion elsewhere.[21] For that Russians have no one to blame but themselves.

Nonetheless the West must share a big part of the blame for the Russian economic debacle, and hence for Putin's rise to power. Post-Soviet Russia was coerced into taking on the full foreign debt of the USSR—a burden reminiscent of the Entente forced on Germany in 1919.[22] Aid was given on the condition that neoliberal "shock therapy" be applied. This ripped out the economic safety net that might have cushioned Russia's capitalist transformation. And when the inevitable crash came, Western investors rushed in to buy up former Soviet assets at fire sale discounts, as did Russian Mafia bosses who became the nucleus of the emerging capitalist class.[23] It is against this backdrop that other antagonisms take their toll.[24] Russia's legitimate sense of grievance is compounded by NATO's eastward advance and its planned missile shield. Clearly Moscow has ample grounds for complaint. Promises made to Soviet leaders in return for dismantling their empire have been shredded.

Putin, however, entered the lists as a seeming moderate. The West thought it had more to fear from hardliners such as Putin's prime minister, Yevgeny Primakov, whose zero-sum impulse was notorious. Putin's desire to "normalize" Russia's foreign relations seemed closer to the outlook of

---

[20] Robert Kagan, *The Return of History and the End of Dreams* (New York: Alfred A. Knopf, 2008), 56.

[21] See Zbigniew Brzezinski, "The Premature Partnership," *Foreign Affairs* 73, no. 2 (March/April 1994): 69 (67–82).

[22] Alfred Kokh, "The West Must not Push Russia Away," *The Christian Science Monitor* (October 15, 2008), http://www.csmonitor.com/2008/1015/p09s01-coop.html

[23] Loren Goldner, "Great Game II: America Lashes Out on the Borders of China and Russia," *Mute: Culture and Politics after the Net* (October 8, 2008), http://www.metamute.org/content/great_game_ii_america_lashes_out_on_the_borders_of_china_and_russia

[24] Even without those provocations, most Russians would have little sense of affiliation with the West. Only 11 percent of Russians live in Moscow or St. Petersburg, where direct Western contacts are more likely, and in a recent survey only 4 percent have any pronounced sense of identification with the West. See Richard Rose and Neil Munro, "Do Russians See their Future in Europe or the CIS?" *Europe-Asia Studies* 60, no. 1 (January 2008): 55–56 (49–66).

Andrei Kozyrev, Russia's first foreign minister, who believed in advancing Russia's interests through cooperation rather than confrontation.[25] Talking of democracy and the rule of law, Putin easily won confidence in Washington. Of course, with the Chechen War going badly, and Russia still reeling from the 1998 crash, this was not the time for renewed polarity. For now the new regime, like Yeltsin's before, would have to wear separate domestic and foreign hats. For good reason Putin cooperated with President Bush after 9/11, and even muted his reaction to NATO's expansion and America's withdrawal from the Antiballistic Missile Treaty of 1972.

In return for Russian cooperation in Central Asia on the eve of the Afghan War, Putin got royal treatment from the White House at a time when Europe was aghast at his actions in Chechnya. Moscow managed to "grandfather in" the Chechen War as part of Washington's war on terrorism.[26] In fact, by invading Afghanistan, America was acting as a virtual proxy for Soviet security interests. As the Russian specialist Toby T. Gati puts it, "Putin now had the Americans doing his business in Afghanistan and he was fighting to the last American."[27] Soon Russian air transports were landing in Kabul, as Moscow charged back into Central Asia's Great Game, courtesy of Washington.

Not until 2003 were Putin's economic coffers and his domestic power base impressive enough to support a more transparent "KGB" agenda, and even then he was slow to take a pronounced anti-Western stand. Global events forced his hand, however. The US Iraq invasion gave him a hard push, as he could not afford to come across as Washington's lackey. Claiming the high moral ground, he grabbed the opportunity to move closer to the other West—that of Chirac and Schröder as opposed to Bush and Blair.[28] Clearly his hope was to forge a Russian–German–French axis to counter US unilateralism, but the ongoing Europeanization of former Soviet space finally made him look for greener geopolitical pastures.

The color revolutions in Georgia, Ukraine, and Kyrgyzstan gave the final push. Zbigniew Brzezinski had long before predicted that Ukraine's turn to

---

[25] Richard Sakwa, "New Cold War on Twenty Year's Crisis? Russia and International Politics," *International Affairs* 84, no. 2 (2008): 242–43 (241–67).

[26] See Carla Anne Robbins, "Mr. Bush Gets Another Look into Mr. Putin's Eyes," *The New York Times* (June 30, 2007), http://www.nytimes.com/2007/06/30/opinion/30sat3.html

[27] Quoted Patrick E. Tyler, "The World: The Morning After Dawns on Moscow," *The New York Times* (December 16, 2001), http://query.nytimes.com/gst/fullpage.html

[28] Robert Service, "A Touch of Menace," *Hoover Digest* no. 1 (2008), http://www. hoover.org/publications/digest/13848482.html and Andrew Kuchins, "New Directions in Russian Foreign Policy: Is the East Wind Prevailing over the West Wind in Moscow?" Wilton Park Conference on Russia, the G-8 Chairmanship, and Beyond, November 29, 2005, http://www.cdi.org/russia/johnson/9314-27.cfm

the West would ensure Russia's equally decisive turn to the East.[29] Between 2003 and 2005, Russia effectively rejoined the Second World, dropping the Westpolitik that had marked the Yeltsin years and even the early Putin years. Moscow and Beijing demanded a fast US exit from Central Asia and drew an ideological line in the sand by defending Uzbekistan after the 2005 Andejan massacre.[30] This "easternization" of Kremlin foreign policy would be matched on the domestic side by a campaign of historical revisionism, including the apotheosis of World War II ("the Great Patriotic War") and the rewriting of high school textbooks to soften or delete representations of Stalin's brutality.[31]

MAN OF THE YEAR

Putin's political success, powered by resource nationalism, bears comparison with the petro-politics of Hugo Chávez of Venezuela, though there are striking differences in terms of their global packaging. Whereas Chávez never made any pretense of fitting into the new world order as envisioned by the Washington Consensus, Putin restrained his refractory inclinations until he could afford to flaunt them as a bargaining chip in the new great game. At that point he played his resource card to thunderous domestic applause. By popular demand, Russia was "turning East."

That reversal put Russia back on the geopolitical map and got Putin onto the cover of *Time* magazine as person of the year for 2007. His stunningly pugnacious Munich speech of February 10, 2007 gave "Old Europe" — which in Robert Kagan's words had been playing Venus to America's Mars — a quick refresher course on geopolitical realities. So too it gave NATO a new lease on life. This should not have been necessary, given Putin's treatment of Chechnya, which in many ways was reminiscent of Mussolini's treatment of Ethiopia. Unfortunately it met roughly the same international indifference.

While the new Kremlinism tamed Boris Yeltsin's kleptocratic "family," it also resurrected the Stalinist anthem, the cult of the sacrosanct army, and the rightful powers of the KGB, now recycled as the FSB.[32] What solidified

---

[29] Zbigniew Brzezinski, *The Grand Chessboard: American Primacy and Its Geopolitical Imperatives* (New York: Basic Books, 1997), 46.

[30] See Dimitri Trenin, "Russia Leaves the West," *Foreign Affairs* 85, no. 4 (July/August 2006): 91 (87–96).

[31] Peter Finn, "From Russia, A Cinematic Double Take on WWII Era," *The Washington Post* (May 31, 2008), A01.

[32] See Sergei Kovalev, "Why Putin Wins," trans., Jamey Gambrell, *The New York Review of Books* 54, no. 18 (November/December 2007), http://www.nybooks.com/articles/20836

Putinism's political base was its reinstatement of the extraordinary power and privileges of the *nomenklatura*.[33] Under Putin the number of state employees doubled, reaching around 1.5 million.[34] This bureaucratic class would become his Pretorian Guard, cheering him on as he and his chosen successor turned the 2008 presidential election into a mockery of even pro forma democracy.

The *nomenklatura* view this democratic forfeiture as a fair price for stability and prosperity. Yet Putinism is anything but the economic panacea they imagine. Two things have saved the new Kremlinism from the public opprobrium it deserves. The first was the marvelous luck of having Yeltsinism as a comparative base. Ironically it was Yeltsin's two good years, 1996 and 1997, that set the stage for the crash of 1998. It was then that Russia's debt passed the tipping point. The default that followed nearly took the global system down with it, and finished Yeltsinism politically.

The second stroke of luck came with surging oil prices, without which the economy would have sunk into Third World oblivion. Revenues shot up as the price per barrel of oil almost tripled.[35] Tellingly, however, investment as a percentage of GDP lagged behind many of the region's fledgling democracies.[36] Russia was becoming a classic case of the "wealth paradox," whereby countries that are richest in natural resources tend to fare worse politically and often even economically.[37] Though Russia's aggregate economy grew more than 6 percent per year for most of Putin's time as president, the general population has not been invited to the party. The story is told by the suicide rate (50 percent higher since the 1990s), alcoholism, drug addiction, and the climate of fear that engulfs all ethnic minorities.[38]

As the working classes fell into penury, Putin accepted the IMF mandate to raise housing and heating costs and cut social services. Why would this

---

[33] See Alexander N. Yakovlev, "Restoration of the *Nomenklatura* in Russia," *New Perspectives Quarterly — NPQ* 21, no. 2 (Spring 2004), http://www.digitalnpq.org/archive/2004_spring/ yakovlev.html

[34] Michael McFaul and Kathryn Stoner-Weiss, "The Myth of the Authoritarian Model: How Putin's Crackdown Holds Russia Back," *Foreign Affairs* 87, no. 1 (January/February, 2008): 74 (68–84).

[35] Amy Knight, "The Truth about Putin and Medvedev," *The New York Review of Books* 55, no. 8 (May 15, 2008), http://www.nybooks.com/articles/21353

[36] See McFaul and Stoner-Weiss, "The Myth of the Authoritarian Model," *op. cit.*

[37] In contrast to Russia's resource route to globalization, China took the road of cheap labor, which it bartered for capital and technology. See Judith Stein, "Russia: Which Capitalist Road?" *Dissent* (Fall 2006), http://dissentmagazine.org/article/?article=693&print=1

[38] Federico Varese, "The Russian Conundrum: Growing Economy, Failing Society," *Dissent* (Spring 2007), http://dissentmagazine.org/article/?article=768&print=1

anti-Western demagogue yield so easily to this very Western intrusion into social policy? The simple answer is that he was not averse to the corporatism that Yeltsin had embraced, but simply undertook to put the Kremlin back in charge. In effect he made himself the corporate CEO-in-chief. Putinism is fascism, pure and simple, and the fact that it is every bit as globalist as Yelsinism was says much about the real nature of today's globalization.

The undertow effect of Russia's resource curse should not blind us to the potency of Putinism as a Second World development model. Its signal advantage—a dexterous linkage of revanchist nationalism with international capitalism[39]—runs against the grain of classic globalist theory, which downplays nationalism in world affairs. Putinism's ardent re-nationalization makes it uniquely attractive to developing countries such as Serbia,[40] which need Western commercial contacts yet are repelled by EU cosmopolitanism. Under Putin, capital no longer calls the shots. Despite globalization, or indeed because of it, Moscow is back in charge. Making profits in Russia means being on good terms with the Kremlin.

It is little wonder that Henry Kissinger and James Baker—former secretaries of state turned corporate power venders—have lent support for the Obama "reset" of US-Russian relations. This is the new frontier of the lucrative political brokerage they engineered in China, and in some ways it is better suited for their brand of cronyism. The Putinist linkage of capitalism and authoritarianism has much in common with China's revised CCPism, except that Beijing lost effective control of its provinces long ago. That dilutes the effectiveness of the Kissinger–Baker style of mercantilism. On the other hand, transnational corporations are benefited by the fact that

---

[39] Many analysts fall into the delusion of thinking Putin's "joiner" impulse softens his Second World reflex. See James M. Goldgeier and Michael McFaul, "Russians as Joiners: Realist and Liberal Connection of Postcommunist Europe," in *After the Collapse of Communism: Comparative Lessons of Transition*, ed. Michael McFaul and Kathryn Stoner-Weiss. (New York: Cambridge University Press, 2004), Chapter 7, 232–56.

[40] Serbia's far-Right Radical Party, now headed by Tomislav Nikolić, venerates Putin and awaits the opportunity to do for Serbia what he has done for Russia, which is to silence opposing parties. See Charles Simic, "The Troubled Birth of Kosovo," *The New York Review of Books* 55, no. 5 (April 3, 2008), http://www.nybooks.com/articles/21190

These Radicals hope to join an anti-Western coalition government in the near future. They welcome Gazprom's controlling interest in Serbia's national oil company and propose making Serbia a hub for Western trade with Russia. Unlike the former Serbian prime minister, Vojislav Koštunica, who is anti-Western in the classic sense of romantic nationalism, Nikolić models on the pragmatism of Putin's globalized nationalism. He may be every bit as reactionary as Milosevic, Mladic, or Karadzic, but Western capitalists know they can deal with him. See Dan Bilefsky, "No Milosevic, He Says, but Serbia's 'Undertaker' Worries the West," *The New York Times* (May 3, 2008), http://www.nytimes.com/2008/05/03/world/europe/03nikolic.html

local fiefdoms brazenly ignore central edicts on social and environmental issues.[41]

A similar centrifugal drift was apparent in Russia under Yeltsin,[42] but Putinism has been working hard to reverse all that. Its renewed centrism is tied to all spheres of business, including the vast Russian underworld.[43] For all the government's talk about fighting corruption, Russia in 2009 stood at 146th out of 177 nations in Transparency International's ranking of global corruption—that is, at about the level of Sierra Leone. Russians pay around $318 billion in bribes each year, or one-third of the country's GDP.[44] That does not prevent some analysts from praising the new Kremlinism for undermining localism, as if that is *prima facie* evidence of progress.[45] This is like praising Mussolini for making the trains run on time. Perhaps Putinism can do the same for Russian air traffic, but opposition leader Garry Kasparov has good reason never to fly on Aeroflot.

The renationalization of corporations like Gazprom and Rosneft was carried out under a patriotic cloak, but certainly not for the general public's benefit.[46] Whether or not official ownership is national or private, the state is now in charge, and the economic clout this affords is prodigious. Gazprom alone controls a fifth of the world's gas production,[47] and along

---

[41] Francis Fukuyama stresses that most rights abuses to Chinese citizens also involve TVEs (township and village enterprises) that were set up after China's economic restructuration in 1978. See Francis Fukuyama, "China's Powerful Weakness," *Los Angeles Times* (April 29, 2008), http://www.latimes.com/ news/opinion/la-oe-fukuyama29apr29, 0,5376622,print.story and Francis Fukuyama, "China, Strong States and Liberty," *New Perspectives Quarterly* (Spring 2008), http://www.digitalnpq.org/articles/global/262/04-28-2008/francis_fukuyama

[42] Alec Razisade,*op. cit.*, 155.

[43] That connection is natural in a country where even the police in most Russian towns are openly in league with organized crime. See Orlando Figs, "Vlad the Great," *New Statesman* (November 29, 2007), http://www.newstatesman.com/print/200711290027

[44] Fred Weir, "Russia Corruption Costs $318 Billion—One-Third of GDP," *The Christian Science Monitor* (November 23, 2009), http://www.csmonitor.com/layout/set/print/content/view/print/263681

[45] John F. Young and Gary N. Wilson, "The View from Below: Local Government and Putin's Reforms," *Europe-Asia Studies* 59, no. 7 (November 2007): 1087 (1071–88).

[46] By fall 2010, the virtual bankruptcy of the state forced Moscow to reverse its course and put 900 state companies up for public sale, including 15 percent of Rosnef and 25 percent of Russian Railways. This time, however, the state will be so solidly in charge that paper ownership will not affect political power relations as it did in the 1990s. See Daniel Amerman, "Russia Earmarks 900 State Firms for Public Sale," *BBC News* (October 21, 2010), http://www.bbc.co.uk/news/business-11594837

[47] Joshua Kurlantzick, "State Inc.," *Boston.com* (March 16, 2008), http://www.boston.com/bostoneglobe/ideas/articles/2008/03/16/state_inc?mode=PF

with Rosneft it provides two-thirds of Russia's federal budget.[48] It seemed obvious as of 2000 that Yeltsin's economic overlords would run this show. That would have had profound geopolitical consequences, for then there would be little chance of a full "turn East" and a consequent consolidation of the new Second World. Yeltsin's oligarchs constituted an inadvertent barrier against an even less democratic Kremlin elite.

Putin tore down that barrier and cleared the way for a far more assertive Kremlinism. He renounced democratic values at home and reached out to like-minded authoritarians abroad. With surprisingly little trouble, he pulled off a veritable revolution, though it cannot be said that no shots were fired. Uncooperative journalists were routinely assassinated. The very unsubtle message was that vocal dissent, or even objective reportage, would no longer be tolerated. And corporate interference would be strictly proscribed. In a prophetic meeting late in 2000 Putin served notice on the corporate oligarchs that henceforth their only business would be business.[49] Nonetheless Putinism ended up fusing business and politics even more tightly, albeit with a role reversal in who answers to whom. As Kasparov wryly asks: "The oligarchs Oleg Derispaska and Roman Abramovich are worth $21 billion each, and Potanin and Prokhorov each have $14 billion. How much do you think the man is worth who has the power to throw them all into prison on the same day?"[50]

DARKEST HOUR

Guy Sorman draws insightful comparisons between Putin and Charles de Gaulle, whose Bonapartism combined ultra-nationalism with aristocratic

---

[48] Miriam Elder, "How the State Got a Grip on Energy, Putting Natural Resources Back in the State's Hands," *The St. Petersburg Times* (March 18, 2008), http://www.sptimes.ru/index.php?story_id=25375 &action_id=2

[49] *Ibid.*

[50] See Garry Kasparov, "Russia is not a Democracy," *Spiegel* interview, *Spiegel Online* (March 15, 2007), http://www.spiegel.de/international/Spiegel/0,1518,druck-471877,00.html

As of 2007 Putin was believed to personally control 37 percent of the shares of Russia's fourth largest oil producer, Surgutneftegaz. That would put the market value of his holdings at $20 billion. He also controls nearly 5 percent of Gazprom, in addition to his 50 percent stake in the oil company Gunvor, through his representative Gennady Timchenko. In 2006, Gunvor's profit came to $8 billion. See David Satter, "Russia Incorporated: Why Vladimir Putin Dare Not Give Up His Position as Capo," *The Weekly Standard* 013, no. 14 (December 17, 2007), http://www.weeklystandard.com/Utilities/printer_preview.asp?idArticle =14461&R=116312D27

and even monarchic traditions.[51] We should also mention the striking resemblance between the political economy of Putinism and that of East Asia's early "miracle" economies. Consider, for example, the iron grip that Korea's President Park Chung Hee held over his nation's chaebol. Those giant conglomerates were never allowed to forget that they were junior partners in Korea's government–chaebol symbiosis.[52] Similarily, Yeltsin's corporatocracy has been tamed, even as the state–corporate bond has been intensified.

The scope of Kremlin, Inc. is suggested by the double lives of its CEOs. It is no accident that two of Putin's deputy prime ministers became the chairmen of Gazprom and Russian Railways. One of these, Dmitry Medvedev, replaced Putin as president. Other Kremlin luminaries took the helm of the second largest oil company, a nuclear fuel giant, and Aeroflot. The minister of industry took over the oil pipeline monopoly, the finance minister was given both the diamond monopoly and the second largest state bank, and the telecoms minister got the biggest mobile phone operation.[53] Collectively Putin's cronies control around 80 percent of Russia's stock market capitalization.[54]

What these glaring conflicts of interest augur for Russian development is sad to contemplate. Two essential ingredients of functional democracy, according to Amartya Sen, are open information and public debate.[55] In the late 1980s President Gorbachev cracked this Senian door with his famous mix of *glasnost* and *perestroika*. Suddenly the dull, statist media of past years gave way to flaming commentaries on Russian politics.[56] However, under Yeltsin's corporatism the political side of Gorbachev's revolution was de-prioritized. Caught in the flux of this rump liberalism, the media began to slide into their present mercantile rut.[57] The counter-revolution had

---

[51] Guy Sorman, "From de Gaulle to Putin," *Project Syndicate* (September 19, 2008), http://www.project-syndicate.org/print_commentary/sorman3/English. Likewise, Pierre Hassner compares Putin to some of the more menacing features of Franklin Roosevelt, who also subdued vexatious oligarchs and extended his rule beyond its normal limits. See Pierre Hassner, *op. cit.*, 7–8.

[52] Songok Han Thornton, "The 'Miracle' Revisited: The De-Radicalization of Korean Political Culture," *New Political Science* 27, no. 2 (June 2005): 161 (161–176).

[53] Perry Anderson, "Russia's Managed Democracy," *London Review of Books* 29, no. 2 (January 25, 2007), http://www.lrb.co.uk/v29/n02/print/ande01_.html

[54] Satter, *op. cit.*

[55] See Songok Han Thornton, "Trial by Development: Senian 'Concurrence' in the New Asian Developmentalism," *New Political Science* 28, no. 3 (September 2006): 353–76.

[56] Michael Specter, "Kremlin, Inc.: Why are Vladimir Putin's Opponents Dying?" *The New Yorker* (January 29, 2007), http://www.newyorker.com/printables/fact/070129fa_fact_specter

[57] *Ibid.*

begun, though inconclusively. If Yeltsin had no fondness for press freedom, it can at least be said that he was an inattentive censor. Journalists were still able to report the horrors of the Chechen War in detail. This gave rise to an overwhelming consensus that the war must end, and gave Russia's power elite a lesson in what to avoid at all costs.

Putin resolved to tame the press, and soon the message was out that the life expectancy of journalists could depend upon the vigor and candor of their reporting on sensitive issues. The most notable case in point was that of the intrepid Anna Politkovskaya, who signed her death warrant by persisting in writing articles critical of Russia's scorched earth policies in Chechnya. It is surely no accident that she was murdered on the president's birthday.[58] In many ways this was a tragic replay of the murder of Yuri Shchekochikhin in the midst of his 2003 investigation of the general prosecutor's office. Some see his assassination as the end of the romantic era of Russian journalism that flowered in the 1980s with perestroika.[59]

After that there was a shocking normality about the high-profile murders of Politkovskaya and Ivan Safronov, a military affairs journalist for *Kommersant* who outraged the government by reporting the launch failures of the Bulava intercontinental ballistic missile, Putin's pet project. Safronov mysteriously fell from a window to his death just as he was about to release a highly sensitive report on Russian arms deliveries to the Middle East. The police immediately ruled this a "suicide."[60] It would have been real news if they had taken the case half seriously.

Putin takes it all in stride, casually dismissing these murders as the work of enemies who want to discredit him, or making no comment whatsoever. The Russian cult of the strongman is so pervasive that suspicion of Putin's complicity in such crimes—including the allegation that he was behind the 1996 apartment bombings that gave him an excuse for the second Chechen War—only raises his popularity.[61] In a slapdash two-for-one sale, Moscow charged that the exiled tycoon and veteran Putin critic Boris Berezovsky ordered the murder of Politkovskaya.[62]

Berezovsky's name was already familiar to British tabloid readers, as he was a close associate of another murdered Putin critic, the former KGB

---

[58] Tom Parfitt, "Assassin's Bullet Kills Fiery Critic of Putin," *Observer* (October 8, 2006), http://oberver.guardian.co.uk/print/0,,329595772-119093,00.html

[59] Nadezhda Azhgikhina, "The Struggle for Press Freedom in Russia: Reflections of a Russian Journalist," *Europe–Asia Studies* 59, no. 8 (December 2007): 1248 (1245–1262).

[60] "Ivan Safronov was Killed," *Kommersant.com* (March 6, 2007), http://www.kommersant.com/p747802/ Ivan_Safronov_arms_trading/

[61] Kovalev, *op. cit.*

[62] See "Berezovsky Blamed in Politkovskaya Murder," *The Moscow Times* (April 4, 2008), http://www.moscowtimes.ru/articles/detail.php?ID=361780&print=Y

agent Aleksander Litvinenko. Litvinenko died in London in 2006 after ingesting polonium 210, a commonly used KGB/FSB poison that is virtually impossible for the general public to obtain. At the time of his death he was collecting information on FSB involvement in the Politkovskaya murder as well as the Beslan school siege and the assassination in Qatar of the former Chechen President Zelimkhan Yandarbiyev.[63]

Outside Russia, Yeltsin's reputation tends to get a posthumous boost from Putin's growing despotism. One rapt apologist, Anders Aslund,[64] credits Russia's current growth to the lasting impact of pre-Putin economic reforms. He goes so far as to defend Yeltsin's oligarchs as creative entrepreneurs who did great things for Russia. He grants that Yeltsin left political reform out of his agenda, but believes this omission was not so important, since in his view (which strangely ignores China's experience in the two-decade aftermath of Tiananmen) no thriving economy can remain authoritarian for very long. For Aslund the crux of Russia's present dilemma is that Putin fell short by failing to become Yeltsin II.

The fact is that few outside observers understood Yeltsin I. On the surface he may have seemed pro-Western, but so was Peter the Great. His authoritarian decrees began a "quiet coup" as early as July 1992, just a half year into his presidency.[65] His real agenda was reflected by the company he kept. The problem with his cronies, in Sergei Kovalev's view, "was not that they were ineffective as democrats, but that in truth they weren't democrats at all."[66] On their advice Yeltsin laid siege to the Russian Parliament in 1993, rewrote the constitution to buttress presidential power, blocked undesirable parties and individuals from competing in regional and national elections, and started two horrific wars in Chechnya.[67]

---

[63] "Russia: British Police Investigating Litvinenko Poisoning Case," *Radio Free Europe/ Radio Liberty* (November 20, 2006), http://www.rferl.org/featurearticleprint/2006/11/ 746f6a6a-88b2-4a6a-ad9d-168e183384d

When a pre-trial hearing finally began for two suspects in the Politkovskaya murder, her lawyer, Karinna Moskalenko, was absent due to mercury poisoning. Her husband found mercury pellets in her car shortly after she fell ill. She had formerly represented Gary Kasparov, the imprisoned oil baron Mikhail Khodorkovsky and Litvinenko. A motion to delay the Politkovskaya hearing in Moscow was denied. See Michael Schwirtz and Alan Cowell, "Russian Lawyer's Illness Investigated," *The New York Times* (October 16, 2008), http://www.nytimes.com/2008/10/16/world/europe/16russia.html

[64] See Anders Aslund, *Russia's Capitalist Revolution: Why Market Reform Succeeded and Democracy Failed* (Washington, DC: Peterson Institute, 2008).

[65] Fred Kaplan, "Blame Yeltsin: The Historical Roots of Vladimir Putin's Power Play," *Slate* (October 2, 2007), http://www.slate.com/toolbar.aspx?action=print&id=2175133

[66] Kovalev, *op. cit.*

[67] McFaul and Stoner-Weiss, "The Myth of the Authoritarian Model," *op. cit.*, 70.

Russia's post-Cold War regional strategy, like its *reconquista* strategy of 1918, first focused on the South Caucasus, putting Chechnya off till later.[68] By the end of 1993 Yeltsin was ready to move north. The risk seemed minimal, as his defense minister assured him that Russia could win a war with the Chechen rebels "in two hours."[69] It dragged on for two years, wrecking Yeltsin's popularity before the coming election campaign.[70] Chechnya became for him what Vietnam had been for Lyndon Johnson. The damage had been done by the time Russian troops withdrew in 1996. Filling the void, the Communist presidential hopeful Zyuganov gained public backing with his vow to restore stability the old-fashioned way. Liberal journalists made the fateful mistake of throwing their unconditional support to Yeltsin, who now more than ever was on the tether of his corporate keepers. This did more damage to Russia's democratic future than anything Zyuganov could have concocted.

What saved Russian democracy, for the moment, was the clumsy ineptitude of Yeltsin's authoritarianism. Putin learned much from those tactical mistakes. The worst of them, from his KGB vantage, was allowing free reportage of the First Chechen War. Some see the Second Chechen War of 1999 as part of a grand strategy to secure a smooth succession,[71] but it also exposed Moscow's long-range intentions in the "near abroad" and beyond. Much was made of the fact that Muslim rebels in the southeast Russian republic of Dagestan used Chechnya as a base camp. The bottom line, however, was that the Kremlin needed the war, and this time the press backed off. The ill-fated Politkovskaya stated that while the first war was the Russian media's finest hour, the second was its darkest.[72]

---

[68] See Cornell, *op. cit.*, 18.

[69] Specter, *op. cit.*

[70] A national poll in 1995 showed a 72 percent disapproval rating of Yeltsin's action in Chechnya, with only 16 percent approving. Joseph L. Nogee and R. Judson Mitchell, *Russian Politics: The Struggle for a New Order* (Boston: Allyn and Bacon, 1997), 125. Part of what saved Yeltsin, despite approval ratings ranging between 5 and 10 percent, was that Russians had simply had their fill of political turnovers. Any incumbent would have enjoyed the same phobic advantage. He won reelection for the simple reason that he was there. Putin too would reap the rewards of democratic fatigue in 2000. As the acting head of state he was effectively the prince-regent. See Kovalev, *op. cit.*

[71] Stephen Blank, "Russia's Project 2008: Reforming the Military and Preparing a Coup," *World Affairs* (September 22, 2006), http://www.encyclopeida.com/doc/1G1-154462673.html

[72] James Meek, "Dispatches from a Savage War," *Guardian* (October 15, 2004), http://www.guardian.co.uk/print/0,5039841-103694,00.html

RETURN OF THE EAST–WEST RIFT

Clearly the old Kremlin is back, and Putin is its personification. When President Medvedev opened his term by proposing an extension of presidential term limits, rumors abounded that he had been installed to ram through constitutional changes on Putin's behalf.[73] Moscow, in any case, is sending a strong signal to Europe and the world that its recharged ambitions reach far beyond the "near abroad." At Munich in February 2007, Putin accused the US of malicious hyperpower ambitions,[74] and in May he added the obligatory comparison with the Third Reich. The next month he argued testily over human rights issues with German Chancellor Angela Merkel, and in July he all but declared a renewed Cold War by ordering that Soviet-style bomber flights be resumed. Already Russia had withdrawn from the Treaty on Conventional Armed Forces in Europe. Finally, after the Litvinenko imbroglio in Britain, diplomats were expelled from both countries.[75]

What should be stressed is the almost seamless bond between Putin's domestic and international agendas. Moscow's new regional assertiveness was as much about Russia as about the "near abroad." Gorbachev had exhibited a similar bond, but in reverse—looking on his neighbors and even NATO as comrades in future democracy.[76] These opposite styles of governance and foreign relations confirm Zbigniew Brzezinski's prediction in 1994 that Russia would have to make a fateful choice between two models of development: it "can be either an empire or a democracy, but it cannot be both."[77] Foreign policy would ultimately hinge on domestic politics.

Yeltsin tried to wear two hats, but found it impossible to compromise democracy at home without reactivating the old Kremlinism abroad. Putin simply finished the job by openly exporting his authoritarian turn.

---

[73] Ellen Barry, "Rumor Mill Sees Groundwork for Another Putin Presidency," *The New York Times* (November 7, 2008), http://www.nytimes.com/2008/11/07/world/europe/07putin.html

[74] Putin quoted in "Not a Cold War, but Cold Tiff," *The Economist* (February 15, 2007), http://economist.com/world/international/PrintFriendly.cfm?story_id=8703054

[75] Nikolaus von Twickel, "In Like a Dove, Out Like a Hawk," *The Moscow Times* (February 22, 2008), http://www.cdi.org/russia/johnson/ 2008-04-17.cfm

[76] Robert Kagan, "The End of the End of History," *The New Republic* (April 23, 2008), http://www.tnr.com/environmentenergy/story.html?id=ee167382-bd16-4b13-beb7-08effela6844

[77] Brzezinski quoted in Thomas F. Remington, *Politics in Russia* (New York: Longman, 1999), 237. Brzezinski again tied the empire question to internal politics in his later classic, *The Grand Chessboard, op. cit.*, 44.

Meanwhile friction mounted between the country's Atlanticists and Eurasianists. The liberal current, as Robert Conquest notes, is rooted in the middle class enlightenment that took place in the 1880s.[78] Yeltsin was torn between the Western tilt of his global diplomacy and the increasingly "Eastern" turn of his domestic and regional policies. Even Putin was initially torn between the two.

More consistent Eurasianists escaped this schizophrenia by "turning East" in all respects. This entailed not only the vigorous prosecution of domestic "state interests" but also the interests of Russians living in former Soviet territory.[79] Putinism finally brought it all together, completing on the world stage the ideological shift that Yeltsin had initiated at home. By getting all its political ducks in line, the new Kremlinism tries to restore the geopolitical reach of the Soviet empire.[80] The problem is that it can only do this with the help of a very dubious ally—China. Much as Hitler and Stalin managed to forge their infamous Nazi–Soviet Pact at the expense of vulnerable neighbors like Poland and Finland, the price for Sino-Russian convergence will be paid by democratic reformists throughout Eurasia.

Tenuous as this alliance is, it could still be the most momentous geopolitical event of our times—every bit as important as the Nixon/Kissinger rapprochement with China of the previous generation. For the first time in 40 years, Russia and China agreed in 2005 to settle their border disputes and to carry out joint military exercises.[81] Thanks to Russia's sale of advanced weaponry and space technology, China is now able to cast an ominous shadow across the whole Asia Pacific, and was able to launch its first astronaut in 2003 and two others in 2005. In December 2006 Russia announced a plan for further cooperation with China's space program.[82] Commercial ties have followed the same vector. Sino-Russian trade reached $28 billion

---

[78] See Robert Conquest, "History and Culture: The Great Terror at 40," *Hoover Institute* (April 2008), http://www.hoover.org/publications/digest/17830254.html

[79] Joseph L. Nogee and R. Judson Mitchell, *Russian Politics: The Struggle for a New Order* (Boston: Allyn and Bacon, 1997), 157.

[80] See Brzezinski, "The Premature Partnership," *op. cit.*, 72.

[81] Marcel de Hass, "Russia-China Security Cooperation," *Power and Interest News Report* (November 27, 2006), http://www.pinr.com/report.php?ac=view_printable&report_id=588&language_id=1

[82] Vladimir Isachenkov, "Space Cooperation with China," *The Moscow Times* (December 27, 2006), 2. As if to rub salt into the wound, America's NASA was forced to admit that from 2010 to 2015 it would not even be able to get an astronaut into space without hitching a ride, just as space tourists do, on Russian Soyuz spacecraft. See John Schwartz, "One Way Up: U.S. Space Plan Relies on Russia," *The New York Times* (October 6, 2008), htpp://www.nytimes.com/2008/10/06/science/space/06gap.html

in 2005, four times the 1998 level, and China's growing demand for energy and natural resources will greatly inflate this figure in the future.[83]

If there is any silver lining here, it is that full awareness of this gathering storm could help Europe and America see past their differences of recent years. And the same applies to democratic nations around the world. Another blessing is the fact that the strength of the new Second World depends on full and lasting cooperation between China and Russia. These erstwhile enemies are still so distrustful of one another that their alliance requires a common adversary just to function at all. Neither party's offensive capabilities are quite what they seem to be, for neither can risk much global brinkmanship with such a dubious "ally" at its back.

That simmering distrust is obvious from the machinations of the two nations' resource politics. Their collision course is suggested by the oil and pipeline deals that both have negotiated with Kazakhstan and Turkmenistan. Granted, the biggest immediate loser in these developments has been America's Chevron, which had enjoyed special Kazak relations for over a decade. Russia, however, must be aware that its present bargaining advantage will evaporate as China moves in. Currently Russia pays Turkmenistan $100 per cubic meter for gas that it resells to Europe for $250.[84] Such blatant exploitation will be impossible to sustain once China gains a solid foothold in the region. Hence a key assumption of Putin's foreign policy—that Russia's major Eurasian threat issues from the West—is fundamentally flawed. Only a dictatorial Kremlin could fail to recognize that a greater danger lies to the East.[85]

In some ways the recession and oil crash of 2008 intensified Russia's closure toward the West. Sensing the country's vulnerability in the face of fluctuating energy prices, Putin tried desperately to establish a global cartel for natural gas. The idea was to link up with big players like Iran, Qatar, Libya, Venezuela, Algeria, and Indonesia to lock in high prices through a de facto "gas OPEC."[86] So it was that Libya's Col. Muammar el-Qaddafi came to Moscow and pitched his Bedouin tent in a Kremlin

---

[83] Kuchins, *op. cit.*

[84] Ian Greenberg, "Russia to Get Central Asian Pipeline," *The New York Times* (May 13, 2007), http://www.nytimes.com/2007/05/13/word/europe/13putin.html

[85] Even a dictatorial Kazakhstan can see that. It has no choice but to do business with China, but makes sure that it balances this risk factor by also throwing energy contracts to Russia and the West. See Pinar İpek, "The Role of Oil and Gas in Kazakhstan's Foreign Policy: Looking East or West?" *Europe-Asia Studies* 59, no. 7 (November 2007): 1179–99.

[86] Fred Weir," Russia Pushes an 'OPEC' for Natural-Gas Nations," *The Christian Science Monitor* (October 30, 2008), http://www.csmonitor.com/World/2008/1030/p01s04-wogn.html

garden, where he invited Putin for tea. The Russians must have known, however, that just two months earlier he was having tea with Secretary of State Condoleezza Rice.[87]

It is a core Putinist assumption that Russia and America are locked in a winner-takes-all "Great Game." This Cold War notion blinds Moscow to the fact that the chief beneficiary of its anti-Western turn is none other than its SCO partner, China. There is a simple reason why Washington finds it difficult to wean Moscow from this geopolitical blunder: the message was delivered in the wrong package. Either it came wrapped in mutual commercial interest or, worse still, in hortatory preachments about shared democratic values. What should be stressed, rather, is the common *geopolitical* necessity of thwarting China's westward advances. Once the Kremlin awakens to the danger it faces from the East, it will not only warm to the West, but could even welcome NATO's eastward expansion.

Putinism misses this point because its ideological guns are all pointed toward the West. To boot America out, it feels compelled to invite China in. Some Kremlin insiders recognize this monumental error.[88] Off the record, they lament that US–Russia relations have fallen into a state of decay that can only serve China's interest. At some point there will be a general awakening to the virtual treason of Putin's "capitulatory" policy toward China, as the dissident Boris Nemtsov calls it.[89] At that point the Kremlin power elite will toss Putinism out. Washington's task is to get them to do so before Central Asia is a de facto Chinese territory.

GLOBALIZATION AS DEMOCRATIC ABORTION

As if to hedge its bet on its Eastern turn, Moscow sent conciliatory signals to the West early in 2008. In mid-February the presidential heir apparent Medvedev spoke before a business group in Siberia, calling for trade liberalization and a broad expansion of personal freedoms. These are nice words, but it must be remembered that Putin too put on a convincing pro-Western display when he first took office. Medvedev can afford to play

---

[87] Andrew E. Kramer, "Qaddafi Discusses Energy Ties With Russia," *The New York Times* (November 3, 2008), http://www.nytimes.com/2008/11/03/world/europe/03russia.html

[88] See Albert L. Weeks, "Why Russia is Warming to the West," *The Christian Science Monitor* (December 15, 2010), http://www.csmonitor.com/layout/set/print/content/view/print/350102

[89] Nemtsov, the co-founder of the Union of Right Forces, goes so far as to declare Putin "a Chinese agent of influence." See Richard Lourie, "Sinophobia," *The Moscow Times* (May 12, 2008), http://www.themoscowtimes.com/articles/detail.php?ID=362653&print=Y

that moderate role since the apparatus of "managed democracy" is already firmly in place.[90]

Just the day before Medvedev's Siberian speech, Putin was once again fulminating against the West and declaring that his eight years in office were free of any trace of failure.[91] Translation: Russia's anti-Western trajectory will persist as long as Putin is the top gun in the Kremlin. For the moment Moscow seems to be edging toward the EU, but whether this is good or bad news depends upon whether this convergence amounts to the Westernization of the Kremlin or the Kremlinization of the EU. Moscow's motive may be partly China-related, but another factor is its Putinist desire to drive a wedge between Washington and Brussels. Even as Medvedev was making his presidential debut, Putin was in France lambasting the US "monster." Clearly he was still in charge, despite the fact that the Russian constitution gives the president sole responsibility for foreign policy. By meeting Putin on these terms, against the G8 tradition of dealing at a presidential level, Sarkozy simply acknowledged the obvious.[92]

Medvedev's encomium for civil society—repeated *ad nauseam* in his speeches, and especially in his November 2008 State of the Nation address—is ludicrous at a time when Putin's opponents are being struck down or imprisoned on a regular basis. The most notable recent victim was Putin's archenemy, the former corporate oligarch Mikhail Khodorkovsky. His reconviction in December 2010 dashes the hope that Putin's power has dissipated. While scores of journalists and human rights advocates have paid with their lives for offending Putin, luckier ones have simply disappeared from the media. In one case a dissenting political analyst, Mikhail G. Delyagin, was digitally erased from a TV show that was about to air, much as Stalin's errant comrades were once airbrushed from Soviet photos. In their haste to get Delyagin off the air, the censors accidently left his legs on the screen, giving us an apt symbol of civil society on the run.

Even leaders of the Communist Party—the only opposition party allowed in parliament—have been vanishing from Russian TV, and the same fate

---

[90] United Russia not only enjoys a majority in the Duma, but as of the 2003 Duma elections it holds enough seats to push through constitutional changes at will. See Stephen K. Wegren and Andrew Konitzer, "Prospects for Managed Democracy in Russia," *Europe-Asia Studies* 59, no. 6 (September 2007): 1025 (1025–47).

[91] C. J. Chivers, "Medvedev Pledges Reform in Russia," *The New York Times* (February 16, 2008), http://www.nytimes.com/2008/02/16/world/europe/16russia.html

[92] Henry Meyer, "Putin Calls U.S. 'Frightening Monster,' Urges French Solidarity," *Bloomberg.com* (May 31, 2008), http://www.bloomberg.com/apps/news?pid=20601087& sid=adHBA_CS6GHg^refer=home

awaits entertainers who perform at opposition rallies.[93] But the Potemkin democracy that survives Putin's presidency is still too much for some Putinists to bear. With impeccable logic they wonder why the government should bother with elections that are merely a troublesome formality. As one party leader puts it, "we are tired of democratic twists and turns... It may sound sacrilegious, but I would propose to suspend all this election business."[94]

Likewise, most Russians are not averse to trading a few democratic formalities for Kremlinesque efficiency and military potency. This explains the popularity of the six-day Blitzkrieg that routed Georgian forces in 2008. With Abkhazia and South Ossetia firmly under its grip, and a former FSB agent inserted as South Ossetia's new prime minister,[95] Russia served notice on the West that its "turn East" was no bluff. In Robert Kagan's view, the wonders that Moscow and Beijing have achieved in the name of development and security have much in common with the 19th century Concert of Europe, which used peace and "stability" to camouflage reactionary designs.[96] Today's "Concert" is taking shape across Eurasia in the form of a revitalized Second World. On the surface this anti-Western alliance may seem rock solid, but that need not be the case. Without robust Western assistance and geopolitical bungling the new Second World will once again be its own worst enemy, fractured by internal rivalries and bled by graft and mismanagement.

Unfortunately, multinational corporations stand ready to rescue the new Kremlinism, just as they saved China's CCP after Tiananmen. That is what Putin is counting on, and toward that end he is using Medvedev as his partner in a very effective game of "good cop–bad cop." The main stage for this public relations ploy has been the World Economic Forum at Davos. It was here in 1996 that the "Davos Pact" was struck between Russia's corporate oligarchs and their Western counterparts, with the implicit aim of drafting a Final Solution for the Russian Left.[97] More broadly it amounted to an accord for the division of spoils from a fully globalized Russia.

---

[93] Clifford J. Levy, "It Isn't Magic: Putin Opponents Are Made to Vanish From TV," *The New York Times* (June 3, 2008), http://www.nytimes.com/2008/06/03/world/europe/03russia.html

[94] Clifford J. Levy, "Putin's Iron Grip on Russia Suffocates Opponents," *The New York Times* (February 24, 2008), http://www.nytimes.com/2008/02/24/world/europe/24putin.html

[95] "La Russie Resserre son emprise sur l'Abkhazie et l'Ossetie du Sud," *Le Monde* (October 25, 2008), http://www.lemonde.fr/europe/article/2008/10/25/la-russie-resserre-son-emprise-sur-l-abkhazie-et-l-ossetie-du-sud_1111028_3214.html

[96] Kagan, "The End of the End of History," *op. cit.*

[97] Alan Cowell, "Russians Work on Their Image at Davos," *The International Herald Tribune* (January 28, 2007), http://www.iht.com/bin/print.php?id=4378800

The 1998 crash and the subsequent rise of Putinism scuttled that arrangement. Putin's corporate seizures and anti-Western rhetoric presaged an East–West schism in both commercial and geopolitical relations. Though Russia would be much discussed at Davos, Moscow sent only low-profile delegations there for several years. That all changed in 2007, when Putin began sending distinct signals that the geoeconomic tide was turning, even as the geopolitical "turn East" was being consummated. In effect, a new pact was on offer, much like the Sino-globalist accord between Beijing and Western corporations.[98] The question was whether Western globalists were ready to buy a package that came wrapped in repression at home and rising aggression abroad.

Putin and Medvedev have good reason to believe that their stick and carrot tactics—the carrot being ripe investment opportunities—will prove irresistible to Western elites. Most corporate CEOs clearly favor a no-questions-asked accommodation with Russia, and that is the prevailing sentiment at Davos. Even Joseph Nye, who admonished Russia that its development as a major power would be at risk if it failed to reform, welcomed the return of a strong delegation from Moscow and backed away from Senator John McCain's plan to oust Russia from the G8.[99] When Medvedev was asked about this idea, he bluntly stated that the question of democracy was irrelevant to the G8, and America was in no shape to lecture Russia on development matters. What the world needs, he suggested, is far less US interference.[100] There was no need to add the implicit point that more Russian interference would be there to fill the void.

In June 2008, shortly before the Georgia invasion, many of the world's energy bosses gathered at St. Petersburg to accept Medvedev's carrots. Michael Klein of Citigroup set the tone with his praise of Russia for having avoided the "resource curse" (not meaning, obviously, the avoidance of a thriving autocracy). For Klein and other US corporate leaders all is well on the Russian front, because Medvedev says so. Some CEOs did grumble a little about Russia's lack of a dependable rule of law, but only as it related to property rights.[101] Meanwhile Medvedev was calling for nothing less

---

[98] See Thornton, "Sino-Globalization," *op. cit.*

[99] Joseph Nye, "Davos Day 4: An Impressive Russian Delegation," *The Huffington Post* (May 31, 2008), http://www.huffingtonpost.com/joseph-nye/davos-day-4-an-impressive_b_39798.html?view=print

[100] Clifford J. Levy, "U.S. Is in No Shape to Give Advice, Medvedev Says," *The New York Times* (July 3, 2008), http://www.nytimes.com/2008/07/03/world/europe/03medvedev.html

[101] Alison Smale, "Money Talks at Russian Forum as Business Leaders See Past Hurdles to Investing," *The New York Times* (June 9, 2008), http://www.nytimes.com/2008/06/09/world/europe/09petersburg.html

than an overhaul of the entire world system, with Russia on offer as a global role model.[102]

Soon that model would be crushed by the falling stock market. Not long before, investors had been bracing for an oil price rise as high as $200 per barrel,[103] but by October 2008 the country's entire oil industry was valued below Brazil's Petrobras, and some banks were trading at less than half their book values.[104] Nor did Putin's Georgia invasion or his corporate bullying help matters.[105] What did help was the fact that Russian currency reserves stood at nearly half a trillion dollars,[106] and Europe's dependence on Russian oil made it very reluctant to challenge Moscow.

Over the stentorian objections of Lithuania, Poland, and other countries that knew Russia all too well, an increasingly German-dominated EU approved a negotiating mandate for a new "partnership" with Russia. This was a step toward a comprehensive free trade agreement once Russia joined the WTO.[107] These Tiananmen-style accommodations bracketed the whole issue of political reform. Although the EU froze partnership deliberations on September 1, 2008, in response to the invasion, 26 out of 27 EU members agreed to resume negotiations that November. Only Lithuania stood its ground.[108]

The collapse of the oil bubble in 2008 only accelerated this convergence. Not only did Russia once again need huge amounts of foreign direct investment (FDI), but this predicament reminded it of how little it trusted China. More than ever President Medvedev looked to the West as a hedge on its Eastern bet. This was possible without any reform provisions because Europe, led by Germany, was already wooing Moscow unconditionally. President Obama's "reset" rhetoric would simply duplicate the capitulation process that Germany's Schröder had arduously promoted.[109]

---

[102] Levy, "U.S. Is in No Shape to Give Advice, Medvedev Says," *op. cit.*

[103] See Clifford G. Gaddy, "Russia's Jerry-Rigged Oil Pump," *The Moscow Times* (October 28, 2008), http://www.themoscowtimes.com/articles/detail.php?ID=371992&print=Y

[104] James Quinn, "Russia Feels Chill Winds of the Global Downturn," *Telegraph* (October 27, 2008), http://www.telegraph.co.uk/finance/financetopics/financialcrisis/3264822/Russia-feels-chill-winds-of-the-global-downturn.html

[105] Charles Clover, "Onward to 1998," *Financial Times* (October 27, 2008), http://www.ft.com/cms/s/ 0/813ed2a0-a3c7-11dd-942c-000077b07658.html

[106] Mark Medish, "Where is Russia?" *The New York Times* (June 22, 2010), http://www.nytimes.com/2010/06/23/opinion/23iht-edmedish.html

[107] "The EU Backs Talks on Russia Pact," *The Moscow Times* (May 27, 2008), http://www.themoscowtimes.com/article/600/42/367756.htm

[108] Stephen Castle, "European Union to Resume Russian Partnership Talks," *The New York Times* (November 11, 2008), http://www.nytimes.com/2008/11/11/world/europe/11union.html

[109] "Will Germany Now Take Centre Stage?" *The Economist* (October 21, 2010), http://www.economist. com/node/17305755/print

Russia was ready to dance, so long as no political concessions were required. Thousands of Western guests got a warm welcome from the Russian president at the 2010 St. Petersburg International Economic Forum. In many ways this was a rollback to Yeltsin-style accords, except that the shadow of Putin hung over the entire proceedings. Medvedev was a gracious host, but what he had to offer was globalization on a Putinist platter. In lieu of political reform and constraint,[110] the West would get an easing of Russia's capital gains tax.[111]

Conventional wisdom after the Cold War has held that there is just one kind of globalization, and despite a few bumps and detours it invariably leads to democratic development. Britain spearheads this mindset, and Europe usually tags along. In stark contrast to the moral realism of the late Robin Cook, Britain's Foreign Secretary William Hague made almost no criticism of the brutal election crackdown of Belarus's president Alexander Lukashenko in December 2010.[112] To its credit, the EU balked on this one. It joined the US in boycotting Lukashenko's inauguration, while the European Parliament passed a resolution calling for strict sanctions against Lukashenko's government.

Russia, right on time, aborted its recent campaign against Lukashenko. The day before his inauguration, Putin promised him $4.1 billion in discounts on Russian oil. Not to be outdone, China rushed to pledge a $5 billion investment in 20 Belarusian projects.[113] Clearly the drift is toward a deeper East–West divide, with Belarus as one of its major fault lines. Set in this context, Hague's neoliberal engagement credo seems woefully dated, and remarkably consistent with the geopolitical preferences of Russia and China. Twenty years of this globalist hokum is enough. In Russia, as in China, massive infusions of global capital and munificent political tolerance

---

[110] In return for red carpet treatment from the EU—punctuated by a proposal by Germany's Chancellor Merkel for an EU–Russia Political and Security Committee and a tripartite summit with Merkel and France's Sarkozy in October 2010—Russia was only asked to assist in resolving tensions in Transnistria (a troubled part of Moldova). What goes without mention is that those tensions are largely the result of Russian-sponsored insurgency. See Judy Dempsey, "Russia Wants to Formalize Relations with E.U.," *The New York Times* (October 17, 2010), http://www.nytimes.com/2010/10/18/world/europe/18iht-germany.html

[111] Alison Smale, "Two Parallel Narratives of Russian Modernization," *The New York Times* (June 21, 2010), http://www.nytimes.com/2010/22/world/europe/22iht-letter.html

[112] John Kampfner, "Who will Fight Europe's Last Dictator?" *The Independent* (December 30, 2010), http://www.independent.co.uk/opinion/commentators/john-kampfner-who-will-fight-europes-last-dictator-2171651.html

[113] Benjamin Bidder, "Lukashenko Looks East for New Friends," *Spiegel Online* (January 21, 2010), http://www.spiegel.de/international/europe/0,1518,druck-740841,00.html

have worked wonders, but not the democratic kind. Globalization on these terms amounts to a rescue operation for endangered authoritarianisms.

It is no big secret that Putinism could never have been launched without the Western support system it inherited from Yeltsinism. Instead of mid-wifing democracy, globalization is again helping to perform a democratic abortion. This process can and must be reversed. It is not enough that Russia be contained, as during the Cold War. To prevent the consolidation of a new Second World, every effort must be made to convince Russian leaders that democracy, far from being Russia's nemesis, could be its best geopolitical ally. Simply put, the real adversary lies to the East.

3

THE NEW CHINA MODEL
Power through Political
Underdevelopment

THE TIANANMEN EFFECT

In the lexicon of the CCP, the enforcement of political silence is called
"harmony," and violations are akin to treason.[1] By far the most "harmonious" date on the Chinese calendar is June 4, the day in 1989 when the new
direction of Chinese development was set in stone. Since then almost no
public discussion of the Tiananmen Massacre has been permitted.[2] As the
20th anniversary of this un-event approached, just one newspaper was
allowed to break silence. The English edition of *The Global Times* ran a story

---

[1] The artist Ai Weiwei was reminded that silence is golden when he received notice
that his brand-new, million dollar Shanghai studio was soon to be demolished due to
a minor infraction in its paperwork. His response was to throw a huge party on the
night before its destruction. More to the point, he let it be known that the dinner menu
would feature 10,000 river crabs, whose Chinese name sounds like "harmony." For
that he was put under immediate house arrest. See John Sunyer, "Ai Weiwei is Placed
Under House Arrest," *New Statesman* (November 5, 2010), http://www.newstatesman.
com/blogs/cultural-capital/2010/ 11/chinese-shanghai-china and John Sunyer, "Ai Weiwei
Under House Arrest," *Straits Times* (November 5, 2010), http://www.straitstimes.com/
BreakingNews/Asia/Story/STIStory_599754.html

[2] Likewise, except during the 1981 show-trial of the Gang of Four, Beijing has blocked
open discussion of the Cultural Revolution.

defending the crackdown as necessary and proper. The article got approval just before press time. After all, few except resident foreigners would read it, and they would have heard much about Tiananmen already. The idea was to make sure they got a proper reeducation.

What is surprising is not just how effective the Tiananmen blackout has been, but also how easy it has been to enforce. Apart from an always refractory Hong Kong—where on June 4, 2009 76,000 people poured out for the largest candlelight vigil since 1990[3]—China weathered the 20th anniversary with hardly a ripple of Tiananmen-related unrest.[4] The CCP's major point of vulnerability is its promise to generate sustained economic mega-growth. So far its ability to deliver that package remains an almost religious article of faith. Nevertheless the long shadow of Tiananmen blankets almost every aspect of Chinese life. Today's CCPism is a direct product of this Tiananmen effect.

John Lee observes how June 1989 marks a critical dividing line in terms of China's political economy. In the years before Tiananmen, Chinese development allowed for a considerable degree of private initiative, especially in the rural sector. Eighty percent of the country's poverty reduction since 1979 came in that period. It was widely expected that China would follow the familiar course of East Asia's authoritarian transitions, a pattern foretold by Samuel Huntington half a century ago. In the course of their iconic transitions, Japan, South Korea and Taiwan pumped most of their investment capital into the private sector. China seemed to be moving in that same general direction, but after Tiananmen it abruptly reversed course.

---

[3] Keith Bradsher, "Hong Kong Democracy March Draws Thousands," *The New York Times* (July 2, 2009), http://www.nytimes.com/2009/07/02/world/asia/02hongkong.html?_r=1

[4] In that same month, the government had a more difficult time handling two internet issues that struck a deeper nerve in the public consciousness. First there was the announcement that all personal computers would have to contain "Green Dam" filtering software. This spawned a heated national debate which the CCP probably welcomed as a diversion from the Tiananmen issue. Briefly the government seemed to be backing away from the new rule, but then it reversed itself. Green Dam will add one more layer of repression to a censorship system that is already the most advanced in the world. The second issue was the case of Deng Yujiao, a karaoke bar girl who stabbed to death a local government official who had demanded sex from her. A massive wave of internet protest got her charges dropped. Doubtless the CCP welcomed the whole tempest, for Deng's supporters were targeting local government vice, and central CCP leaders had their own problems in dealing with local officials. This case not only provided a convenient distraction from the Tiananmen issue, but allowed the central government to appear just and conciliatory at this sensitive moment.

Today over 70 percent of available capital is soaked up by state-controlled enterprises, and that percentage is rising.[5]

Likewise the number of government officials is rising. In the 1980s there were less than 20 million of these notoriously sluggish functionaries. That number doubled in the 1990s, and by 2004 there were over 46 million. Lee notes, moreover, that of the 35 largest companies listed on the Shanghai Stock Exchange, 30 are majority-owned by the state or state-controlled institutions. The government holds 50 percent of all the shares of listed companies. To put it bluntly, China is not just another Asian tiger, much less a budding liberal economy. It is the archetype of state corporatism,[6] and it has no incentive to become anything else. Expecting it to liberalize itself is quixotic at best. As its global influence grows, the China model is more likely to de-liberalize the developing world than to adapt the ways and means of the West.

Inside China the Tiananmen effect is so pervasive that, like all hegemonic devices, its power is best measured by its invisibility, or in this case its in-audibility. By way of compensation, its draconian force is often matched by government flexibility on a wide range of non-political issues. One benefi-ciary has been China's thriving porn industry. Religious or spiritual groups like the Catholic Church and Falun Gong have not been so fortunate, since the government fears their institutional scope and international connections. It is not enough that they are basically apolitical. Their organizational ability is enough to label them subversive.

Even in Taiwan, where two decades of faltering democracy have reduced overt repression, the Tiananmen issue has been adroitly downplayed. One likely reason is Tiananmen's striking resemblance to Taiwan's own "2–28" (February 28) incident of 1947, when Kuomintang (KMT) forces slaugh-tered an estimated 10,000 Formosans,[7] or four times the estimated victims of Tiananmen. Countless more died in the subsequent white terror, which never really ended until martial law was lifted four decades later.

Thereafter the KMT has been forced to make substantial concessions, as it lacks the hegemonic grip on society that the CCP enjoys in China. Its envy of its Chinese counterpart is suggested by its rush to merge the two operations under the rubric of a government-sponsored "reunification"

---

[5] John Lee, "Is China Really an 'East Asian Success Story'?" *Policy* (Winter 2009), http://www.cis.org.au/ Policy/winter09/lee-winter09.html

[6] *Ibid.*

[7] Tillman Durdin, "Formosa Killings are Put at 10,000," *The New York Times* (March 29, 1947), http://www.taiwande.org/hst-1947.htm

movement.[8] Since no organization could be expected to favor its own demise, it is obvious that KMT stalwarts regard reunification as an upgrade rather than a surrender. They expect the post-unification KMT to become the Taiwan branch of the CCP, with themselves in complete control of the island. Their chief political competitor, the Democratic Progressive Party (DPP), would be given early retirement, as would Taiwan democracy.

Seeing how the KMT mishandled the ghost of 2–28, the CCP is making sure that the ghost of Tiananmen stays in its grave. The party has recourse to two major devices: carefully managed nationalism and the post-Tiananmen economic bargain, with double-digit growth given in exchange for political apathy. Clearly most Chinese consider this a fair trade. To raise the issue of Tiananmen would be to throw bolts into the gears of the country's economic engine. Silence, then, is literally golden. This helps to explain why so little action is required to keep information in China under wraps. The job of censorship is effectively outsourced to the market. The commercialization of censorship allows the government to step back and let editors and advertisers do the job.[9]

THE CCP's WESTERN FRIENDS AND FOES

On any developmental scale that includes politics, China's rating would tumble. Yasheng Huang and Minxin Pei set the record straight about China's dazzling progress, dismissing the idea of a Chinese "miracle" economy. In the "miracle" years of East Asian states, corruption was certainly rife, but

---

[8] "Reunification" institutions are springing up on many Taiwan university campuses, and prospective faculty members in the country's very few political science departments are carefully vetted for any oppositional leaning. As in China, open discussion is regarded as subversive.

[9] Christopher Walker and Sarah Cook, "China's Commercialization of Censorship," *Far Eastern Economic Review* (May 2, 2009), http://www.feer.com/politics/2009/may56/Chinas-Commercialization-of-Censorship

In Taiwan, likewise, silence is golden where the China question is concerned. Here too, the issue of Tiananmen is a clear case in point. It has required little in the way of raw suppression by the KMT-dominated media. Public interest is simply lacking. By electing Ma Ying-Jeou as their openly pro-Chinese president in March 2008, a solid majority of Taiwanese manifested their desire to subordinate democratic priorities to economic ones. Korea did much the same by putting Lee Myung Bak in the presidential Blue House in February 2008. Whereas Ma is a strong advocate of reunification between the two Chinas, Lee is in the opposite camp concerning "sunshine" policies toward North Korea. Nonetheless, Ma and Lee share something much more emblematic of our times: an unqualified politics of the cash register.

in terms of sheer scale the PRC's current "land grab" bureaucracy takes the prize. Between 1989 and 2001, while rural incomes fell, China embarked on a "reverse Robin Hood" policy that included raises and other perquisites for civil servants.[10] Democracy would have made these urban-bureaucratic enrichment programs scandalous, and for that very reason the country's pampered classes are content with authoritarian rule.

The question is how far party-affiliated privilege can be pushed before resistance pressures reach explosive levels. Even as China presumably surpassed all the Asian competition, a curious anomaly arose. While Western economists and Sinologists were fixated on the country's rocketing GDP, basic education and health care were crumbling in both rural areas and in migrant slums within the cities. Now, in a country that once prided itself on almost complete literacy, 30 percent of rural children leave school as illiterates.[11] Social pressure is building, and not just in the restless countryside. There is general consternation regarding China's insolvent banks, its decrepit state-owned enterprises (SOEs), and crime-ridden stock market.

Gordon Chang sees little hope, therefore, for the durability of the present regime. How long can order prevail when the party fails to provide for society's most basic needs?[12] Can revolt be far away when Dickensian poverty is coupled with surging urban ostentation? Conspicuous consumption could prove more dangerous to the regime than the Falun Gong ever was. What the CCP most fears, however, is the social upheaval that would follow any lasting economic downturn. Only that could push affluent classes into opposition. Thus the party has had to give priority to business interests over all competing concerns, such as the amelioration of rural and working-class conditions.

Huang, Pei, and Chang all target the myth of China's salutary capitalist transition. In rural areas, especially, China has actually regressed since the 1980s in terms of social welfare and even entrepreneurial development. The nation's celebrated growth has been state-directed and largely oblivious to human needs. Viewed in this way, urban marvels like Shanghai function as shimmering Potemkin villages, diverting attention from pressing crises like environmental meltdown, social inequality, and a court system that answers directly to political bosses. GDP figures mask the "other China" that happens to include the majority of Chinese.

---

[10] Yasheng Huang, *Capitalism with Chinese Characteristics: Entrepreneurship and the State* (Cambridge, UK: Cambridge University Press, 2008), 282.

[11] *Ibid.*, 43.

[12] Gordon Chang, *The Coming Collapse of China* (London: Arrow Books, 2002), 274 and 284.

Should China begin to unravel domestically, the CCP could come to depend for its very existence upon the externalization of internal crises. This is one more reason why Washington feels compelled to assist Beijing in its endless search for security. That of course raises China's threat potential even higher. The question is how to get off this merry-go-round of engagement through empowerment. Liberal institutionalists believe authoritarian regimes like the PRC will eventually come to see their interests as better served by liberal and peaceful means than by belligerence. They are not bothered by the prospect of an unreformed China being ushered into the highest ranks of international decision making, for liberalism as they conceive it is infectious. The only danger would be in delaying the reformation of wayward nations by keeping them out of the "international club."

Will Hutton, by contrast, worries that inviting an unreformed China to "the top table" will erode the international rule of law.[13] We must agree with him that a rogue power like China is much more likely to alter global institutions than to be altered by them. Our nemesis in this regard is the Princeton Project, which lives in a fictional universe where power politics is giving way to a world without real enemies. We are given to believe that no regime can resist the lure of a properly structured "international socialization," with America providing the de facto blueprint for world order. The idea is to magnify Washington's influence by muting its spoken agenda while rolling out a red carpet of commercial advantages to would-be adversaries. No pressure is recommended or needed, and by this logic it would be counterproductive. The trick is simply to give retrograde nations more incentives for cooperation than for confrontation.[14]

The project's founding editors, John Ikenberry and Anne-Marie Slaughter, dismiss the adverse relations of traditional geopolitics. Taking Beijing's "New Diplomacy" at face value,[15] they end up very close to pro-China "realists" like Kissinger and Brzezinski, and to strange amphibians like Susan Shirk, a former State Department watchdog who faults China on a wide range of issues yet advises a conciliatory policy. Shirk is motivated primarily by fear of what the sleeping dragon might do if provoked, whereas Kissinger

---

[13] Will Hutton, "Does the Future Really Belong to China?" *Prospect Magazine* 130 (January 2007), http://www.prospect=magazine.co.uk/article_details.php?id=8174

[14] G. John Ikenberry, "The Rise of China and the Future of the West," *Foreign Affairs* 87, no. 1 (January/February 2008): 25 (23–37).

[15] It does not phase these Sino-optimists that this same kind of "engagement" handed the Burmese junta almost unqualified support from ASEAN, even after the brutal crackdown of September 2007. The ASEAN appeasement took the heat off the junta and made it impossible for Western sanctions to have any reform impact. See William H. Thornton, "Burma's Geopolitical Revival: A Post-Realist View of the Saffron Rising," *World Affairs: The Journal of International Issues* 12, no. 1 (spring 2008): 122–51.

is obviously inspired by the stupendous commissions he gets from renting the China connections of his consulting firm, Kissinger Associates.

It is hardly surprising that Kissinger took a leading role in sweeping Tiananmen under the table. So too he was adamant that China's pre-Olympic crackdown on human rights should be ignored, despite the fact that reform was a non-negotiable condition for granting China the Olympics in the first place. The story of these bounced checks traces to the early 1990s, the time of China's first Olympics bid. Even Shirk seems to grant, between the lines, that there is something awry here. She reminds us that a common Chinese billboard slogan of that period was "a more open China for the 2000 Olympics."[16] It speaks volumes that the head of China's Olympics campaign was Beijing's mayor Chen Xitong, an architect of the Tiananmen crackdown.

True to form, Shirk's main concern was that the CCP might lose face if China did not win the bid. Jiang Zemin was indeed embarrassed when the International Olympic Committee (IOC) turned down the Chinese application for 2000. Shirk fretted over the fact that resentment persisted even after China won the bid for 2008.[17] Her firm advice—which is even more axiomatic for the Obama administration than it was under Bush—is to never make China's rulers feel the least bit threatened or pressured. All talk of democratization and human rights should be stanched,[18] Shirk believes, for our security lies in the CCP's sense of security.

By 2000, in the wake of the Asian Crash, China was taking the fore in Asia both economically and militarily. The Hainan incident of April 2001 suggested the direction that East–West relations might have gone if this trend had not been interrupted by 9/11 and the subsequent "war on terror." That turn of events put both Washington and Beijing in a cooperative mood, sidelining the Hainan incident. Nothing, however, had fundamentally changed about China's larger strategy.

John Mearsheimer gives us a convincing portrait of China as an emerging Asian hegemon and a loose cannon on the global deck. Present "engagement" policies compound the problem by assisting in the development of this economic powerhouse. Mearsheimer argues that Beijing "will almost certainly translate its economic might into military might and make a run at dominating Northeast Asia."[19] The same goes for Southeast, South and

---

[16] Susan L. Shirk, *China: Fragile Superpower* (New York: Oxford University Press, 2001), 226.

[17] *Ibid.*, 226–27.

[18] *Ibid.*, 262.

[19] John J. Mearsheimer, *The Tragedy of Great Power Politics* (New York: W. W. Norton, 2001), 4.

Central Asia, though the tactics will vary according to the circumstance. Though Beijing has so far used soft power very effectively, the hard power option is coming out of hiding. Eventually the myth of China's peaceful rise will crumble, but by then its power will be secure.

Pessimists like Mearsheimer are very much in the minority camp. Engagement proponents reign supreme in policy-making circles. Witness Anne-Marie Slaughter when she was head of policy planning at the State Department. Many such Sino-optimists will grant that the current Beijing Consensus leaves much to be desired, but they believe the China model will be self-correcting after a few more years of double-digit growth. There is, moreover, a much more assertive set of Sino-apologists who hold that any attempt to judge China's actions by "Western" standards of democracy and human rights is an exercise in orientalist hubris. John Gray, for example, takes obvious multicultural satisfaction in China's rise.[20]

More standard "Left" critiques charge realists like Mearsheimer with latter-day colonialism. Immanuel Wallerstein considers any moral or political criticism of China a tactical ruse to gain a better bargaining position for commercial negotiation: "naval maneuvers in the China Sea or U.S. Congressmen berating China's record on human rights may be seen as part of the bargaining."[21] Randall Peerenboom goes even farther, not only accusing China critics of having ulterior motives, but insisting that all criticism based on human rights is a product of xenophobic prejudice. It rests, he believes, on a double standard whereby the faults of China's development strategy are registered while those of democratic India are conveniently ignored.[22] What is astonishing about this "argument" is that—unlike neo-liberals who look forward to a new and improved China through global trade, or liberal internationalists who expect a transformed China through institutional engagement—the Wallersteins and Peerenbooms defend the China model *as is*.

The more common China apology, however, issues from the capitalist Right rather than the Left. Basically it is a spinoff from globalist wishful thinking of the 1990s. From this vantage the advent of China's post-Tiananmen "fourth generation" will lead to the promised land of liberal progressivism by incorporating the rising entrepreneurial classes. That was not what Jiang Zemin had in mind when he broached his "Three Respects" dictum in a

---

[20] See John Gray, "China and the End of Westernisation," *The Guardian* (June 23, 2009), http://www.guardian.co.uk/commentisfree/2009/jun/23/china-rise-west-history

[21] Immanuel Wallerstein, "Commentary No. 35," Fernand Braudel Center, Binghamton University (March 1, 2000), http://fbc.binghampton.edu-35en.htm

[22] Randall Peerenboom, *China Modernizes: Threat to the West or Model for the Rest?* (Oxford: Oxford University Press, 2007), Chapter 5, 163–83.

speech of July 1, 2001.[23] Jiang wanted capitalists to join the Communist Party so as to co-opt them. Casting off any idealistic baggage that Sino-globalism might still contain, he moved beyond Deng Xiaoping's "black cat, white cat" pragmatism to an even more economistic stress on growth.[24] This accorded with Zhu Rongji's economic priorities, which have since been fully implemented by Wen Jiabao.

Jiang completed China's capitalist transformation by ridding Dengism of its last traces of socialistic idealism. This raw economism reached fruition in the Zhu/Wen model of authoritarian capitalism. To comprehend its dynamics is to understand why Sino-globalization is the major challenge to Senian "development as freedom." The world's autocrats look to the China model as a way to have growth without political reform, while less privileged classes are drawn to it as a way to escape the neoliberal devil they know. So long as the choice is between the inveterate Washington Consensus and the upstart Beijing Consensus, the dark horse wins by default. What is needed is a real alternative, a true third way, to reignite the lost cause of social democratization. Any genuine People Power would be anathema to Sino-globalization.

If America can bring itself to embrace this grassroots democratism, rather than the ersatz "reform" of neoliberalism, the China model will find itself on the losing side of history. Oblivious to any such third way possibilities, international institutionalists like Ikenberry and Slaughter seek to pacify global adversaries through their empowerment. These perpetual optimists miss the fact that a new Cold War is taking shape in terms of values as well as power politics. The most pressing geopolitical challenge of our times escapes them.[25] Whereas they expect reform to follow almost automatically from the right kind of engagement, Gordon Chang and Minxin Pei argue with equal optimism that reform will issue from a collapsing CCP.

We are closer to James Mann in that we reject both forms of optimism. Both assume that Chinese authoritarianism is doomed, but this begs the question of what is on hand to replace it. After 2008, the neoliberal competition is on life support. The Great Recession has been a veritable triumph for the China model. Chang is certainly right that a Chinese economic collapse

---

[23] Lowell Dittmer, "Chinese Leadership Succession to the Fourth Generation," in *China After Jiang*, ed. Gang Lin and Xiaobo Hu (Washington, DC: Woodrow Wilson Center Press and Stanford, CA: Stanford University Press, 2003), 26 (11–37).

[24] *Ibid.*, 30.

[25] When we put the question of a renewed Cold War to Ikenberry at a May 2009 conference in Korea, he fired back with a splenetic "No!"—almost like the famous scream of Howard Dean during his failed presidential bid of 2004. Clearly this issue strikes a nerve.

would make the Dubai crash look miniscule,[26] but even that might not bring down the CCP or destroy the global appeal of the China model, given the fact that neoliberal globalism is the only obvious alternative. At the very least we need to hedge our bets by preparing for the real possibility that the CCP might weather the coming storm. Indeed, it could emerge as a much more virulent adversary after the eclipse of market democracy's attraction as a developmental catalyst.

Our concern is that the negative optimism of Chang and Pei will void policy debate over what to do about a sustainably authoritarian China. We must avoid lending support to the perilous wager that the unreformed Party is doomed and therefore is nothing to fear. Presently the Party is reforming itself in the opposite direction: becoming more autocratic as it gains power and wealth. The imaginary "China" that has been addressed by America's policy makers is expected, through trade alone, to undergo sweeping liberal transformation. James Mann notes that this bipartisan delusion, held by Bill Clinton and George Bush alike,[27] has so far been proved dead wrong.

A new wave of authoritarianism is turning globalization to on its head: keeping and even intensifying its capitalist element, while ditching its democratic trappings. Slaughter and Ikenberry fail to see how their liberal institutional case against liberal activism is a gift to authoritarian capitalists the world over. So too they fail to recognize China as the geopolitical foe that it is. Like Susan Shirk, we take China as an enormous security concern. We depart from her, however, in our conviction that security mandates a strong and principled response to the PRC as well as the China model. In our view an ardent defense of rights will reduce rather than heighten the chance of war with China and other Second World powers. The greatest threat is a dictatorial China that meets no challenge.

Shirk is right to avoid needless antagonism, but wrong to think that appeasement is the solution to rising tensions. Placating Chinese leaders will only embolden them. The best route out of this policy morass is moral realism. Just as it is possible to share Shirk's security concern without abandoning human rights, it is also possible to support the liberal objectives of the Princeton Project while shedding its institutional utopianism. As Edward Friedman puts it, there is "far less of a challenge to China from democracy than there is a challenge to democracy from China."[28]

---

[26] Gordon G. Chang, "China: The Next Big Crash," *New Perspectives Quarterly* 27, no. 2 (spring 2010): 10–12.

[27] James Mann, *The China Fantasy: How our Leaders Explain Away Chinese Repression* (New York: Viking, 2007), 2.

[28] Edward Friedman, "China: A Threat to or Threatened by Democracy?" *Dissent* (Winter 2009), http://dissentmagazine.org/article/?article=1318

The liberal–democratic mandate that we draw from Amartya Sen—and from James Mann with special regard to China—meets its antithesis in the Asian exceptionalism of Kishore Mahbubani. For him East–West parity is not enough. To fulfill its manifest destiny, the Asian century he celebrates must shove the West off the global stage.[29] This puts even liberal institutionalists on guard. We agree with Slaughter that Mahbubani's East–West power inversion not only belittles the West but also most of the Global South.[30] The win-win assumption of globalist economism sees both East and West, as well as South and North, as beneficiaries of a neoliberal world order. This nostrum is being pulverized by a new generation of Asianists who are ready to take charge of globalization and send the West packing.

THE SOCIAL MEANING OF CCP CORPORATISM

For too many years it was taken for granted that globalization carries benefits that apply equally to all trading nations. Critics who assailed this premise were branded antiglobalists and banished from liberal development discourse. What took shape through the Clinton and Bush years was an inner circle of true believers who refused to alter this neoliberal master plan. That hubris, which was the raw essence of the Washington Consensus, ensured that Sino-globalization and other reactionary development models were never registered as serious competition.

In 2008 this house of cards came tumbling down. The proximate cause may have been the US housing bubble, but that was itself a product of low-cost mortgages and easy credit that depended upon China's purchase of America's explosive debt. Belatedly Washington was catching on to the fact that something was terribly awry. China had fueled its growth engine by exporting undervalued goods. This not only made for huge US trade deficits, but also smothered the export hopes of other developing countries. The whole global system was being wrecked by Beijing.

As an eleventh-hour reflex, Treasury Secretary Henry Paulson flew to Beijing in December 2008 to urge China to bring its exports under control and to stop manipulating its currency. Beijing had cooperated to some degree after a similar plea was made in 2005. That time the Chinese currency was allowed to appreciate from its 2005 level of 8.25 renminbi to the

---

[29] Kishore Mahbubani, *The New Asian Hemisphere: The Irresistible Shift of Global Power to the East* (New York: Public Affairs, 2008).

[30] Anne-Marie Slaughter, "The Debate on East vs. West Continues," *The Washington Note* (May 2008), http://www.thewashingtonnote.com/archives/2008/05/the_debate_on-e/

dollar to 6.83 in 2008. However, in response to the recession, China not only froze the renminbi,[31] but raised tax rebates for exports.[32]

Meanwhile Chinese popular opinion faults Beijing for being too cooperative. Many Chinese are asking why their nation should bankroll the consumption habits of its major geopolitical competitor. China's official foreign exchange reserves at the beginning of 2009 were just under $2,000 billion,[33] but experts at the Council on Foreign Relations put the real figure at around $2,300 billion, or more than $1,600 for every Chinese citizen. That is not far beneath the country's average income. In 2008, with its economy already under great stress, China lent America another $400 billion, bringing its total credit to around $1,700 billion. $5 billion of this had been invested through the China Investment Cooperation (CIC) in Morgan Stanley before its collapse. The CIC was also ensnared in the Reserve Primary Fund, with links to the bankrupt Lehman Brothers.[34]

Of course, China reaps much more from its loans than their stated dividends. While its lending habits serve to keep the American door wide open for Chinese exports, it also gains tremendous influence over Washington. As a debtor nation, America will not be inclined to put much reform pressure on its major creditor. But there is another reason for Washington's disinclination to press this matter. The decision to terminate annual most favored nation (MFN) assessments was prompted by the pervasive belief among pundits and policy makers that political reformation is a natural process within capitalist societies. If commerce automatically breeds democratic liberalism, why disturb delicate trade relations with needless talk of reform?

The root assumption behind America's China policy was provided by Seymour Martin Lipset's postulate that affluence is the guarantor of democratization. Many who accept the democratic transitions of South Korea and Taiwan as proof of this thesis refuse to accept China as its disproof. It is an article of faith that China, despite appearances, *must* be following the Taiwan and South Korean path. Consider the case of Henry S. Rowen's GDP determinism. In 1996, on the basis of GDP data alone, Rowen predicted that China would be a "free" country by 2015. He has since changed that estimate

[31] "Will China Listen?" *The New York Times* (March 17, 2010), http://www.nytimes.com/2010/03/17/opinion/17wed1.html

[32] "Obama's Dependence on China," *The Christian Science Monitor* (December 9, 2008), http://www.csmonitor.com/2008/1209/p08s01-comv.html

[33] "Smaller Increase in China's Foreign Reserves in Quarter," *The New York Times* (July 11, 2010), http://www.nytimes.com/2010/07/12/business/global/12yuan.html

[34] Geoff Dyer, "China's Dollar Dilemma," *Financial Times* (February 22, 2009), http://www.ft.com/cms/s/0/299e404c-011b-11de-8f6e-000077b07658.html?nclick_check=1

to "partially free," but still holds that full freedom will follow by 2025.[35] The picture he paints is of a relatively smooth transition to democracy, far less traumatic than the still fragile transitions of Taiwan and Korea.

It is a grave mistake to treat China as just a hugely inflated Taiwan. Taiwan's KMT can only dream of the CCP's uncontested power. Over time the minority status of the KMT's "mainlander" constituency forced it to make social and democratic concessions, starting with land reform and culminating in a multiparty system. Rising affluence led to the emergence of a civil society that would eventually make political demands, despite the risk of imprisonment and even death in the early years. The result was a viable political opposition.[36] It helped that in its martial law days Taiwan's nascent middle class was made up largely of non-mainlanders who were not so easy to co-opt as China's affluent classes have been.[37] The newly globalized CCP is now stronger than ever, with no viable rivals in sight. As Martin Jacques stresses, China has a strong "civilizational" preference for "harmony" and "stability" over the deliberative rancor of democracy, and Jacques fully concurs with the official CCP view that development should be concerned almost exclusively with economics, not tangential matters such as democracy.[38] CCPism is so steeped in this "civilizational" bent that to resist it would require a cultural as well as political revolution.

This deep-rooted authoritarianism gives China its comparative advantage over democratic India in attracting foreign capital. The party generously offers its "harmonizing" services to TNCs that are glad to do business in a country where "free enterprise" means freedom from destabilizing factors such as democracy, independent unions, fair wages, environmental protection, etc. With collective bargaining and protest strictly forbidden, only individuals can file lawful complaints, and one who does so will be summarily fired and often will end up in a mental ward getting electric shocks and massive drug injections, even as mentally ill people go untreated. It takes just one official's signature to have someone committed to an asylum

---

[35] Henry S. Rowen, "When Will Chinese People Be Free?" *Journal of Democracy* 18, no. 3 (July 2007): 38 (38–52).

[36] See Linda Chao and Ramon H. Myers, *The First Chinese Democracy: Political Life in the Republic of China on Taiwan* (Baltimore, Moldova: The Johns Hopkins University Press, 1998), 70.

[37] Likewise, oppositionalism was too deeply ingrained in postcolonial Korea to permit very effective cooptation. See Songok Han Thornton, "The 'Miracle' Revisited: The De-Radicalization of Korean Political Culture," *New Political Science: A Journal of Politics & Culture* 27, no. 2 (June 2005): 161–76.

[38] Martin Jacques, *When China Rules the World: The Rise of the Middle Kingdom and the End of the Western World* (London and New York: Penguin Books, 2009), 213–14.

or one of the infamous "black jails" that are scattered across China. The inmates of these prisons had no formal arrest, trial, or conviction, and there is no mechanism for appeal.[39]

Granted, there is always hope for concerted resistance. As protests grow larger, it will be impossible for the state to incarcerate everyone. Robert Gifford believes that the bleeding of rural China is reaching a critical juncture. The party itself estimated that in 2007 there were more than 200 rural protests per day, most of them motivated by gross corruption and inequality, and since then the numbers have certainly grown. The lack of an independent legal system voids any chance of a just and peaceful settlement of these disputes.[40] Likewise, as Alexandra Harney stresses, the China boom has cost the urban proletariat dearly.[41] These are the very workers who are commonly said to be the prime beneficiaries of the Deng revolution. Their opinion on the matter is not registered, and their independent organization is strictly prohibited.

Journalists, politicians, and academics constantly remind us of how millions of former peasants have been "lifted out of poverty" by the CCP system. Many fatuous commentators laud the Party for its "moderation" and "pragmatism," and some carry the argument to effusive extremes that more resemble Party hoopla than political analysis. One of these panegyrics, which somehow ended up in the *New York Times*, credited the CCP with safeguarding not only property rights but even "individual liberties." Needless to say the author, from Fudan University, takes a dim view of Liu Xioabo's Nobel Peace Prize, which prompted his essay.[42] He is joined in this opinion by the 19 governments that turned down their invitations

---

[39] Sharon LaFraniere, "Assertive Chinese Held in Mental Wards," *The New York Times* (November 11, 2010), http://www.nytimes.com/2010/11/12/world/asia/12psych.html?src=me

[40] Robert Gifford, *China Road: A Journey into the Future of a Rising Power* (New York: Random House, 2007), 16.

[41] See Alexandra Harney, *The China Price: The True Cost of Chinese Competitive Advantage* (London: Penguin Press, 2008), *passim*.

[42] See Eric Li, "A Color Revolution in China? Keep It Red," *The New York Times* (December 6, 2010), http://www.nytimes.com/2010/12/07/opinion/07iht-edli.html

Li's idea that the CCP deserves praise for its protection of "individual liberties" is too risible for comment. As for his notion that the party is a guardian of property rights, the question is whose rights. Those with the right government connections are indeed protected. Within Chinese firms, likewise, major operational decisions are ultimately decided by the state. As one Western observer put it, "In China you're dealing with the government. In India you're dealing with companies." See "Being Eaten by the Dragon," *The Economist* (November 11, 2010), http://www. economist.com/node/17460954/print

to attend the awards ceremony in Oslo.[43] The list of those countries is tantamount to an honor roll of the authoritarian block that we call the new Second World.

In the words of Václav Havel and Desmond Tutu, "the story of this year's Nobel peace prize laureate, Dr Liu Xiaobo, is sadly emblematic of the Chinese government's intolerance to individual expression."[44] Paradoxically, as Liu's friend Bao Tong notes, it is Liu and his Charter 08 colleagues who actually uphold the core values of the Chinese Constitution, and particularly Article 33's guarantee of equality before the law. The chief enemies of those tenets were Mao and Deng, the respective architects of the Cultural Revolution and the Tiananmen Massacre.[45] The Nobel Prize debacle took a bizarre turn when Beijing, desperate to save face, not only cracked down harder than ever on dissent, but quickly staged a rival "Confucian peace prize" ceremony.[46] The prize went to the KMT party hack Lien Chan, whose venality and political bungling cost him his popularity even within his own Taiwan party.

Gifford and Harney offer potent correctives for the "miracle" myth that supports CCPism. Far from the salvation story that is endlessly circulated in globalist circles, most of China's new urban workforce was more booted out than "lifted out" of their agrarian communities. Their forced march into industrial China has usually been a trail of woe, marked by the kind of living and working conditions that English sweatshop workers suffered

---

[43] David Barboza, "China Moves to Block Foreign News on Nobel Prize Ceremony," *The New York Times* (December 9, 2010), http://www.nytimes.com/2010/12/10/world/asia/10china.html

[44] Václav Havel and Desmond Tutu, "China Must Release Liu Xiaobo—or Lose Its Credibility," *The Guardian* (December 5, 2010), http://www.guardian.co.uk/commentisfree/2010/dec/05/liu-xiabao-nobel-havel-tutu

[45] Bao Tong, "Rights for All, Through Peaceful Means," *The New York Times* (December 6, 2010), http://www.nytimes.com/2010/12/07/opinion/07iht-edbao.html

It should be added that the Cultural Revolution was in many respects a by-product of the Great Famine, which was Mao's real masterpiece. As Frank Dikötter puts it, the famine "was not merely an isolated episode in the making of modern China. It was its turning point. The subsequent Cultural Revolution was the leader's attempt to take revenge on the colleagues who had dared to oppose him during the Great Leap Forward." See Frank Dikötter, "Mao's Great Leap to Famine," *The New York Times* (December 15, 2010), http://www.nytimes.com/2010/12/16/opinion/16-eddikotter16.html

It should also be stressed that the current CCP has never repudiated this masterpiece. Like Tiananmen, it is an organic part of the Party's structure—past, present, and future.

[46] Will Hutton, "China's Fury over the Nobel Showed Weakness, not Strength," *Guardian* (December 12, 2010), http://www.guardian.co.uk/commentisfree/2010/dec/12/will-hutton-china-economy

in the early industrial era. Those fortunate enough to get regular factory work may feel almost blessed. Others must make do with day labor that leaves them on the very edge of subsistence.

Armies of these hapless itinerants were put to work preparing Beijing and other cities for China's Olympic coming-out party. As the opening date drew near, migrant laborers were not invited to the party. A massive "clean-up" operation summarily evicted them from the cities they had worked so hard to prepare. Nor were they the only "clean-up" victims. Street vendors suffered the same fate, and some of the oldest residential sections of Beijing were demolished, along with around 2,500 religious sites.

The urban elite used the Olympics as an excuse to cut out the very heart of the city's traditional social fabric. It was a cruel irony that this demolition work was carried out by soon-to-be evicted migrant workers. This recalls the way the Ming emperor Yongle used 200,000 press-ganged workers to construct the original city that was now being deconstructed under the name of modernization. It was also ironic that the Cultural Relics Bureau, officially dedicated to cultural preservation, was given the job of supervising this cultural pillage.

The Olympic binge was just the latest battle in a virtual war on urban underclasses. The government admits having evicted 500,000 Beijing residents between 1990 and 2003, and unofficial estimates reach to 1.25 million.[47] The Olympics simply shifted the process into high gear. Across China a peasant labor force of around 1.3 million toiled day and night in the thick of smog, urban blight, and unimaginable stress on about 7,000 construction projects. Between 2,000 and 3,000 workers died *per day* in the name of a clean and green "people's Olympics."[48]

SINO-COLONIAL TESTING GROUND

What CCPism has done to China's own working classes, in the name of "uplifting," the China model is now doing to workers throughout the developing world. Nowhere is this recipe for oppression applied so aggressively as in Africa, which by no accident is emerging as the new frontier of Sino-globalization. Belatedly the West is realizing the error of its disinterest in Africa, and is trying to stage a comeback. This policy reversal is

---

[47] Michael Meyer, "The Death and Life of Old Beijing," *Architectural Record* (July 2008), http://www.archrecord.construction.com/features/beijing/

[48] "Going, Gone," *The Economist* (July 31, 2008), http://www.economist.com/books/Printer Friendly.cfm?story_id=11837639

going to stoke intense competition between the rival capitalisms of East and West. Just as the Cold War was mostly waged through distant proxy wars in the Third World, a new "Great Game" is taking shape in Africa, Central Asia and other resource-rich regions on the global periphery. Part of what makes Africa so geopolitically volatile is that its foreign relations are unsettled. There is no pan-African equivalent of the Monroe Doctrine, and the resources at issue are so valuable that diplomatic compromise may be impossible.

China's African ventures must be understood in the context of the limiting factors that China faces elsewhere. By expanding Westward into Central Asia, China is not only stepping on ex-Soviet turf but on Muslim cultural politics, and for the moment it will tread lightly. Likewise it will be on its best behavior in Latin America, given the North American competition. It knows that in the Middle East the geopolitical stakes are too high (too oil-saturated) for bumptious action, and in East Asia constraint is enforced by a residual Cold War balance of power. Finally, in South and Southeast Asia there is so much historical wariness toward the Chinese dragon that most regional players will think twice before giving the boot to the West. Even Vietnam is reaching out to its former foe, America.

In John Mearsheimer's view, China's primary ambition is to establish the kind of Asian hegemony that the US has maintained in Latin America. There are, however, clear signs that China has much broader ambitions. One clue to its global designs is its concentration on Africa, which could become its most prominent sphere of influence in coming years. China comes to Africa with the signal advantage of having no reform commitment. By contrast, the pride of the West's new Africa agenda is the Millennium Challenge Account (MCA), which would selectively reward the good conduct of developing countries with favorable aid packages. Given China's counter offers, many African countries are simply refusing Western aid.

Critics charge that the West's reform conditionality is a form of soft imperialism, as if China's raw mercantilism is not imperialistic. One very vocal example is the Zambian economist Dambisa Moyo, who blames the West for having an "obsession with democracy" that leads to ruinous battles between political factions and interest groups. It is not surprising that this former World Bank and Goldman Sachs functionary would exalt free-enterprise solutions to Africa's ills.[49] What is strange is that she could cling to this neoliberal position even as she simultaneously recommends China's state capitalism as the continent's developmental savior.

---

[49] See Dambisa Moyo, *Dead Aid: Why Aid is not Working and how there is a Better Way for Africa* (London: Allen Lane, 2009).

Somehow she misses the fact that Chinese statism is in many respects the very antithesis of the neoliberalism she extols.

Granted, neoliberal and Sino-globalist development models do have some crucial features in common. First and foremost they share an aversion to the moral element that has crept into Western development discourse in recent years. Like the victims of Nigeria's petro-political ecocide, the residents of Bhopal, India have learned the hard way that Western neoliberals pay little heed to the corporate responsibility they tout in theory. Likewise the soft power of the China model is anything but the value-free instrument it claims to be. Indeed, it is more value-packed than the Western corporate competition, which has no interest beyond quick profits. The cement of today's Sino-African relations is located in a shared respect for authoritarian order. This deeply ideological commitment is certainly not averse to profits, but it is even more interested in power politics.

To be sure, China gets a "late comer" boost from the sordid reputation that Western firms and institutions have earned in Africa over decades. As in Latin America, the whole neoliberal apparatus is implicated. "Structural adjustment" programs (SAPs) of the 1980s and 1990s were said to cure statist maladies such as corruption, market distortion and general economic malaise. Economic benefits that were supposed to "trickle down" to all classes continuously trickled up. What neoliberalism actually accomplished was to entrench crony capitalism, deepen inequality, and retard economic growth. Africa had negative per capita growth from 1980 to 2000,[50] even as some of the worst African rulers secured a respectful place in the global economy. This made a mockery of the neoliberal boast that globalization favors democratic development.

That anti-democratic reflex has contributed greatly to the relegation of social services to foreign aid agencies and non-governmental organizations (NGOs).[51] Worse, this was happening just as the West was losing interest in Africa's social needs after the Cold War. Foreign aid reductions were an ironic by-product of world peace. It therefore became all the more important to make every penny count, which meant that the quality of governance would count more than ever. Aid critics like Moyo and William Easterly only depart from this script in that they believe aid precludes good governance.

---

[50] Gordon McCord, Jeffrey D. Sachs, and Wing Thye Woo, "Understanding African Poverty: Beyond the Washington Consensus to the Millennium Development Goals Approach," in *Africa in the World Economy: The National, Regional and International Challenges* (The Hague: Fondad, 2005), 23–54.

[51] James Ferguson, *Global Shadows: Africa in the Neoliberal World Order* (Durham and London: Duke University Press, 2006), 10–12.

Aid optimists, by contrast, often think that attaching the right conditions could render aid an effective reform tool. The IMF and World Bank finally began applying some ethical oversight to Western businesses operating abroad. Richard Behar describes how in recent years American companies have been vexed by higher moral and environmental standards. Under the Foreign Corrupt Practices Act, the Justice Department and the FBI are empowered to go after violators, while the Sarbanes-Oxley law tightens financial regulation.[52]

Paradoxically, the main beneficiary of these reform initiatives has been China. The new ethical bent of the West turned China's amorality into a huge commercial and geopolitical asset. A 2007 World Bank study found that sub-Saharan Africa led every other region on earth in terms of business graft.[53] However, most data on Chinese corruption was simply unavailable. It is telling that so many African leaders now look to China as their developmental mentor. By defining hegemony as any form of meddling in another country's internal affairs, China puts an ingenious anti-hegemonic spin on its ethical indifference.[54] Its present advantage, then, is not just a matter of its deep-pockets focus on the region. There is some truth in the adage that "no good deed goes unpunished." For once the West did something right, and for that it is losing the competition in Africa's race to the bottom.

AFRICA AS A POST-GLOBALIST OPPORTUNITY

For decades African regimes have operated in the interest of a small elite that uses the government to beat down any possible opposition. The dark truth that few globalists care to admit is that globalization courts this elite and renders it immune to reform pressure. Even Jeffrey Sachs, who argues fervently for more aid, prefers to blame Africa's woes on geography rather than atrocious governance.[55] Others try to evade the whole question of governmental defects. That was the unstated theme of the France-Africa

---

[52] Richard Behar, "China Surpasses U.S. as Leader in Sub-Sahara," *Fast Company. com* (June 1, 2008), http://www.fastcompany.com/magazine/126/endgame-hypocrisy-blindness-and-the-doomsday-scenario.html

[53] Richard Behar, "Special Report: China Storms Africa," *Fast Company.com* (June 1, 2008), http://www.fastcompnay.com/node/849662/print

[54] Ian Taylor, *China and Africa: Engagement and Compromise* (London and New York: Routledge, 2006), 197.

[55] William Easterly, "Geography Lessons: Correcting Sachs on African Economic Development," *Huffington Post* (June 12, 2010), http://www.huffingtonpost.com/william-easterly/geography-lessons-correct_b_208879.html

Summit which convened in 2010 on the French Riviera. Seventeen African countries gained their independence in 1960, 14 from France alone, yet none saw fit to spotlight their achievements on this 50th anniversary. Lengthy discussion of the postcolonial experience would have called attention to the indigenous oppression that took the place of colonialism.[56]

Though many follow Tony Blair and the "save Africa" singer Bono in calling for more aid and exhorting the West to look after Africa, there is little to show for the $294 billion in loans that went to sub-Saharan Africa from 1970 to 2002. $268 billion has been repaid, but the remaining debt plus interest comes to a crushing $210 billion.[57] Worse still a 2005 report from the Blair Commission for Africa estimated that an amount greater than half of Africa's external debt had been shunted into foreign bank accounts over this period. Other studies paint an even bleaker picture, charging that for every dollar loaned to Africa between 1970 and 1996, 80 cents ended up in private Western accounts. The total is put at over $500 billion, yet Western governments (no doubt acting at the behest of the banks) make little or no attempt to repatriate these stolen funds.[58]

Despite his objection to aid in general, Easterly offers some pithy advice on how to make aid more effective. First and foremost, make sure that it goes to poor people, not poor governments.[59] Oddly that is not far from the social-responsibility tenet that Easterly famously rejects. Paul Collier carries this cautionary principle to its logical conclusion: not with a call to end aid, but rather for tough conditionality. While he agrees with most aid critics that large amounts of no-strings-attached assistance will discourage government accountability, his solution is to make aid contingent upon transparency and fair elections.[60]

Pierre Englebert takes this tough-love approach even farther by urging the international community to de-recognize nations that seriously violate human rights, destroy the environment, and rob the public. By this standard

---

[56] Adam Nossiter, "African States Weigh 50 Bittersweet Years of Independence," *The New York Times* (June 4, 2010), http://www.nytimes.com/2010/06/05/world/africa/05africa.html

[57] Eric Wiedemann and Thilo Thielke, "Choking on Aid Money in Africa," *Das Spiegel 27/2005* (July 4, 2005), http://www.spiegel.de/international/spiegel/0,1518,36360,00html

[58] Behar, "China Surpasses U.S. as Leader in Sub-Sahara," *op. cit.*

[59] Easterly, *op. cit.*

[60] Paul Collier, "Time to Turn Off the Aid Tap?" *The Independent* (January 30, 2009), http://license.icopyright.net/user/viewFreeUse.act?fuid=ODY5Njk2OA%3D%3D

Others like Paul Romer demand only transparency, so as to escape the developmental undertow that they associate with democracy. Only in terms of degree is this elitist development model distinguished from Singapore school authoritarianism.

the nightmare regimes of Sudan, Chad, Congo, and Equatorial Guinea would simply cease to exist as sovereign states. International excommunication would compel rogue governments to seek support from their own people. It says much about the general state of African political development that Englebert finds it necessary to cite the breakaway state of Somaliland, which technically is not even a nation, as his key democratic example. Since 2003, this semi-state has had a fairly elected president, and the contrast with Somalia could hardly be more graphic. Englebert believes this grand exception owes much to the fact that the Somali National Movement, which fought the Somali dictator Siad Barre, failed to gain international recognition in the early 1990s.[61] That failure became a blessing in disguise, for it compelled the National Movement to adopt more participatory policies and institutions.[62]

Somaliland is so unusual that it serves as little more than the exception that proves the dictatorial rule. By underwriting Africa's worst rulers, China forfeits all claim to concern for Africans in general, yet puts itself on the winning side of African globalization. The best known case in point is Sudan, which is the hottest spot on Africa's geopolitical chessboard. Western attempts at sanctions over the Darfur crisis paved the way for China's virtual monopoly over Sudan's oil trade. Here and elsewhere Beijing has been well rewarded for refusing to follow the West in making aid conditional upon reform.[63] The harder the West works at its ethical agenda, the more China profits.

Countless other hotspots warrant attention. In February 2007 President Hu Jintao made a game-changing tour through eight African countries, signing contracts, forgiving debts and extending millions in interest-free loans. Within a week of this foray, President Bush announced a new military command, AFRICOM, to plug up America's strategic gap in Africa.[64] The contrast between the two initiatives could hardly have been more striking.

---

[61] "Somaliland's Elections: Not So Failing," *The Economist* (July 1, 2010), http://www.economist.com/node/16488840/print

[62] Englebert's classic case in point is Taiwan, which in the 1970s was effectively de-recognized as the flipside of China's international upgrade. The pressure this put on Taiwan's corrupt and repressive KMT forced it to seek more domestic legitimacy and eventually to open the country up for a measure of democracy and the abolition of martial law. Pierre Englebert, " To Save Africa, Reject its Nations," *The New York Times* (June 11, 2010), http://www.nytimes.com/2010/06/12/opinion/12englebert.html

[63] See Scott Baldauf, "Hu's Trip to Sudan Tests China-Africa Ties," *The Christian Science Monitor* (February 2, 2007), http://www.csmonitor.com/2007/0202/p06s01-woaf.html

[64] Paul McLeary, "A Different Kind of Great Game," *Foreign Policy* (February 2007), http://www.foreignpolicy.com/story/cms.php?story_id=3744

African leaders tend to see the American initiative as invasive, whereas China is lauded as the consummate ally in development. Beijing's support for Africa's political horror show is worn like a postcolonial badge of honor. There is some irony in the fact that Washington's effort to stabilize the continent militarily could easily redound to China's commercial benefit, much as American military operations in Afghanistan help to protect Chinese investments there.

Nevertheless there could be a serious flaw in China's Third World strategy. Hu's 2007 Africa trip exposed the fact that China's game plan revolves almost entirely around the top-heavy mechanisms of crony capitalism. This makes it highly vulnerable to democratic challenges from below. Hu was met by a rash of protests against China's irresponsible dealings. In Zambia, for example, his travel plan was disrupted by the threat of demonstrations against the low wages and unsafe working conditions at Chinese-operated copper mines. These complaints had become issues in the previous fall's presidential campaign. So too, in late 2006 a Chinese energy company in Gabon had been forced to halt its environmentally destructive drilling practices; and in South Africa there were very effective protests against the massive influx of Chinese textiles and consumer goods.[65]

It was becoming obvious to many Africans that dealing with China is anything but the win-win, no-strings-attached engagement that Beijing advertises. While the China model well serves a privileged few and lends security to loathsome regimes, it crushes local enterprises and locks in resource contracts that preclude better negotiations in the future. China eventually yielded ground in the face of South Africa's anti-import campaign, but not before it had threatfully invoked its WTO rights.[66] Other countries have been hit even harder. In Nigeria and Ghana the domestic textile and consumer products industries were wrecked by Chinese imports.[67] China knows that such capital-starved countries cannot resist its inroads.

The message at Beijing's November 2006 African Summit was that China offered investment and funded projects that "respected sovereignty," which is to say they made no reform demands on local rulers and their cronies. By 2008 there were over 800 Chinese state-owned or state-controlled corporations active in Africa, while China's Export-Import Bank was funding over 300 projects in at least 36 countries. Already Chinese aid was thought to exceed that of the World Bank. This was a devastating blow to Western institutions seeking reform leverage. A whole decade of work on

---

[65] *Ibid.*

[66] Princeton N. Lyman, "China's Rising Role in Africa," *Council on Foreign Relations* (July 21, 2005), http://www.cfr.org/publication/8436/chinas_rising_role_in_africa.html

[67] *Ibid.*

human rights and government transparency was all but nullified,[68] and that is not to mention the commercial and geopolitical damage.

The biggest losers, however, have been African workers and small business owners whose governments leave them in the lurch. The sheer volume of Chinese trade—$100 billion annually by 2010[69]—explains why African governments are structuring their operations around Chinese needs. That means scuttling any thought of protective action on behalf of domestic companies and local workers. Stories abound of workers being horrendously overworked and underpaid by Chinese employers. Smaller Chinese firms frequently disappear without even paying workers for months of grueling labor.[70] The cozy relationship between African politicians and their Chinese cronies removes any chance of legal remedies.

Though inter-elite collusion is a big factor here,[71] it is more the symptom than the cause of this globalist malady. Even more than neoliberalism, Sino-globalism is a formula for the recolonization of the Third World. There is a silver lining, however, in the utter indifference of elites to general social welfare, for it advertises the system's fatal flaw. As anger swells from below, a window of opportunity is opened for democratic action. It must be asked why the West is not doing more to reap this post-globalist opportunity.

Regretfully, Western globalism hinges on the equally top-down formula of "trickle down" distribution. It profoundly distrusts any politics that might promote real equality. That slams the door on social democracy. Many are coming to agree with Paul Romer that democracy per se (not just globalist market democracy) is a developmental obstacle. His idea is to circumvent Africa's crisis of local governance by establishing "charter cities:" enclaves run entirely by foreign managers.[72] If this democratic rollback is the best remedy the West can offer for the crisis of Third World governance, it is a safe bet that the China model will be the winner in Africa and most of the developing world. Only a post-globalist First World can hope to match the Second World competition.

---

[68] Richard Behar, "China Saps Mozambique of Timber Resources," *Fast Company.com* (June 1, 2008), http://www.fastcompany.com/magazine/126/mozambique-a-chain-saw-for-every-tree.html

[69] Howard French, "The Next Empire," *The Atlantic* (May 2010), http://www.theatlantic.com/magazine/print/2010/05/the-next-empire/8018/

[70] Behar, "China Saps Mozambique of Timber Resources," *op. cit.*

[71] Bright B. Simons, "Deciphering the Sino-Africa Saga," *Asia Times* (February 19, 2009), http://www.atimes.com/atimes/China/KB19Ad01.html

[72] See Sebastian Mallaby, "The Politically Incorrect Guide to Ending Poverty," *The Atlantic* (July/August 2010), http://www.theatlantic.com/magazine/archive/20101/07/the-politically-incorrect-guide-toending-poverty/8134/

4

TIBET'S LONG SHADOW
China, India, and the Cold War over "Asian Values"

THE MANCHURIZATION OF TIBET

On September 30, 2006, a 17-year-old Tibetan nun named Kelsang Namtso was gunned down by Chinese military personnel at Nagpa Pass near the China–Nepal border. For seventeen days she and her companions had drudged through rough and freezing Himalayan terrain in an effort to reach Buddhist havens outside Tibet. To have made it this far was something of a miracle. The group had been told there would be just two days of walking, and carried only that much food.[1] A night crossing would have been highly advisable, to avoid detection, but to ease the ordeal for children in the group they risked a daylight passage. This made them easy targets on the open snowfield that lay between them and the border.[2] A survivor who escaped by hiding for hours in the snow said the shooting lasted three hours.[3]

---

[1] "Interview with Two Survivors of the Nangpa Pass Shooting," *Human Rights Watch* (November 20, 2006), http://www.hrw.org/en/news/2006/11/20/china-interview-two-survivors-nangpa-pass-shooting

[2] Leonard Doyle, "China Tries to Gag Climbers Who Saw Tibet Killings," *The Independent* (October 11, 2006), http://license.icopyright.net/user/viewFreeUse.act?fuid=MzM1Mzg4Mw%3D%3D

[3] "Interview with Two Survivors," *op. cit.*

There must have been similar but unreported killings before, since several thousand Tibetans were attempting the crossing each year.[4] This time, however, there happened to be foreign witnesses. Mountain climbers on Mount Cho Oyu watched in horror as marksmen just 300 yards from them targeted the helpless refugees. A Slovenian climber took an unforgettable photo of Kelsang Namtso lying dead in the snow, her backpack some distance behind her.[5] She must have crawled those last yards before collapsing. Remarkably, several dozen refugees made it through the pass that day, including a seven-year-old girl, but other children and one old man were captured and marched directly through the Cho Oyu camp, now under heavy military guard.

The surprising thing is that few of the foreign witnesses were willing to speak out. An anonymous American climber expressed revulsion at this self-censorship. Climbing is big business here, and it depends upon the good graces of both Nepal and China. Just to be sure this was understood, Chinese diplomats in Kathmandu tracked down most of the witnesses to debrief them,[6] but that precaution was hardly necessary. The commercial priorities of these climbers suggest in microcosm how the whole issue of Tibet has been finessed by China. The global community has taken a de facto vow of silence regarding Chinese state terrorism. Lately, however, Tibetans have been putting this globalist bargain to the test. They know that time is not on their side, for Han Chinese immigration is weakening their demographic grip on their land. Somehow they must break through the wall of silence that allows the West to trade in good conscience with their persecutors.

The 2008 Beijing Olympics looked like their best shot at global attention. That March, on the 49th anniversary of the 1959 Tibetan uprising, the biggest protests in a generation erupted across Tibet. Chinese troops were primed for violent action rather than mere crowd control. After they crushed the peaceful demonstrations of monks and their supporters in Lhasa, more volcanic protests erupted far and wide. Pent-up frustrations

---

[4] A refugee center in India usually takes in 2,500 to 3,000 Tibetans per year, but intense Chinese surveillance caused that number to drop to a mere 550 in 2008. See Edward Wong, "Tibetan Monks Tell Tale of Escape from China," *The New York Times* (June 21, 2009), http://www.nytimes.com/2009/06/21/world/asia/21tibet.html

[5] This picture was dispatched online through the Explorer's Web. See "Image of Nun's Body in Snow at Nangpa Pass," *International Campaign for Tibet* (October 11, 2006), http://www.savetibet.org/media-center/ict-news-reports/image-nuns-body-snow-nangpa-pass

[6] Doyle, *op. cit.*

from decades of brutal oppression exploded in the streets, to no avail. Only strong and sustained international pressure could put a brake on Chinese injustice here and throughout the Tibet Autonomous Region (TAR). This was precluded by the see-no-evil "engagement" policies of Western governments.

Though Washington did file complaints about the brutality, these were so anemic as to have a reverse effect: reassuring Beijing that Tibet had been written off as China's internal affair. By no means would the crackdown be allowed to mar the Olympics. To underscore that fact, President Bush made a point of attending the opening ceremonies, all but walking on the graves of the estimated 220 Tibetan protesters who gave their lives in a futile plea for international support. Another 1,300 were injured and around 7,000 arrested, 1,000 of whom would still be missing a year later.[7]

All this happened just as China was being quietly dropped from the US top ten list of human rights violators.[8] The message was painfully clear. As had happened after the Tiananmen massacre twenty years before, America and the international business community were washing their hands of the matter. In the case of Tiananmen it took a couple of years for business to get back to normal. This time, it never stopped being normal.

Though China spent decades honing its anti-imperialist image, it could accomplish this remarkable public relations feat only by blacking out its actions in Tibet (including the largely Tibetan Qinghai Province) and other occupied areas such as East Turkestan (that is, Xinjiang), Inner Mongolia, Manchuria, and border zones like Aksai Chin, a large section of Kashmir that China seized from India in the 1962 war.[9] The greatest friction point, however, is Tawang, in the disputed border zone of India's Arunachal Pradesh state.

Things heated up in 2008, when the Dalai Lama declared Tawang a legitimate part of India. This position found support in the 1914 Treaty between Britain and Tibet, which has never been recognized by China. Beijing insists that the area still belongs to Tibet, which in turn belongs to China. This became a global issue in March 2009, when India sought a $2.9 billion loan from the Asian Development Bank. As a member of the bank's board, China

[7] Edward Wong, "Dalai Lama Says China Has Turned Tibet Into a 'Hell on Earth'," *The New York Times* (March 11, 2009), http://www.nytimes.com/2009/03/11/world/asia/11tibet.html

[8] "China Terrorizes Tibet," *The New York Times* (March 18, 2008), http://www.nytimes.com/2008/03/18/opinion/18tue3.html

[9] Nick Easen, "Aksai Chin: China's Disputed Slice of Kashmir," *CNN.com* (May 25, 2002), http://edition.cnn.com/2002/WORLD/asiapcf/east/05/24/aksai.chin

tried unsuccessfully to block the loan on the grounds that $60 million of it was earmarked for use by the renegade state of Arunachal Pradesh.[10]

The tragic case of the Manchus serves as a warning to all China's minorities of what awaits them if present policies continue. Today's Manchus constitute a minuscule minority within their own homeland—a mere 3 or 4 percent of the population in most areas. As of 2007 there were less than 100 Manchus who even spoke their own language. This is pure ethnocide, and a similar fate awaits indigenous people throughout the occupied areas of "China."[11] Collectively those occupied zones cover about the same area as China's non-occupied regions.

Tibet, however, is the international focal point of the whole issue, and China knows that to yield an inch on this one would set a precedent for "splitist" activism elsewhere. As the sordid truth about Tibet leaks out, China tries to justify its occupation by adopting the pose of a benign colonizer. It must stress its generous "development" of a savage land, yet the very process that opens the country up exposes the government's brutality and cultural ravages. Beijing's latest gift to its ungrateful pupils is a new Tibetan holiday: Serfs' Emancipation Day. Thus China dons the stereotypically Western pose of enlightened mentor to benighted natives. Any Han shopkeeper is considered culturally superior to meditative monks who have spent decades studying Buddhist texts.

TIBET AND XINJIANG AT THE BARRICADES

The government's problem is that the spirituality and erudition of Tibetan monks does not render them as socially reclusive as might be expected. They are often engaged in civic affairs, including civil disobedience. Even their purely humanitarian work is a thorn in Beijing's side, as became clear after the earthquake of April 14, 2010 in Qinghai Province. In stark contrast to the government's shamefully slow response to the disaster, hundreds and perhaps thousands of monks rushed into the area to save lives, render emergency assistance and handle the hundreds of burials that could not be delayed. Once public officials and military personnel eventually arrived and

---

[10] See Edward Wong, "China and India Dispute Enclave on Edge of Tibet," *The New York Times* (September 4, 2009), http://www.nytimes.com/2009/09/04/world/asia/04chinaindia.html

[11] See "CTA's Response to Beijing's Comments on De-Militarisation and 'Ethnic Cleaning'," *Tibet Net* (September 5, 2009), http://www.phayul.com/news/article.aspx?article=CTA%E2%80%99s+Response+to+Beijing%E2%80%99s+Comments+on+De-Militarisation+and+%E2%80%98Ethnic+Cleaning%E2%80%99&id=25456

began operations, the monks were ordered out of the area, for the job they were doing made a mockery of the media's portrait of Tibetans as helplessly backward people who depended on Han management and authority.[12]

China's neocolonial script inverts the current Western adulation of Tibet as the last preserve of a mystic and unsullied East. Like something out of *Lost Horizon*, Tibet is often looked upon as the antidote for a spiritually moribund West. Increasingly, though, it is taking on the role of a political antidote as well, for this is the main cultural redoubt of the "Other Asia" that Willem van Schendel has dubbed "Zomia" — an extended ethnosphere that defies all the stereotypes we have regarding Asian values. Drake Bennet describes Zomia as an arc of cultural resistance reaching from the Vietnamese highlands to the Tibetan plateau. These "hill people" have long been vilified by other Asians for their insubordination and egalitarianism.[13] By crushing Tibet, the crown jewel of Zomian counter-culture, China is doing its best to root out the last vestiges of this 2000-year-old tradition of Asian anti-authoritarianism.

As a political force, "Tibet" also subsumes the Dalai Lama's government in exile and the Tibetan expatriate community. Both have absorbed so much democratic thought and practice—partly from Western influence, but no less from their adopted Indian home—that their spiritual aversion to Chinese materialism is wedded to a potent political resistance. Very much as the nascent democratization of Taiwan raised the stakes of the "two Chinas" conflict on the PRC's eastern flank, Tibet does so on its western flank. If this downtrodden and culturally besieged people can democratize themselves, albeit in exile, what excuse does a world power like China have for its unyielding authoritarianism?

Despite his very accommodating attitudes, the Dalai Lama's global popularity has kept the suffering of Tibet on the radar screen of international consciousness. Any hope of reconciliation between Beijing and Tibet's exile government in Dharamsala evaporated when the Dalai Lama and his followers embraced democratic principles. It is the amalgamation of native "Zomian" recalcitrance and modern democratic values that renders

---

[12] Michael Wines, "China Asks Monks to Leave Quake Area," *The New York Times* (April 23, 2010), http://www.nytimes.com/2010/04/24/world/asia/24quake.html

The truth could not be shunted from view, as would have been the case if the quake had been centered inside TAR, which is off-limits to foreign journalists. See "Earthquake in China's Qinghai Province Kill Hundreds of People," *The Economist* (April 14, 2010), http://www.economist.com/world/asia/displayStory.cfm? story_id =5904336&source=most_commented

[13] Drake Bennett, "The Mystery of Zomia," *Boston.com* (December 9, 2009), http://www. boston.com/bostonglobe/ideas/articles/2009/12/06/the_mystery_of_zomia/

Tibet a greater threat to the Chinese regime than a semi-democratic Hong Kong ever was. Beijing pays Tibetan culture the backhanded compliment of making its repression a top governmental priority.

No doubt Tibetan democratization concerns not only the Chinese but also those Tibetans who play along with the colonial system, either as puppet administrators or in other service capacities. These professional turncoats, who bear comparison to Tibetan collaborators prior to the 1959 revolution,[14] would lose their special privileges in a democratic and autonomous Tibet. The tragic outcome of the 1959 rising had a solidifying effect on Tibetan politics. While the Chinese won militarily, they lost any possible legitimacy in the eyes of ordinary Tibetans. Previously there had been sharp division among Tibetans on the issue of the Chinese occupation. There was the potential here for a civil war between pro-Chinese and anti-Chinese factions. Afterwards, however, Chinese policies were so barbaric as to create a blanket opposition.

Beijing insists that elite Buddhist institutions have always exploited tractable peasants, who in China's view have been mere slaves to their religious overlords. Hence Tibetans should appreciate their dual "liberation," at once political and religious. Martin A. Mills demolishes this colonial propaganda by certifying the existence of a surprisingly independent and egalitarian local culture. While Buddhist institutions certainly influence the general culture, they are very much affected by it in turn.[15] This reciprocal influence explains the astonishing fortitude of Tibetan values and institutions in the face of the most brutal imperialism imaginable.

A similar blend of secular and religious elements was seen in the Polish Solidarity movement, where veneration for the Polish-born Pope John Paul II (Papa Wojtyla to the Poles) helped to cement resistance against

---

[14] That first major rising and its progeny have been represented by Western sympathizers as classic cases of "horizontal," ethnic-based resistance, in contrast to the vertical and hierarchical structure of most pre-modern rebellions. Martin A. Mills contrasts the standard model of horizontal radicalism, as located in Ronald Schwartz's *Circle of Protest*, with the apparent verticalism of Tsering Shakya's *The Dragon in the Land of Snows*, where pre-modern forms of politicization remain solidly in place. Shakya's interpretation has been unwelcome to Tibetan sympathizers because it seems to reinforce the Chinese insistence that the resistance has been vertically structured and hence less progressive. In fact, as Mills duly notes, Shakya spotlights the way the Chinese themselves cultivated reactionary elements by coopting Tibetan elites in the 1950s and after. See Martin A. Mills, review of *The Dragon in the Land of Snows: A History of Modern Tibet Since 1947*, by Tsering Shakya, *Journal of Buddhist Ethics* 6 (1999): 208 (205–14).

[15] This is the observation of Gray Tuttle in his "Review of Mills's *Identity, Ritual, and State in Tibetan Buddhism: The Foundations of Authority in Gelukpa Monasticism*," *The Journal of Asian Studies* 63 (2004): 1124 (1122–24).

Soviet occupation.[16] Moreover, just as the Vatican's role in Poland became emblematic of its robust outreach to the Third World, and was registered in Moscow as a dire threat,[17] Beijing has good reason to fear the Dalai Lama's global popularity. China's grip on Tibet will never be secure until this global–local cord is cut. The regime's embarrassment is all the more acute because revolution from below was China's mantra—just one of the many Maoist fictions that are better left unexamined. By contrast, grassroots revolution has been Tibet's reality. As Mills aptly puts it, "Chinese Marxists have sought to quash the very thing they claim to champion."[18]

Militarily and demographically the occupation is more secure than ever, but in terms of both global and local norms it is more fiercely contested than it has been for decades. China is in the throes of a double public relations nightmare: the religious one that has haunted the occupation from the first, plus the democratic one that it is fast emerging. In April 2009 both houses of the US Congress passed sweeping bipartisan resolutions condemning China's Tibetan crackdown—the Senate unanimously and the House by a 413-1 margin.[19] No sanctions were imposed, however, and China felt sure that its top-creditor status would immunize it against any serious pressure from Washington.

So far Beijing has been right about that. Aside from the occasional verbal remonstrance or toothless resolution, it is unlikely that much will be done on the human rights front by America or the international community. Nonetheless the tenacity of Tibetan resistance puts China in an awkward situation. It can either crackdown harder than ever, at the cost of its soft-power image, or ease up at the cost of its military prestige. Rather like Mussolini's misadventures in Africa, the need to end this ugly spectacle is so great that Beijing will be tempted to apply even harsher tactics, especially since tough measures have proven immensely popular among China's Han majority.

---

[16] The same blend of religious and political values cemented the Polish underground during the Nazi occupation. So too it buttressed the late Polish President Lech Kaczynski in his two-front contest with Russian imperialists to the East and EU apparatchiks to the West. President Kaczynski has argued for staunch NATO support for Georgia and Ukraine, and for a missile shield on Polish soil. See Judy Dempsey and Diane Cardwell, "Kaczynski Often a Source of Tension within E.U.," *The New York Times* (April 10, 2010), http://www.nytimes.com/2010/04/11/world/europe/11kaczynsiki.html

[17] Norman Davies, *Heart of Europe: The Past in Poland's Present* (Oxford: Oxford University Press, 2001), new edition, 364.

[18] Martin A. Mills, *Identity, Ritual, and State in Tibetan Buddhism: The Foundations of Authority in Gelukpa Monasticism* (London: Routledge-Curzon, 2003), 347.

[19] House resolution 226 of March 11, 2009 also urged the administration to make Tibetan identity and human rights a top priority issue on its agenda. See "H. Res 226," http://www.opencongress.org/bill/111-hr266/show

Public support for intransigence toward Tibet has encouraged Beijing to step up its repression against another vexing minority: the Muslim Uighurs in Xinjiang. Presently the Turkic-speaking Uighurs comprise a little less than half of the 20 million Xinjiang population, and heavy Han migration is tipping the demographic scales against them. Already they have been reduced to a minority status in the regional capital of Urumqi. In terms of economic and political opportunity, they have every reason to feel oppressed, even without considering their futile desire for independence under the name of East Turkestan.

Smoldering tensions between Uighurs and Han Chinese exploded in June 2009 at a Guangdong Province factory. After a group of Uighur men was accused of raping two Han women, outraged Han workers blitzed a Uighur dormitory. A video widely distributed on the internet showed many lifeless bodies in the aftermath. News of this vigilante assault infuriated Uighurs throughout the world. Public protests in Xinjiang brought Han mobs into the streets, pushing Xinjiang to the brink of civil war.

Unlike other Chinese provinces, where leaders are rotated periodically, Xinjiang has been run almost as a political fiefdom. Uighurs are not the only ones dissatisfied with this arrangement. Han protesters have been demanding the removal of the infamous party boss, Wan Lequan, who has held top positions since 1991 and dominated the regional party for 15 years. Wan's police–state mentality has stunted economic growth and damaged Han as well as minority interests. The whole region suffers from the kind of "resource curse" that plagues many underdeveloped countries. While state-owned oil companies like PetroChina rake in huge profits, Xinjiang residents get little or nothing from it, and for added insult must pay some of the highest gas and petroleum prices in China. Since the area's pipeline subsidies are registered in Shanghai, that is where the taxes go, leaving Xinjiang with little more than the social and environmental costs of "development."[20]

China's inroads in Tibet and Xinjiang offer a window on what lies in store for any people who fall under Chinese power and exhibit even a modicum of resistance. This should very much concern China's neighbors, for Beijing is now laying claim to a regional sphere of influence on at least the scale of America's Monroe Doctrine in its prime.[21] This will put China on a collision course with other regional powers such as Russia and Japan, but none so much as India.

---

[20] Kathrin Hille, "Xinjiang Ethnic Groups United in Hostility Towards Leaders," *Financial Times* (September 5 and 6, 2009), 4.

[21] Robert Kaplan, "The Geography of Chinese Power: How Far Can Beijing Reach on Land and Sea?" *Foreign Affairs* 89, no. 3 (May/June 2010): 38 (22–41).

INDIA AS SUPERPOWER

Using Tibet as one of its main staging grounds, China is going on the offensive in South Asia. Its unambiguous objective is the encirclement of India. As Robert Kaplan sees it, the Indian Ocean is already a prime locus of twenty-first century tensions. This puts Americans at a considerable cognitive disadvantage, for they have difficulty comprehending this part of the world even topographically, much less culturally or geostrategically. Indeed, they have little grasp of "the entire arc of Islam, from the Sahara Desert to the Indian archipelago."[22] The whole region is seen as little more than a way-station for energy transfer from the Middle East to the Asian Pacific Rim.

Even in that respect the Chinese have been thinking far ahead of the West with their "string of pearls" strategy for controlling the northern seaboard of the Indian Ocean. These "pearls" include bases in Pakistan, a fueling station in Sri Lanka, a container operation in Bangladesh, numerous surveillance facilities on islands in the Bay of Bengal, roads, pipelines and waterways in Burma (where the junta rakes in millions in Chinese military aid), and a prospective canal through Thailand to link the Indian Ocean with the Pacific.[23]

Indian strategists know full well that the Chinese are trying to surround them, while Beijing in turn has no doubt that Washington wants to enlist India in a pan-Asian encirclement of China. Both suspicions are accurate. Even President Clinton, with China more in mind than North Korea, tightened US–Japan strategic relations, and showed great tolerance toward India after its 1998 nuclear tests. As the Indian prime minister Vajpayee explained to Clinton, these tests were motivated more by the rising China threat than by the perennial Pakistan menace.[24] So too China was the driving force behind the astonishing upgrade of US–Indian relations.

Tellingly, Washington has backed nuclear privileges for India that are strictly against current nonproliferation rules. US–Indian nuclear negotiations between 2005 and 2008 suggest an urgency on Washington's part that can only be explained by the China factor. India, however, is having to nearly invert its geopolitical priorities to forge a solid Indo-American bond. Even when Delhi's foreign policy was officially non-aligned, it was in fact tilted heavily toward the Soviet Union. Once again India seems to be warming toward Moscow, and is making large purchases of Russian arms.

---

[22] Robert Kaplan, "Center Stage for the Twenty-First Century: Power Plays in the Indian Ocean," *Foreign Affairs* 88, no. 2 (March/April 2009): 17 (16–32).

[23] *Ibid.*, 22.

[24] David Scott, "The Great Power 'Great Game' between India and China: 'The Logic of Geography'," *Geopolitics* 13 (2008): 4 (1–26).

Meanwhile its rapprochement with America is meeting a wall of domestic resistance, especially on the part of the Indian Left.

Few of these recalcitrants seem to comprehend the geopolitical stakes involved. Most persist in the Cold War habit of seeing America as the devil incarnate and China as their ideological shield mate, even as this putative comrade installs missile systems in Tibet, all aimed at Indian cities. India poses no comparable threat to Beijing or Shanghai.[25] Fortunately Prime Minster Singh takes a very pragmatic view of the matter. He knows that the nuclear deal gives India greater security against China as well as Pakistan, and also affords India a place at the global bargaining table.

Any realist would have to welcome that opportunity, but even an idealist should not categorically reject a deal that gives India the chance to make a real difference on the world stage. Delhi can now help to shape world affairs rather than retreat from them in the manner of the old Non-Aligned Movement. It remains to be seen, of course, whether this will make a morally significant difference. Arundhati Roy believes the 20-year war in Kashmir, which has left 70,000 dead, removes all doubt as to India's democratic hypocrisy.[26] Definitely India has lost its moral compass. Under its Armed Forces (Special Powers) Act (AFSPA), the military has been given almost unlimited powers in problem areas like Manipur, where the celebrated activist Irom Chanu Sharmila has been fasting for years in protest against military abuse.[27] Even the UN Commissioner for Human Rights has called for AFSPA's repeal. If India does not heed these entreaties it could end up as just another case of reactionary modernization, which sadly is the norm throughout Asia.

It is all the more imperative for India, as a budding nuclear power, to keep its moral balance. Europe looks askance at India's nuclear buildup, and faults the U.S. for promoting this nuclear exception. There is no question that the US–sponsored Nuclear Suppliers Group (NSG) exemption ruling of September 2008 weakened the anti-proliferation consensus of the group. Washington exerted so much pressure to get India's Nonproliferation Treaty (NPT) waiver that upon its ratification there was complete silence among the attending members: no clapping or congratulations, and plenty of palpable resentment.[28] Everyone knew that allowing India to buy

---

[25] *Ibid.*, 5.

[26] Arundhati Roy, "What Have We Done to Democracy?" *Tom Dispatch* (September 27, 2009), http://www.tomdispatch.com/post/175119/arundhati_roy_is_democracy_metling

[27] "Irom Sharmila Awarded Tagore Peace Prize," *The Hindu* (September 12, 2010), http://www.thehindu.com/news/national/article627268.ece

[28] "India Nuclear Trade Waiver Approved," *The New York Times* (September 6, 2008), http://www.nytimes.com/reuters/world/international-nuclear-india-suppliers.html

foreign nuclear fuel for civilian purposes freed its domestic fuel for bomb-building. Delhi has not only refrained from signing the NPT, but has even declined to sign the Comprehensive Test Ban Treaty (CTBT).[29] Moreover, unlike America, Russia, Britain, France, and China, India refuses to put a cap on plutonium and uranium production for military uses.[30] India was not required to freeze its arsenal or to stop producing bomb material. After waiting three years for better terms, Bush's lame duck administration simply muted these issues.[31]

Sordid as that blank-check diplomacy may seem, the fact remains that the nuclear deal was essential to any viable balance of power in South Asia. Unfortunately many Indian critics fail to register that hard reality. For them the bull in this literal China shop is the issue of US affiliation. The Indian Left remains oblivious to the fact that today's China, far from being a socialist ally, is a preeminent capitalist power, and is also the world's most ardent and effective proponent of authoritarian development.[32] Nor should it be forgotten that China is the most steadfast ally of a very unreformed Pakistan, one of the world's most unabashed nuclear proliferators.

What turned the nuclear deal into a domestic political crisis was the personal war of wills between Singh and his United Progressive Alliance (UPA) arch-rival Prakash Karat. It is astonishing that these two were ever able to sit together in the ruling coalition.[33] For Karat, an unabashed admirer of Stalin, the prime measure of socialist commitment is the strength of one's anti-American animus. In November 2006, when the antagonism within the

---

[29] The Bharatiya Janata Party (BJP) charged that Singh secretly agreed to a de facto ban, and there is evidence to support this claim. For its part, Washington could not terminate the deal if India conducted a live bomb test. On Singh's deal, see Smita Gupta, "Man in the Core," *Outlook India* (September 22, 2008), http://www.outlookindia.com/fullprint. asp?choice=1&fodname=20080922&fname=Cover and on Washington's qualifier, see Rama Lakshmi, "U.S. Letter Puts India's Premier on Defensive over Nuclear Deal," *Washington Post* (September 5, 2008), A15.

[30] "Time to Decide," *The Economist* (August 28, 2008), http://www.economist.com/opinion/PrinterFriendly.cfm?story_id=12009694

To be fair, this is more suggestive of India's reluctance to lie about its nuclear production than of China's compliance with its promises.

[31] "No Rush, Please," *The New York Times* (July 5, 2008), editorial, http://www.nytimes.com/2008/07/05/opinion/05sat3.html

[32] Minxin Pei, *China's Trapped Transition: The Limits of Developmental Autocracy* (Cambridge, MA: Harvard University Press, 2006) and Songok Han Thornton and William H. Thornton, *Development Without Freedom: The Politics of Asian Globalization* (Aldershot, UK: Ashgate, 2008), Chapters 6 and 7.

[33] See Monobina Gupta, "Manmohan and Karat—Two Antipodal Faces of a Debate," *Thaindian News* (June 24, 2008), http://www.thaindian.com/newsportal/politics/manmohan-and-karat-two-antipodal-faces-of-a-ebate-2_10063910.html

coalition reached a white heat, one commentator wryly noted that India's progressives were now cursed by getting what they had always hoped for: politicians who put principles above elections.[34] Principles, however, were hardly the main pieces on this chessboard. After being opposed to India having the bomb in the first place, Karat then insisted on the nation's right to conduct unlimited nuclear tests.[35] His foremost concern, along with winning a personal battle with Singh, was to keep India out of the prospective democratic world order that he associates with US hegemony.

It is not just the Left that has a problem with India's emerging superpower status. The issue is complicated by the Nehruvian tradition of denigrating military power in general. Even Nehru, after his disastrous war with China in 1962, had to admit that pacifism could be a double-edged moral sword. Instead of deterring war, India's credulity and military weakness had invited it. The moral factor in an effective geopolitics—or, from a Nehruvian vantage, the realist component of any moral foreign policy—must be put front and center. Realists sometimes charge that pacifism is a symptom of the "mini-state syndrome" whereby weak nations turn their inadequacy into a virtue. From our moral realist perspective, however, idealists as well as realists should take a lesson from Nehru's pacifist ball and chain. When the very word "power" is stigmatized,[36] the moral potential of power politics is voided.

DELHI'S GEOPOLITICAL OPTIONS

What Indian strategists must bear in mind is that China's military might and geopolitical ambitions are far greater than they were in 1962. In 2008 alone the PRC officially budgeted $60 billion for its military. Pentagon sources estimate that the real figure is double that, which means it is seven times the Indian defense budget.[37] China's naval exercises with Pakistan in the Indian Ocean in 2005 marked its first such venture outside PRC territorial waters.

---

[34] Vir Sanghvi, "The Kamikaze Approach," *Hindustan Times* (November 4, 2006), http://www.hindustantimes.com/StoryPage/Print.aspx?Id=04a14del-de30-462a-807f-4cdc7ec8249d

[35] Rajinder Puri, "Karate Chop," *Outlook India* (July 4, 2008), http://www.outlookindia.com/fullprint.asp?choice=1&fodname=20080701&fname=puri&sid=1

[36] See Harsh V. Pant, "India's Power Challenge," *Outlook India* (June 25, 2008), http://www.outlookindia.com/article.aspx?237751

[37] Anand Giridharadas, "Land of Gandhi Asserts Itself as Global Military Power," *The New York Times* (September 22, 2008), http://www.nytimes.com/2008/09/22/world/asia/22india.html

Meanwhile China has made improvements to the Karakorum Highway, its land route to Pakistan. To the east, it has entered discussions with Thailand concerning a canal to directly link the South China Sea to the Bay of Bengal, thus bypassing the vulnerable Malacca Straits. Likewise it is extremely active in Burma and has begun forging military ties with Bangladesh, while to the south it is setting up both commercial and military ties with Sri Lanka.[38] Nothing is more disturbing, however, than its military build-up in Tibet, which puts Indian cities like Delhi and Calcutta within missile range. The crowning touch was the opening of the Lhasa-to-Golmund railway in the summer of 2006. Many analysts regard this as the most important strategic development in the area since the 1950s.[39]

On geopolitical grounds alone, the China development model looks enticing to many Third World nations. New Delhi itself is now tempted to ditch its own model in favor of China's game of containment through "congagement."[40] On the surface there has been talk of a "strategic partnership," including joint military exercises. We are left to wonder who the target of such joint action could be, since India's most implacable enemy, Pakistan, is China's all-weather ally. Only commercially does the "partnership" idea make any sense. With annual trade between the two reaching $40 billion, China has replaced America as India's major trade partner.[41]

That is where the fairy tale ends. Singh and his ministers are surely watching as dark clouds build on the Sino-Indian horizon, even in commercial affairs. India's formerly healthy trade balance now shows a $10 billion deficit, thanks largely to the China factor. But it is in the geopolitical sphere that the "partnership" notion comes completely unraveled. The Chinese military made dozens or even hundreds of border incursions in 2008 alone,[42] pointedly reminding Delhi that Beijing has never renounced its claim to tens of thousands of square miles of Indian territory, plus 23,612 square miles of occupied territory in Jammu and Kashmir, courtesy of Pakistan's illegal boundary agreement with China in 1963.[43] Lest there be any doubt

---

[38] David Scott, *op. cit.*, 6–7.

[39] *Ibid.*, 5.

[40] *Ibid.*, 4.

[41] Jeff M. Smith, "India as a US Hedge against China," *Asia Times*, August 7, 2008, http://www.atimes.com/atimes/South_Asia/JH07Df01.html

[42] Repeated incursions into the Leh area jumped from 140 in 2007 to 280 in 2008. See Ben Arnoldy, "Growing Number of China Incursions into India Lead to a Strategy Change," *The Christian Science Monitor* (September 29, 2009), http://www.csmonitor.com/2009/0929/p06s06-wosc.html

[43] Dipanjan Roy Chaudhury, "India and China: Competitors or Partners?" *World Press* (July 31, 2007), http://www.worldpress.org/Asia/2882.cfm

as to Beijing's intentions, its ambassador to India flatly declared in 2006 that the whole state of Arunachal Pradesh is Chinese territory.[44]

It is little wonder, then, that Delhi has been looking favorably on closer military relations with Washington.[45] US arms sales to India have swelled in recent years. This caught world attention in August 2008 when the Pentagon approved the first US missile sale to India—two dozen Harpoon II anti-ship missiles, with a price tag of $170 million.[46] These purchases confirm that India has not forgotten the lessons of 1962. It is well aware that more is involved here than a simple border dispute.[47] In South Asia, as in most of the developing world, China is the geopolitical "game changer."

Clearly India is at a crossroads in its domestic and foreign policy. While edging toward stronger relations with democratic powers like America, it seems to be moving in the opposite direction regionally. A glaring case in point is its policy shift toward Burma, whose deposed president Aung San Suu Kyi once got strong moral support from democratic India. An entirely new set of Indo-Burmese relations was engineered by the BJP and shamelessly reaffirmed by the UPA after 2004.[48] Just six months after the brutal 2007 crackdown on protesting monks, Prime Minister Singh extended a warm welcome to the junta's second in command, General Maung Aye.[49] Likewise the Dalai Lama has lost much of the moral support he once enjoyed from Delhi. Many Indian realists defend these reversals as a necessary adjustment to hard regional realities. The bottom line is that the old Indian foreign policy—grounded on the admittedly quixotic dream of nonalignment—is defunct. China is everything these realists want India to be.

This attitude is reflected in India's rapt embrace of a BRIC diplomacy that tacitly endorses Chinese and Russian ways and means. But in some respects it simply reconfirms the noxious developmental slant of India's postcolonial years. This reactionary element is camouflaged by the equally

---

[44] Smith, *op. cit.*

[45] The BJP, however, is much more hawkish in this regard, and strongly criticizes the present government for appeasing China. See Somini Sengupta, "India Tiptoes in China's Footsteps to Compete but Not Offend," *The New York Times* (April 4, 2008), http://www.nytimes.com/2008/04/04/world/asia/ 04india.html

[46] "U.S. to Sell Harpoon Missiles to India," *The Hindu* (September 11, 2008), http://www.thehindu.com/2008/09/11/stories/2008091155481200.htm

[47] This interpretation is supported by recently released CIA documents on the Sino-Indian war. See "India's Interests at Stake in Relationship with China," *PINR* (July 30, 2007), http://www.pinr.com/report.php??ac=view_report&report_id=669&language_id=1

[48] William H. Thornton, "Burma's Geopolitical Revival: A Post-Realist View of the Saffron Rising," *World Affairs: The Journal of International Issues* 12, no. 1 (Spring 2008): 137 (122–51).

[49] Somini Sengupta, *op. cit.*

odious record of so many neoliberal development schemes. At the second BRIC Summit, held in Brasilia in April 2010, Brazil's President Lula Da Silva claimed the high moral ground of egalitarianism and transparency in the wake of the horrendous failures of "Washington Consensus" development programs.[50] That was just days before the government won its case against 14 indigenous tribes who were attempting to block Lula's pet infrastructure project, the Belo Monte hydroelectric plant, which will be the world's third largest dam, just behind China's infamous Three Gorges Dam. In terms of ecological and ethnological destruction, the Belo Monte project will be second to none. This, moreover, is just the beginning. Lula's $500 billion infrastructure plan will promote another dozen dams in the Amazon basin.[51]

The futile protests of local Amazon tribes are reminiscent of the hopeless protests of India's dispossessed victims of countless Nehruvian dam projects. The "bigger is better" syndrome that suffuses the new BRIC orthodoxy seeks cover behind a new Third Worldism, but what this development model actually promotes is another century of raw, "bigger is better" GDPism, the very opposite of the model that eco-minded dissidents like Vandana Shiva and Arundhati Roy have broached. The bitter irony is that the Belo Monte contracts were authorized just before Earth Day.

Our position is that People Power, not BRICish GDPism, is the best card Delhi has in its geopolitical hand. Already India has achieved a major geopolitical upgrade in the wake of China's rise, simply by virtue of its residual democratic credentials.[52] In 2005 Delhi and Washington jointly launched the UN Democracy Fund, and both are leaders in the 120-nation Community of Democracies.[53] This pro-democratic vision has its perfect antithesis in Beijing's flagrant regional intrusions. After the electoral victory of Nepal's Maoists in spring 2008, China clearly hoped to use Nepal as another entry point into South Asia, much as it uses Burma as a bridge into Southeast Asia.

---

[50] Luiz Inácio Lula Da Silva, "BRIC Countries Must Forge a Transparent System of Global Governance," *The Christian Science Monitor* (April 16, 2010), http://www.csmonitor.com/Commentary/Global-Viewpoint/2010/0416/Brazilian-President-Lula-BRIC-countries-must-forge-a-transparent-system-of-global-governance

[51] Andrew Downie, "In Earth Day Setback, Brazil OKs Dam that will Flood Swath of Amazon," *The Christian Science Monitor* (April 22, 2010), http://www.csmonitor.com/World/Americas/2010/0422/ In-Earth-Day-setback-Brazil-OKs-dam-that-will-flood-swath-of-Amazon

[52] On that democratic upgrade, see Amrita Narlikar, "All that Glitters is not Gold: India's Rise to Power," *Third World Quarterly* 28, no. 5 (2007): 987 (983–96).

[53] R. Nicolas Burns, "America's Strategic Opportunity with India," *Foreign Affairs* 86, no. 6 (November/December 2007): 140 (131–46).

The competition over Nepal will be fierce. So far the new government of President Ram Baran Yadav and Prime Minister Puspa Kamal Dahal, known as Prachanda, has not taken a strictly hostile stance toward India, though a sweeping review of previous treaty arrangements is in progress. Since 1998 Beijing has conducted active and growing military exchanges with Nepal,[54] and already it is talking of extending its Tibetan road network and its rail line to Kathmandu. A Maoist-led Nepal could snugly fit the needs of China's "Look South" policy, serving Beijing as a proxy in the South Asian Association for Regional Co-operation (SAARC) conferences.

However, there is also the possibility that Beijing could be reading too much into the pro-China tilt of these Maoist leaders. The larger meaning of Nepal's political sea change may derive from its democratic rather than Naxalite element. In that case India's influence could still prevail. To capitalize on this opportunity, Delhi needs to exhibit a far more just and egalitarian attitude toward its own Naxalite movement. Doing so might convince Nepal's Naxilites that they have much less to fear from democratic–capitalist India than from authoritarian–capitalist China.

Another geopolitical friction point is Africa, where India's influence has plummeted relative to China. Beijing holds the advantage in terms of deep-pocket diplomacy, though India has the advantage of a more established diaspora, and until recently its FDI to Africa actually exceeded China's.[55] It is China's noxious politics rather than its commercial prowess that explains its success in dealing with African regimes. It is surging ahead for all the wrong reasons. As part of its "Greater Peripheral" strategy, it recently pumped $5 billion in aid to 48 African nations.[56] It did this, of course, with artful disregard of the internal affairs of these countries. This wins China warm relations with a rogue's gallery of autocratic leaders in resource-rich nations.

The real news, though, is that grassroots animosities are building fast against such Sino-cronyism. Political reformers in Africa could be won over by a reformist India that plays its democratic hand astutely. Unfortunately Delhi is moving in the opposite direction. Rather than renewing its own anti-colonial legacy, it is trying to mimic China's utterly amoral approach. Thus India is at a vital crossroads in its foreign as well as domestic affairs, and its choices will rock the world. It could make a huge humanitarian

---

[54] B. Raman, "Maoists in Nepal: Implications for India," *Outlook India* (August 12, 2008), http.//www.outlookindia.com/full.asp?fodname=20080812$fname=raman&sid=1

[55] Harry G. Broadman, "China and India Go to Africa: New Deals in the Developing World," *Foreign Affairs* 87, no. 2 (March/April 2008): *passim* (95–109).

[56] Chaudhury, *op. cit.*

contribution by exporting its knowledge base in health, education, and democratic processes. Or it could reinforce the current drift toward Sino-globalization.

A modest step in the right direction was taken by foreign minister Pranab Mukherjee, who set up an e-network for sharing Indian expertise with a host of African countries.[57] We should also mention India's crucial role in providing affordable drugs for poor countries. Doctors Without Borders gets 84 percent of its HIV and AIDS drugs from India.[58] In this case profits happen to coincide with virtue. Like the tortoise and the hare, India could win its race with China if its leaders refuse to enter a commercial or strategic race to the bottom. In its rush to move from the geopolitics of a porcupine to that of a nuclear-armed tiger (to borrow C. Raja Mohan's metaphor),[59] India should not forget that its greatest strength lies in its soft power.

CHINA GETS TOUGH

The best traditions of India cannot be reconciled with globalization as we know it. To bring those values to the fore will require a moral realist post-globalization where virtue and national interest coincide. On this plane India's democratic status can pay rich geopolitical dividends. Japan was slow to forgive India's nuclear weapons test of 1998, and as of 2006 its $6.5 billion trade with India was only about 4 percent of its China trade. Nonetheless, Tokyo has begun to take an interest in democratic India as a balancing agent against an increasingly worrisome China.

American neoliberals, too, are reaching out to India as never before. Lately they are starting to realize that China is not going to become a responsible "stake-holder" in the existing world order. Rather, its newfound economic confidence is energizing its nationalism and militarism. Anti-Japanese sentiment has surged, even as anti-Chinese feelings are cresting

---

[57] Sudha Ramachandran, "India Pushes People Power in Africa," *Asia Times* (2007), http://www.atimes.com/atimes/printN.html

[58] The Swiss company Novartis recently sued in an Indian court to block distribution of a generic substitute for its leukemia drug, Gleevec. Fortunately Novartis lost, to the great relief of AID organizations, which dubbed this a landmark victory for "patients over patents." See Amelia Gentleman, "Setback for Novartis in India Over Drug Patent," *The New York Times* (August 7, 2007), http://www.nytimes.com/2007/08/07/business/worldbusiness/07drug.thml

[59] C. Raja Mohan, *Crossing the Rubicon: The Shaping of India's Foreign Policy* (New Delhi: Viking, 2003), 260–63.

in Japan.[60] Consequently Japan is starting to see India as one of its most promising allies. Many ASEAN nations are likewise looking toward India as a hedge against China. India's budding sea power is welcome, and shared naval exercises are becoming common—for example with Singapore (for more than a decade), Indonesia (since 2004), and Thailand (since 2006). In 2007 India joined the US, Japan, Australia and Singapore in a large joint exercise in the Bay of Bengal.[61]

China meanwhile has cut a fresh nuclear deal with Pakistan, and has closed the circle around India by tightening its ties with Dhaka and Kathmandu. Needless to say this was not its official policy. Many have taken at face value Premier Wen Jiabao's announcement of a pending "strategic partnership" with India, issued during his New Delhi visit of April 2005. Even the putative realist C. Raja Mohan commented in 2006 that former tensions between these rising titans "have become receding memories."[62] To feed this illusion, China has held out the possibility of India's membership in the SCO, but only in return for China's invitation to join the SAARC.[63] That is hardly a good trade, since China's potential for influencing SAARC is far greater than India's chance of denting SCO policies.

These surface amenities bear ominous resemblance to the rhetoric that preceded the 1962 war. The difference is that India and China are now world-class geoeconomic powers. If things go wrong, the global repercussions will be enormous. The salient fact is that China is nearly always the aggressor, with India kept on the defensive. Nehru's slowness in grasping China's imperial intentions contributed greatly to the 1962 disaster, and today many progressive-minded Indians are making the same blunder. Thinking that international commerce is a global panacea, they fail to recognize that the capitalist affluence of today's China makes it all the more dangerous. Both poles of current Indian politics are highly deluded. While the Left downgrades the China threat on the fossilized assumption that the

---

[60] Heather Timmons, "As Japan and India Forge Economic Ties, a Counterweight to China is Seen," *The New York Times* (August 21, 2007), http://www.nytimes.com/2007/08/21/business/worldbusiness/2rupee.html

[61] Sudha Ramachandran, "India's Quiet Sea Power," *Asia Times*, http://www.atimes.com/atimes/printN.html

[62] C. Raja Mohan, "India and the Balance of Power," *Foreign Affairs* 85, no. 4 (July/August 2006): 21–22 and 24 (17–32). By 2010, Mohan's earlier perspective—which could probably best be described as "neo-Curzonian," after the former Viceroy to the Raj, Lord George Curzon, whose approach would favor "multi-alignment" with major powers had clearly given way to an unambiguous alliance with Washington against future Chinese domination. See C. Raja Mohan, "The Return of the Raj," *The American Interest* (May–June 2010), http://www.the-american-interest.com/article.cfm?piece=803

[63] Chaudhury, *op. cit.*

CCP is still somehow socialistic and progressive, the Right downgrades it on the equally ludicrous assumption that one capitalist nation cannot seriously imperil another capitalist nation.

So too, Southeast Asian nations have been in denial of the multiplier effect that Chinese economic growth is having on Asian insecurity. Even now, as Beijing drops its soft-power pose at flash points such as the Spratly islands, Beijing is welcomed into the commercial inner circle at ASEAN and other regional forums. Nonetheless there is mounting concern over China's escalating power. Even in the midst of a prolonged recession, ASEAN member-states have been pumping billions into new weaponry, including submarines, since land or air strikes against China would be all but impossible.

Thanks to China's understated image as the prime source of Asian insecurity, Russia is reaping windfall profits as the military vendor of choice for many ASEAN nations. This concern even extends to Burma, which has had extremely cordial relations with the PRC. It is paying $600 million for 20 Russian MiG-29s, while Malaysia shops for submarines and Vietnam is ready to pay $2 billion for subs and fighters.[64] Meanwhile ASEAN countries are glad to have joint military exercises with India. It hardly needs to be said that the target of these war games is not the US Navy.

Given that China is increasingly on the military radar screen of these countries, America has a strategic opportunity that so far it has scarcely tapped. Rather than harp on "anti-terrorism," which is of small concern to most ASEAN nations, a more stalwart position regarding China and Taiwan would be advisable. As Robert Kaplan observes, America cannot afford complacency on this issue:

> If the United States simply abandons Taiwan to Beijing, then Japan, South Korea, the Philippines, Australia and other U.S. allies in the Pacific will begin to doubt the strength of Washington's commitments. That could encourage these states to move closer to China and thus allow the emergence of a Greater China of truly hemispheric proportions.[65]

In fact, this is already happening.

America's geopolitical retreat from the region leaves a void which China is fast filling. This helps to explain Beijing's shift from the vaunted "soft power" that seemed to serve it well until recently. A book on China's "charm

---

[64] William Boot, "What's Behind ASEAN's Arms Race?" *The Irrawaddy* 18, no. 2 (February 2010), http://www.irrawaddy.org/print_article.php?art_id=17689

[65] Robert D. Kaplan, "The Geography of Chinese Power," *The New York Times* (April 20, 2010), http://www.nytimes.com/2010/04/20/opinion/20iht-edkaplan.html

offensive" declared in 2004 that the "charmed" nations of the Pacific Rim "have not recognized the downsides of Beijing's power."[66] In fact, they are petrified. Even the opening ceremonies of the Olympics said more about national potency than international harmony. But China's new militancy was most graphically witnessed on October 1, 2009 in celebrations of the PRC's 60th anniversary. This veritable war dance featured two hundred thousand soldiers and school children marching in what looked like a remake of Leni Riefenstahl's *Triumph of the Will*.

Needless to say, this is not what globalization was supposed to produce, but it is precisely what Deng Xiaoping's economic program had in mind from the start: the unqualified triumph of the Party and the nation. Contrary to the standard neoliberal view of Dengism, which stresses economic pragmatism, double-digit GDP growth is not the end of Sino-globalization. It is the means. Even Mearsheimer has tended to understate Beijing's objectives when he spotlights its regional ambitions. China makes sure that its most "global" military advances get maximum public attention. Two of its recent revelations—operational anti-ship ballistic missiles and a radar-evading stealth fighter[67]—could be geostrategic "game changers." Clearly the PRC is staking its claim to the bipolar role that the Soviet Union vacated at the end of the Cold War.

CONTESTED ASIANISMS

Granted, India is also converting economic growth into an engine of geopolitical advantage.[68] There is, however, a signal difference between Sino-globalization and Indo-globalization. While India is burdened with democratic institutions, China is entirely free of that ball and chain. Many are starting to see CCPism as an effective and durable instrument for rapid modernization. And the concomitant suspicion is growing that India's liberal incubus dooms the country to slow growth and permanent geopolitical inertia. To close this wealth and power gap, many Indian entrepreneurs and strategists want to adopt the China model as much as possible.

There are instrumental as well as intrinsic reasons to question the wisdom of that idea. The jury is still out on the sustainability of the China model.

---

[66] Joshua Kurlantzick, *Charm Offensive: How China's Soft Power is Transforming the World* (New Haven and London: Yale University Press, 2007), xi.

[67] Michael Wines, "China Rolls Out Its First Stealth Aircraft," *The Times of India* (January 6, 2011), http://timesofindia.indiatimes.com/world/china/China-rolls-out-its-first-stealth-fighter-aircraft/articleshow/7226713.cms

[68] David Scott, *op. cit.*, 15.

As we have seen, Gordon Chang agrees with Minxin Pei that this seem-ing "miracle" is a mirage. In Chang's view the CCP is so guarded against political liberalization that it weeds out real leaders, leaving insipid bureau-crats like Hu and Wen at the helm.[69] These functionaries not only resist political progress, but ignore China's most pressing problems until they morph into insuperable crises. In the short run this myopia may actually fuel the economy. Many still regard the absence of worker's rights and environmental regulation as an economic advantage. But there is a point where social repression and environmental holocaust will spell economic ruin, and in China that will trigger a political cataclysm. Even a moderate economic setback could bring down the whole system, whereas in India an economic recession would at most spell the replacement of one party by another. Chang believes that China has already reached the tipping point of its largely ersatz development.[70]

The very opposite view is taken by Martin Jacques, for whom the big news of recent years has been the full revival of the Chinese "civilization-state."[71] It is beyond dispute that this most obdurate form of Asian values is now in the driver's seat of globalization. The question is how far its politi-cal agenda will reach. Is liberal democracy as we have known it simply in recess or in permanent retreat? And will liberal resistance issue only from the West? Could there be a liberal Asianism waiting in the wings, modeled perhaps on Indian democracy at its best?

While our sympathies lean toward Chang and Pei, we must agree with Jacques that a paradigm shift has taken place in our global outlook. First, the assumption that globalization is tantamount to Westernization has been exploded. So too we agree that the coming era is going to be one of

---

[69] In August 2010, on the occasion of Shenzhen's 13th anniversary as a special economic zone, Prime Minister Wen gave a speech that once again raised hopes in the naïve West that top-down reform was imminent. Wen's lame duck advocacy of a moderate political opening—including some degree of judicial and press independence, as well as limited election reform—has been quickly and easily scuttled, as he surely knew it would be. He himself has taken no action on behalf of real democratic dissidents like the imprisoned Nobel Laureate Liu Xiaobo. On the rapid silencing of Wen's reform gambit, see Michael Wines and Sharon LaFraniere, "Chinese Article Seems to Chide Leader," *The New York Times* (October 27, 2010, http://www.nytimes.com/2010/10/28/world/asia/28china.html and "The Dog that Didn't Bark," *The Economist* (November 11, 2010), http://www.economist.com/node/17461050/print

[70] Gordon G. Chang, "The Party's Over: China's Endgame," *World Affairs* (March/April 2010), http://www.worldaffairsjournal.org/articles/2010-MarApr/full-Chang-MA-2010.html

[71] Martin Jacques, *When China Rules the World: The Rise of the Middle Kingdom and the End of the Western World* (London and New York: Penguin Books, 2009), 13.

contested modernities.[72] The catch is that among these competitors, Jacques expects Sino-modernity to take an increasingly dominant role—hence his hyperbolic title, *When China Rules the World*. Here we radically depart from him, for in our view China's cultural bluster is an impediment to any kind of global order except that of raw imperialism. And at this multilateral moment, when soft power "rules the world," China's style could be its own worst enemy.

Beijing's dubious strategy, which is little more than a cultural atavism, may succeed against the Tibetans, but applying it on a pan-Asian scale is quite another matter. China is prone to the same kind of hubris that marred Japan's relations with other Asian countries through the war years and even into the "miracle" era. Eventually this "civilizational" conceit is going to meet major resistance. All the ingredients are here for a geopolitical standoff that will make the old Cold War look attractive in terms of its manageability. Even when couched in the seemingly innocuous terms of BRICism, China's stress on Procrustean "harmony" rather than liberal pluralism is going to put the First and Second Worlds on a collision course.

Our global prognosis, however, is not entirely pessimistic. Unlike Jacques, we do not take it for granted that the economic rise of the East means that China will dominate Asia, let alone "rule the world." Other Asians will not take lightly the idea of stepping out of the era of Western colonization only to rush headlong into the waiting arms of Chinese imperialism. Rim nations have already been put on edge by China's tribute-state conception of regional "harmony." The rudiments of an anti-China coalition are in place, linking such otherwise disparate powers as India and Japan.[73] In coming years this Asian rebound effect could get support from democratic nations throughout the world. Some kind of league of democracies is going to be necessary, given the authoritarian world order that is taking shape.

This new Second World has its prototype in the current SCO, but is rapidly expanding to include African and Latin American autocracies. For the moment China has the upper hand in what amounts to a new Cold War, but we are not totally fatalistic about the long-term democratic prospect.

---

[72] *Ibid.*, 144.

[73] Robert Kaplan skirts this issue in his recent book, *Monsoon*, which focuses on the geopolitics of the Indian Ocean. This is odd in view of Kaplan's early stance in favor of extreme vigilance and even a "Second Cold War" in response to China's rising bellicosity. See for example, his 2005 *Atlantic* essay, "How We Would Fight China." Now he proposes taking China as a geo-maritime partner. This weather vane reversal is all the more curious in view of the fact that China, more than ever, has taken off its "soft power" gloves in the last few years. Perhaps, like the late Christopher Hitchens, Kaplan just likes playing the contrarian role.

After all, the Soviets seemed for a long time to have the upper hand in the first Cold War. George Kennan's "X Article" laid out an effective long-term strategy for geopolitical containment in 1947, and we are broaching a similar geocultural strategy for confronting Sino-globalization and the resurgent Second World. Much will depend on Asia's reaction to China's rise. As will be shown in Chapter 6, India is the crucial swing state at that regional level. The telling factor will be Delhi's posture toward social democracy at home and abroad.

In the case of Burma, to which we now turn, India has regretfully been leaning heavily toward ASEAN's pro-junta commercialism. This policy reversal forfeits the democratic core of Indo-globalization, and for what? Delhi cannot hope to beat Beijing at its own Sino-globalist game. India's forte is still soft power, which is fortunate since that will probably be the most potent form of power in the coming post-globalist era. If raw coercion could not work for imperial Japan at the peak of its military supremacy, there is little chance it will work for China in a multilateral age, or at least not in the very long run.

Chang and Pei will doubtless be right about that—eventually. The problem is dealing in the interim with a rogue nation that is not only the world's largest exporter and its second largest economy, but is fast becoming the most imitated model of Third World development. For that reason our implacable adversary in coming decades will not just be the PRC, but the new Second World that is being cast in its image. Our task is not to exhort the developing world, much less to threaten it with preemptive strikes if it refuses to cast itself in our First World image. The challenge is to offer it an objectively better model to serve its own needs. Neoliberal globalization has been all about us, and ironically it has not even served us very well, if by "us" we mean the democratic majority. A truly capacious globalization, which is to say a post-globalization, must serve the needs of most people on earth. That is an idea worth trying, and there is no better place to start than in India.

5

TIBET OF THE SOUTH
Burma as Geopolitical Testing Ground

THE GEOPOLITICS OF SINO-DEPENDENCY

In fall 2007 the idea took hold among human rights advocates that China could be enlisted as a pressure mechanism for reforming Burma.[1] Some thought this could be accomplished through friendly persuasion, but less naïve reformists recognized that some form of unfriendly persuasion would be necessary. Their weapon of choice was the 2008 Beijing Olympics. Suddenly the Burma crisis overtook the Darfur crisis as the major focus of the "Genocide Olympics" campaign. The name "Saffron Olympics" was increasingly heard, with reference to the saffron robes worn by hundreds of monks who boldly demonstrated against the Burmese junta and were crushed by the crackdown that started on September 26.

There is a cardinal difference, however, between the likely outcomes of the Burma and Darfur stratagems. Burma is now so vital to its region geopolitically, not just economically, that China cannot budge on this one.[2] It is not surprising that this fact was missed by human rights organizers, for

---

[1] Throughout this book, except in direct quotations, the names Burma and Rangoon will be kept instead of Myanmar and Yangon, which are the inventions of the illegal military regime that has done everything within its power to snuff out the Burmese democracy movement.

[2] See "China: Myanmar as the New Sudan," *IntelliBriefs* (October 1, 2007), http://intellibriefs.blogspot.com/2007/10/china-myanmar-as-new-sudan.html

until recently Burma has not been prime real estate on the map of Western geopolitics. ASEAN had a better map, and tried to bring this wayward nation into their orbit before it fell irretrievably into China's.

Burma's geopolitical debut is in fact a revival. Early in the Cold War, Korea and Burma were regarded as matching bookends for the envelopment of China. Nationalist Chinese troops, funded by the CIA, staged at least seven futile "invasions" of China from Burmese base camps before Rangoon's complaints at the UN induced the US to abort the operation. The last Kuomintang units were driven into Thailand in 1961 with the help of 20,000 People's Liberation Army (PLA) soldiers.[3] One thing that prevented this Sino-Burmese alliance from becoming a full-fledged dependency was Beijing's preoccupation with its Soviet menace to the north and its Indian nemesis to the southwest. China was in no position to press itself on Burma.

So too there was Burma's extreme non-aligned proclivity, which exceeded even India's. This independence streak had nothing to do with Nehruvian ideals. It was rooted in a determination on the part of the new rulers to share no part of the spoils of governance with any foreign power. Such domestic neocolonialism was costly, however. Burma bought its non-alignment at the price of crippling isolation. While India slipped into aid dependency with the Soviets, Burma under Ne Win's Burma Socialist Programme Party (BSPP) preferred assistance from peripheral sources like Israel and Yugoslavia.[4] In 1979 it even broke with the Non-Aligned Movement itself, which it regarded as too closely linked to the Eastern Bloc. Though it maintained close ties with China, a puppet-state relationship was out of the question.

Burma's neutrality took it so far off the Cold War map that it was rarely even mentioned in studies of regional security. That insularity was much admired in the UN General Assembly,[5] and helps to explain why a Burmese, U. Thant, was unanimously elected twice as the UN Secretary-General. The irony is that the end of the Cold War spelled the end of Burma's

---

[3] Andrew Selth, "Burma and Superpower Rivalries in the Asia-Pacific," *Naval War College Review* (Spring 2002), http://findarticles.com/articles/mi_mOJIW/is_2_55/ai_88174228/print

[4] The rumor always simmered that Ne Win had continued to pull the junta's strings after the BSPP was overthrown. Hopes were raised, therefore, that things might improve in Burma after his death at 92 in December 2002. But, as one political observer quipped, the only thing that changed was that his wife became a widow. See "Former Myanmar President Ne Win Dies at 92," *Asian Political News* (December 9, 2002), http://findarticles.com/p/articles/mi-m0WDQ/is_2002_Dec_9/ai_95100432

[5] Selth, *op. cit.*

geopolitical exception. With Moscow's power in recess, Southeast Asia lost a clandestine ally. This coincided, moreover, with democratic reform movements throughout East and Southeast Asia. Burma's generals scrambled to ward off this grim prospect. It came down to a choice between two evils: democracy within or cooptation without.

Domestic reform pressures forced Rangoon to accept China as its de facto guardian. Free at last from its Soviet incubus, the PRC could afford to take more interest in the rest of Asia.[6] Burma became its pick of the litter—an easy grab, with a plethora of natural resources. This former icon of nonalignment is fast becoming another Chinese tribute state,[7] almost a Tibet of the South. In recent years two million Chinese have settled here, which was not too complicated in a country where passports can be bought on the black market and business can be conducted in Chinese yuan.[8]

While Southeast Asia looks on this China connection with alarm, India looks on it with real panic. Consider Burma's geostrategic importance from an Indian perspective. Rimmed by two inveterate enemies, Pakistan and China, India must pay close attention to its eastern flank. As China tightens its grip on Burma, it not only gets insider extraction privileges for a huge stock of natural resources, but stands to gain easy access to the Bay of Bengal and the Indian Ocean. This extends the encirclement of India and puts a future Chinese blue-water navy within striking range of the Malacca Straits, one of the world's most strategic hotspots.[9] Neither the Sino-Indian treaty of 1993, which agreed to reduce troop levels in the border zones, nor the joint ("Hand-in-Hand") military exercises of 2007 could paper over the mutual antipathy between these rising titans. That is good for Burma, since

---

[6] Bruce Elleman, review of *The Geopolitics of East Asia: The Search for Equilibrium*, by Robyn Lim, *Naval War College Review*, Winter 2004, http://finadarticles.com/p/articles/mi_m0JIW/is_1_57/ai_113755357

[7] See Kanbawza Win, "*Hpao Lan Hpar* Got a Heart Attack," *The New Era Journal* (January 6, 2008), http://www.khitpyaing.org/english_page/december07/kanbawzawin_13-12-07.php

[8] Jürgen Kremb, "Anatomy of Burma," *Spiegel Online* (October 24, 2007), http://www.spiegel.de/international/world/0,1518,513302,00.html

[9] Meanwhile, to complete the "containment" of India, China has moved aggressively to fill the void created by failing US policies in the Middle East and Afghanistan. By tightly affiliating itself with the US–Israeli axis of Middle East relations, India forfeited its energy negotiations with Iran, giving China an inside track here as well. Thus China Petroleum was able to close a $2 billion deal with the Iranian Oil Ministry in December 2007, even as China bypassed India to win mammoth copper mining contracts with Afghanistan. See M. K. Bhadrakumar, "China Leaves the US and India Trailing," *Asia Times* (December 15, 2007), http://www.atimes.com/atimes/China/IL15Ad01.html

any semblance of Burmese independence depends upon the durability of Sino-Indian distrust.

If Burma is China's bridge into South Asia, so too it is ASEAN's, and the China factor makes this "passage to India" all the more imperative. Suffice it to say that ASEAN had more than commercial motives for admitting Burma as a member in July 1997. As it turned out, this was the very month of the Asian Crash. Until then the ideology of Asian values (defined negatively as a rejection of the West's fixation on democracy and human rights) was a key component in ASEAN's indifference to the horrors of Burma's internal affairs. Talk of "engaging" Burma so as to encourage its political transformation was mere window dressing.

SANCTIONS, ENGAGEMENT, AND OTHER LIES

Even as post-Crash reformism crested in ASEAN nations, no significant pressure was brought to bear on the infamous SPDC (State Peace and Development Council) that shut down the democratic aspirations of Burma's largely Buddhist civil society. Instead, ASEAN glibly accepted the SPDC's promises of reform, such as its professed "road map to democracy," which turned out to be an endless detour. Both ASEAN and the international community have been satisfied with the relative liberation of Burma's economy, which ironically has spawned inflation, shrunk the middle class, and raised both income inequality and poverty in general.[10]

It was only when economic liberalization stalled that Western powers began to take a harder line against the junta. America's position has been cosmetic at best. Its post-9/11 Patriot Act targets any Burmese refugee who has given any form of "material support" to an organization such as the Karen National Union (KNU), which forcefully resists the junta. Thus pro-democratic resistance has been labeled as "terrorism" by Washington and the SPDC alike.[11]

If there was ever any ambiguity about the junta's position on eventual democratization, it evaporated in October 2004, when every SPDC member who showed any reformist inclination was purged. This included Prime Minister Khin Nyunt as well as like-minded cabinet members such as

---

[10] Bridget Welsh, "Sanctions Worsen Burmese Poverty," *International Herald Tribune* (August 8, 2003), http://www.iht.com/cgi-bin/generic.cgi?template=articleprint. tmphlh&ArticleId=105592

[11] Anna Husarska, "The Patriot Act's Terrible Toll," *The New Republic* (July 24, 2006), http://www.tnr. com/docprint.mhtml?i=20060724&s=husarska072406

Foreign Minister Win Aung and Home Minister Tin Hlaing.[12] More than ever it was clear that to back the SPDC was to support authoritarian oppression. Just a month after the crackdown of September 2007, ASEAN showed its true stripes by accepting the junta's flippant promise of a progressive constitution as reason enough to extend "engagement" policies indefinitely and unconditionally. It went without saying that ethnic minorities and pro-democracy organizations would have no part in drafting this new law of the land.[13]

Reactionary Asian values thus remain in the driver's seat of ASEAN foreign relations—and why not? Did not Western powers, egged on by bloated multinationals, soon forgive China for Tiananmen? So too they are looking the other way as Cambodia's Prime Minister Hun Sen consolidates his de facto dictatorship, using elections as a tool of international legitimacy while any real opposition is crushed.[14] Probably the SPDC had Cambodia in mind when it decided to allow its own rigged elections in 2010.

Still, it is the China model that casts the longest authoritarian shadow. If the West can forgive and forget Tiananmen, why should Burmese generals be held to full account for their bloody 1988 coup and their refusal to accept the results of the May 1990 election? Were Aung San Suu Kyi's 15 years of house arrest (as of her release in November 2010) so different from Zhao Ziyang's lifelong house arrest after he showed sympathy for the students at Tiananmen? Was it not hypocritical for America to stay on cozy terms with the CCP while condemning Burma's SLORC (the State Law and Order Restoration Council, as the SPDC was called until 1997)?

Likewise Washington was stooping to the ASEAN level when it allowed a US petroleum company, Unocal, to profit from forced labor and relocations exacted by the Burmese military in support of a $2.1 billion pipeline project.[15] Now Chevron (which bought Unocal in 2005) and its French partner

---

[12] "Myanmar" (covering events of 2004), *Amnesty International*, http:web.amnesty. org/web/web.nsf/print/A59772B951CC391E80256FE3004C77C3. Lee Kuan Yew, the godfather of Singaporean soft authoritarianism, claims that he personally won Khin Nyunt over to the idea of opening the junta up to global interaction, in the manner of Suharto's Golkar Party. See Lee Kuan Yew, "Myanmar's Generals Cant's Survive," *New Perspectives Quarterly* 24, no. 4 (Fall 2007), http://www.digitainpq.org/articles/global/212/10-11-2007/leekuanyew

[13] "Burma: Time for ASEAN to Bite the Bullet," *ALTSEAN: Alternative ASEAN Network On Burma* (November 18, 2007).

[14] Dustin Roasa, "Cambodia's Democratic Warrior," *The New Republic* (December 2, 2010), http://www.tnr.com/article/world/79558/cambodias-democratic-warrior-mu-sochua-political-reform

[15] These facts were documented by Earth Rights International in support of a class action suit filed against Unocal in 1996. See Anna Shelton, "Storyteller for Human

Total can actually profit from tougher sanctions against Burma, since these will eliminate future Western competition while prior contracts are safely "grandfathered."[16] By continuing to operate in Burma, these corporations funnel billions in taxes and fees to the junta.[17] It would be utterly hypocritical for Washington to declare war on Al Qaeda-type terrorism while ignoring the whole issue of state terrorists like Senior General Than Shwe and his genocidal comrades.

Granted, the Unocal affair is not the last word on America's Burma policy. US sanctions have at least sent the message that Burma leaves much to be desired. American hypocrisy is still better than the full complicity of ASEAN, which treats the SPDC as a legitimate government and business partner.[18] Perhaps ASEAN's engagement policies could still be defended as

---

Right," *The Progressive* (September 1999), http://findarticles.com/p/articles/mi_m1295/is_9_63/ai_55671576

Students across America began pressing their universities to divest Unocal stock, as well as that of Unocal's partner in the project, the French company, Total. See Marilyn Berlin Snell, "Pump Politics—Bold Strokes," *Sierra* (May/June 2002), http://findarticles.com/p/articles/mi_mi1525/is_3_87/ai_85281761

When Unocal was brought to trial in California, under the Alien Tort Claims Act, it tried to shift the blame to its subsidiaries, but finally settled the case with confidential compensation to the victims. See "Unocal, Myanmar Villagers Settle Suit," *Bloomberg News* (March 21, 2005). Total tried to escape blame in a similar trial in France by way of an even more startling defense. Against the charge of using forced child labor on its pipeline project, it claimed that this was impossible, since the pipes were too heavy for children to carry. In fact, the children were used to cut trees, dig ditches and carry equipment. See Eric Inciyan and Jean-Claude Pomonti, "Kouchner, Total et la Birmanie," *Le Monde* (January 5, 2004), http://www.lemonde.fr/web/imprimer_ article/ 0,1-0@2-3230,348020,0.html

[16] Sara Founders, "Myanmar: Washington's Geopolitics and the Straits of Malacca," *Workers World* (October 28, 2007), http://www.workers.org/2007/world/myanmar-1101/

However, Chevron could lose tax credits under a bill approved by a congressional committee on October 23. See Cherian Thomas, "Asian Leader, Seeking Myanmar's Gas, May Go Soft on Sanctions," *Bloomberg.com* (November 19, 2007), http://www.bloomberg.com/apps/news?pid=20601091&sid=aQKMX8vMfado&refer=india#

[17] Avni Patel, "Amid Deaths, Censorship, Oil Companies Continue Myanmar Operation," *ABC News* (October 3, 2007), http://blogs.abcnews.com/theblotter/2007/10/amid-deaths.cen.html

[18] This effectively abandons the duly elected General Secretary Daw Aung San Suu Kyi and her NLD (National League for Democracy), as well as other reform groups such as the exiled NCGUB (National Coalition Government of Burma), headquartered in Washington, D.C. From the early 1990s the NCGUB came out against all forms of aid to Burma, whereas the NLD has been more open to carefully supervised aid to the people. In practical terms, however, the two policies are nearly identical. By stipulating that aid must be equitably distributed without regard to political affiliation, the NLD effectively denies all aid, since the junta would never allow equitable distribution to its potential

of the mid-1990s, when SLORC seemed to be yielding a little to international pressure. In 1994 the generals initiated face-to-face talks with Suu Kyi.[19] This tiny ray of hope was magnified under the imaginative lens of those years, a time when faith was still vested in the so-called "third wave" of global democratization. The US, Europe, and Japan were following much the same "engagement" path in inviting Russia to join their club of First World elites at the global bargaining table.

A decade later it would be clear that unconditional engagement had failed as miserably in Russia's case as it has in China's. Likewise, as Michael Green and Derek Mitchell point out, the incontestable verdict is now in that neither US-style sanctions nor ASEAN-style constructive engagement is working in Burma's case.[20] While ASEAN did issue some tepid criticism of SPDC orders to fire on peaceful protestors in September 2007, Prime Minister Lee Hsien Loong of Singapore (which then held the ASEAN chairmanship) was quick to call for still more constructive engagement.[21]

In practical effect, US–Burma policies have come to the same dead end. Unless they are universally applied, sanctions simply freeze the status quo.[22] They could never work without hard and sustained pressure on India and ASEAN to impose matching sanctions, and on China to stop bolstering Burma's military buildup. It is no accident that the junta's confidence has grown in tandem with the PRC's economic rise. Along with Russia and Ukraine, China is the chief supplier of Burma's startling militarization.[23] When China's annual MFN evaluation was dropped in advance of its WTO entry, Washington lost its best pressure point on China, yet a wide range of diplomatic mechanisms were still available. None have been put to serious use on Burma's behalf.

---

enemies. See "Myanmar: The Politics of Humanitarian Aid—Executive Summary and Recommendations," *ICG Asia Report*, no. 32 (April 2, 2002): 4–5. Even if the Saffron democracy movement had succeeded, the international aid that would have poured in could have divided ethnic groups and fomented further civil strife, much as World Bank policies have done in Bosnia-Herzegovina. See Yuki Akimoto, *Opportunities and Pitfalls: Preparing for Burma's Economic Transition* (New York: Open Society Institute, 2006), 48.

[19] *Amnesty International 2002 Report on Myanmar*, AI Index: POL 10/001/2002.

[20] Michael Green and Derek Mitchell, "Asia's Forgotten Crisis: A New Approach to Burma," *Foreign Affairs* 86, no. 6 (November/December 2007): 148 (147–58).

[21] Josh D. Friedman, "Deuces High: How the US can Bring an End to Myanmar's Crackdown on Democracy," *World Press* (November 29, 2007), http://www.worldpress.org/Asia/3002.cfm

[22] "Myanmar: Sanctions, Engagement or Another Way Forward?" *International Crisis Group* (April 26, 2004), http://www.crisisgroup.org/home/index.cfm?id=2677&1=1

[23] Jane Perlez, "Power and Politics in Myanmar," *International Herald Tribune* (November 16, 2006), http://www.iht.com/bin/print.php?id=3561993

Clearly Washington has been using Burma for image purposes. This should not be surprising, given the recent US record on democracy promotion in general.[24] Laura Bush may have been sincere in broadcasting her concern over Burma's human rights conditions, but all the while her husband's administration kept its silence on equally heinous conditions in Egypt, Pakistan and a host of other unmentionables; and the implicit pledge behind Obama's "reset" mentality is a marked reduction in human rights pressure worldwide. When China's violent crackdown on protestors in Tibet spawned another round of demands for an Olympic boycott, Bush remained silent, pointedly refusing to alter his plan to join hands with Hu Jintao at the Olympic opening ceremonies.[25]

Much as Hitler used the 1936 Olympics to stage a major propaganda coup, China was using the 2008 Olympics to normalize its most heinous domestic and foreign policies.[26] There seemed to be a huge contrast between Bush's relatively tough stance on Burma and his flaccid response to Tibet, but in fact the two were not so far apart. Although US sanctions were ostensibly tightened after the rearrest of Aung San Suu Kyi in May 2003, it was perfectly understood that such actions would have no impact without matching measures by Burma's neighbors. The US position was no more than a public relations ploy to deflect attention from so many American sellouts in other parts of the world.

THE SAFFRON RISING

Unfortunately the Burmese people did not understand this subterfuge. They swallowed the idea that the world's most powerful nation was solidly on their side, ready and waiting for their democratic gambit. In the late summer of 2007 the world looked on in dismay as thousands of Burmese took to the streets, unarmed against seasoned killers. The train of events that led to the Saffron Rising began with government waste and corruption, but especially with one project. Countless millions were spent moving the country's capital from Rangoon to the appropriately named Naypyidaw (meaning royal city), which had to be built from scratch, complete with an obligatory golf course. This functional equivalent of Versailles was remote

---

[24] See Thomas Carothers, *U.S. Democracy Promotion During and After Bush* (Washington, D.C.: Carnegie Endowment for International Peace, 2007), 14.

[25] Sheryl Gay Stolberg and Somini Sengupta, "Bush Silent, but Others Speak Out on Tibet Crackdown," *The New York Times* (March 22, 2008), http://www.nytimes.com/2008/3/22/world/asia/22prexy.html

[26] Anne Applebaum, "Olympic Fallacies," *The Washington Post* (March 25, 2008), A15.

enough to isolate civil servants from the social ferment that was building in the cities as prices rose and food stocks dropped. Needless to say, government employees would be unhappy about this relocation. To secure their loyalty, lower ranking officials got a five-fold pay increase, while senior ones got a raise of 1,200 percent.[27] The junta decided to cover these costs with a fuel price adjustment: a 500 percent hike on compressed natural gas and about 100 percent on petrol and diesel.[28]

What began on August 19 as a protest over that price hike morphed into a full-fledged democratic movement as legions of saffron-robed monks joined the demonstrations, led by the All Burma Monks's Alliance.[29] They knew that the military (Tatmadaw) they confronted — the second largest in Southeast Asia after Vietnam's, and double the size of the forces facing the protesters in 1988[30] — was capable of unspeakable atrocities. Most Chinese students at Tiananmen believed the PLA would not fire on unarmed demonstrators, but few of Burma's Saffron protesters had any such delusions. This was a military that was known to use prisoners as human mine sweepers, and between 1996 and 2006 had destroyed 2,700 ethnic villages. Firing on unarmed demonstrators was not going to be a soul-wrenching task for them.

What, then, did the protestors expect that could be worth this degree of risk? To whom was their perilous statement addressed? Surely it was not being sent to the junta itself, nor to any power the generals were likely to listen to, such as China. Thus the first mystery that hung over the Saffron demonstrations was what their practical objective was. This question is

---

[27] Kremb, "Anatomy of Burma," *op. cit.*

[28] This was in fact the second round of a hike that began two years before. Inflation had soared in October 2005 when the government raised fuel prices more than 600 percent. Commodity prices again shot up after civil servants were given a ten-fold salary increase to stanch their grumbling over the move of the capital to Naypyidaw. See "Burma: Time for ASEAN to Bite the Bullet," *op. cit.* Immediately after the fuel hike, taxi drivers doubled their fares and bus rates quadrupled. See "Transport Costs Soar after Myanmar Fuel Price Hike," *Agence France Presse* (October 24, 2005), http://www.burmanet.org/news/2005/10/24/agence-france-presse-transport-costs-soar-after-myanmar-fuel-price-hike/

[29] The Buddhist factor was critical for this democratic transformation. The original march, on August 19, had no broader agenda than the fuel issue. There were no slogans or banners, nor was there any shooting. The 500 marchers were simply symbolically joining those people who would now have to walk to work, not being able to afford public transportation. See "Hundreds Protest in Myanmar over Fuel Price Hike," *The Shwe Gas Movement* (August 20, 2007), http://www.shwe.org/docs/hundreds-protest-in-myanmar-over-fuel-price-hike/ and Jürgen Kremb, "People Will Never Forgive the Murders," *Der Spiegel*, no. 41 (October 8, 2007), http://www.spiegel.de/international/world/0,1518,druck-510074,00.html

[30] Selth, *op. cit.*

hard to answer because of the amorphous nature of the protests. Numerically, at least, the monks and the soldiers were equally matched, at around 400,000 each. While the soldiers had guns, the monks had public support,[31] and that was not a negligible weapon. The fact that most monks return to ordinary life after a few years gives them close ties with civil society.[32] The torch of opposition had now passed from the party politics of the National League for Democracy (NLD) to a deeper cultural politics that could not so easily be contained.

This also helps to explain a second mystery, which was why the crackdown that followed was so severe. Contrast the crackdown of 2000 on the NLD, which followed on the heels of two years of relative civility on the junta's part. By then Western critics had developed "crackdown fatigue," such that few bothered to speak out on the latest anti-NLD actions. Indeed, the regime was even rewarded, as Western business lobbies seized upon the 2000 setback as proof that sanctions were not working.[33] So long as repression was kept moderate by these malevolent standards, world reaction would be limited. Why sacrifice that advantage by pushing the present crackdown into overdrive?

There is no way to know how many of the protesters were murdered. Among the army divisions sent in on September 25 was the 22nd, which had distinguished itself in 1988 by firing on unarmed demonstrators.[34] At first the junta claimed to have killed only 10 of the 2007 protesters, but residents near one crematorium in Rangoon counted 71 bodies on the night of September 26,[35] and independent sources put the death toll at around 200 in the first few days.[36] Moreover, with thousands still detained or missing, and 1,400 monks known to be in custody as of October 7, countless deaths could be going unreported.

This aggression was encouraged by the military's successes in its decades-long civil war with rural minorities. Seventeen armed ethnic groups have

---

[31] Kenneth Denby, "Monks Defended by Power of the People," *Times* (October 4, 2007), http://www.timesonline.co.uk/tol/news/world/asia/article2583600.ece

[32] "On the Brink: Myanmar's Protests," *The Economist* (September 27, 2007), http://www.economist.com/PrinterFriendly.cfm?story_id=9868041

[33] Robert Horn, "From Bad to Worse," *Time Asia* 156, no. 11 (September 18, 2000), http://www.time.com/time/asia/magazine/2000/0918/burma.junta.html

[34] "Myanmar's Monks Resume Street Protests, Defying Junta's Order," *Deseret News* of Salt Lake City (September 25, 2007), http://findarticles.com/articles/mi_qn4188/is_20070925/ai_n20518195

[35] *Burma Bulletin*, 10 (October 2007).

[36] See Kyi May Kaung, "Burma Post-Clampdown: What Should be Done?" *The American Prospect* (November 1, 2007), http://www.prospect.org/cs/articles?articles=burma_post_clamddown_what_should_be_done

officially suspended their struggle by signing ceasefire agreements, and intense pressure is being brought to bear on the few remaining active groups.[37] A report in the *New Era Journal* indicates that while ethnic nationalities largely sat out the 1988 rising, they have been more involved in the present resistance.[38] That point needs further examination, but clearly it is a case of too little, too late. Had this cooperation developed before those seventeen groups were sidelined, the Saffron Rising could have had a different result.

With most ethnic resistance terminated, the junta could now turn the brunt of its might on a more proximate enemy: the urban and deeply Buddhistic opposition that refuses to surrender the election results of 1990. This hostility, however, goes beyond the anti-democratic animus that the regime has long applied to Aung San Suu Kyi and the NLD. Their largely secular challenge is certainly feared and despised, but the wrath vented on these recalcitrant monks has exceeded even that. One must agree with Donald Seekins that the special venom directed at the monks in fall, 2007 was born of their deeper threat to the regime's legitimacy. Their upturned rice bowls not only signified a rejection of the junta's style of governance, but of its very "Burmeseness."[39]

ANOTHER EAST IS POSSIBLE

True to the adage that generals always fight the previous war, the Burmese generals turned the gruesome tactics of their minority wars on marchers who were simply telling the government what its puppet press would not report: that its new fuel edicts were pushing an already impoverished population to the brink of starvation. While the price of rice shot up, the black market exchange value of the kyat plummeted.[40] With inflation at over 90 percent, the average family now spends over 70 percent of its income

---

[37] "Burma Stepping Up Attacks on Insurgents," *Democratic Voice of Burma* (December 10, 2007), http://english.dvb.no/print_news.php?id=754

[38] Michael Beer, "Burma Resistance Much Stronger than 1988," *New Era Journal* (December 15, 2007), http://www.khitpyaing.org/english_page/October07/michaelbeer_2-10-07.php

[39] Donald M. Seekins, "The Geopolitics and Economics of Burma's Military Regime, 1962–2007," *Japan Focus* (November 12, 2007) in Znet, http://www.zmag.org/content/print_article.cfm?itemID= 14263&sectionID=1

[40] The black market exchange rate of the kyat fell from 200 to the dollar in 1997 to 900 in 2006 and 1,500 in October 2007. See Christopher Johnson and Simon Montlake, "With More Sanctions, Burmese Chafe under Further Isolation," *The Christian Science Monitor* (October 15, 2007), http://www.csmonitor.com/2007/1015/p04s01-woap.html

on food,[41] and many are able to afford only one meal per day. Despite a perennial rice shortage, the government has attempted to increase the export of rice to finance its often frivolous imports.[42] Such policies widen still farther the immense gulf between the country's haves and have-nots. With most medical services limited to the rich and regime-connected, the vast majority are left without even rudimentary health care. This explains why Burma, with but a fraction of India's population, has more malaria deaths. Tuberculosis and AIDS are also rampant, and extreme malnutrition is becoming common in urban areas.[43] Meanwhile the bulk of the country's natural resource sales go into military funding and junta-connected bank accounts.

Little is done to hide the kleptocratic extravagance of the generals and their cronies. Early in 2007 Than Shwe treated his daughter to a wedding costing an estimated $300,000, complete with diamond-studied jewelry, showers of champagne, and gaudy photographs of the newlyweds in front of a golden bed. A secret video of this "let them eat cake" festival found its way to Burma's Thai-based alternative newspaper, *The Irrawaddy*,[44] and from there to YouTube. Even Singapore's senior autocrat, Lee Kuan Yew, found this galling: "the daughter was like a Christmas tree! Flaunting these excesses must push a hungry and impoverished people to revolt."[45] A 2005 UN study concluded that if food prices rose by 15 to 20 percent, half the Burmese population would end up below the poverty line. This undoubtedly happened with the fuel price escalations of 2005 and 2007.[46]

Remarkably this famished country has an impressive literacy rate, which by some estimates is as high as 80 percent.[47] That ray of social hope owes more to Buddhistic values than to the government's paltry support for education.[48]

---

[41] Kremb, "Anatomy of Burma," *op. cit.*

[42] Larry Jagan, "Deepening Crisis Poses Major Security Threat," *The Bangkok Post* (August 30, 2002), http://www.burmafund.org/Perspectives/083002-LJagen-Deepening%20crisis.htm

[43] Perlez, *op. cit.*

[44] Fergal Keane, "The Sweet Contagion of freedom will Outlast Bloodshed in Burma," *The Spectator* (October 6, 2007), http://findarticles.com/p/articles/mi_qa3724/is_20071006/ai_n21059780/print

[45] Lee Kuan Yew, *op. cit.*

[46] The ensuing food crisis was even worse in minority areas that were riven by civil war. In the Karen State, for example, the recent offensive has displaced 76,000 and left 25,000 on the brink of starvation. See "Burma: Time for ASEAN to Bite the Bullet," *op. cit.*

[47] Joshua Kurlantzick, "Regime Unchanged: How Burma's Ruling Junta has Endured," *The Washington Monthly* (December 2006), http://findarticles.com/p/articles/mi_mi1316/is_12_38/ai_n6880251/print

[48] Although Burma is officially a party to the Convention on the Rights of the Child (CRC), which mandates free public education and financial assistance for those in need,

This may also help to explain why most Burmese outside the junta and the military fervently support democracy. Women are especially aware that democracy could well serve them by restoring their former social status. In Burma's traditional culture they enjoyed a status almost unprecedented in Asia.[49] Burma, then, embodies two antithetical political cultures. That of the present government, like the so-called Asian values school of Singapore fame, resists all democratization except the most "guided" and pro forma varieties. But Burma is also home to the simmering grassroots progressivism that erupted in 1988 and 2007. The mere mention of those years is enough to set the region's authoritarians on edge, much as the Tunisian rising of January 2011 has set the whole Arab world on edge.

Western development thought is likewise bifurcated where non-economic issues are concerned. A minority position holds that support must be given to reform elements in developing nations, but the more dominant school calls for full engagement with China and other dictatorial regimes without much concern for political niceties like free speech and human rights.[50] Marvin Ott and David Steinberg apply this engagement approach to Burma specifically. Ott argues on standard realist premises that US sanctions have failed geopolitically by driving Burma into the waiting arms of China.[51] Steinberg puts a more humane face on the argument by stressing that sanctions have failed in both economic and human rights terms. Hence they should be replaced with a policy modeled on ASEAN's friendly persuasion.[52] We are left to wonder how Steinberg reaches the conclusion that ASEAN's approach has fared any better than Western sanctions have.

Taken together, Ott's amoral realism and Steinberg's friendly economism privilege stability and profit maximization over freedom, exactly as Sino-globalism does. The East is effectively reduced to a happy hunting ground for economic and geopolitical advantage. That is the East which Niall Ferguson has in mind when he charges that the signal geopolitical

---

the fact is that Burmese parents must directly cover the cost of primary education for their children. As a result, only about a third of Burmese children complete their five years of primary school, and only two percent finish high school. See Foreign Affairs Committee of the All Burma Federation of Student Unions, *Education Report 2002*, May, 2003.

[49] Cheryll Barron, "Burma: Feminist Utopia?" *Prospect Magazine*, 139 (October 2007), http://www.prospect-magazine.co.uk/printarticle.php?id=9839

[50] This school is typified by William Overholt's neoliberal paean to unconstrained economism. Overholt dismisses democracy promotion by linking it to militarist foreign policy. See William H. Overholt, *Asia, America, and the Transformation of Geopolitics*, Cambridge, UK: Cambridge University Press, 2007.

[51] Marvin C. Ott, "Southeast Asian Security Challenges: America's Response?," *Strategic Forum* (October 2006), http://findarticles.com/p/articles/mi_m0QZY/is_n16850411

[52] David I. Steinberg, "Burma: Feel-Good US Sanctions Wrongheaded," *Yale Global Online* (May 19, 2004), http://yaleglobal.yale.edu/article.print?id=3901

event of our era, eclipsing even the fall of the Soviet Union, was Deng's ruthless suppression of liberal impulses at Tiananmen.[53] This paved the way for the present China model, hinging as it does on the Sino-globalist merger of capitalism and Asian authoritarianism.

The Burma crisis, however, proves that another East is possible. That so many were willing to risk so much for freedom and social justice sends a message of astonishing defiance not only against the Burmese junta, but against the idea that repression can be taken as the normal course of Asian affairs. In terms of that message, so daring and yet almost entirely nonviolent, the Saffron Rising was in a league with Gandhi's civil disobedience. Yet there was a sad difference in terms of the final product. Like the students at Tiananmen, Burma's dissident monks grossly overestimated the democratic convictions of the audience they addressed. They threw their fate to global and regional players who cared little about Burma except as a resource hub or geopolitical stomping ground. Nothing these protesters did was going to turn the tide of world affairs in this era of raw economism and flagging liberal influence.

A HOME-GROWN COBRA

To be sure, the monks' naivety regarding power politics does not dent the meaning of their courage and sacrifice. At the very least we owe them the respect of recognizing their motives and actions as their own. When they joined the marches, with their rice bowls inverted to symbolize moral condemnation, they were effectively ex-communicating the military government. William Engdahl's nominally "Left" accusation that US interests were the prime movers behind the demonstrations both insults the protestors and pays an unwitting and unjustified compliment to US undercover operations.[54] The Bush administration not only lacked the competence to be such an undercover mover and shaker, but had no interest in the kind of People Power that was rocking Burma. What Engdahl and his ilk cannot imagine is that the Saffron Rising was a home-grown and religiously inspired phenomenon. Interestingly, the junta shares this same incredulity. Like Engdahl it insists that the Rising was made in the USA.[55] No real

---

[53] Niall Ferguson, "The Triumph of the East," *New Statesman* (June 26, 2006), http://www.newstatesman.com/200606260034

[54] See F. William Engdahl, "The Geopolitical Stakes of 'Saffron Revolution,'" *Asia Times* (October 17, 2007), http://www.atimes.com/atimes/SoutheastAsia/IJ17Ae01.html

[55] As evidence of this, it is simply noted that the staff of the US Embassy in Rangoon was increased shortly before the Rising. See Aung Zaw, "Than Shwe: The Main in the Iron

evidence is adduced to support this allegation. It rests primarily on the orientalist assumption that it *must* be so, for a poor, undeveloped country like Burma could not possibly generate such democratic conviction as was seen in September 2007.

The Dalai Lama, who expressed full support for the demonstrators,[56] knows better. He implicitly agrees with Amartya Sen that another Asia is possible. What spawned the Saffron Rising was not outside agitation or funding, but spontaneous outrage at the insufferable social conditions under the junta. The spark that set it off was the brutalization of several monks in Pakokku, a small town in Mideast Burma which was especially hard hit by the fuel hikes because it was so poor already. Unable to afford rice, most residents had to eat pancakes made from cheaper rice meal. The Chin people of this region have long been in open rebellion, which may explain why the junta chose Pakokku to set an example for others to consider. Several monks were tied to lamp posts and savagely beaten. Revulsion at this incident, and at the whole Burmese malady, led to the formation of the All Burma Monks Alliance, which turned a mere fuel protest into the Saffron Rising.[57] On three consecutive days the protest marches grew larger, reaching an estimated 100,000 in Rangoon on September 25. Suffice it to say that this movement was not a US export.

As the protests turned political, placards were seen calling for UN intervention. There seemed to be little awareness that any such proposed action would be summarily vetoed by China. Nonetheless there was a certain logic to the monks' expectation of external assistance of some kind. What requires explanation is why Burma's neighbors, with their culturally embedded fear of Chinese imperialism, would not try to counter Beijing's influence by throwing their support to what the PRC fears most: a genuine democracy movement on its southern border. This would effectively put a cobra in China's chamber pot. Although it is a home-grown cobra, it still needs international backing, or at the very least neutrality. That means putting an end to the support that regional powers are showering on the junta. India and the ASEAN nations reap short-term benefits from friendly relations with the generals, but in this geopolitical race to the bottom they are sure to be the losers in the long run.

Mask," *The Irrawaddy Online* (October 31, 2007), http://www.irrawaddy.org/print_page. php?art_id=9165

[56] Gavin Rabinowitz, "Dalai Lama Condemns Crackdown on Buddhist Monks in Burma," *Burma Digest* (November 28, 2007), http://burmadigest.info/2007/11/28/dalai-lama-condamns-crackdown-on-buddhist-monks-in-burma/

[57] Kremb, "Anatomy of Burma," *op. cit.*

Beijing understandably views democratization as anathema to its interests, but India is foolish to play by these rules. As of the early 1990s, India staunchly supported Burma's democratic movement, and even gave Aung San Suu Kyi its coveted Jawaharlal Nehru Award in 1993.[58] But a new set of Indo-Burmese relations—forged by the fascist BJP and shamelessly upheld by the Congress Party after 2004—represents a blend of geopolitical ambition and geoeconomic greed.[59] New Delhi fails to recognize that its strong comparative advantage, as the intelligence guru B. Raman argues, lies in the integration of India's foreign policy with its widely respected democratic commitments.

Raman urges India to reclaim its pre-globalist policy standards by reaching out to Burma's civil society, just as it once did toward dissenting elements in Zia al-Haq's Pakistan and Suharto's Indonesia.[60] By selling a wide range of arms to the junta, including tanks, helicopters and artillery, India barters its former good name for fast profits that could dry up as Burma slips further into the Chinese orbit. Already Burma has withdrawn the "preferential buyer" status of the Gas Authority of India Limited (GAIL) in favor of PetroChina for key Andaman Sea gas fields.[61] India took the wrong lesson from its ebbing influence. Instead of reverting to its soft power policies of years past, it decided to go farther than ever in placating the junta. It abandoned Aung San Suu Kyi and any semblance of a moral foreign policy. Even while the September 2007 crackdown was in progress, India's petroleum minister went to Burma to sign a deep-water exploration deal.[62]

ASEAN FAMILY VALUES

Like India, most ASEAN nations are defining themselves by their closure toward Burma's democratic movement. Their standard line is yet another

---

[58] Cherian Thomas, *op. cit.*

[59] Marie Lall argues that India's main concern is energy security, which in our view misses the equally important geopolitical element. See Marie Lall, "Indo-Myanmar Relations in the Era of Pipeline Diplomacy," *Contemporary Southeast Asia: A Journal of International and Strategic Affairs*, Vol. 28, No. 3 (December 2006): 424–46.

[60] B. Raman, "Myanmar's Ethical and Strategic Dimensions," *Global News Blog*, July 20, 2007, http://globalnewsblog.com/wp/?cat=12

[61] "Pipeline Politics: India and Myanmar," *PINR: Power and Internet News Report* (September 10, 2007), http://www.pinr.com/report.php?ac=view_printable&report_id=679&language_id=1

[62] Pankaj Mishra, "The Revolt of the Monks," *The New York Review* (February 14, 2008), 38 (36–38).

call for dialogue between the SPDC and the NLD, despite the fact that this approach proved utterly fruitless in 1994 and again after October 2000. In the latter case, a confidential but well-publicized dialogue with Suu Kyi continued through most of 2001.[63] By then it was obvious to even the most optimistic Burma-watchers that dialogue alone was anything but a road to reform. It was basically a diversion that served the junta's interest by making it appear open-minded and equitable.

A glaring question mark had been placed on ASEAN's objectives when it admitted Cambodia, Laos, and Burma as new members. At that high tide of the Asian miracle, shortly before the Asian Financial Crisis, it could still be asked if democracy would eventually count as a factor in Asian development. At least this possibility had not been ruled out. Such benign ambiguity was obliterated by ASEAN's position on Burma at the 2007 Summit. Despite a vain attempt to sweep the issue aside,[64] it became obvious that the organization's basic values were not fundamentally at odds with the SPDC's.[65]

Like a mafia godfather forgiving an overzealous mobster, ASEAN's Secretary-General Ong Keng Yong averred that "Burma is 'part of our family'."[66] These dubious "family values" have not changed since ASEAN took its classic stand for inaction at the nadir of the East Timor crisis. Then as now the sole concern was "stability," and as Amy Chua admonishes in *World on Fire*,[67] democratization in most underdeveloped countries is a veritable factory for instability. This argument squarely fits the Singapore-school mantra that privileges static Asian values which just by coincidence always serve the interest of the ruling classes.

However, measured by a different set of Asian values, ASEAN's interests would be far better served by democracy in places like Burma. Stability-through-repression does nothing to keep China at bay. Just as Taiwan's democratization, halting as it is, makes peaceful reunification with China

---

[63] *Amnesty International 2002 Report on Myanmar, op. cit.*

[64] In doing so they likewise spurned a US Senate resolution calling for the expulsion or at least the suspension of the junta from ASEAN. See Amy Kazmin, "Failure to Push Burma Undermines ASEAN," *Financial Times* (November 19, 2007), http://www.ft.com/cms/s/0/334de10a-9683-11dc-b2da-0000779fd2ac,dwp_uuid=61365390-7032-11dc-a6d1-0000779fd2ac,print=yes.html

[65] This was even more obvious at the 2007 Summit than it was in 2006, when Burma was passed over for its turn as the ASEAN chair.

[66] Kazmin, *op. cit.*

[67] Amy Chua, *World on Fire: How Exporting Free Market Democracy Breeds Ethnic Hatred and Global Instability*, New York: Doubleday, 2003, *passim*. In the name of protecting ethnic minorities, such as the Chinese minority in her native Philippines, Chua makes a tendentious and convoluted case against democratic reform in general.

difficult, a democratic Burma would provide a firewall against Chinese encroachment throughout the region. It is a question of whether ASEAN stands for anything more than "bigger is better" economism. The new ASEAN charter was supposed to provide a blueprint for an EU-style community by 2015,[68] but it remained to be seen if ASEAN had any intention of emulating the liberal democratic side of the EU model.

Clearly the main attraction of the EU formula was its commercial and geopolitical rather than democratic attributes. Japan under Shinzo Abe broached a similar and equally suspect liberal strategy in an effort to encircle China with an "arc of freedom."[69] ASEAN's original charter proposal (known to the public through leaked drafts) suggests that it too was trying to erect an ideological barrier against Sino-hegemony. The Burma case, however, marks ASEAN's retreat into old ideological habits. It knows too well that any censure of Burma could boomerang on its own internal affairs. Although it initially expressed "revulsion" at the September crackdown (whereas India simply promised to "monitor the situation"),[70] it ended up supporting the junta's right to do as it pleases.

So it was that a *Financial Times* editorial accused ASEAN of having an "ethical vacuum at its heart." There is no question about its financial complicity in Burma's killing fields. While its leaders tend to frame the Burma crisis as a culture clash between East and West, the real clash is between the generals and their people. The *Financial Times* pointed out that most Southeast Asians, if consulted, would be "as vocal as Europeans or Americans in supporting the enforcement of human rights for Burmese and other Asians."[71]

Not surprisingly, Tokyo would soon back away from Abe's Eurasian "arc." Under Yasuo Fukuda Japan revived the "Fukuda Doctrine" set forth by Yasuo's father in the 1970s. Once again close relations with China took

---

[68] Wayne Arnold, "Southeast Asian Pact Exposes Rifts," *The New York Times* (November 21, 2007), http://www.nytimes.com/2007/11/21/world/asia/21asean.html

[69] Taro Aso, "Arc of Freedom and Prosperity: Japan's Expanding Diplomatic Horizons," in a speech to the Japan Institute of International Affairs, *The Ministry of Foreign Affairs of Japan* (November 30, 2006), http://www.mofa.go.jp/announce/fm/aso/speech0611.html

Accordingly, Japan cancelled a $4.7 million grant to Burma in the wake of the 2007 crackdown. Strangely, however, it took no position for or against further sanctions. Southeast Asia remains the weakest link in this geopolitical chain, thanks in no small part to ASEAN's unwillingness or inability to confront China directly. See Norman Bordadora, "ASEAN Charter OK Hinges on Suu Kyi Release," *Inquirer* (November 20, 2007), http://newsinfor.inquirer.net/inquirerheadlines/nation/view_article.php?article_id=101985

[70] "The Saffron Olympics," *The Washington Post* (September 29, 2007), p. A18.

[71] "Southeast Asia's Toothless Charter," *Financial Times* (November 19, 2007), http://www.ft.com/cms/s/0/b76c2806-96c5-11dc-b231-0000779fd2ac.html?nclick_check=1

priority, while human rights were shelved.[72] How this would affect Japan's stance on Burma was not hard to guess. It was never likely that Abe's "arc" could have much value as a geopolitical balancing agent unless it was defined in moral realist rather than globalist terms.[73]

BURMA AS POST-REALIST TEST SITE

The ASEAN members had taken a much tougher stand on the China threat in the midst of the Mischief Reef conflict of 1995. That, however, was at the peak of the region's "miracle years," and before China's own miracle was on full display. In the wake of the Asian Crash, ASEAN and especially Indonesia were less equipped to confront China when the conflict resurfaced in 1998. Already the Asian balance of power was tilting in China's favor. The quarter-century retreat of America from Southeast Asian affairs had made the region an easy target for Chinese empowerment.[74]

Waning US influence was reflected in the way China, India, and most ASEAN nations brushed off Washington's call for economic and diplomatic action against the Burmese junta in the aftermath of the 2007 crisis.[75] While the economic side of this power shift has taken headlines—for example, with the establishment in 2010 of the ASEAN–China Free Trade Area (ACFTA)[76]—the military side goes without saying, given China's double-digit annual increases in military spending.

---

[72] "The Return of the Fukuda Doctrine," *The Economist* (December 13, 2007), http:// www.economist.com/world/asia/PrinterFriendly.cfm?story_id=10286958. In fact, Abe himself was more politic in his China relations than his predecessor Junichiro Koizumi, who seemed to enjoy irking Beijing with his infamous visits to the Yasukuni Shrine and his insistence that Article 9 of the Japanese Constitution be repealed, thus releasing Japan's military from its purely defensive restraints. See Joseph S. Nye, "The Rise of Liberal Japan," *Project Syndicate* (June 2007), http://www.project-syndicate.org/print_commentary/nye46/English

[73] Neoliberal globalism has had no trouble co-existing with Sino-globalization. Likewise, the neoliberalization of Japan has blended easily with the neo-statist thrust of Japanese thought. See Takahashi Tetsuya, interviewed by Lee Hyo Duk and translated by Norma Field, "Philosophy as Activism in Neo-Liberal, Neo-Nationalist Japan," *Japan Focus* (November 3, 2007), http://japanfocus.org/products/topdf/2566

[74] Marvin C. Ott, "Southeast Asian Security Challenges: America's Response?," from *Strategic Forum*, No. 222 (October 2006), http://findarticles.com/articles/mi_m0QZY/ is_222/ai_n16850411/print

[75] Seth Mydans, "Months After Protests, Myanmar Junta in Control," *The New York Times* (December 8, 2007), http://www.nytimes.com/2007/12/08/world/asia/08myanmar.html

[76] See "ASEAN-China Trade Ties Close, Rosy," *China View* (December 8, 2007), http:// news.xinhuanet. com/English/2007-12/08/content_7218384.htm

Gullible Western leaders,[77] and even Aung San Suu Kyi herself, looked to Beijing of all places for assistance in curbing the military's brutality. It somehow escaped their notice how strikingly similar the anti-Buddhist tactics of the junta were to those of the Chinese in Tibet and elsewhere. More even than North Korea, Burma had become a Chinese puppet state. This gave China the edge over India and South Korea in its bid for Burma's new pipelines and offshore natural gas fields.[78] It goes without saying that Beijing's political influence flowed through those same pipes. In April 2006 plans were ratified for China to lay a pipeline across Burma from a deepwater port off Sittwe (on an island at the confluence of the Kaladan, Myu, and Lemyo Rivers) to the Chinese province of Yunnan. That would enable China to import Middle Eastern oil without passing through the highly vulnerable Malacca Straits.[79]

These commercial and military ties with China go far to explain the junta's turn toward rabidly anti-Buddhist tactics. In the short run, at least, this very un-Burmese action has been effective. Two months after the Saffron Crackdown began, the streets were hauntingly quiet. Arrests continued almost daily, and hundreds of monks were missing,[80] but the monasteries in Rangoon were pacified. In words that echoed the Bush administration briefings on the invasion of Iraq, Information Minister Kyaw Hsan boasted of the military's successful "pre-emptive strikes" to remove "destructive elements."[81]

Meanwhile the government offered huge bribes to senior monks who played along, and many took the bait. No one could seriously think at that point that the generals were going to respond favorably to the overturned bowls of unruly monks or the wishful remonstrance of world leaders.

---

[77] In some cases this hope may have been tactical, as when New Zealand's prime minister Helen Clark, after meeting with China's Premier Wen Jiabao at the Singapore Summit, expressed great confidence in China's good will regarding U.N. efforts in Burma. Surely she knew that China was the biggest obstacle there was to effective U.N. action, but she evidently considered dialogue a better option than truthful derogations. It was well and good for her to play the amiable role in a game of good cop/bad cop. The problem is that the West presently has no bad cop where China is concerned. On Clark's Chinese overtures, see "Clark Confident China is behind UN Role in Myanmar," *TV3* from New Zealand (November 21, 2007), http://www.tv3.co.nz/tabid/213/Default. aspx?&articleID=39668

[78] "Myanmar's Pipeline Politics," *The Economist* (March 23, 2007), http://www. economist.com/agend/PrinterFriendly.cfm?story_id=8908775

[79] Perlez, *op. cit.*

[80] Lennox Samuels, "The Silence of the Monasteries," *Newsweek* (November 19, 2007), http://www.newsweek.com/id/71266

[81] Mydans, *op. cit.*

They would prefer to cut most non-commercial ties rather than relinquish their absolutism.[82] This isolation further eroded any benefit that could have been expected from Saffron politics. Realizing the futility of civil disobedience, some monks began contemplating a fundamental change of tactics so as to fight fire with fire, in the spirit of Christian liberation theology. Secular organizations like the All Burma Federation of Student Unions (ABFSU) were also gravitating toward forceful resistance.[83] This was more in line with the All Burma Students' Democratic Front (ABSDF), which in theory at least has been militant since its inception in November 1988.[84] Unfortunately ethnic distrust made it difficult for ABSDF to work closely with minority opposition groups.[85] One of the junta's best tools of repression has been its divide and conquer strategy.

Three months after the crackdown, the US Congress stiffened sanctions to the point that they could actually make a difference, costing Burma hundreds of millions per year in lost revenue from sales in gems and timber. The EU likewise slapped an embargo on gemstones, timber, and metals, and expanded its existing arms embargo, travel ban and asset freeze.[86] Such actions are vitiated, however, by the refusal of neighboring Asian countries to impose even moderate sanctions on the junta. Thus Burma sits on a crucial fault line dividing the developmental goals of East and West. So too, for

---

[82] Typical of this isolationism was the government's decision to raise the annual satellite television levy from $5 to $800, or one million kyat. As usual, this was done without prior announcement. People only learned of it when they went to pay their bills. Those seeking a new license would have to pay two million kyat. Most were not able to afford the cost, and were left with nothing but state-controlled MRTV. See Aung Hla Tun, "Myanmar Junta Hikes Satellite TV Fees," *Reuters* (January 2, 2008), http://www.reuters.com/article/idUSBKK1591520080102; and "Myanmar: Article Riles Censors," *The New York Times* (January 18, 2008), http://www.nytimes.com/2008/01/18/world/asia/18briefs-newspaper.html

[83] See, for example, Myway Oo Way, "No Redeemer Can be Found," *The New Era Journal* (November 30, 2007), translated from the Burmese by an anonymous associate of ours. Such opposition would have been far more effective if it could have allied itself with the seasoned resistance movements of minority groups. Unfortunately these movements met only indifference from the general public. Their enemy was not just the government, but the "Burmafication" credo that got tacit approval from the Burmese majority. It is understandable, therefore, that minority groups did not rush to support the Saffron Rising.

[84] The actual degree of its violence is highly disputed, however. Naturally the SPDC calls it a terrorist organization, but this charge has no factual substantiation.

[85] "Unwanted and Unprotected: Burmese Refugees in Thailand," *Human Rights Watch*, Vol. 10, No. 6 (c) (September 1998), http://hrw.org/reports98/thai/Thai989-04.htm

[86] "EU Ratchets up Burmese Sanctions," *BBC News* (November 19, 2007), http://news.bbc.co.uk/go/pr/fr/-/2/hi/asia-pacific/7102033.stm

better or worse, the country is regaining its lost geopolitical stature of the early 1950s. This makes it the perfect test site for what Canada's foreign minister Maxime Bernier called a new "international realism," joining humanitarian concern with power politics.[87] This is synonymous with our "moral realism," and is the antithesis of both ASEANism and globalism as they relate to Burma.

SHOWDOWN AT THE SINGAPORE SUMMIT

Surprisingly, ASEAN itself seemed to be moving in the direction of moral realism in January 2007 when it set about framing a new charter that purportedly would uphold democracy and human rights as universal values. That turned out to be empty rhetoric. For ASEAN, as for globalists in general, Burma's cheap energy resources and other economic attractions trump democratic reformism.[88] Already close to 75 percent of Burma's exports go to ASEAN members. If that degree of "engagement" is not enough to give ASEAN political leverage, it is hard to imagine how much more would be required to get the job done.[89] In fact, the thrust of "engagement" has pushed in the opposite direction. Instead of ASEAN gaining influence over the Burmese generals, they have been pulling ASEAN's geoeconomic strings, much as the PRC has been pulling Washington's strings in the global arena.[90]

When Burma objected to the reform mandate of the proposed ASEAN Constitution, all enforcement provisions were removed. So too a scheduled summit briefing on the Burma crisis by UN envoy Ibrahim Gambari was cancelled, despite the fact that Gambari had shown himself to be the very model of appeasement in the midst of the Saffron Crackdown. Malaysian foreign minister Syed Hamid Said stated unabashedly that "Myanmar objected and we base our decisions on consensus."[91] Hence Burma was

---

[87] "Realism and Our Stand on Burma," *Canada.com* (November 19, 2007), http://www.canada.com/reginaleaderpost/news/viewpoints/story.html?id=93bb35d5-4793-4b15-99e0-8ec47afe39dc

[88] This fuel-economics interpretation was expressed by Subramanyam Chandrashekhar, director of the South Asia Analysis Group of New Delhi. See Cherian Thomas, *op. cit.*

[89] Wayne Arnold, "Surprise Pressure from Myanmar's Neighbors," *The New York Times* (November 20, 2007), http://www.nytimes.com/2007/11/20/world/asia/20asean.html

[90] For example, restrictions on the export of sensitive technologies with crucial military applications are being eased to please China and its US suppliers. See Steven R. Weisman, "Some China Firms Avoid U.S. Technology Transfer Licenses," *International Herald Tribune* (January 1, 2008), http://www.iht.com/bin/printfriendly.php?id=8978324

[91] "ASEAN Consensus U.N. Envoy's Briefing on Burma," *World News Australia* (November 20, 2007), http://naca.sbs.com.au/worldnewsaustralia/asean_cancels_un_envoy39s_briefing_on_burma_135353

allowed to decide whether any action against Burma was appropriate. Not to be outdone, ASEAN Secretary-General Ong Keng Yong served up the excuse that Gambari's presence would have been too much of a "distraction."[92] He then added, as if it had to be said, that ASEAN did not "want to come across as being too confrontational."[93]

To their credit, Washington and the EU did push in the opposite direction. The US trade representative Susan Schwab charged that the "reputation and credibility of ASEAN as an organization has been called into question because of the situation in Burma."[94] Only one ASEAN nation, the Philippines, stood apart. Since the Philippines is not known for its humanitarian priorities, it is obvious that some potent backroom pressure was applied by Washington to inspire this break from the ranks.[95] Just hours after the US criticized ASEAN over the Burma issue, Philippine President Gloria Macapagal Arroyo (of all people)[96] declared that Manila would not ratify the new charter if substantive action were not taken on the Burma crisis.[97]

Not surprisingly a very different stance was taken by Indonesia. It had already made its position toward Burma clear in February 2007 when it offered advanced training to Burmese military officers and even held out the possibility of joint military exercises between the two nations.[98] President Susilo Bambang Yudhoyono went so far as to declare that nothing would

---

[92] "ASEAN Says No to Gambari to Please Myanmar," *AsiaNews.it* (November 20, 2007), http://www.asianews.it/index.php?l=en+art=10849+geo=15+size=A

[93] "Southeast Asian Leaders Adopt Charter," *The New York Times* (November 20, 2007), http://www.nytimes.com/aponline/world/AP-Myanmar-Southeast-Asia.html

[94] Wayne Arnold, "Surprise Pressure from Myanmar's Neighbors," *op. cit.* A similar EU-ASEAN F.T.A. appeared to be stalled. See Norman Bordadora, *op. cit.* A cooperation agreement between the EU and ASEAN had been blocked ever since ASEAN admitted Burma as a member in July 1997. See "Myanmar," *Amnesty International Report 2000.*

[95] A year before the 2007 crackdown, US Ambassador to the U.N. John Bolton had pushed to get the Burma Crisis on the Security Council agenda. Previously there had been opposition to the mere discussion of the subject. See "U.S. Proposes adding Myanmar to U.N. Security Council Agenda," *Japan Policy & Politics* (September 4, 2006), http://findarticles.com/p/articles/mi_m0XPQ/is_2006_Sept_4/ai_n6704213

[96] Human rights advocates and Philippine opposition legislators have recently charged senior officials in Arroyo's administration with responsibility for the kidnapping, torture and murder of hundreds of political activists. See Carlos H. Conde, "Calls for Philippine Officials to Step Down over Killings," *The New York Times* (November 29, 2007), http://www.nytimes.com/2007/11/29/world/asia/ 29phils.html

[97] See Norman Bordadora, *op. cit.*

[98] "Indonesia to Offer Training for Myanmar Military Officers," *Kyodo News International* (February 19, 2007), http://www.findarticles.com/p/articles/mi_m0WDQ/is_2007_Feb_19/ai_n1862034

be done without the participation of China.[99] Giving China a de facto veto over pro-democracy and pro-Buddhist initiatives was an exercise in black humor, rather like putting Hitler in charge of a relief agency for Jewish refugees. Chinese Premier Wen Jia Bao put the final nail in the coffin by taking this occasion to praise what he regarded as the positive developments in Burma.[100]

No amount of moral exhortation will alter ASEAN's priorities. Its members are not going to endorse a pro-democracy movement in Burma or anywhere else unless it is manifestly in their geopolitical interest, for clearly they do not see it as being in their commercial interest. Our hope is that they are sufficiently concerned about the regional balance of power to eventually see that a counter-PRC initiative has power as well as virtue on its side. In that case they might toughen their stance, for no ASEAN nation, not even Burma under its present management, wants to become a Chinese vassal state.

To avert that dread prospect, the US will quietly be invited back as a balancing power in Southeast Asia. It would help enormously if Washington could repair its tattered image as a global force for good, not just for profit and power. Fortunately the choice is not between purely ethical and realist concerns. Burma offers the perfect locus for a post-realist compromise. The stance of America, India, and all democratic nations toward Burma will show how far they are willing to go for the principles they profess. This is where Senian "development as freedom" collides head-on with its authoritarian nemesis.[101]

There can be no doubt that the stakes in the ongoing Burma crisis are global in scope and carry profound implications for future international policy. Just as it is no longer feasible to treat geoeconomics in neoliberal purity, free from geopolitics, so too it is no longer possible to segregate geopolitics as an airtight policy zone, free of social, cultural and ethical inputs. Burma involves a geopolitics of hope as well as trepidation. The Saffron protesters of 2007 may have been tactically naïve, but they did succeed in putting Burma on the global map, if only as a question mark.

By trying to bury this issue, ASEAN exposed its own contribution to Burma's political catastrophe. The Singapore summit became an exercise

---

[99] "RI not to Join Other Nations in Imposing Sanctions on Myanmar," *Now Public* (November 22, 2007), http://www.nowpublic.com/politics/ri-not-join-other-nations-imposing-sanctions-myanmar

[100] "Southeast Asian Leaders Adopt Charter," *op. cit.*

[101] Concerning this global clash, see Songok Han Thornton and William H. Thornton, *Development Without Freedom: The Politics of Asian Globalization*, Aldershot, UK: Ashgate Publishing, 2008.

in craven appeasement—a Munich for our times—but its lasting message was what it failed to achieve. It could not snuff out the "Other Asia" that stepped forward in Burma in September 2007. Nor could it lend legitimacy to a decrepit dictatorship that finally, in a desperate bid for respectability, staged the pseudo-elections of November 2010.

Nothing could redeem the junta after Cyclone Nargis in May 2008. The generals not only refused international aid, but even prevented Burmese citizens from helping starving victims in the Irrawaddy Delta. This is a government that stuffs the coffers of its military elite while spending less than one percent of its budget on education and health care.[102] The Obama administration's plan to "engage" this regime, in perfect ASEAN style, will simply add fuel to the authoritarian fire. What Burma needs is open and sustained support for its democratic opposition. Here, as in China, globalist appeasement serves only to normalize oppression.

---

[102] Howard W. French, "Looking for Hope in Burma," *The New York Review of Books* (December 23, 2010), http://www.nybooks.com/articles/archives/2010/dec/23/looking-hope-burma/

6

INDO-GLOBALIZATION
India and the Crisis of
Asian Democracy

NEHRU'S LEGACY

Speaking at the Indian History Congress of 2007, 150 years after the Revolt of 1857, Kerala's chief minister V. S. Achuthanandan condemned the new imperialism that was engulfing India under the rubric of globalization.[1] His message could not have been more at odds with the globalist celebration that was staged the year before at the World Economic Forum in Davos. There the spotlight had been on Asia's rising titans, China and India, with rapt attention given to their two billion potential customers.[2] But it was China that stole the show, and since then it quite literally has been stealing globalization.

By the end of 2005 China had surpassed France, Italy, and Britain to become the world's fourth-largest economy, and in 2009 it overtook Germany to become the third largest. Finally, in 2010, it bypassed Japan as the second largest. Not surprisingly it is becoming the prime role model for the whole developing world, including India. Already the Singh administration has

---

[1] C. Gouridasan Nair, "India Sliding into Neo-Imperialism: VS," *The Hindu* (November 3, 2007), http://www.thehindu.com/2007/03/11/stories/2007031118170100.htm

[2] See Trudy Rubin, "India's Messy Democracy or China's Model of Economics?" *Journal Sentinel (JS) Online* (March 11, 2006), http://www.jsonline.com/story/index.aspx?id=407319

followed China's example in setting up special economic zones and waiving social protections. In 2008 China became India's major trade partner, though the present winners in Indo-globalization also include Western firms like Wal-Mart, Tesco, and Carrefour. The manifest losers are local businesses, common workers, and the environment.[3]

No one at Davos is going to mention that it is precisely China's economic success that cements social injustice and underwrites a sweeping crackdown on dissent. There is no hiding the fact that this vaunted development formula not only works despite its political defects, but may work even better because of them. That revelation would seem to put the economic efficacy of all democratic development in doubt. What must be stressed, however, is that the China model is not the incontrovertible success story it purports to be. The CCP depends upon continued "miracle" growth for its legitimacy, yet that same economic boom unleashes forces that make CCP leaders feel highly vulnerable.[4] In this respect the regime remains a median power, just as Gerald Segal depicted it in his classic study of China during the 1990s.

To be sure, much has changed since then, and now all of Asia is in a state of angst over what to do about the waking dragon next door. Does this mean that Segal was completely off the mark? In fact, his assessment would still be accurate if the exogenous factor of FDI had not come to China's rescue.[5] It is certainly not because of good governance, advanced technology, quality control, or even cheap labor that authoritarian China has managed to attract ten times more FDI than democratic India.[6] The unsavory truth is

---

[3] See Martine Bulard, "An Elephant Can Run Very Fast: India's Boundless Ambitions," *Le Monde Diplomatique* (January 2007), http://mondedeplo.com/2007/01/02india

[4] Susan Shirk, *China—Fragile Superpower: How China's Internal Politics Could Derail Its Peaceful Rise* (Oxford, UK: Oxford University Press, 2007), 269.

[5] As Segal put it, "China is a second-rank middle power that has mastered the art of diplomatic theater. . . . Only when we finally understand how little China matters will we be able to craft a sensible policy toward it." See Gerald Segal, "Does China Matter?" *Foreign Affairs* 78, no. 5 (September/October 1999): 24–36.

[6] With the third largest technical and scientific manpower in the world, India does better in these areas. In 2005, 40 percent of its FDI was in information technology, as opposed to China's 11 percent; and India's overall FDI has almost tripled from $5.5 billion in 2005 to $15.7 billion in the 2006–07 period. See Ch. Paramaiah and Vinod Anand, "Prospering India, But for Whom?" *Mainstream* (March 10, 2008), http://www.mainstreamweekly.net/article569.htm and Martine Bulard, *op. cit.* China's present problem may be the reverse of India's: a plethora of FDI, and for all the wrong reasons. Despite China's tight currency controls, "hot money" is pouring in. Even as the use of this money for fixed investment fell by 6 percent, net FDI inflow shot up by 60 percent between mid-2007 and mid-2008. The incentive, clearly, is speculative exploitation of the interest rate gap between dollars and yuan: 2 percent for the former as opposed to

that foreign investors and TNCs have a special affinity for a certain kind of dictatorial regime. In the case of China it is easy to see the bottom-line reasons for this preference. For those with the right connections (*guanxi*), labor and infrastructure needs are met without resistance or delay, and with no thought of human rights or environmental impact.

To compete on this level, Indian leaders feel pressed to put social and political development on hold. In our opinion this is a serious and unnecessary error. Already India's economy has been growing at an 8 percent rate, and a Goldman Sachs study predicts that within three decades India will be the number three economy in the world, after America and China.[7] Even that glowing projection may underrate India's prospect relative to China, for it misses the role of intangibles such as free democratic exchange. If Amartya Sen is right about the long-term economic advantage of democratic values and institutions,[8] India could outperform China in the next generation, especially in quality of living terms. That will not happen, however, if India trades in its democratic traditions for a growth formula borrowed from authoritarian China or neoliberal America.

Sadly, that substitution is already well under way. Development on these top-down terms all but abandons the 300 million Indians who subsist in abject poverty.[9] When the World Bank raised its official poverty line from the income level of $1 a day to $1.25 at 2005 purchasing power parity (PPP), the global poverty estimate shot up from 16 to 26 percent.[10] Meanwhile the Indian percentage almost doubled, jumping from 24.3 to 41.6. That puts India's official poverty figure at 456 million.[11] Indian academics can quibble

---

4 percent for the latter. Dollars are sucked in by the lure of this almost risk-free profit. But, of course, what pours in may also exit rapidly, as many Rim nations learned the hard way at the time of the 1997 Asian crash. India's slow pace of FDI growth could well be a blessing in disguise. Concerning China's hot money problem, see "Hot and Bothered," *The Economist* (June 26, 2008), http://www.economist.com/finance/PrinterFriendly.cfm?story_id=1639442

[7] Amrita Narlikar, "All that Glitters is not Gold: India's Rise to Power," *Third World Quarterly* 28, no. 5 (2007): 984 (983–96).

[8] Amartya Sen, *Development as Freedom* (New York: Alfred A. Knopf, 1999), 148.

[9] William H. Thornton and Songok Han Thornton, "The Price of Alignment: India in the New Asian Drama," *Journal of Developing Societies* 22, no. 4 (December 2006): 405 (401–20).

[10] Moreover, this startling reassessment was based on 2005 data which does not take into account the soaring food and energy prices that followed. See "An Even Poorer World," *The New York Times* (September 2, 2008), http://www.nytimes.com/2008/09/02/opinion/02tue3.html

[11] Raghav Gaiha, "Poverty of Statistics," *Outlook India* (September 15, 2008), http://www.outlookindia.com/fullprint.asp?choice=1&fodname=20080915&fname=Column+Raghav+%28F%29&sid=1

about this statistical adjustment, but the bottom line is that the country has higher malnutrition levels than sub-Saharan Africa.[12] One in three of the world's malnourished children lives here. Grinding poverty is rife even in Mumbai, the nation's financial capital, though the states of Kerala and Tamil Nadu do a better job of providing for basic needs.[13] This proves that while there are no easy solutions, policy does matter.

A recent World Health Organization report (*Closing the Gap in a Generation*, 2008) shows that the right social priorities rather than economic growth alone are of prime importance for closing the social gap in health and education. This effectively destroys the developmental premises of the Washington Consensus, where stress is put on the "trickle down" benefits of raw growth.[14] Unfortunately India is moving fast in the opposite direction: disowning the rich store of endemic values that have been the bedrock of its democratic tradition. A veritable academic industry now dedicates itself to selling economic liberalization. One such apologist for the New India, Sumit Ganguly, grants (in an understatement bordering on black humor) that globalization "has not lifted every household" and "reform has created losers as well as winners." Nonetheless he contends that democracy is "bolstered" by the nation's globalist transformation.[15]

What is missing from this neoliberal panegyric is any mention of globalization's broader effects, including an epidemic of farmer suicides, the spread of Maoist Naxalism across the rural heartland, and the recent spike of Muslim terrorism. The Indian press reports these events with little or no attention to their root causes. The same journalists who recently pressed for a massive financial sector bailout from the Reserve Bank of India (RBI) railed against the much smaller assistance being offered distressed farmers by the

---

[12] M. G. Srinath, "India Offers Students Free Midday Meals as Incentive to Stay in School," *Worldpress.org* (August 6, 2008), http://www.worldpress.org/print_article. cfm?article_id=3340&dont=yes

[13] Nirmala Lakshman, "Where are the Children?" *The Hindu* (August 15, 2007), http:// www.hinduonnet. com/af/india00/stories/2007081550250800.htm

The case of Kerala is especially significant since it lacks a large commercial and industrial base. However, Kerala too is being sucked into the remorseless engine of globalization. Under the throes of rising living costs, the state has come to depend largely on remittances from Keralites working abroad.

[14] See Peter Wilby, "Inequality Kills," *New Statesman* (September 4, 2008), http://www. newstatesman.com/society/2008/09/health-social-report-cuba

[15] Sumit Ganguly, "India's Unlikely Democracy: Six Decades of Independence," *Journal of Democracy* 18, no. 2 (April 2007): 37 (30–40); see also Ganguly's mentors Assema Sinha, *The India—A Divided Leviathan* (Bloomington, IL: Indiana University Press, 2004) and Rob Jenkins, *Democratic Politics and Economic Reform in India* (Cambridge, UK: Cambridge University Press, 1999).

finance ministry after years of almost total neglect.[16] How much damage these academic and journalistic evasions do to Indian democracy depends upon one's assessment of how much actual democracy there is to subvert. Some question how far India has ever gone beyond pro forma democratic regimes like Singapore under the PAP or Malaysia under United Malays National Organisation (UMNO).

To answer this question we must revisit the economic disaster zone of post-Independence India. Measured by any progressive yardstick, Nehru's India gets mixed reviews at best. Its principle of nonalignment rates admiration,[17] yet in practice Nehru did much to align India with the USSR. He seemed to think it was a choice between Soviet macroism and a Gandhian embargo on modern development. There was, indeed, an almost oedipal dimension to Nehru's love affair with Moscow. It seemed that to make room for his own project Nehru had to bury Gandhi's. India has been paying for that patricide ever since. The main casualty has been the "Other India"—the 800 million "have nots" who live very much as they did in Gandhi's day and who are airbrushed from global and local representations of "Shining India."[18] This readily dispensable "other"—the same "vast majority" that Michael Harrington described three decades before in his book of this title[19]—has been left behind by the major models of modernization and globalization alike.

One of the main beneficiaries of early Indian modernization was Nehru's family dynasty. We now know that Nehru's daughter Indira owed much of her political success to KGB assistance. A critical chapter in her rise to power was the Moscow-induced support her faction of the Congress Party got in 1969 from the Communist Party of India (CPI). What most Indians consider her greatest achievement—India's smashing success in its 14-day war with Pakistan—owed much to Soviet military assistance. Soviet cash flowed into her political coffers throughout her career, in return for which she danced to Moscow's music.[20]

---

[16] Devinder Sharma, "The Question to be Asked: 'Where will the Money Come From?'," *Dissident Voice* (October 14, 2008), http: www.dissidentvoice.org:80/2008/10/the-question-to-be-asked-"where-will-the-money-come-from"

[17] The Non-Aligned Movement (NAM) is commonly regarded as independent India's greatest contribution to world politics. See Prithvi Ram Mudiam, "The Nehruvian Model and the Post-Cold War World," *World Affairs* 10, no. 2 (Summer 2006): 36–46.

[18] Cynthia Fuchs Epstein and Howard Epstein, "Revisiting a Vast Majority: A Journal from India," *Dissent* (Summer 2008), http://dissentmagazine.org/article/?article=1227

[19] Michael Harrington, *The Vast Majority* (New York: Simon and Schuster, 1972).

[20] See Christopher Andrew and Vasili Mitrokhin, "Indira's India and the KGB," *Times Online* (September 17, 2005), http://www.timesonline.co.uk/printFriendly/0,,1-1461-1782367-1461,00.html

The Nehru legacy also included the "license raj" that well served India's political elite but sapped the country's commercial vitality and all but ensured its "Hindu rate of growth." It is somewhat ironic, therefore, that Nehruvian development harped on nothing so much as mega growth, which was to be achieved through that engine of chronic stagnation, Soviet-style central planning. The problem was that Nehru so feared religious extremism on the one hand and Gandhism on the other that he thought it necessary to personally dictate all high-level planning. Lacking the power within his party to pull this off, he shifted responsibility for economic policy to a planning commission that he could better control.[21]

Thus planning in India went its separate and utterly undemocratic way, rather as the Ministry of International Trade and Industry (MITI) did in Japan. Gunnar Myrdal traced the deeper roots of this cult of planning to the pre-Independence linkage of colonialism with *laissez faire* policies. The new nationalism inverted that association, as if to prove its postcolonial virtue by way of statist fiat.[22] It hardly mattered what impact this might have on the usually compliant underclass to which most Indians belong. The "Other India" knows modernization mainly as an instrument of neo-colonization.

A NOT-SO-SHINING INDIA

It is no surprise, then, that the benefits of today's Indo-globalization have bypassed those most in need: the nearly 70 percent of the work force that remains locked in agriculture,[23] most at a subsistence level. Only about 1.3 million of the total workforce (estimates range between 400 and 500 million, nine tenths of which work on the land or in local trades) have any real stake in India's new economy. While that globalized sector lifts the aggregate economy toward nearly double-digit growth, there will be little of China's labor-intensive industrialization to take up the slack as 70 million Indians enter the workforce over the next five years.[24] This will push the political system to a juncture where its neocolonial devices can no longer

---

[21] Sudipota Kaviraj, "Dilemmas of Democratic Development in India," in *Democracy and Development: Theory and Practice*, ed. Adrian Leftwich (Cambridge, UK: Polity Press, 1996), 117 (114–38).

[22] See Gunnar Myrdal, *Asian Drama: An Inquiry into the Poverty of Nations, Volume II* (New York: Pantheon, 1968), 722.

[23] Narlikar, *op. cit.*, 990.

[24] Pankaj Mishra, "Impasse in India," *The New York Review of Books* 54, no. 11 (June 28, 2007), http://www.nybooks.com/articles/20339

be camouflaged. Indian democracy will have to either fulfill some part of its egalitarian promise or revert to a politics of spiteful diversion.

Granted, the voting public has sometimes applied a brake to elitist governance, as when Prime Minister Indira Gandhi responded to mounting opposition by getting martial law declared in June 1975. That cost her the election of January 1977,[25] but more commonly the country's electoral rituals have well served its neocolonials by lending them badly needed legitimacy. Even nonalignment, Nehru's major claim to progressive standing, is now up for auction. Increasingly India blends the worst kind of Nehruvian macroism with a new globalist alignment. One result is an unprecedented land grab that leaves more and more small farmers jobless and homeless. The corporate-controlled media paints these changes as a bracing story of social progress, leading Arundhati Roy to declare Indian democracy "the biggest publicity scam of this century."[26]

The danger of this blanket indictment is that it could underrate, and thus fail to protect, what Indian democracy has done right. Amartya Sen gives the system due credit for preventing, by way of open information access and entitlement guarantees, the famines that were common under British rule.[27] And no less it deserves credit for a degree of religious and multicultural tolerance that is notoriously absent in most neighboring countries. Pakistan, Bangladesh, Nepal, and Sri Lanka have officially shackled democracy to reactionary religious hierarchies.[28]

Of course, India also slid in this direction in the 1990s under the lead of the BJP. The reelection of the infamous Narendra Modi as Gujarat's chief

---

Also, Pankaj Mishra, "The Myth of the New India," *The New York Times* (July 6, 2006), http://www.nytimes.com/2006/07/06/opinion/06mishra.html and Epstein and Epstein, *op. cit.*

[25] More recently, this same democratic brake was applied to the BJP's brand of Hindu politics. The relative absence of this brake in Pakistan suggests, by way of contrast, how crucial the Indian example is as a model for Third World development. See William H. Thornton, *New World Empire: Civil Islam, Terrorism, and the Making of Neoglobalism* (Lanham, MD: Rowman and Littlefield, 2005), 104–11.

[26] Quoted in Atul Cowshish, "Arundhati Roy Denounces Indian Democracy," *Asian Tribune* (July 6, 2006), http://www.asiantribune.com/inbox.php?q=node/937

[27] Sen stresses, however, that this salutary role of democratic freedom is by no means unique to India, for "there has never been a famine in a functioning multiparty democracy." Sen, *Development as Freedom, op. cit.*, 169, 178, and 180.

[28] Mukul Kesavan, "India's Model Democracy," *BBC News* (August 15, 2007), http://news.bbc.co.uk/go/pr/fr/-/2/hi/south_aisa/6943598.stm

Sen underscores India's native propensity for religious and ethnic tolerance. See especially *The Argumentative Indian*, and for his rebuttal to cultural imperialists like Niall Ferguson see his "Imperial Illusions," *The New Republic* (December 31, 2007), http://www.tnr.com/bookstarts/story.html?id= 21fc429e-2d7d-4e4d-9009-4603a9857f47

minister shows that the danger is still very much alive and well. In the name of *Hindutva*—a Hindu equivalent of Nazi *Völkergemeinschaft*—the BJP and its Sangh Parivar cohorts peddle an ironically European strain of national identity. If the whole country buys this package, it will ignite a civil war very much like the one that long raged in Sri Lanka. A sample of that grim prospect was provided by the Gujarat atrocities of February and March 2002. Under cover of Washington-inspired anti-terrorism, Hindu purists such as Modi, and even ex-prime minister Atal Bihari Vajpayee, condoned Hindutva and tacitly endorsed a ghastly mixture of business and massacre.[29]

India's electorate got the point and in May 2004 booted the BJP out. *Hindutva*, however, was only half of what many voters thought they were rejecting. Their other target was the BJP's myth of a globalist "Shining India." To the dismay of those who thought they were electing Sonia Gandhi (the widow of Rajiv Gandhi, Indira's son) as prime minister, the other India found itself saddled with the arch-globalist Manmohan Singh. Even Congress Party MPs were stunned,[30] and their Communist allies in the UPA ruling coalition had reason to feel betrayed.

It was Singh who, as Narasimha Rao's finance minister, had been the chief architect of India's globalist turn of the early 1990s. Now he was back in full stride, along with his own finance minister Palaniappan Chidambaram, architect of the neoliberal "dream budget" of 1997.[31] As a board member of Vedanta (the infamous multinational mining company that is presently raping Orissa's environment), Chidambaram is the very archetype of today's colonial plunder. His vision of development includes the virtual forced migration of five hundred million Indians from the countryside into cities. This is part of the unprecedented land grab that Arundhati Roy calls the reversal of post-independence land reform.[32] Singh and his lieutenants must be credited with an amazing feat of political alchemy: the conversion of a clear anti-globalist mandate into yet another victory for "market democracy."

---

[29] Mishra, "Impasse in India," *op. cit.*

[30] See Amy Goodman [interview with Arundhati Roy], "Arundhati Roy on the Indian Elections, Her Support for the Iraqi Resistance & the Privatization of War," *Democracy Now* (May 19, 2004), http://www.democracynow.org/2004/5/19/arundhati_roy_on_the_indian_elections

[31] "What's Holding India Back?" *The Economist* (March 6, 2008), http://www.economist.com/opinion/PrinterFriendly.cfm?story_id=10808493

[32] Arundhati Roy, "Is There Life After Democracy?" *Dawn.com* (July 5, 2009), http://news.dawn.com/wps/wcm/connect/dawn-content-library/dawn/news/world/06-is-there-life-after-democracy-rs-07

This virtual coup d'état got almost no critical comment from Western media. Singh would go as the belle of the ball to the World Economic Forum, while the world press treated his hostile takeover as an unambiguous triumph over BJP fascism. The most trenchant critique of Indo-globalism has come in the form of rural meltdown. In little more than two decades there have been over 180,000 farmer suicides,[33] each one amounting to a "vote" on what globalization means for the other India. By no accident these suicides are more frequent where agriculture is most modernized, forcing farmers to pay lenders unaffordably high prices for seeds, fertilizers, and pesticides.[34] In a country with more indigenous billionaires than any except the US, one in three of the 1.1 billion population subsists on less than $1 per day.[35] These are not the wages of substantive democracy, or even sustainable plutocracy. More from desperation than from urban hope, millions are flocking to cities which are already straining to house their exploding underclasses. Most who are lucky enough to find steady work will end up in illegal and hence dangerous tenement houses,[36] light years removed from the Shining India we associate with double-digit growth.

Indian governance is trapped in a no-man's-land of too much and too little. The state is at once too invasive to satisfy global investors yet too weak or indifferent to give much relief to those in distress—most notably

---

[33] Roy, "Is There Life After Democracy?" *op. cit.* A more conservative estimate puts the figure at something over 150,000 in two decades. See "Write-Offs as High as an Elephant's Eye," *The Economist* (March 6, 2008), http://www.economist.com/world/asia/PrinterFriendly.cfm?story_id=10809412

[34] Sue Bolton, "India: Socialists Call for People's Resistance, Left Resurgence," *Green Left Weekly*, no. 736 (January 23, 2008), http://www.greenleft.org.au/2008/736/38121

[35] Kevin Watkins, "When Globalization Leaves People Behind," *The International Herald Tribune* (February 12, 2006), http://www.iht.com/articles/2006/02/12/opinion/edwatkins.php

This figure was actually optimistic. Some reports estimate that half the population survives on far less. See Somini Sengupta, "Economic Boom Fails to Generate Optimism in India," *The New York Times* (August 16, 2007), http://www.nytimes.com/2007/08/16/world/asia/16india.html

Conservative estimates show 700 million living on less than $2 per day. See Kirsty Hughes, "India's Poverty: Help the Poor Help Themselves," *International Herald Tribune* (May 9, 2005), http://p://www.iht.com/articles/2005/05/08/opinion/edhughes.php and Satya Sivaraman, "Development-India: Democracy in Conflict with Free Market Policy," *IPS News* (January 24, 2008), http://ipsnews.net/news.asp?idnews=40900 and "Rural Poverty in India," *Rural Poverty Portal.org* (updated April 2, 2007), http://www.ruralpovertyportal.org/english/regions/asia/ind/index.htm

[36] Lydia Polgreen, "New Arrivals Strain India's Cities to Breaking Point," *The New York Times* (November 30, 2010), http://www.nytimes.com/2010/12/01/world/asia/01delhi.html

the 200 million Dalits of the scheduled classes. The quotas that helped lift some of these "untouchables" out of dire poverty are now sought by new waves of economic casualties.[37] They have a point, for the country's most grating social divisions are no longer those of caste, religion, or tribe, but of the burgeoning income gap. Globalized India will sink or swim by how well it negotiates the coming clash between haves and have-nots. Perhaps Amartya Sen is right about the end of literal famines, but no country in the world has so much malnutrition as India.[38] With 50 percent of Indian children underfed,[39] even as the nation exports cereal, talk of a "Shining India" is just another way of saying "let them eat cake."

COLLISION COURSE

Such crushing deprivation puts the other India on a collision course with the power elite, for this is a country where even the poor have ubiquitous voting habits.[40] One thing that has helped contain radical impulses is the conservatism of village communities. This helps to explain why, until recently, there was less violence here than in urban lower class life.[41] More than in most developing countries, India's ancient villages have managed to hold their own in the face of modern culture shock. Urbanites tend to view traditional rural structures (known in the stifling professional lingo as ILGIs, or "informal local governance institutions") as simply backward and oppressive. But some studies have noted their valuable supplementary role in India's "messy" democracy.[42] Whatever their other merits or defects, "ILGIs" do function as violence inhibitors. Globalization is fast dismantling these bulwarks of social restraint. While many insolvent farmers end up in urban ghettos, others are cast into an even deeper rural penury. These castaways become the "free radicals" of an increasingly volatile rural meltdown.

The BJP ingeniously defuses this social time bomb by way of an old colonial trick: substituting religious venom for class war. One of the

---

[37] Somini Sengupta, "Crusader Sees Wealth as Cure for India Caste Bias," *The New York Times* (August 30, 2008), http://www.nytimes.com/2008/08/30/world/asia/30caste.html

[38] Watkins, *op. cit.*

[39] Martine Bulard, *op. cit.*

[40] Ashutosh Varshney, "India's Democratic Challenge," *Foreign Affairs* 86, no. 2 (March/April, 2007): 94 (93–106).

[41] Kripa Ananth Pur, "Rivalry or Synergy? Formal and Informal Local Governance in Rural India," *Development and Change* 38, no. 3 (2007): 407 (401–21).

[42] *Ibid.*, 414.

party's most horrific elders, Lal Krishna Advani, is still its main decider, and globalists who find the present government too "social democratic" can once more reach out to the BJP for a business-friendly corrective.[43] It is uncertain how long the Congress party can cap social tensions, since it has no religious card to play against growing social unrest. Already Maoist Naxalites control much of the countryside. In Orissa, for example, 10 out of 30 districts were under Naxal control by 2005.[44] As insurrection spreads in the poorest regions, Prime Minister Singh has more than once declared Naxalite violence the nation's most pressing crisis, even worse than sectarian violence in Kashmir.

Talk of a rising India almost always omits reference to Naxalism. If it is mentioned at all, it is treated as the source of the rural problem rather than its most glaring symptom. The question is whether this radical energy can be rechanneled into the democratic fold. Officially the Naxalites call for a "democratic" revolution, but not by democratic means. Indians are closely watching the long-term effects of the Maoist electoral victory of 2008 in Nepal. A key question is whether it amounts to a step forward or backward in democratic terms. Maoists, after all, were instrumental in toppling Nepal's 250-year royal order. Will their present success afford a sustained democratic opening or signal a new authoritarian turn? If moderate political parties are sidelined in Nepal, a dark lesson will be drawn. If not, the question will be why India cannot reach a similar rapprochement with its Naxalites.

Perhaps to avert panic—or to ward off the prospect of having to really confront rural poverty and social injustice—India's home minister Shivraj Patil claimed that the Naxal problem affected only 2 percent of the country's villages and that violence was under control everywhere except Chhattisgarh.[45] In fact the conflict is also rampant in West Bengal, Jharkhand, Bihar, and Orissa. In many cases security forces have been reduced to merely "holding the fort," and even that is sometimes impossible. In Orissa the police were forced to vacate 12,000 out of 30,000 posts, and in several districts they prudently refused to wear their uniforms.

---

[43] J. Sri Raman, "A Shadow Prime Minister on a 'Strategic Partnership," *Truthout* (March 28, 2008), http://www.truthout.org/docs_2006/printer_032808T.shtml

[44] Prafulla Das, "A Naxalite Corridor," *Frontline* 22, no. 14 (July 2–15, 2005), http://www.hinduonnet.com/fline/fl2214/stories/20050715002403700.htm

[45] "Naxal Menace Should not be Exaggerated: Shivraj Patil," *The Times of India* (March 20, 2008), http://timesofindia.indiatimes.com/Naxal_menance_should_not_be_exaggerated_Shivraj_Patil/articleshow/2882465.cms and Nihar Nayak, "Naxalites Resolve to Focus on Urban Areas," *IDSA: Institute for Defense Studies & Analyses* (March 6, 2007), http://www.idsa.in/publications/stratcomments/NiharNayak060307.htm

Matters are indeed worse in Chhattisgarh, where 16 of the state's 20 police districts are deemed Naxalite-infested. Officially there were 531 armed incidents and 413 deaths here In 2007.[46] Police must often post 24-hour sentries in machine gun watchtowers, constantly scanning the area with searchlights at night. In just one raid, in March 2007, 55 security personnel were killed.[47] But the real victims are villagers trapped in a no-man's-land between the Naxalites and the hired militia. A government-funded paramilitary organization, *Salwa Judum*, drives citizens into camps, destroying their homes, crops, and livestock so as to leave them no choice but to cooperate. Meanwhile the Maoists attack the camps to force them to flee. Hundreds have been killed in this crossfire in Chhattisgarh alone, and some estimates put *Salwa Judum* victims in the thousands.[48]

Patil's dismissive attitude is belied by the government's new offensive, Operation Green Hunt, which was launched in October 2010. 50,000 troops are now battling the rebels in five states.[49] By understating the Naxal reach, Patil had unwittingly downplayed the rural trauma that fuels it. This was a gift to the Naxalite cause, for the main culprits behind India's rural nightmare are poverty and concomitant social injustice. Emphatically this is not just a law enforcement issue, and Green Hunt is no solution. So far the most robust assistance measure for the millions who have lost their land and their livelihood has been the National Rural Employment Guarantee Scheme (NREGS). This provides 100 days of employment per year at the minimum wage of about a dollar per day for each rural household. Paltry as that seems to be, it can make the difference between subsistence and starvation. As of April 2008 NREGS was expanded to cover the whole nation, making it one of the world's biggest development projects.[50] Unfortunately the program is most desperately needed in areas with the worst government, so it is sure to founder in mismanagement and corruption.[51]

---

[46] Prem Shankar Jha, "The State as Landlord," *Outlook India* (March 17, 2008), http://www.outlookindia.com/author.asp?id=subsection&name=Prem+Shankar+Jha&subsection=Opinion&section=National

[47] Nitin Mahajan, "Taking on Naxalas: Both Hands Tied: Part one Chhattisgarh," *The Indian Express* (February 24, 2008), http://www.indianexpress.com/printerFriendly/276456.html

[48] Nandini Sundar, "It's Not Just War," *Outlook India* (March 24, 2008), http://www.outlookindia.com/www.outlookindia.com/author.asp?name=Nandini+Sundar

[49] "India Maoist Rebels 'Killed in Gunbattle," BBC News (January 28, 2011), http://www.bbc.co.uk/news/world-south-asia-12304693

[50] Mian Ridge, "India's Jobs Plan Goes Nationwide," *The Christian Science Monitor* (April 8, 2008), http://www.csmonitor.com/2008/0408/p06s02-wosc.html

[51] Jill McGivering, "Is India's Rural Poverty Plan Working?" *BBC News* (April 22, 2006), http://news.bbc.co.uk/go/pr/fr/-/2/hi/south_asia/4927436.stm

There are, however, more dubious programs on the drawing board. For example, Chidambaram has proposed that the debts of 30 million small farmers simply be cancelled. This has the putative advantage of bypassing the usual bureaucratic labyrinth, but it will be extremely costly, at one percent of India's GNP. Moreover, it will serve only those who were well enough off to get loans in the first place.[52] The primary beneficiaries will be banks that otherwise would never have been repaid for their bad loans.

Granted, some belated assistance is also being allocated in the areas of education and health care. As of 2005 the education budget was raised substantially, and the dearth of rural medicine was addressed by a health spending hike from 1 to 3 percent of national income.[53] These programs are minuscule, however, in comparison to the scope of the rural crisis. Though Naxalism is the direct product of social injustice, so far the government's main response has been counter-terrorism rather than serious economic redress. A prime weapon in this rural class war is the militia movement, which tellingly gets equal support from the BJP and the Congress party. That unlikely alliance makes sense when it is considered that both are agents of India's economic liberalization. Even *Salwa Judum* can be seen as a byproduct of globalization insofar as it specializes in containing the resistance that globalist policies generate.

In March 2007 the pseudo-Left government of West Bengal paid militia units to perpetrate one of the worst non-religious pogroms of recent times: the Nandigram massacre. Villagers who dared to resist land appropriations for a special economic zone (SEZ) were put under siege. Fourteen died when police stormed the village barricades.[54] Resistance became so intense that authorities refused to go near the place. Roads and bridges were sabotaged, cutting the whole area off from the outside world.[55] Finally West Bengal had to suspend the operation.[56]

More often state governments suspend negotiation and the rule of law. This recourse to state terror rather than social welfare is a panic response that guarantees the Naxalites all the recruits they need.[57] Already the movement controls about 20 percent of India's forests, and in recent years it has

---

[52] "What's Holding India Back?" *op. cit.*

[53] "Naxal Menace Should not be Exaggerated: Shivraj Patil," *op. cit.*

[54] Leah Temper and Joan Martinez-Alier, "Is India Too Poor to be Green?" *Economic and Political Weekly* 42, no. 17 (April 28, 2007): 1490 (1489–92).

[55] Rajesh Narayanan, "Nandigram Carnage: A Black Chapter in Indian History," *Merinews* (March 23, 2007), http://www.merinews.com/catFull.jsp?articleID=124554&c atID=2&category=India&rtFlg=rtFlg

[56] Temper and Martinez-Alier, "Is India Too Poor to be Green?" *op. cit.*, 1492.

[57] Curiously, the BJP, which has specialized in anti-Muslim state terrorism, has come out against the kind of brutal police action that was seen at Nandigram. See *Ibid.*

been extending its reach at the rate of about two districts per week,[58] largely in reaction to SEZ land seizures and the environmental carnage of mega-mining. At this point it would be hard for the government to shift to a reform strategy, because tribal communities have seen it all before: amelioratory laws that were passed but never enforced. False promises have soured the rural poor on the whole democratic process, pushing them into the waiting arms of Naxalite organizers.

THE STRANGE ECLIPSE
OF CLASS-FOCUSED POLITICS

Even as the modernization of Indian agriculture reduces employment per unit of output, the rural population is exploding. Shunting surplus labor into cities will simply convert a rural crisis into an urban one, for few of these migrants will be able to secure adequate employment. Those who cannot will have to resort to either crime or begging, and the government's present crackdown on begging will only promote crime. One of the most unsavory aspects of the new economism has been this tendency to target the poor rather than poverty itself.

New Delhi, for example, has a special Beggar's court empowered to prosecute indigents even when no crime has been committed. It gives one to ten year sentences simply for having no visible means of livelihood. Ten years is what a violent felon would get in a regular court. Those who are blind or otherwise seriously handicapped, and therefore unemployable, can effectively get a life sentence. Though begging has been a crime here since 1961, it was rarely punished before, partly because mendicancy has a place in the country's religious tradition. This new breed of "justice" was supposed to help Delhi achieve a polished look prior to the city's hosting of the Commonwealth Games in 2010.[59]

Similar clean-up operations, which often target Muslim communities, are in progress in most major cities.[60] In 2005 a large number of Mumbai's

---

[58] Das, *op. cit.*

[59] Mian Ridge, "New Delhi Cleanup Sends in the Beggar Raid Teams," *Christian Science Monitor* (March 4, 2008), http://www.csmonitor.com/2008/0304/p01s03-wosc.html

[60] Indiscriminate arrests have compounded the prejudice Muslims already suffered in terms of healthcare, education, and job opportunities. The direct result is the rise of the "Indian Mujahideen," whose terrorism is inwardly focused, with little connection to Al Qaeda or other outside organizations. See Mark Sappenfield, "India Faced with Home-Grown Terrorism," *Christian Science Monitor* (September 26, 2008), http://www. csmonitor.com/2008/0926/p07s02-wosc.html

lower class neighborhoods were razed, rendering 400,000 people homeless.[61] Meanwhile, just outside the city, large tracts of actively farmed but officially "unproductive" land were seized by the state government for conversion into SEZs, pushing still more ex-farmers into the city. In effect the state was serving as a broker for private investors, most notably Reliance Industries Limited (RIL). Knowing that land values would skyrocket once an SEZ materialized, RIL got farmers evicted while the cost was still dirt cheap. Sonia Gandhi and at least two national ministers declared, to no effect, that farmland should never be seized for SEZs.[62] Nor has there been any better result from grassroots protest actions like hunger strikes and demonstrations. One such demonstration, in September 2006, brought out 35,000 farmer protestors, with no result whatsoever.

Corporate land grabs have been taking place all across India. Around 220 SEZs were set up between 2000 and 2007,[63] with another 250 on the drawing board in 21 states.[64] Meanwhile mining companies have been seizing land throughout the mineral belt of Northeast and Central India. The social and environmental impact of these operations reaches far beyond the range of actual land seizure. Their primary victims tend to be Adivasis—indigenous tribal people who comprise about 8 percent of the national population (22 percent in Orissa)[65] but suffer 55 percent of the evictions. They seldom have any legal recourse, since they have no formal title to the land and forests of their ancestors.[66]

India's rural crisis has reached such a scale that the usual Naxalite question must be reversed. Instead of asking how the movement became so widespread, we should wonder why it is not wider still. And why did it subside for a long period? What we are now witnessing is its second coming. The original Naxalite upsurge began as a radical socialist rebellion in West Bengal in 1967. Though it was stoked by members of the Communist Party of India (Marxist), or CPI(M), it was brutally crushed by a West Bengal government that itself was under CPI(M) leadership. That betrayal led to one of many schisms that have marred the Indian Left.

One of the most radical Naxal branches took shape in Andhra Pradesh under the People's War Group, or PWG. Led by Kondapalli Seetharamaiah,

---

[61] Hughes, *op. cit.*

[62] Dionne Bunsha, "Rural Resistance," *Frontline—India's National Magazine* 23 (20, October 7–20, 2006), http://www.flonnet.com/fl2320/stories/20061020004700900.htm

[63] Joan Martinez-Alier and Leah Temper, "When Development and Tradition Clash," *International Herald Tribune* (April 27, 2007), http://www.iht.com/articles/2007/04/27/opinion/edalier.php

[64] Nayak, *op. cit.*

[65] Das, *op. cit.*

[66] Martinez-Alier and Temper, "When Development and Tradition Clash," *op. cit.*

the PWG sought to merge in 1980 with 40 or so Naxalite factions, but the more grassroots and uncompromising Maoist Communist Centre (MCC) made this impossible. The two groups vied with each other until armed clashes erupted between them in the late 1990s. Naxalites remember the 1998–99 period as their "black chapter."[67] A cease-fire was declared in January 2000, and in September 2004 the MCC and PWG finally united to form the formidable CPI (Maoist).

Only the social ravages of globalization could have brought about this remarkable merger. The political system can no longer hide its neocolonial stripes. Worse still, the system includes many "Left" affiliates like the "communist" government of West Bengal. Granted, the hard lesson of Nandigram taught Chief Minister Buddhadeb Bhattacharjee to use less brazen tactics. His Left Front government now tries to mediate industrial disputes between corporations and land holders. But while landed farmers and absentee landlords may get some compensation, sharecroppers and other agricultural workers are not so fortunate.

This negotiated-settlement approach was recently put to the test in the case of a Tata Motors project in Singur, West Bengal. Tata was building a plant to manufacture the Nano, the world's cheapest car, but wanted to do it on the world's cheapest land. A genuine (if rather nuanced) Leftist, the Trinamool Congress chief Mamata Banerjee, accused the "communist" ruling party of compelling 2,000 farmers to sell their land against their will. For the first time in thirty years of Left Front rule, the West Bengal government felt compelled to really negotiate a land decision with the opposition. There was symbolic significance, also, in the presence of the fair-minded Governor Gopalkrishna Gandhi, the grandson of Mahatma Gandhi.[68] Unfortunately Gandhi was powerless, and Bhattacharjee let it be known that he intended to continue the Tata project "at any cost."[69] What turned the tables against Bhattacharjee was not the negotiation process, which he could easily control, but the prospect of Naxal-style retaliation if the land theft proceeded. Citing safety concerns, Tata Motors decided to move production elsewhere.[70]

---

[67] K. V. Kurmanath, "PW, MCC Put 'Black Chapter' Behind," *The Hindu Business Line* (October 16, 2004), http://www.thehindubusinessline.com/2004/10/16/stories/2004101602181700.htm

[68] Raktima Bose, "People Betrayed, Alleges Mamata," *The Hindu* (September 17, 2008), http://www.theindu.com/2008/09/17/stories/2008091756331300.htm

[69] "Singur is an Exception: Buddhadeb," *The Hindu* (September 11, 2008), http://www.theindu.com/2008/09/11/stories/2008091160881200.htm

[70] "India: Automaker Abandons Site," *The New York Times* (October 4, 2008), http://www.nytimes.com/2008/10/04/world/asia/04briefs-AUTOMAKERABA_BRF.html

In his frustration, Bhattacharjee admitted that the project's prime supporters were "the educated youth" who stood to benefit from the industrial restructuration of society.[71] Perhaps "Nanofication" would be a better word. For this rising bourgeois class, the issue of socioeconomic justice is out of fashion. Class-driven discourse has given way to identity politics, despite the fact that income disparity has been climbing exponentially.[72] As in Marx's day, the lower classes themselves have little comprehension of the forces behind their privation. Those who make it out of poverty tend to identify with higher social ranks, breaking all association with those they left behind. For example, the Dalit writer Chandra Bhan Prasad, a former Maoist, now sings the praises of the new economy.[73] The rural poor have a choice of two psychological exist doors: *Sangh Parivar* machinations, on the one side, or Naxal indoctrination on the other.

Apart from a few stalwart radicals, who resist globalization and stubbornly defy India's warming toward Washington, the Left Front has found it efficacious to strike an anti-BJP alliance with the pro-globalist Congress Party. This marriage of convenience was seriously jeopardized by Singh's nuclear rapprochement with Washington. For him the deal represented not just a crucial step toward India's energy security, but also a mark of its geopolitical maturity.[74] He had to tread carefully, however, so as to avoid a forced election in the midst of a severe food crisis. With over half of all Indians living on less than $2 per day, nuclear deals and multilateral agreements have little voter appeal. The UPA governing coalition had a shock in May 2008 when the BJP won elections in the southern state of Karnataka. This was Congress's ninth loss out of eleven state elections since January 2007, and it left no doubt that the BJP's power was migrating south.[75]

---

[71] "Singur is an Exception: Buddhadeb," *op. cit.*

[72] Andre Beteille, "The Paradox of Democracy," *The Times of India* (June 27, 2008), http://timesofindia.com/Editorial/The_Paradox_Of_Democracy/articleshow/3169607.cms

A similar shift can be been seen in the Indian academic world, where class issues have been largely superseded by a combination of poststructural and postcolonial (PSPC) theory. Marxism or any other class-focused analysis is not just marginalized by PSPC, but almost proscribed. This blackout has been as strongly enforced by the nominal "Left" as by the globalist Right. The result is a generational divide whereby academics who took their graduate training after the 1970s tend to be indifferent to the class divisions that are ripping India apart. See Vivek Chibber, "On the Decline of Class Analysis in South Asian Studies," *Critical Asian Studies* 38, no. 4 (2006): 358 (357–87).

[73] Sengupta, "Crusader Sees Wealth as Cure for India Caste Bias," *op. cit.*

[74] Smita Gupta, "One Man on an Island," *Outlook India* (July 7, 2008), http://www.outlookindia.com/full.asp?fodname=20080707&fname=Cover+Story+%28F%29&sid=1

[75] Mian Ridge, "India at an Impasse over Civilian Nuclear Deal," *The Christian Science Monitor* (June 26, 2008), http://www.csmonitor.com/2008/0626/p07s02-wosc.html

The BJP resurrection has been a factor in the spate of anti-Christian riots across the country. These began in Orissa in August 2008, in response to the murder of a Hindu priest. Although Maoist Naxalites claimed responsibility for the crime, the Bajrang Dal (a youth wing of the *Vishwa Hindu Parishad*, or VHP) preferred to blame local Christians, and took revenge by burning their churches and homes. Tens of thousands have fled to refugee camps. By September the pogram had spread to the states of Madhya Pradesh, Kerala, and Karnataka,[76] and became even more intense in some parts of Orissa. In the Kandhamal district, 80 churches and prayer houses were torched, along with 1,400 Christian homes, making for another 13,500 refugees. Those who did not escape were savagely beaten and often killed.[77] By targeting Christians rather than combative Muslims or Naxalites, the BJP has found a perfect scapegoat. In nearly all these cases the real motive has less to do with religion than with jealous rage over the opportunities that converted Christians can obtain through church-provided educational programs. The worse the general economic climate becomes, the more this rage is inflamed.[78]

Even as Singh's centrist politics comes under assault from the religious Right, his UPA affiliates on the Left have been turning against him, irate over his nuclear deal with Washington. His leadership was dramatically saved when a regional Left party, the Samajwadi (famous for its best-known lawmaker, the "bandit queen"), suddenly swung its support to the UPA, making for the Congress victory of July 22, 2008.[79] Singh's standing was further restored after the NSG gave a green light to his nuclear deal in September.[80] Nonetheless the UPA crisis of 2008 underscored the nation's fractured perspective on the direction it should take at home and abroad. More than at any time since its independence, India seems to have lost its way. There is some irony in the fact that it could suffer this vertigo exactly as it emerges as a global power.

---

[76] Mian Ridge, "Anti-Christian Attacks Flare in India," *The Christian Science Monitor* (September 24, 2008), http://www.csmonitor.com/2008/0924/p07s03-wosc.html

[77] Hari Kumar and Heather Timmons, "Violence in India is Fueled by Religious and Economic Divide," *The New York Times* (September 4, 2008), http://www.nytimes.com/2008/09/04/world/asia/04chrstians.html

[78] *Ibid.*

[79] See "RPT-Samajwadi Who? All Eyes on India Regional Party," *Reuters* (July 3, 2008), http://www.reuters.com/article/latestCrisis/idUSSP250451

[80] Smita Gupta, "Man in the Core," *Outlook India* (September 22, 2008), http://www.outlookindia.com/fullprint.asp?choice=1&fodname=20080922&fname=Cover

The political Left finally stood up against Congress's neocolonial estab-lishment,[81] but not on behalf of the poor. Its main target was Singh's US relations. The poor ended up with even less representation than before. So long as the Left Front's cooperation was critical to UPA rule, some degree of class counterpoint was exerted domestically. However, after the Samajwadi Party came aboard, allowing the UPA to survive without CPI(M) backing, the Left in general was thrown into political exile. Whether Congress retains power or is replaced by the BJP, the clear victor will be unreformed globalization.

CAN INDO-GLOBALIZATION
BE DEMOCRATIZED?

It is our contention that a much reformed Indo-globalization—one that charts its own moral course, independent of both American and Chinese models—could lay the foundation for a global Third Way. First, though, India must get its own house in order. That means coming to terms with its Naxal and Hindu excesses, which are the result of having forgotten the lessons of Gandhism. Anti-Naxalite policies that amount to state terrorism have pushed the nation close to civil war in at least ten Indian states.[82] The Maoist success in Nepal puts India under pressure to justify its blanket clo-sure toward Naxalism. The use of outlaw militias has been a grave mistake, rather like trying to extinguish a fire with gasoline.

Of course, the Naxalites invited this venomous reaction through their own cult of violence, which systematically inverts Gandhian ethics. They consider the message of the Mahatma nothing but "a cruel hoax perpetrated on a gullible, long-suffering, population..."[83] From this Naxal vantage the two largest communist parties have been shamefully coopted by the neo-colonial establishment, and unfortunately there is much empirical basis for that conclusion. Communist legislators often refrain from contesting the neoliberal drift of the Congress Party, while Congress in turn declines

---

[81] Recognizing that the Congress and UPA base was shrinking, the CPI(M) General Secretary Prakash Karat vowed to openly challenge the Congress, but the BJP had good reason to celebrate this action. See "We'll Vote Against the UPS Government," *Outlook India* (July 14, 2008), http://www.outlookindia.com/fullprint.asp?choice=&fodname=20 080714&fname=Cover+Story+%28F%29&sid=2

[82] Somini Sengupta, "India Maoists Kill 49 in Raid on Police Post," *The New York Times* (March 16, 2007), http://www.nytimes.com/2007/03/16/world/asia/16india.html

[83] Rabinchra Ray, *The Naxalites and Their Ideology* (New Delhi: Oxford University Press, 2002), second edition, xv.

to challenge even the most caustic Communist actions, such as the pro-globalist warlordism of West Bengal's CPI(M).[84] This quid pro quo leaves no doubt in the minds of Naxalites that the parliamentary deck is stacked against the poor.

With the state governments of West Bengal, Tripura, and Kerala under CPI(M) management, and with none consistently at odds with Congress party globalism, Maoists see themselves as the only authentic Left.[85] The government seems to confirm that judgment by denying Naxalites the tolerance shown other Left parties. Their brand of communism is banned in some states, and their members are everywhere subject to secret arrest under today's equivalent of the old black laws. This departure from the nation's liberal tradition could easily metastasize, for members of any opposition organization can now be tagged "Maoist" and arrested.[86] What is really under assault, therefore, is Indian pluralism. It must be asked how long India's social and political diversity can survive the homogenizing gauntlet of globalization.

Notwithstanding the horrors of the Naxal crisis, there is ground for hope on the side of democratic Left resistance. Consider the decisive gains of the communists in state legislatures in mid-2006, even as the nation was celebrating its newfound capitalist stardom.[87] The "other India" is standing its ground at countless local flashpoints. A good example was a protest at Gurgaon, a town in northern Haryana that is well-known as the home of the Great Mall, an icon of upscale consumerism. For "Old Gurgaon" to make its stand here, of all places, gave symbolic power to the event.

As has happened in so many Chinese protests, the Indian police responded harshly and even brutally, but there was a cardinal difference. Here it all ended up on prime time news in New Delhi.[88] Time will

---

[84] Martha C. Nussbaum, "Violence on the Left: Nandigram and the Communists of West Bengal," *Dissent* (Spring 2008), http://dissentmagazine.org/article//article=1157

[85] Bolton, *op. cit.*

[86] "Civil Liberties and People's Movements under Attack in India: The 'Maoist' Scare," *Monthly Review* (March 2008), editorial, http://mrzine.monthlyreview.org/amr 210308p.html

[87] Mishra, "The Myth of the New India," *op. cit.*

[88] P. Sainath, "Class War in Gurgaon," *Counterpunch* (July 29, 2005), http://www.thewe. cc/contents/more/archieve2005/july/coke_india_poster.htm

Other such flashpoints include the sites of several Coca Cola plants, which are accused of ecological destruction and severe water depletion. Protesters from dozens of villages have forged links with American campus activists to publicize the issue. See Haider Rizvi, "Coke Slammed at Shareholders Meeting for Practices in India," *Common Dreams News Center* (April 21, 2006), *OneWorld.net,* http://www.thewe.cc/contents/more/archive2005/ july/coke_india_poster.htm

tell if that informational advantage can survive the increasing collusion between big corporations, politicians and the media.[89] Since the thoroughly "incorporated" middle classes are clearly content with a coopted press, any hope for preserving India's free speech tradition rests with the democratic participation of lower, "un-incorporated" classes. It is this flickering hope that could redeem Indo-globalization and render it a badly needed alternative for the developing world—a model driven by People Power rather than capital.

Sumit Ganguly correctly notes that "India's democratic consolidation challenges the current expert consensus that some 'floor' level of economic growth is needed before democracy can consolidate."[90] But then, seemingly unaware of the contradiction, he goes on to sing the praises of the market democracy that is putting capital back in charge. He believes this new economism will produce "a bulwark of support for liberal democracy in the form of a more educated and cosmopolitan middle class."[91] Which is it? If sweeping market liberalization is necessary for new India's democratization, then we are back to the old consensus that Ganguly himself refuted. If, however, Indian democracy is already "consolidated," why call in reinforcements *ex post facto* from a mode of globalization that has done more to "deconsolidate" Indian democracy than all the floods, malnutrition, and religious strife of the last half century?

Fortunately this democratic erosion has not completely unhinged India's free press. In China, by contrast, countervailing traditions and institutions have been almost obliterated, courtesy of the Cultural Revolution and the less conspicuous but equally relentless repression of Sino-capitalism.[92] There is no doubt that the other India will fight back against globalist colonization. The question is whether this resistance can be brought into the fold of mainstream Indian politics. Or will it take the rabidly undemocratic path

---

Such efforts conspicuously failed in the infamous Bhopal case. Locals still suffer and die from the area's toxic seepage. Government officials apparently fear that forcing Dow Chemical (which bought Union Carbide in 2001) to fund an adequate cleanup operation would deter future investment. See Somini Sengupta, "Decades Later, Toxic Sludge Torments Bhopal," *The New York Times* (July 7, 2008), http://www.nytimes.com/2008/07/07/world/asia/07bhopal.html

[89] See Pankaj Mishra, "The Rotting of New India," *The Guardian* (December 1, 2010), http://www.guardiam.co.uk/commentisfree/2010/dec/01/rotting-new-india-scandal

[90] Ganguly, *op. cit.*, 33.

[91] *Ibid.*, 39.

[92] On the contrast between India and China, see Pankaj Mishra, "A New Sort of Superpower," *New Statesman* (January 30, 2006), http://www.newstatesman.com/200601300015

of revolutionary Naxalism? That would not only enfeeble the Indian Left, but would devitalize the whole political process, which needs this radical infusion as much now as it did in 1857 or 1947.

As Americans begin to register the fact that Chinese authoritarianism is not the fleeting phenomenon they once imagined, their respect for Indian democracy is sure to grow. It would be a tragic irony if in the meantime India had reversed course and modeled itself on the PRC. India has in fact been blessed by Washington's delay in warming to New Delhi after the Cold War. To appreciate this paradox we must recognize the curse that Washington's globalist affections have spelled for Russia and China, where democratic development was stunted or totally aborted. Western capital encouraged that retrenchment by bankrolling the CCP after Tiananmen and by fueling the energy binge that bred Putinism. India had the good luck to be left off this dubious priority list. That gives it a chance to reexamine its own priorities in the light of Russian and Chinese maldevelopment.

This latecomer advantage has been wasted by both the BJP and Congress parties, which have busied themselves at imitating the growth models first of Washington and now of Beijing. Either way, the other India has been left behind and often left homeless. What makes this a vital global issue is not just the fact that cheap labor, ruinous mining, and fast-track industrialization serve the global market. In 2004 the state of Orissa—home to countless mining operations, coal plants, refineries, iron factories, and over 50 steel plants—accounted for about one percent of the world's greenhouse emissions.[93] This puts Orissa's Naxal resistance in a different light. We are forced to recognize that, however inadvertently, such local opposition is a proxy for the battles we all should be waging against the corporate demolition of our natural world. When thirteen Orissa residents were shot in January 2006 for resisting the construction of yet another steel plant on their land, they were inadvertent casualties in a global war for environmental sustainability as well as social justice. Here, as throughout the Global South, the poor and dispossessed serve as the proverbial canary in our globalist mine shaft.

The issue is not should this eco-social pillage be contested, but *how*. At first glance, Gandhism and Naxalism give antithetical answers to that question, for clearly they are at opposite poles ethically. Yet what they share is no less important. Both embrace the distinctly Indian dream of agrarian-centered egalitarianism. To be true to itself, Indo-globalization must reconfigure that dream for our times. Indian idealism and realism converge here, for there really is no choice in the matter. An economy that casts over

---

[93] Temper and Martinez-Alier, "Is India Too Poor to Be Green?" *op. cit.*, 1490–91.

450 million citizens into hopeless destitution is a recipe for national debility and even revolution. To escape this quagmire, India must find a way to integrate the "other India" with the "Shining India" that controls the media and nearly all policy decisions. Whatever the cost, this is an investment India cannot afford not to make.

7

RACE TO THE BOTTOM
Globalization with Chinese Characteristics

THE WAGES OF "ENGAGEMENT"

The "Other America" that Michael Harrington spotlighted in the 1960s is no longer the peripheral sector he described. Long before the 2008 recession, outsourcing and other globalist malfunctions had mainstreamed downward mobility, rendering the American "other" a misnomer. 5,000 plant closings between 2004 and 2008 effectively "othered" the very heart of working America. Though the recession officially ended in June 2009, jobs kept hemorrhaging, even as corporate profits soared. There was, therefore, a complete divorce between Wall Street's economic numbers and Main Street's "lived economy."[1]

That same disjuncture between growth data and the human factor is apparent wherever transnational corporatism takes hold, be it in Mumbai, Shenzhen, or Detroit. Over the last few years, as India's growth rate approached 9 percent, 180,000 farmers committed suicide.[2] In China

---

[1] See Paul Clemens, "The Ghost of 'Old G.M.'," *The New York Times* (November 17, 2010), http://www.nytimes.com/2010/11/18/opinion/18clemens.html

[2] Arundhati Roy, "Is There Life After Democracy?" *Dawn* (July 5, 2009), http://news.dawn.com/wps/wcm/connect/dawn-content-library/dawn/news/world/06-is-there-life-after-democracy-rs-07

an even higher growth rate has been coupled with a drop in rural income as well as a programmatic deterioration of life-quality infrastructure such as schools and hospitals. Villagers who fall ill often find medical treatment so far beyond their means that the choice is between death or bankruptcy.[3] Healthy farmers have little choice but to migrate to Eastern cities in search of work, much of it day labor. It is the travail of this vast underclass that has made the Chinese "miracle" possible.

Meanwhile in America globalist corporatism has become so politically entrenched that it no longer requires the neoliberal camouflage of years past. The new corporate order—marked by "too big to fail" bailouts and a Supreme Court that seems to give its first allegiance to corporate rights—can dispense with the democratic mythology of classic globalists like Francis Fukuyama. That idealism is now as dated as the communist mythology it vanquished. It lives on in the popular imagination for the simple reason that there is nothing to put in its place. It is all the more absolute and perplexing because it is taken as being beyond dispute: TINAesque.

This decrepit myth holds that the end of the Cold War was a victory for mankind, not just Wall Street, and thus must spell the "end of history" in the sense of ideological strife. Initially the whole West danced to this music. Neoliberal and cosmopolitan globalists could bicker over what to do with the ailing remnants of social democracy, but they came together on the merits of a new world order premised on robust capitalism and a virtual ban on radical alternatives. "Globalization" was the process whereby this "reform" agenda was to be imposed on the whole developing world.

Well, not quite all of it. Exceptions would be made where big enough profits were at stake. Thus the Asia Pacific was initially spared the neoliberal restructuration that Latin America had suffered since the early 1980s. That double standard was removed after the Asian Crash, when the region's bankrupt nations were effectively "Latinized." The glaring exception was China, which was showered with FDI with few strings attached. This sent a compelling message to developing nations concerning the advantages of authoritarian capitalism.

There can be no doubt that Russia's recoil from liberal democracy in the last decade was partly a response to China's unparalleled success story. However, Russia's own political economy cannot be ruled out as an alluring development model in its own right. If shorn of its heinous excesses—such as Prime Minister Putin's vow to crush the skulls of any

---

[3] Aditya Chakraborty, "Is China Really the New Superpower on the Block?" *Guardian* (November 9, 2010), http://www.guardian.co.uk/commentisfree/2010/nov/09/is-china-really-new-superpower

protesters who defy his rules concerning unapproved demonstrations[4]—the Russian model could offer a more saleable formula for authoritarian governance in resource-rich areas such as Africa. This Potemkin democracy could lower the oppositional heat while avoiding international angst over obvious despotism.

There is some question, then, as to whether the China model will prevail in Africa or other "postcolonial" regions where a democratic façade can be useful.[5] Even Teodoro Obiang Nguema Mbasogo, Equatorial Guinea's de facto president-for-life, finally got the message. Having embezzled over $600 million of the country's oil profits,[6] Obiang has now hired Lanny Davis (former special counsel to President Clinton) for $1 million a year to help clean up his international image. Davis began by advising his new boss that he could raise his international credibility by winning his next election by only 51 percent instead of his usual 98.[7]

Why, then, has the Chinese development model been beating the global competition? The biggest reason is Western "engagement." In its formative stages, at least, the success of the China model heavily depended upon America's support for its economic dynamism, if not its very existence. Not even the colonial horrors of Tibet or Xinjiang could stem the neoliberal lust for China's cheap labor, fiat management, and market potential. Human

---

[4] Luke Harding, "Vladimir Putin Says 'Unsanctioned' Protesters Can Expect Police Brutality," *The Guardian* (August 30, 2010), http://www.guardian.co.uk/world/2010/30/vladimir-putin-protesters-police-brutality

In defiance of Putin's threat, hundreds of protesters poured out for an August 31, 2010 demonstration staged by the "Strategy 31" organization. This movement takes its name from Article 31 of the 1993 Russian Constitution, which guarantees civic freedoms such as the right to assemble. See Fred Weir, "Russian Protesters Defy Putin Warning—and Meet Tough Response," *Christian Science Monitor* (August 31, 2010), http://www.csmonitor.com/World/Europe/2010/0831/Russian-protesters-defy-Putin-warning-and-meet-tough-response

[5] Even China finds it necessary to play the democratic game to some extent. Like Mao before, and like Singapore's Lee Kuan Yew more recently, Beijing is trying to invent a new "democracy with Chinese characteristics" to complement its special brand of state capitalism.

[6] George B. N. Ayittey, "The Worst of the Worst," *Foreign Policy* (July/August 2010), http://www.foreignpolicy.com/articles/2010/06/21/the_worst_of_the_worst

[7] Celia W. Dugger, "African Leader Hires Adviser and Seeks an Image Change," *The New York Times* (June 28, 2010), http://www.nytimes.com/2010/06/29/world/africa/29obiang.html

Meanwhile Washington is pressing UNESCO to cancel its participation in another of Obiang's public relations schemes: his munificent UNESCO-Obiang Prize for scientific achievement. See Steve Erlanger, "U.S. Calls for Withdrawal of United Nations Prize Financed by a West African Dictator," *The New York Times* (October 8, 2010), http://www.nytimes.com/2010/10/09/world/europe/09unesco.html

rights could still get a nominal hearing so long as rights violations took place in the global outback of Sudan or Burma,[8] but sovereignty trumps rights when it comes to prime capitalist turf like China or Russia. China, moreover, offers the added bonus of unrelenting social discipline.

This tool is so effective that it tends to be invisible to pro-China economists like James Galbraith and Alice Amsden. Indeed, a whole genre of Western scholarship mistakes Chinese repression for "social harmony." Daniel A. Bell goes so far as to propose a global "Social Harmony Index" to measure countries according to how well they conform to the China model. What he fails to mention is the police state and gulag that are more central to this system than the "meritocracy" he lauds.[9] Thus the most virulent state capitalism on earth is fully legitimized within a much revised globalism.[10]

Whether the blueprint is provided by Beijing or Moscow, the rudiments are now in place for a formidable Second World order. Its defining feature is the reduction of development to raw economic growth, free of Western impediments like free speech and civil rights. This sweeping de-liberalization fits the demographics of global poverty. With nearly half the world's population living on less than $2.50 a day, freedom is not going to be a top priority for the bottom three billion. Nor can we expect much more interest in the subject from the 80 percent of the world's population living on less than $10 a day.[11] The irony is that a democratic vote within this bloated economic bracket could easily put democratic values out to pasture. For those near or below the poverty line, democracy has not only lost its luster, but is likely to be associated with the neocolonial power structures that spell dependency and repression for the voiceless half of the world's population.[12]

---

[8] Indeed, the issue of human rights in Burma has been sidelined under Obama, who has joined ASEAN in "engaging" the Burmese junta. See Philip Bowring, "A Comeback in the Pacific," *The New York Times* (September 23, 2010), http://www.nytimes.com/2010/09/24/iht-edbowring.html

[9] Daniel A. Bell, "Developing China's Soft Power," *The New York Times* (September 23, 2010), http:www.nytimes.com/2010/09/24/opinion/24iht-edbell.html

[10] Only in the wake of the 2008 Great Recession did the geopolitical and geoeconomic price of this accommodation come under broad scrutiny, primarily from the Right. For example, see David Brooks, "The Larger Struggle," *The New York Times* (June 14, 2010), http://www.nytimes.com/2010/06/15/opinion/15brooks.html

[11] Those statistics are conservative, insofar as they were gathered prior to the 2008 recession. See Anup Shah, "Poverty Facts and Stats," *Global Issues* (updated March 28, 2010), http://www.globalissues.org/article/26/poverty-facts-and-stats

[12] See Roger Cohen, "Democracy Still Matters," *The New York Times* (September 20, 2010), http://www.nytimes.com/2010/09/21/opinion/21iht-edcohen.html

What about those on the affluent side of the global spectrum? The classic modernist assumption—straight out of Seymour Martin Lipset's *Political Man*—was that democratic transformation will follow naturally from economic development. What this conventional wisdom ignores is the prevailing politics of development in countries that lack liberal traditions such as universal suffrage, human rights and independent judiciaries. In such cases social status does not issue so much from hard work or professional merit as from political connections. Will the privileged classes of Second World countries go to bat for democratic reforms that would deprive them of their present distributive advantages? Making matters worse, democratic systems around the world are now floundering economically. Desperate democratic leaders look to China, with its double-digit growth and its massive financial reserves, as the indispensible engine of global recovery.[13]

So it is that the democratic First World has enthusiastically "engaged" the Second World, running trade deficits that foster a new mode of globalization. One form of tribute being paid to Beijing by America and the West is prodigious disinterest in China's repression and foreign machinations. The Obama administration came into office determined to retire the very idea of confrontational diplomacy, be it with China, Russia, Iran, or even North Korea.[14] Calling for an unconditional "reset" of relations with Moscow and an almost total ban on criticism of Chinese rights abuse, Obama took the neoliberal cult of "engagement" to new heights. The message this sent to the Third World was quite simply that authoritarianism pays.

Though it earned the new president an instant-mix Nobel Peace Prize, the Obama Doctrine is by no means original. Its basic assumptions are lifted straight out of the Clinton administration playbook that normalized commercial relations with the butchers of Tiananmen. Soon China got its long-sought "most-favored nation" status, after which it was fast-tracked into the WTO. This would make economic sanctions difficult to apply. For all practical purposes state capitalism, or what may fairly be described

---

[13] Graham and Dodd Investor, "Why China Could Lead Us into Another Depression," *Seeking Alpha* (June 30, 2010), http://seekingalpha.com/article/212467-why-china-could-lead-us-into-another-depression

[14] In the wake of the *Cheonan* incident (North Korea's torpedo attack on a South Korean warship), the Obama administration found itself without any comfortable policy options, and soon began thinking of extending its standard engagement strategy toward the North. The irony is that it was precisely the failure of its similar China engagement that brought Washington to this impasse, for it is common knowledge that Beijing has the North in its pocket economically. Concerning the engagement trap, see Mark Landler, "U.S. Considers Possibility of Engaging North Korea," *The New York Times* (August 27, 2010), http//www.nytimes.com/2010/08/28/world/asia/28diplo.html

as 21st century fascism, was ushered into the international community unconditionally.

Domestic repression was thus condoned, but that left the ponderous question of how the West would react to naked aggression by state capitalist powers across national borders. China's ongoing aggressions against Tibet and East Turkistan (aka Xinjiang) do not register as imperialism because the international community has yielded completely to the Chinese claim of full and rightful sovereignty over these formerly independent territories. The same could be said for Russia's scorched-earth campaigns in Chechnya, which the West dismissed as legitimate anti-terrorist actions.

It was quite another matter when Russia invaded Georgia in August 2008. With America already mired in two costly and demoralizing wars, Russia correctly guessed that there would be no serious repercussions from the Western side. Stunned Europeans dared not even call this an invasion. Many evaded the whole issue of a NATO response by laying blame for the war on the admittedly rash conduct of the Georgian president Mikheil Saakashvili. He made for a convenient scapegoat, but putting him in a class with Putin was farcical.

Europeans who had known decades of Soviet occupation tended to take a very different view of the matter. For them an assertive NATO was a patent necessity, not a Cold War anachronism, and Georgia was a proxy for Europe's neglected geopolitical imperatives. From this vantage it was obvious that the war was a product of Putinism, pure and simple. Nor should the invasion have been any great surprise. Much as the Nazi blitzkrieg on Czechoslovakia had its trial run in the Spanish Civil War, Putinism exposed its true colors in the Chechen nightmare. As the Russian journalist Anna Politkovskaya made clear, at the cost of her life, Russia's renewed foreign aggression was the flip side of its domestic repression: "Putin, a product of the country's murkiest intelligence service, has failed to transcend his origins and stop acting like a KGB officer."[15]

Politkovskaya was not "pro-Western" in the shallow sense of giving a blanket endorsement to Western policies. Indeed, she recognized that to a large degree the Western political establishment was more the problem than the solution to Russia's woes. The Russian pogrom on Chechnya, for example, was conducted even as the IMF and World Bank lavished funds on Russia. The Clinton administration cared only about cementing its commercial relations with Putin's fledgling regime. While Grozny was being reduced to a wasteland by carpet bombing—strictly in violation of

---

[15] Anna Politkovskaya, *Putin's Russia: Rise in a Failing Democracy*, trans. Arch Tait (New York: Henry Holt & Company, 2004), "Author's note."

Geneva Convention rules about indiscriminant bombing—Secretary of State Madeleine Albright was in Moscow praising Putin's leadership qualities.[16]

DEMOCRACY AS STRATEGIC OPPORTUNITY

As usual, the US and its Western allies have been content to succor authoritarians whenever it served their interests. This liberal apostasy is now coming back to haunt, but America—embroiled in war, recession, and geopolitical eclipse—is in no position to reverse course. To deal effectively with the current global recession, or with crucial geo-moral issues such as the need for sanctions on Burma, Sudan, or North Korea, it has been necessary to repeatedly solicit China's assistance, usually to no avail. The Bush administration put so much stress on "anti-terrorist" cooperation that it ended up giving support for any kind of anti-Islamic action. If the Islamic world holds the U.S. more responsible for this injustice than other offending nations, it is partly because more was expected from America. Likewise, pro-democrats in Central Asia expected more, as did Tibetans, Uighurs, Burmese, Acehnese, West Papuans, etc. One reason democratization has stagnated globally is this unconscionable lack of concern on the part of the world's leading democracy.

At this point, however, there is a big question as to how much difference even a concerned Washington could make in many of the world's disputed zones. America's geopolitical impotence emboldens Russia in its "near abroad." Its concern is more with China's reaction than NATO's. The silver lining on the Georgia invasion is the fracture it revealed within SCO ranks. The good news was that Russia was not nearly so committed to this anti-Western pact as many supposed. By going its own way, Moscow shocked the East and West alike, and cast some welcome doubt on the durability of the SCO as a prototype for the Second World Order.

Nonetheless the invasion was a crushing blow to the West. One of the most strident critics of the new Russian aggression is Vladimer Papava, a former Georgian minister of economy who faults the West for its reluctance to admit that the Cold War *never ended*.[17] For him it was merely frozen, and now it is rapidly thawing out. We must agree with Papava that the

---

[16] "War Crimes in Chechnya and the Response of the West," *Human Rights Watch* (February 29, 2000), http://www.hrw.org/en/news/2000/02/29/war-crimes-chechnya-and-response-west

[17] Vladimer Papava, "The End of the Frozen Cold War?" *Caucasian Review of International Affairs* 3, no. 1 (Winter 2009), http://www.cria-online.org/6_9.html

Georgian crisis will be an ill omen if nothing is done to counter the new wave of authoritarianism that is engulfing Eurasia.

History has turned diametrically against the color revolutions that just a few years ago pulled nascent democracies toward the West. Many in the ex-Soviet sphere—up to 70 percent of Tajiks, for example[18]—express longing for Soviet rule, and recent political upheavals point in the same direction. The overthrow of Kurmanbek Bakiyev in Kyrgyzstan pushed that country closer to Russia, and by May 2010, with the presidential victory of Viktor Yanukovych over Yulia Tymoshenko, Ukraine too was falling back into Russia's grip. Georgia was the grand exception to this trend, and look where that got it.

Nonetheless it is important not to overly "Sovietize" the Russian rebound. Papava usefully resuscitates geopolitical awareness, but goes too far in equating today's Russia with the USSR. Bruce Gilley, by contrast, still sees Russia's democratic turn of the 1990s as giving it an instrumental edge over China.[19] Whatever the economic effects of democratization may be—and many believe China holds a strong authoritarian advantage—it will be hard for Putinists to completely purge Russia's democratic element. A potent opposition (albeit most likely from the Bolshevik side) could arise in Russia if the economy hits rock bottom, whereas in China it would take a literal revolution to reach that boiling point. Even Putin's United Russia regime needs some degree of democratic approval, which explains Putin's continuous public relations campaign. So far this democratic encumbrance has only made the Kremlin more wary of Western influence. The fact remains, however, that Russia's greatest geopolitical nemesis is China, not NATO. If America and the West can drive that fact home, Moscow's split with China and the SCO can be accelerated.

That strategic opportunity will be missed, however, if Russia's authoritarian drift is not squarely confronted. Obama's white-flag diplomacy—calling for a complete "reset" of US–Russian relations, with little or nothing asked in return—only rewards Russian aggression. Conversely, Papava's hard-line reaction clings too narrowly to the paradigm of the old Cold War. Edward Lucas offers a more dexterous geopolitics, though he too blasts the West for its failure to confront hard facts:

> ...the most catastrophic mistake the outside world has made since 1991 is to assume that Russia is steadily becoming a 'normal' country. From this

---

[18] Iason Athanasiadis, "Tajikistan Pines for Old Soviet Union Strength," *The Christian Science Monitor* (May 27, 2010), http://www.csmonitor.com/World/Global-News/2010/0527/Tajikistan-pines-for-old-Soviet-Union-strength

[19] Martin Jacques, *When China Rules the World: The Rise of the Middle Kingdom and the End of the Western World* (London: Penguin Group, 2009), 214.

Panglossian point of view, any problems that arise are mere bumps in the road that will be left behind in the inexorable progress toward Western-style freedom and legality.[20]

Our main difference with Lucas is that we move beyond a national focus on Russia or China to the more generic issue of authoritarian capitalism, which to us is a byproduct of the raw economism that neoliberalism and Sino-globalism jointly foster. What distinguishes these two economisms is the false neoliberal tenet that capitalism as such generates liberal democratization. As James Mann cogently argues in *The China Fantasy*[21], the rise of the PRC contains no democratic teleology.

This "end of history" mythology has blinded globalists to what is taking place in China, Russia and other neo-authoritarian laboratories. To this day Fukuyama refuses to abandon his iconic "endism."[22] That intransigence—grounded in an abiding faith in capitalism as the natural spawning ground of democracy, human rights, and the common good—handicaps a wide range of Western judgments about China, including that of the hard Left, which paradoxically ends up as a glee club for state capitalism. Doug Henwood, for example, sees almost all criticism of China as xenophobic "yellow perilism."[23] Thus, in one of the strangest of strange bedfellows scenarios, the neoliberal Right joins the anti-American Left in defending China against any kind of containment or conditionality.

The idea that multilateralism is inherently progressive, no matter who sits at the global bargaining table, is one of the most dangerous fallacies of 21st century thought. Papava and Lucas explode that notion in the case of Russia, and doing the same for China is just a matter of pulling away its globalist veil. The cardinal fact is that "history" has come back with a vengeance. In *Development Without Freedom*[24] we laid blame for this recidivism on the curious symbiosis of Western globalism and reactionary Asian values. Regretfully we found it necessary to depart substantially from our developmental mentor, Amartya Sen, for Sen failed to acknowledge that neoliberal

---

[20] Edward Lucas, *The New Cold War: Putin's Russia and the Threat to the West* (Hampshire, UK: Palgrave Macmillan, 2009), 6.

[21] James Mann, *The China Fantasy: How our Leaders Explain Away Chinese Repression* (New York: Viking, 2007).

[22] Francis Fukuyama, interviewed by Nathan Gardels, "Societies Don't Have to be Secular to be Modern," *The Christian Science Monitor* (October 21, 2009), http://www.csmonitor.com/2009/1021/p09s07-coop.htm?print=true

[23] See Robert Dreyfuss, "China in the Driver's Seat," *The Nation* (September 2, 2010), http://www.thenation.com/article/154484/china-drivers-seat

[24] Songok Han Thornton and William H. Thornton, *Development Without Freedom: The Politics of Asian Globalization* (Aldershot, UK: Ashgate, 2008).

globalism was a willing sponsor of the anti-democratic turn of capitalism in China, Russia and much of the politically undeveloping world.

WAKING DRAGON

Now only the most obdurate paleo-globalists can fail to see that repressive countries can be fully globalized without absorbing a trace of political liberalism. Indeed, it was the globalist energy market that spared Putinist Russia the kind of political reform that was broached by Mikhail Gorbachev, and it was China's massive export trade that came to the rescue of the flagging CCP after Tiananmen. A rising and well-remunerated host of Sino-globalist cheerleaders lay stress on the changes that are occurring within the CCP, but the major change has been the Party's embrace of the new professional and entrepreneurial classes—Jiang Zemin's "red capitalists." This cooptation spells the end of hope for middle class resistance to CCPism.

Far from withering away in the wake of capitalist "reform," the CCP is mushrooming into a mega-party that controls Chinese social and economic life more inclusively than ever. As Ian Bremmer notes, career paths are more than ever forged on the party's anvil, such that college students are flooding to join the party to improve their vocational prospects.[25] This melding of political and economic power structures is producing a highly consolidated upper class that is everything the original CCP was sworn to prevent—viz., a universal capitalist class. The result is a two-tiered caste system fueled by legions of underpaid and virtually rightless migrant workers.[26] A third tier, made up of ethnic minorities like the Tibetans and the Uighurs, functions as a vital emotional outlet for the vast Han underclass. It gives them something to look down on, much as the institutionalized racism of America's Jim Crow South gave lower class whites a way to inflate their impoverished egos without wage increases.

By no means can the socioeconomic injustice of the new China model be blamed entirely on "Asian cronyism" or other "Asian values." Throughout the globalist era, Western corporatism has supported CCPism. If the biggest losers in this partnership have been China's lower classes, their plight is structurally bound up with that of Western workers whose jobs have been outsourced. These twin afflictions are not just economically determined, however. No less they are political products, and even moral ones, for the

---

[25] Ian Bremmer, *The End of the Free Market: Who Wins the War Between States and Corporations?* (New York: Penguin Group (Portfolio), 2010), 132.

[26] Stefan Halper, *The Beijing Consensus: How China's Authoritarian Model Will Dominate the Twenty-First Century* (New York: Basic Books, 2010), 162.

West's decision to pursue unlimited trade with authoritarian powers is an act of collective (not just corporate) moral dereliction.

We may fairly call this the Wal-Mart syndrome, for it is rooted in America's lust for bargain prices at any moral cost. The shopping public is indifferent to the working conditions of Chinese labor, including prison slave labor. But of course the China model has also been propped up by corporate greed and bad geopolitical judgment. That gift to authoritarian capitalism is one of the self-inflicted wounds that Stephen Walt alludes to in his dire warning concerning the coming decline of the West.[27] The fact is that the corporate West has been burying the democratic West, albeit with a spade "made in China."

For twenty years, globalism has been increasingly defined by the curious coalition of CCPism and Western corporatism. Academic as well as media impressions of Sino-American relations have downplayed the grating political incompatibilities of the two systems. Usually that disparity has been dismissed as a temporary obstruction in the process of global convergence. There is growing recognition, however, that this ideological chasm is here to stay. In Bremmer's view we are watching the emergence of an almost Manichean West/East schism, as Western globalism fights for its life against its erstwhile partner.[28] It is possible for him to draw this stark, geo-cultural dichotomy because, like Fukuyama, he fails to register the equally entrenched conflict between Western corporatism and Western democracy. He rightly levels blame on Chinese and Russian statisms, but conveniently ignores the self-inflicted nature of the West's decline, as Walt treats it.

Likewise he misses the amelioratory possibilities that we perceive on the post-globalist horizon. In the face of the growing contest between the Washington Consensus and the Beijing Consensus, the time is ripe for a global third way. Bremmer's critique of authoritarian capitalism is timely and constructive, but offers no credible alternative to the brand of globalization that most of the developing world has rightly come to despise. As a Wall Street consultant, Bremmer is of course going to downplay Western corporate responsibility for world recession and a host of other maladies, such as global warming, explosive income disparity, and environmental holocaust. The gross defects of his corporatism are so well-known in the Third World, and so widely deplored, that China enjoys a tremendous "dark horse" advantage.

---

[27] Stephen M. Walt, "The End of the World as We Know it?" *Foreign Policy* (May 13, 2010), http://walt.foroeignpolicy.com/posts/2010/05/13/the_end_of_the_world_as_we_know_it

[28] See Bremmer, *op. cit.*

That free ride cannot last long. A reversal will set in once the developing world gets to know China better. A preview of this rebound effect is provided by labor relations at China's Shougang Corporation in Peru. Since 1992, workers here have been locked in often violent confrontation with their Chinese overlords.[29] These workers are not deluded by Beijing's promise of a "win-win" accord with Latin America. It is only a matter of time before the word spreads about the real nature of "South-South" relations on China's terms. The question is whether America and the West will be ready to offer the South a better deal in the form of a genuine Third Way.

Fortunately for China, most American internationalists are clinging to an utterly discredited brand of globalism that happens to include a glowing assessment of the Chinese competition. The same old neoliberal bromides spill from a host of Sino-apologists like Susan Shirk and Michael Spence, the World Bank's development guru. Spence believes that an economically moribund America needs to learn the art of effective governance from China's great leaders.[30] Even as Beijing snuffs out dissent and cracks down harder than ever on the Internet, Shirk insists that there is no cause for alarm, for the less savory aspects of the China model have little global appeal and in any case Beijing is fast reforming.[31] Daniel Bell and Robert Lawrence Kuhn likewise paint a rosy picture of ever-expanding popular participation in China's "intra-Party democracy." Kuhn has ample reason to appreciate the CCP, for like Henry Kissinger he is making a fortune in consultancy fees that are in fact loan payments for the use of his personal contacts (*guanxi*) with high-ranking Chinese apparatchiks.

It is significant that an inner circle globalist like Bremmer would break ranks with these Sinophiles by challenging some of globalism's most cherished false assumptions. Fortunately he is not alone in his disillusionment. Disengagement from an unreformed China is now very much "in the air," even in the corporate world. Google's threat to withdraw from China in 2010 signaled the beginning of a tidal shift in corporate thinking about the whole China connection. Granted, Google later vacillated, as did Rio Tinto

---

[29] Simon Romero, "Tensions over Chinese Mining Venture in Peru," *The New York Times* (August 14, 2010), http://www.nytimes.com/2010/08/15/world/americas/15chinaperu.html

[30] Michael Spence, interviewed by Nathan Gardels, "China's Resilience is an Economic Gut Check for America," *The Christian Science Monitor* (August 23, 2010), http://www.csmonitor.com/Commentary/Global-Viewpoint/2010/0823/China-s-resilience-is-an-economic-gut-check-for-America

[31] See, for example, Shirk's Pollyanna argument in her August 2010 debate with Stefan Halper: "The China Model," *The Economist* (August 4, 2010), http://www.economist.com/debate/days/view/553

after its fleeting attempt to escape the gravitational pull of China's commodities power.[32] By July 2010 Rio had capitulated, signing a mammoth deal with Chinalco (Aluminum Corporation of China) for co-investment in Africa and elsewhere.[33]

Nonetheless there are mounting rumors of insurrection among the 50,000 American companies operating in China. Many are coming to realize the folly of their inordinate expectations. At a moment of understated frustration, the CEO of General Electric (GE) expressed doubt that Chinese officials want any foreign company to be successful.[34] GE—which invested $70 million in the Beijing Olympics and is also a huge contributor to the US Pavilion at the Shanghai World Expo—is said to be moving part of its China production to Kentucky.[35] Other firms are sure to explore similar exit strategies as they come under increasing pressure to relinquish secret technology as a condition of their Chinese operations. Even the consistently pro-China branches of the American Chamber of Commerce and the European Union Chamber of Commerce have expressed concern (better late than never) over China's commercial extortion.[36] Such policies are already costing America billions of dollars and thousands of lost jobs.[37] This is not even to mention the security costs of high-technology transfers that have direct military applications, which GE is notoriously engaged in even as it talks (perhaps simply for bargaining advantage) about an exit strategy from China.

The crux of the problem cannot be solved simply by exiting China, for it is the China model rather than the PRC alone that poses the greatest challenge to the West. As Bremmer puts it, Western firms "are now forced

---

[32] See Ambrose Evans-Pritchard, "Hot Political Summer as China Throttles Rare Metal Supply and Claims South China Sea," *The Telegraphy* (August 1, 2010), http://www.telegraph.co.uk/finance/comment/ambroseevans_pritchard/7921209/Hot-political-summer-as-China-throttles-rare-metal-supply-and-claims-South-China-Sea.html

[33] See David Barboza, "Rio Tinto Puts on a New Face in its Relations with China," *The New York Times* (August 20, 2010), http://www.nytimes.com/2010/08/21/business/global/21rio.html

[34] Simon Tay, "Interdependency Theory: China, India, and the West," *Foreign Affairs* (September/October 2010), http://www.foreignaffairs.com/print/66678?page=show

[35] Ambrose Evans-Pritchard, "Western Profits Wilt on China's Surging Wages," *The Telegraph* (August 18, 2010), http://www.telegraph.co.uk/finance/china-business/7952675/Western-profits-wilt-on-Chinas-surging-wages.html

[36] He Qinglian, "Once Friendly, Foreign Companies in China Have Second Thoughts," *The Epoch Times* (updated August 21, 2010), http://www.theepochtimes.com/n2/content/view/41113/

[37] "Grand Theft Electric Auto, and other Chinese Industrial Robbery," *The Christian Science Monitor* (September 17, 2010), http://www.csmonitor.com/layout/set/print/content/view/print/326560

to compete all over the world against companies armed with enormous financial and political support from their home governments."[38] It follows that globalization can no longer be regarded as a singular and inherently progressive phenomenon, with all roads leading to the Washington Consensus. Communism is defunct, but the same cannot be said of dictatorship.[39] Already, globalization is split along the lines that Bremmer outlines: the "free market" versus "state capitalism."

Beijing had a head start in exploiting this divide insofar as it was never deluded by neoliberal visions of global convergence. The trick was to keep China's ultra-nationalist objectives out of sight. Martin Jacques takes this laundered imagery at face value, tracing what he considers a dependably moderate PRC foreign policy to China's essence as a civilizational state.[40] Though he does not share the neoliberal faith that China is on its way to becoming like us, he validates the standard neoliberal conclusion that post-Deng China is too pragmatic and profit-minded to pose a major threat. Given its economic thirst, coupled with its civilizational preference for stability, China can be trusted to wield its global power in a responsible manner.

Bremmer, by contrast, takes a corporate road to a very different conclusion. Although his analysis is still steeped in neoliberal assumptions about what the world needs, he gives no quarter to the glib, pro-China agenda of today's (neo)liberal internationalism. According to this story line, Beijing's hard-power plays of years past failed miserably and were reversed by the globalized and hence pacified PRC that emerged in the 1990s.[41] While the myth of China's "peaceful rise" is packaged as common knowledge, its domestic repression is brushed aside as mere growing pains.

So too recent reversals in China's foreign affairs are systematically ignored. Everyone knows that the sleeping dragon is now wide awake economically, yet somehow the notion persists that geopolitically China is a pet dragon interested only in GDP growth. The new century is not shaping up the way neoliberals predicted, and certainly China is not marching to a Western drummer.[42] Washington and Brussels have been pushed together

---

[38] Scott Horton, "The End of the Free Market: Six Questions for Ian Bremmer," *Harper's Magazine* (May 7, 2010), http://harpers.org/archive/2010/05/hbc-90006994

[39] Bremmer, *The End of the Free Market, op. cit.*, 8.

[40] Martin Jacques, *When China Rules the World: The Rise of the Middle Kingdom and the End of the Western World* (London: Penguin Group, 2009), 270–24.

[41] See Joshua Kurlantzick, *Charm Offensive: How China's Soft Power Is Transforming the World* (New Haven, CT: Yale University Press, 2007), 37–39.

[42] Experts date the shift between 2004 and 2006. See Baohui Zhang, "Chinese Foreign Policy in Transition: Trends and Implications," *Journal of Current Chinese Affairs* 39, no. 2 (2010): 40–41 (39–68).

in desperate opposition to Beijing's currency manipulation,[43] which is now being mimicked by other nations.[44] What few realize is that currency is a weapon of mass destruction in the emerging globalist Cold War.

Meanwhile many other alarm bells are ringing. French President Jacques Chirac was delighted in 2003 when China signed on to the EU's GPS system, which he saw as part of a "multipolar" challenge to US techno-hegemony. Perhaps Chirac was thinking along the lines of Parag Khanna's geopolitical triad, whereby China and Europe achieve a new global equilibrium by dislodging America's unipolarity.[45] Unfortunately China wasted no time in exposing its very "polar" intentions. It not only turned loose its formidable army of hackers on the Dalai Lama's computer system, but soon took on Europe in a GPS turf war.[46] The idea was to appropriate the same GPS frequency used by Europe, with the clear aim of blocking reception from European satellites.

Stunned by this unexpected security threat, the Europeans denied China a seat on the Supervisory Authority which owns the "Galileo" GPS system. This tepid response only served to embolden Beijing, which soon turned its hacking operations on foreign corporate networks inside China. Surprisingly Google struck back, threatening to close down its China branch. Even more surprisingly it got vocal support from the State Department. Doubtless part of the reason is that the US government—far more than the public is aware—has also been a target of China's escalating cyberwarfare, especially in highly sensitive military areas.[47] It is said that China's blue laser technology may already have moved it ahead of America in some areas of quantum messaging and cyber tactics, with grave implications for US naval operations.[48] We doubt, however, that it is actually winning this race. A more likely scenario is that Chinese hacking operations have stolen highly classified US military technology that is unknown to the public.

---

[43] David Leonhardt, "Protectionism by China is Biggest Since World War II," *The New York Times* (October 8, 2010), http://economix.blogs.nytimes.com/2010/10/08/biggest-protectionism-since-world-war-ii

[44] David E. Sanger, "More Countries Adopt China's Tactics on Currency," *The New York Times* (October 3, 2010), http://www.nytimes.com/2010/10/04/world/04currency.html

[45] Parag Khanna, *The Second World: Empires and Influence in the New Global Order* (New York: Random House, 2008), 340.

[46] See Peter Ford, "China Asserts Itself in GPS Turf War," *The Christian Science Monitor* (March 25, 2009), http://features.csmonitor.com/innovation/2009/03/25/China-asserts-itself-in-gps-turf-war

[47] John Pomfret, "Economic Powerhouse China Focuses on its Military Might," *The Washington Post* (August 17, 2010), A6.

[48] Christopher Shay, "China's Great (Quantum) Leap Forward," *Time* (September 9, 2010), http://www.time.com/time/printout/0,8816,2016687,00.html

So too China's soon-to-be operational anti-ship ballistic missiles (ASBMs)—with a range of 1,000 miles, as opposed to the 600 mile range of a US cruise missile—send a clarion geopolitical message to Asia and the West alike. ASBMs are much faster than a cruise, and far more lethal. Not only does the US Navy have no defense against them, but also (officially, at least) has none in development.[49] This alone could terminate the US dominance of the Western Pacific and check its ability to defend Taiwan. Tensions spiked in this area in 2010,[50] raising a question that was hardly even contemplated a year before: what direction will neighboring countries take when forced to choose between a full-blown arms race or a geopolitical downgrade to the status of de facto Chinese tribute state?

This strained atmosphere has not only dimmed hopes for "G2" bilateralism between Washington and Beijing,[51] but has cast a dark shadow over globalization in general. China's budding economic hubris invites a hardening of its geopolitics and a concomitant indifference to First World opinion. Sometimes Beijing even seems to deliberately cultivate an odious image, as when it set aside its pre-Olympics amity campaign and, at this of all times, brutally cracked down on Tibet. Then, soon after the Olympics, it all but flaunted its new fleet of mobile execution vans.[52] Their ghastly debut served at once as a warning to local troublemakers and an advertisement to international transplant customers in search of freshly harvested body parts from executed convicts.[53]

These departures mark the end of the soft-power phase of China's rise—its "charm offensive," as Joshua Kurlantzick dubs it.[54] While much of

---

[49] Seth Cropsey, "Keeping the Pacific Pacific," *Foreign Affairs* (September/October 2010), http://www.foreignaffairs.com/print/66713

[50] Alfred W. McCoy, "The Decline and Fall of the American Empire," *The Nation* (December 6, 2010), http://www.thenation.com/article/156851/decline-and-fall-american-empire

[51] Geoff Dyer and Daniel Dombey, "Shadow Cast Over Hopes for US-China 'G2,'" *Financial Times* (January 14, 2010), http://www.ft.com/cms/s/0/b09172ac-0135-11df-8c54-00144feabdc0.html#axzz 195agX8P7

[52] Andrew Malone, "China's Hi-Tech 'Death Van' where Criminals are Executed and then their Organs are Sold on Black Market," *Mail Online* (March 27, 2009), http://www.dailymail.co.uk/news/worldnews/article-1165416/Chinas-hi-tech-death-van-criminals-executed-organs-sold-black-market.html

[53] An added attraction was the fact that most of these organs were known to have been stolen from health-minded Falun Gong prisoners of conscience. This trade, which is largely run by the military, is documented in David Matas and David Kilgour, *Bloody Harvest: Revised Report into the Allegations of Organ Harvesting of Falun Gong Practitioners in China* (January 2007), available online in eighteen languages at david-kilgour.com

[54] Joshua Kurlantzick, *Charm Offensive: How China's Soft Power is Transforming the World* (New Haven: Yale University Press), 2007.

the West is in denial, a far more aggressive PRC is on display in places like the South China Sea, where Beijing has been winning almost by default. It simply has not met the kind of regional resistance it once did.[55] Its Southeast Asian rivals have effectively passed the hot potato to Washington. Clearly Rim countries need a strong American presence; yet to placate China they have blocked Washington's input to ASEAN and other Rim organizations.

Recently, however, there have been signs of renewed regional resolve. Japan's clash with China over fishing rights in the East China Sea sent a tsunami of anxiety across the whole Asia Pacific, and meanwhile China arrested nine Vietnamese fishermen near the disputed Paracel Islands in the South China Sea.[56] Soon ASEAN members, in a complete reversal of their former drift, were requesting US mediation in the maritime imbroglio. Against China's insistence that these matters be handled bilaterally, the US State Department is being welcomed as a multilateral umpire.[57] The question is what kind of umpire a bankrupt America can be in the face of China's burgeoning economic and military might.[58]

Denying America a solid diplomatic foothold while inviting its greater military presence was always schizophrenic, but in many ways the ASEAN nations simply duplicated Washington's own equivocation toward China. Even as Washington sells weaponry to Taiwan, it continues to fuel the Strait crisis by promoting the economic and institutional empowerment of the PRC. These mixed signals from the world's foremost democratic leader can hardly encourage Rim nations to take a principled stand against China. Geopolitical ambiguity is very much in China's interest, so it too sends mixed signals. In September 2010 it went back to making verbal overtures to both Washington and US corporations.[59] So too it resumed military

---

[55] Du Tran, "Unbalanced Bargaining Game with China," *Japan Times* (February 24, 2009), http://search.japantimes.co.jp/print/eo20090224a3.html

[56] "Vietnam Demands China Release 9 Fishermen," *The Associated Press* (October 6, 2010), http://www.wten.com/Global/story.asp?S=13276559

[57] Edward Wong, "China's Disputes in Asia Buttress Influence of U.S.," *The New York Times* (September 22, 2010), http://www.nytimes.com/2010/09/23/world/asia/23china.html

[58] It is little wonder that South Korea, in the aftermath of North Korea's December 2010 shelling of Yeonpyeong Island, began making fawning diplomatic overtures toward China, which it assumed had preponderant influence over Pyongyang. See Ahn Young-joon, "South Korea Moves to Boost Ties with China in Wake of North Korea Attacks," *The Christian Science Monitor* (December 16, 2010), http://www.csmonitor.com/World/Asia-Pacific/2010/1216/South-Korea-moves-to-boost-ties-with-China-in-wake-of-North-Korea-attacks

[59] Keith Bradsher, "China Moves to Ease Strain with U.S.," *The New York Times* (September 8, 2010), http://www.nytimes.com/2010/09/09/world/asia/09china.html

exchanges with the Pentagon, even as it launched provocative war-games in the Yellow Sea, just days before scheduled US–South Korean anti-sub exercises commenced in the same area.[60]

These actions bespeak a full commitment to what John Mearsheimer calls the "unpeaceful rise."[61] Nowhere are China's real intentions more graphically exposed than in its effort to forge a full naval capability, including a modern carrier fleet. At first sight this blue-water gambit seems preposterous, given the conspicuous superiority of the US Navy. As for Taiwan, its proximity makes a carrier presence not only unnecessary but even a military liability. Obviously China's military ambitions are going global. The rapid development of its nuclear submarine fleet, coupled with its rising ASBM threat, leaves no doubt that the prime target is the US Navy.[62]

The mixed signals Washington often gets from Beijing crested in 2006. After Beijing was praised for its putative cooperation on North Korea's nuclear threat, the commander of the US Pacific fleet was sent to China to set up a military exchange program. It was surely no accident that at this very moment a Chinese Song-class submarine, packing wake-homing torpedoes and anti-ship cruise missiles,[63] set about stalking the US carrier Kitty Hawk. To ensure the greatest possible diplomatic splash, the sub surfaced within easy firing range of the carrier fleet.[64]

Again, as a predictable test of the new Obama administration, a naval spat erupted in March 2009 near Hainan Island. Increasingly China uses civilian ships as pawns in these unconventional war games. This time a flotilla of Chinese "fishing" boats surrounded and "played chicken" with an unarmed US surveillance ship. On the surface this action seemed less combustible than the Bush administration's Hainan Incident of April 2001, for no lives were lost and no hostages were taken. The difference is

---

Later in September, Premier Wen Jiabao extended similar overtures to US companies that have been grumbling about unfair policies in China. Reported on CNN (Hong Kong), September 23, 2010.

[60] Shay, *op. cit.*

[61] John J. Mearsheimer, "China's Unpeaceful Rice," *Current History* (April 2000): 160–62.

[62] Pomfret, *op cit.*

[63] China's cruise missiles are now much safer from air-to-air missile defense, thanks to China's extensive espionage. Recently an American defense consultant was convicted of selling this vital technology to Beijing for $84,000. See "U.S. Engineer Guilty in China Spy Case," *UPI.com* (August 10, 2010), http://www.upi.com/Top-News/US/2010/08/10/US-engineer-guilty-in-China-spy-case/UPI-89011281461613/

[64] Sally Peck, "Chinese Sub Secretly Stalks US Fleet," *The Telegraph* (November 13, 2006), http://www.telegraph.co.uk/news/worldnews/1534011/Chinese-sub-secretly-stalks-US-fleet.html

that post-recession China feels much less constrained than it did in 2001. America now needs Chinese credit so badly that it might be willing to trade a considerable chunk of its military and geopolitical capital for China's financial cooperation. It is common knowledge that without a decisive US presence, the South China Sea would already be a Chinese lake. Beijing hopes Washington will conclude that the US economy is worth the South China Sea, with Taiwan next on the acquisitions list.

POWER VACUUM

China's ability to juggle policy contradictions is part of what has distinguished its power politics from Russia's. Ironically, Putin's tactics must be credited with having more transparency, in the sense of his more openly advertised bellicosity. The problem is that Russia's economy is so petrol dependent that its geopolitical power trades like a commodity. This worked to Moscow's advantage so long as the oil and gas boom lasted, but came back to haunt in 2008 when commodity prices plummeted and Western bank credit vanished. With inflation in double digits and the former trade surplus evaporating, the Kremlin's economic promises went up in smoke.[65]

Even Russia's flagship company, Gazprom, which early in 2008 aspired to being the largest and most powerful corporation in the world, would need a government bailout to stay afloat.[66] By 2010 it and other top Russian companies were still teetering on the edge of bankruptcy. While billions were pumped into failing banks and state-controlled conglomerates, small and medium companies were left to wither on the vine.[67] Even less was

---

[65] Arkady Ostrovsky, "Swaggering on," *The Economist* (November 19, 2008), http://www.economist.com/PrinterFriendly.cfm?story_id=12494494

[66] Andrew E. Kramer, "Gazprom, Once Mighty, Is Reeling," *The New York Times* (December 30, 2008), http://www.nytimes.com/2008/12/30/business/worldbusiness/30gazprom.html. By late January 2009 the Central Bank was trying to defend a 30 percent devaluation of the ruble from the previous year's high, so as to improve the trade balance, but a future dive in oil prices would be devastating. See James Beadle, "Placing Big Get on Oil," *The Moscow Times* (January 29, 2009), http://www.moscowtimes.ru/articles/detail.php?ID=374017&print=Y

Even the rebound in oil prices that took place in 2010 did not repair the economic and political damage that had been done. Low growth and further state collapse was expected in 2011 and 2012. See Carnegie Endowment, "Russia: Unstable Economy and Political Crisis," *Seeking Alpha* (December 23, 2010), http://seekingalpha.com/article/243366-russia-unstable-economy-and-political-crisis

[67] Fraser Cameron, "Dead-End Russia," *The New York Times* (February 11, 2010), http://www.nytimes. com/2010/02/11/opinion/11iht-edcameron.html

done to soften the social impact of a falling ruble or to assist the unemployed.[68] The result was a spate of anti-government demonstrations, most staged by communists who oddly demanded greater civil freedom as well as nationalization. Most emphatically, though, they called for further de-Westernization and a "Russia without Putin."[69]

Coupling those objectives is an unsubtle way of lumping Putin in with Yeltsin. This has not worked, for Putin is a grand master of image construction. He keeps his ratings up by staging macho demonstrations of his capabilities in everything from judo to aerial firefighting. Meanwhile he avoids the fray of daily affairs, leaving Medvedev the task of explaining all the setbacks.[70] Unfortunately the buck still stops with Putin, who is in the awkward position of needing the West almost as much as Yeltsin did. Under attack from far Left factions like the Communist and Bolshevik parties, and no doubt aware of how fragile his alliance is with China, this champion of Russian Orthodoxy has been forced to walk some distance in Yeltsin's occidental shoes.

Clearly he does not like the fit. His ambivalence was on full display in January 2009 when he went to the World Economic Forum in Davos as a keynote speaker. Since part of his mission was to get a portion of Russia's debt ($540 billion as of October 2008) written off,[71] he was in no position to berate Washington over the recession or anything else, and he began his speech by promising not to do so. However, the scorpion just had to sting. In the very next breath he charged

> . . . that only a year ago, from this rostrum, we heard the words of American representatives about the fundamental stability and cloudless prospects of the US economy. But today, the pride of Wall Street—the investment banks—have practically stopped existing. . . This example alone reflects the real state of affairs better than any criticism.[72]

---

[68] Michael Schwirtz and Clifford J. Levy, "As Economy Sinks, Russians Protest," *The New York Times* (February 1, 2009), http://www.nytimes.com/2009/02/01/world/europe/01russia.html

[69] Mansur Mirovalev, "Protesters Rally Against Kremlin's Economic Course," *Forbes* (January 31, 2009), http://www.forbes.com/topstories/feeds/ap/2009/01/31/ap59991263.htmlFORBES

[70] Nikolai Petrov, "Taking the Hit for Putin," *The Moscow Times* (March 3, 2009), http://www. themoscowtimes.com/articles/detail.php?ID=374976&print=Y

[71] Dmitry Sidorov, "Vladimir Putin Wants Your Money," *Forbes* (February 6, 2009), http://www.forbes.com/2009/02/06/putin-davos-debt-opinions-contributors_0206_dmitry_sidorov.html

[72] Vladimir Putin, "Putin's Speech at Davos World Economic Forum," *Russia Today* (January 28, 2009), http://themoscowtimes.com/opinion/article/taking-the-hit-for-putin/374976.html

China's Premier Wen Jiabao could not resist chiming in on the subject of America's excessive consumption and financial extravagance, as if China had not been the major beneficiary of both.[73]

Accustomed as we are to Putin's indecorum, Wen's barb seems more emblematic of a global power shift. François Godement charges that the West has been unwittingly assisting China in "hollowing out" the international system that was supposed to tame it. Instead of becoming the "responsible stakeholder" that neoliberals envisioned, Beijing is pulling international institutions into its Second World orbit. Godement's proposed solution is "reciprocal engagement," which means hard political conditionality.[74] Unfortunately the "hollowing out" that he laments may already have reached an institutional tipping point. Whether that is good or bad news for the Third World depends upon what fills the resulting power vacuum.

On the Left there is a pervasive assumption that anything would be better than the American devil we know. After all, Washington for decades played a quasi-development game with heinous puppet dictators like Marcos, Suharto, and Pinochet, all under the rubric of Kissingeresque "realism."[75] Nor did this practice end with the Cold War. Neoliberalism's unqualified "engagement" with post-Tiananmen China and with pseudo-democratic Russia only reconfirmed the moral bankruptcy of American foreign policy. It is no wonder that Kissinger himself became a boisterous advocate of neoliberal engagement. Nothing much changed as the policy torch was passed from the amoralism of Cold War realism to that of globalism.

More recently relations with Africa have been paraded as a partial exception to this rule. But the attempt to implant a modicum of reform conditionality in African policies was a sad case of too little, too late. Perhaps this moral posture was possible because Africa was thought to be so incorrigible that reform conditions would never be met. Or, as was clearly the case in Rwanda prior to the 1994 holocaust, the conditions imposed were recklessly politicized, giving impetus to Western-backed insurgents

---

[73] Then, as a surreal postscript that says much about the new global pecking order, ex-president Bill Clinton (as if he had nothing to do with the neoliberal defects under assault) trumpeted that "the Chinese Premier was right..." See Jenny Booth, "Playing the Davos Blame Game," *Times Online* (January 29, 2009), http://business.timesonline.co.uk/tol/business/economics/wef/article5612801.ece

[74] François Godement, "A Global China Policy," *European Council on Foreign Relations—ECFR/22* (June 2010): 2.

[75] See William H. Thornton, *New World Empire: Civil Islam, Terrorism, and the Making of Neoglobalism* (Lanham, MD: Rowman & Littlefield, 2005), 157.

(Kagame's RPF) at the expense of the ruling coalition (FAR). The result was genocidal rage on the part of the Hutu-backed FAR.[76] In any case, Western policy makers have tended to view Africa after the Cold War as a side show. The Chinese were much faster in grasping Africa's geoeconomic import as well as its authoritarian dynamics.

Many Western analysts are now coming to similar conclusions. Where they differ is in their belief that "good governance" still counts for sustainable development. Paul Romer, as we have seen, would solve the dilemma of social disorder and commercial unaccountability by offering Africa a neocolonial package plan that gives up on indigenous reform and runs designated SEZs by Western managerial fiat. The assumption here is that democracy has been the weak link in the West's developmental chain. Romer's package resembles Singapore-style globalism, which amounts to Westernized economic institutions without any Western political baggage. We should note, however, that even Singapore sees fit to keep its democratic façade in place, as does Moscow. It is Sino-globalization that jettisons this pretense.

Eventually Africans will come to see that the supposedly neutral China model is actually more stringently conditional than Western programs that openly spell out their conditions. Regional organizations still claim the postcolonial high ground, but their record belies this pose. The case of Zimbabwe's Robert Mugabe is all too typical. He has exerted so much control over the Southern African Development Community (SADC) that the organization will rubber stamp anything he does. Recently it lent support to his stonewalling of the Global Political Agreement (GPA) and ended its August 2010 summit by calling for the removal of all international sanctions against Mugabe.[77]

Ad hoc regional solutions fare no better. In the case of the Democratic Republic of the Congo (DRC), the involvement of Uganda and Rwanda has exacerbated a bloody civil war. Both of these intruders have plundered DRC resources and fanned ethnic animosities. It may fairly be asked where Western governments and media were during all this trauma. The same

---

[76] It is still an open question how much of the resulting genocide was planned in advance by the Rwandan Armed Forces (FAR) and how much of it was committed by the Rwandan Patriotic Front (RPF). What is obvious is the fact that Kagame's present government is doing everything it can to keep these questions from being raised. See Oliver Kearns, "Polarizing the Debate over Rwanda," *ZNET* (June 29, 2010), http://www.zcommunications.org/polarising-the-debate-over-rwanda-by-oliver-kearns

[77] See Kholwani Nyathi, "Southern Africa: Mugabe Wins Big at SADC Summit," *All Africa.com* (August 22, 2010), http://allafrica.com/stories/201008231144.html

US administrations that charged into Yugoslavia and Iraq with such deep-pocket conviction have been conspicuously absent from Africa.[78]

What is sorely needed here and throughout the Third World is full democratic engagement, coupled with a much heavier injection of the right kind of conditional assistance. Ideally this would be applied on a multilateral basis, though doing so under UN auspices is out of the question, given China's veto power in the Security Council. Thus the West faces a moral paradox: to "do the right thing" for failed states, or in Africa's case for a failed continent, may require stepping outside existing legal structures that privilege sovereignty over democratic values. A far more humanistic policy direction was broached in 1993 by UN Secretary-General Boutros Boutros-Ghali. This initiative found expression in the Vienna Declaration and Programme of Action of 1993, which amounted to a democratic Bill of Rights.[79]

THE POST-GLOBALIST IMPERATIVE

That strikingly liberal code of conduct had its trial run in Kosovo. Recourse had to be taken to NATO rather than the UN, and not surprisingly there has been broad resistance to this precedent-setting departure. A huge reactionary bloc refuses to recognize Kosovo's independence from Serbia. The two sides of the issue provide a measure of the current balance of power between the First and Second Worlds. It is telling that only 69 of the 192 countries in the UN General Assembly take the US/EU side on the matter. A two-thirds majority would be necessary to give Kosovo UN membership, and even that would be nullified by the certain veto of China and Russia in the Security Council. It hardly matters that in July 2008 the top UN court backed the legality of Kosovo's declaration of independence.[80]

Having gained effective control of the UN, the Second World is fast consolidating its power in the G20 and other international bodies. If liberal values are to have any place in world affairs, some form of counter organization, such as a League of Democracies, is a liberal imperative.

---

[78] See "The Civil War in the Democratic Republic of Congo," *Africa Resource* (May 30, 2007; updated February 18, 2010), http://www.africaresource.com/index. php?option=com_content&view=article&id= 306

[79] Roland Axtmann, "Democracy and Globality," *STSS—Studies of Transition States and Societies* 2, no. 1 (June 2010): 26 (22–35).

[80] Dusan Stojanovic, "After UN Court Ruling, Fears of Global Separatism," *Google.com* (July 23, 2010), http://www.google.com/hostednews/ap/article/ ALeqM5id6fpJYD9tvwpyuobS8jGb_hVlugD9H4SIV03

The potency of this idea is suggested by the hostility it meets from anti-democratic quarters. Sergey Karaganov, a ranking Russian scholar of foreign affairs, may be right that a league would increase tensions between the West and what he calls "the Second New World"[81]—in other words, our new Second World.

From a Putinist perspective this tension would prevent international affairs from entering a new "era of cooperation," though it hardly needs to be said that Moscow's notion of cooperation amounts to Western capitulation. Lately Russia has been getting little but "cooperation" from its energy clients in "Old Europe," while Europe's "juniors" bitterly protest the retreat of the EU from its former liberal commitments. Estonian President Toomas Hendrik Ilves charges that Brussels is now "virtually complicit with Moscow" in its plan to roll back democratic gains in the former Soviet sphere.[82] However, the grand prize for Second World "cooperation" goes to the former German Chancellor Gerhard Schröder, who is now a consultant for Gazprom.

We would argue that this erosion of democratic resolve is not only detrimental to Europe's long-term interests, but to Russia's as well. The worst case scenario for Russian geopolitics is the ongoing Sinofication of Central Asia. For the Chinese this region is even more critical than Africa, since they see it as the locus of *Lebensraum* as well as affordable resources. Whereas Hitler flatly stated that "Russian territory is our India,"[83] Beijing has the good sense not to spell out its intentions. The brighter minds in the Kremlin nevertheless know that Putin has been pointing his geopolitical guns in the wrong direction. Some may even recognize, *sotto voce*, that the best way to check the westward march of Chinese hegemony would be to support the democratic transformation of the region.

It is true that in some cases democratization could favor radical Islamization. The classic case of Algeria comes to mind, and in Pakistan local democratic institutions have given impetus to Sharia law. In Central Asia, however, democracy is more likely to favor civil Islam. What most disturbs Moscow and Beijing alike is that a moderate and progressive

---

[81] Sergej Karaganov, "The New Russia is no Longer a Crippled Giant," *Spiegel Online* (November 14, 2008), http://www.spiegel.de/international/world/0,1518,druck-590412,00.html

[82] "The EU is Virtually Complicit with Moscow," *Spiegel* interview with Estonian President Ilves, *Spiegel Online* (November 3, 2008), http://www.spiegel.de/international/europe/0,1518,druck-588047,00.html

[83] Jürgen Zimmerer, "Colonialism and the Holocaust—Towards an Archeology of Genocide," *Development Dialogue*, no. 50 (December 2008): 95 (95–123).

Islamism would conduce to good Western relations.[84] Civil Islam could be the West's best ally in its dual contest with China and Russia. A high price has been paid, therefore, for Washington's blanket hostility toward Islamism after 9/11.[85] If the West were to play these democratic and Islamic cards wisely, and in tandem, the Second World would not only lose much of Eurasia, but would have a much harder time controlling Islamic resistance within its own borders.

The West, meanwhile, has an even greater geopolitical trump card in the inherent rivalry between Russia and China. It was certainly no accident that Russia's attack on Georgia coincided with the Beijing Olympics. China was incensed, and most Central Asian nations were sorely disturbed. Hence the SCO refused to condone the action or to recognize the subsequent independence of South Ossetia and Abkhazia. Even Russia's pet dictatorship, Belarus — which gets an estimated $8 billion in annual subsidies from Russia — refused to do Moscow's bidding this time.[86] It was a rare event to have NATO and the SCO in agreement on something besides Muslim terrorism. Nonetheless Russia proceeded to consolidate its gains. In August 2010, exactly two years after the invasion, Russian S-300 missiles were openly planted in Abkhazia and South Ossetia.[87] Like a wolf marking its territory, Moscow was sending a message to China as well as NATO.

Russian strategists must know that their SCO alliance with China is no more than a short-term expedient. The Kremlin cannot fail to see that China's gain in Eurasia will be Russia's irreparable loss. Even some hardcore realists must recognize that if Russia were to lose its grip on Central Asia, it would be far better to forfeit it to the forces of democratization, even with links to Washington and Brussels, than to let Beijing take it. Moscow's choice can be compared to London's as it faced the end of the

---

[84] This was clearly the case until very recently with Turkey's Erdoğan administration. Turkey's recent split with the West was largely a product of the West's blanket support for Israel. By way of reaction, Turkey joined with Brazil to broker a nuclear deal with Iran, and likewise voted with Brazil against UN Security Council sanctions against Iran. See James Traub, "Turkish Dilemma," *Foreign Policy* (June 15, 2010), http://www. foreignpolicy.com/articles/2010/06/15/turkish_dilemma

[85] See Thornton, *New World Empire, op. cit.*, Chapter 5.

[86] Fred Weir, "Why Russia's Medvedev is Lashing Out at Belarus's Lukashenko," *The Christian Science Monitor* (October 6, 2010), http://www.csmonitor.com/layout/set/print/content/view/print/330487

[87] Dmitry Solovyov, "Russia Deploys Missiles to Protect Georgia Rebels," *Reuters* (August 11, 2010), http://www.reuters.com/assets/print?aid=USTRE67A26520100811 and "Georgia Says Russia Deployed S-300 Missiles in South Ossetia," *Radio Free Europe/Radio Liberty* (August 25, 2010), http://www.rferl.org/content/Georia-Says_Russia_Deployed_S300_Missiles_In_South_Ossetia/2137662.html

British empire in the twentieth century. As Arnold Toynbee saw it, the question was whether power would be relinquished to the US, Russia, Germany, or Japan. America was the far less onerous choice. Now, the West can use a similar "lesser evil" stratagem to lure Russia back into the democratic camp.

So far America's forays into Central Asia have had the opposite effect. Despite grating conflicts of interest, China and Russia have been pushed together in what amounts to a shotgun marriage. So too there is a short-term economic incentive behind this Second World accord, in that China covets Russia's resources and technology while Russia desperately needs China's cash. For Moscow it comes down to a question of short-term gain versus long-term disaster. Nina L. Khrushcheva (the great-granddaughter of Nikita Khrushchev) argues that if Russia's anti-Western drift continues for the next 20 years, China will swallow Siberia and the whole Far East.[88] Meanwhile the Sino-centric SCO is fast evolving from a regional economic and security organization into the spearhead of a new Great Game against the West. The problem for Russia is that it is starting to look like a pawn on this Chinese chessboard.

China will win this game by default if the West fails to mount an intelligent and determined counter-offensive. With the ravages of neoliberal globalization in clear view, the developing world will be tempted to embrace the China model, but this dark-horse advantage will not last long. Even more than neoliberalization, Sino-globalization is a factory for horrific inequality. It will ensure so much distributive injustice that the working classes of the Third World will finally balk at its economics, and hopefully its politics as well. At some point they will catch on to the fact that neither First nor Second World globalism is serving their interest.

The question is whether this great awakening will come in time, before China-style mechanisms of repression are solidly in place. Stripped of democratic choice, the world's developmental politics will increasingly resemble CCP or Putinist politics. Too late Amartya Sen's basic axiom concerning the instrumental value of democracy will be understood at a grassroots level. Unfortunately Sen himself missed the fact that neoliberal globalization also erodes developmental freedom. It is time to move beyond both neoliberal and authoritarian development by way of a radically democratic post-globalism.

---

[88] Nina L. Khrushcheva, "Russia's Rotting Empire," *World Policy Journal* (Fall 2008): 117 (109–17).

8

FREEDOM WITHOUT BORDERS
Lessons of the Arab Revolt
for the Globalist West[1]

THE LIBYAN PRECEDENT

When we began writing this book, arguing for a conjoint First and Third World geopolitics, hope was all we could offer. Early in 2011, however, much of what we were hoping for started to materialize. To the dismay of nearly all Western observers,[2] the greatest pro-democratic movement of our times erupted from one of the most unlikely places: the Arab Street.

---

[1] This chapter (originally titled "The New Democratic Imperative: Cultural Studies in a New Key") and the Arab Spring sections of the Conclusion were written by William Thornton while on a research sabbatical from National Cheng Kung University. He wishes to thank NCKU for its assistance and encouragement.

[2] One notable exception was Emmanuel Todd, who along with Yousef Courbage predicted an Arab revolution four years before it came. We respect Todd's demographic prescience, but profoundly differ with his treatment of Islamism, as will be discussed later in the chapter. For a good overview of his thesis see Emmanuel Todd, "A Look at the Root Causes of the Arab Revolution," *Spiegel Online* (May 20, 2011), http://www.spiegel.de/international/world/0,1518,763537,00.html

Another such exception came from Walid Phares, who has advised members of Congress and the European Parliament. His book, *The Coming Revolution*, predicted broad regional resistance, but also warned of a radical Islamist undercurrent that could easily seize control of the revolts and negate their democratic character. See *The Coming Revolution: Struggle for Freedom in the Middle East* (New York: Simon & Schuster, 2010).

Sweeping quickly out of Tunisia into Egypt and a host of neighboring police states—Yemen, Bahrain, Syria, Jordan, Oman, Libya, Morocco,[3] Algeria, Iraq, and (in terms of defensive reaction) Saudi Arabia[4]—the Arab Spring mocks the implanted democracy that has failed so egregiously in Iraq and Afghanistan.[5] For Washington this amounts to "shock and awe" in reverse, as any assault on Middle East and North Africa (MENA) power structures is *ipso facto* a condemnation of US foreign policy.

Who could have imagined in March 2010, when the Arab League hosted its first summit in Libya, that within a year this venue would be ground zero in UN-approved air strikes invited by the League itself? That request of March 12, 2011 was the first in a series of diplomatic game changers. The League could almost always be counted on to oppose any kind of

---

[3] As of July 1, Morocco's constitutional referendum turned the nation into a limited democracy, complete with an elected president and congress, equal rights for women, and protection for religious minorities. It remains to be seen how all this will pan out in practice, since the king will still appoint the prime minister and control the military. Nonetheless these reforms warrant a more positive reaction than the one word comment that came from the US State Department: "encouraging." The Arab world is fully aware that the Obama administration is no friend of Arab democracy. What's truly "encouraging" is the fact that Morocco did not require Western guidance or intervention to launch this democratic initiative. See Richard Miniter, "Why Is Obama's State Department Uneasy About Democracy?" *Forbes* (July 7, 2011), http:blogs.forbes.com/ richardminiter/2011/07/07/why-is-obamas-state-department-uneasy-about-democracy/ and "In Arab Spring, Truth Can Beget Freedom," *The Christian Science Monitor* (June 20, 2011), http://www.csmonitor.com/Commentary/the-monitors-view/2011/0620/In-Arab-Spring-truth-can-beget-freedom; and Ahmed Charai and Joseph Braude, "All Hail the (Democratic) King," *The New York Times* (July 11, 2011), http://www.nytimes. com/2011/07/12/opinion/12Charai.html

[4] Witness King Abdullah's $130 billion spending hike. See Susanne Koelbl, "Saudi Arabia's Silent Battle to Halt History," *Spiegel Online* (June 14, 2011), http://www.spiegel. de/international/world/0,1518,768368,00.html and Steffen Hertog, "The Cost of Counter-Revolution in the GCC," *Foreign Policy* (March 31, 2011), http://mideast.foreignpolicy. com/posts/2011/05/31/the_costs_of_counter_revolution_ in_the_gcc

[5] Here we treat the new "Arab Street" and the "Arab Spring" as mutually reinforcing entities. For some this is an overly optimistic view of the region's democratic potential. Stanley Kurtz, for example, regards the "Street" and the "Spring" as antithetical forces. For him it is always 1952, the year of the popular rising that overthrew Egypt's ailing democracy. Not only Egypt but the whole Arab world is in his view locked in a perpetual replay of that reactionary turn. Egypt's constitutional referendum of March 2011, which effectively voted down a full democratic transformation, was just the latest rerun of the 1952 syndrome. We agree that the referendum bears comparison with 1952, but largely by way of contrast. The protesters who stood their ground at Tahrir Square were quite literally on a different "Street." In Egypt, as in the whole region, we find two opposing Streets—one of reform and one of reaction. See Stanley Kurtz, "Is There an Arab Spring?" *National Review Online* (March 21, 2011), http://www.nationalreview.com/corner/262618/ there-arab-spring-stanley-kurtz

popular resistance or foreign intervention, yet now it was calling for the unthinkable: foreign intervention in support of popular resistance. Without that invitation the UN's preemptive action would have been summarily vetoed by China and Russia in the Security Council, just as they would later block any action in support of the Syrian opposition. Russia's decision to abstain from the Libyan vote was critical, since China rarely takes contrarian positions without Russian cover.[6]

Thus the Libyan resistance got an incredibly lucky break, ushering in the first case of UN-approved military action to prevent a massacre.[7] Council Resolution 1973, passed on March 17, put teeth into the UN's "Responsibility to Protect" (R2P) resolution of 2005. There was even a positive connotation in the resolution's main limitation. 1973 authorized concerned states "to take all necessary measures," other than occupation, to protect civilians. That qualifier ensured that this branch of the Arab Revolt would remain the business of Arabs. The international community was there only to guarantee that Libya would not become another Rwanda or Srebrenica.[8]

That grim possibility was all the more likely in view of the fact that Colonel Muammar Gaddafi was beefing up his military with massive infusions of foreign mercenaries who had no qualms about killing the locals. According to a 1989 non-binding resolution of the UN General Assembly

---

[6] This order had to come from the very top. Even Sergey Lavrov, the Russian foreign minister, seemed to have no idea what his country was about to do. Shortly before he had told Hillary Clinton that Russia would "never never" permit a "no-fly zone" over Libya. That made sense insofar as this was Putin's position on the matter. Ordinarily Putin's position would be Russia's, but this time President Medvedev publically broke with his mentor and exercised his constitutional right to decide foreign policy. See Ryan Lizz, "The Consequentialist: How the Arab Spring Remade Obama's Foreign Policy," *The New Yorker* (May 2, 2011), http://www.newyorker.com/reporting/2011/05/02/110502fa_fact_lizza and Gregory L. White, "Medvedev, Putin Clash over Libya," *The Wall Street Journal* (March 22, 2011), http://online.wsj.com/article/SB10001424052748704355304576214803505330690.html

Beijing sorely regretted that it did not break ranks with Russia on this occasion. See Philip Stephens, "Working Out What China Wants," *Financial Times* (June 30, 2011), http://www.ft.com/intl/cms/s/0/33c093e4-a363-11e0-8990-00144 feabdc0.html#axzz1R3C9ad37

[7] Lizz, *op. cit.*

[8] Some, however, believe that NATO's limited mandate compromised its R2P responsibilities. Chris Parry, a former Royal Navy rear admiral, holds that the Libya campaign — run on the cheap, and by committee — defied strategic logic. Not only were ground troops precluded for political reasons, but infrastructure targets that propped up Gaddafi's regime were proscribed. Hence a complete rethink of the mission is badly needed. See Nick Hopkins, "NATO's Mission in Libya Needs a Complete Rethink, Says Former Admiral," *The Guardian* (May 22, 2011), http://www.guardian.co.uk/world/2011/may/22/nato-mission-libya-rethink-admiral

(Resolution 44/34), hiring these mercenaries was in itself a criminal act against the Libyan people.[9] In effect the country had already been invaded. Hence, any countervailing assistance from the international community need not be construed as an intrusion into the internal affairs of Libya. Gaddafi had already rendered the civil war international by hiring his foreign thugs.

What made 1973 seem so controversial was the bias stacked against it after the Bush "freedom agenda" made a mockery of all liberal intervention. Russia and China were not the only roadblocks. NATO was split by Germany's shocking abstention in the council vote, which cost precious time and earned praise from Gaddafi himself.[10] The rebel capital at Benghazi was then just hours from collapse and sure annihilation.[11] Echoing Rwanda's genocidal radio exhortations of 1994, Gaddafi called the protesters rats and cockroaches who must die. Doubtless that genocidal rant helped Bernard-Henri Lévy to galvanize French support for what some have called "Lévy's war." At this eleventh hour he connected President Sarkozy with the rebel National Transitional Council (NTC). This led to Hillary Clinton's meeting in Paris a few days later with the de facto rebel leader, Mahmoud Jibril, and soon British prime minister David Cameron was clamoring for air strikes. The French air force took immediate action once the UN approval came through.

In view of Europe's reputation for playing Venus to America's Mars, this was startling news. An even bigger surprise, however, was the League's green light. Although most League members detested Gaddafi—who had burned his last bridge with Saudi Arabia by allegedly plotting the assassination of the then Crown Prince Abdullah in 2003[12]—they had to be mindful of what an opposition victory would portent for their own ruling classes. This was a political litmus test for the whole MENA region, and arguably for the whole Third World. Compared to Gaddafi, Tunisia's Ben Ali and Egypt's Hosni Mubarak had been authoritarian light weights.[13] If Gaddafi

---

[9] Louis Klarevas, "Libya's Stranger Solders," *The New Republic* (February 26, 2011), http://www.tnr.com/article/world/84250/qaddafi-libya-mercenaries-united-nations

[10] Severin Weiland and Roland Nelles, "Germany has Marginalised Itself over Libya," *The Guardian* (March 18, 2011), http://www.guardian.co.uk/commentisfree/2011/mar/18/libya-germany-un-security-council

[11] Ulrich Fichtner, "Berlin's Hesitancy in the UN and the World," *Spiegel Online* (April 15, 2011), http://www.spiegel.de/international/world/0,1518,druck-756782,00.html

[12] Ellen Knickmeyer, "A Five-Star Retirement Home for Dictators," *Foreign Policy* (June 23, 2011), http://www.foreignpolicy.com/articles/2011/06/23/a_five_star_retirement_home_for_dictators

[13] This point is effectively made by Michael Totten, who was never deluded about reform possibilities in Libya. See Michael J. Totten, "Libya's Legacy," *The New*

could be toppled, despite his draconian tactics, no dictator would be safe and the whole League would be on borrowed time. It is possible that the League and the Gulf Cooperation Council (GCC) were bargaining on a flaccid response from the West. In that case Gaddafi would crush the opposition and terminate the Arab Spring's domino effect.

Whatever its real motives, the League's glimmer of support for the Libyan rebels was not extended to Syria, where protestors were under much the same axe.[14] It did not take long for that ambivalence to impact Libya as well. Shortly after NATO's air mission began, the League's Secretary-General, Amr Moussa, threatened to withdraw approval for the whole operation. Oddly this reversal came and went in just two days. In his March 21 meeting with UN Secretary-General Ban Ki-Moon, Moussa reconfirmed the League's support,[15] begging the question of what took place behind closed doors.

Much like East European communist apparatchiks who reinvented themselves as "reformists" after 1989, Moussa is doing a fine job of casting off his authoritarian epaulets. He was Mubarak's foreign minister from 1991 to 2001 and for the last decade has headed the autocratic Arab League. Nonetheless he is now the front-runner for the presidency of a proto-democratic Egypt.[16] Clearly he is playing both sides of the revolutionary fence. The League retraction he engineered was almost certainly a power play on behalf of the Old Guard to get assurance that Western intervention would not be extended to other conflict zones. That would include the Syrian debacle, which by late May had seen over 900 protesters killed and another 10,000 imprisoned.[17] The regime of Bashar al-Assad (aka the "Syrial Killer")[18] showed none of the diffidence one would expect in the

Republic (February 23, 2011), http://www.tnr.com/article/world/83992/qaddafi-libya-protests-iran

[14] The only military participant in the UN action has been Qatar, the home base of Al Jazeera, though the United Arab Emirates was a robust provider of humanitarian aid. Qatar may have some non-humanitarian motives. It quickly brokered a $100 million sale of Libyan crude oil from the rebel zone. See Alex Delmar-Morgan, Nathan Hodge and Charles Levinson, "Allies Clash on Libya Stalemate," _The Wall Street Journal_ (April 14, 2011), http://online.wsj.com/article/SB10001424052748703730104576260832626131842.html

[15] Martin Chulov, "Arab League to Reiterate Backing for Libya No-Fly Zone," _The Guardian_ (March 22, 2011), http://www.guardian.co.uk/world/2011/mar/22/arab-league-libya-no-fly

[16] Dan Ephron, "Egypt's Rising Power Player," _Newsweek_ (July 11, 2011), http://www.newsweek.com/2011/07/10/why-amr-moussa-is-egypt-s-presidential-frontrunner.html

[17] Abu Dhabi, "Arab Spring Hit by New Violence," _The Sydney Morning Herald_ (May 23, 2011), http://www.smh.com.au/world/arab-spring-hit-by-new-violence-20110522-1eyv4.html

[18] So named by the editorial cartoonist Robert Arial.

wake of NATO's Libyan gambit. Obviously Assad understood that Libya was a special case. One of the few concessions his regime was willing to make was a slight delay in its almost comical bid to sit on the UN Human Rights Council. For the moment Syria let Kuwait take its place, but with the clear intention to reapply in 2013. The irony is that Kuwait would vote almost the same way Syria would, and on some issues, such as women's rights, would probably be more regressive.[19]

Only three League members—Qatar, Jordan, and the United Arab Emirates—provided early military support for the Libyan rebels, and those three together assigned only 125 personnel to the operation.[20] Turkey, with its close commercial ties to Gaddafi, initially opposed the project, but finally sent some light naval support for non-combatant purposes.[21] What was far more important was the diplomatic sway of the more agreeable League members. This was especially true of Qatar, which became the second nation after France to recognize the rebels in Benghazi as Libya's legitimate government. Qatar itself might have felt relatively immune to the League's general fear of a Libyan precedent, since this mini-nation happens to have the highest per capita GDP (at $145,300 per person) of any country in the world.[22] Who would revolt against such largesse? Nonetheless, for all its globalist trappings, Doha is as fundamentally authoritarian as Tripoli or Damascus. Even as it hosted Al-Jazeera TV, Qatar's al-Thani ruling family canceled plans for an elected parliament and did not hesitate to back Persian Gulf neighbors in the suppression of Bahrain's demonstrations.[23]

WASHINGTON AND THE NEW ARAB STREET

There is no question that League members were using Libya as a fig leaf to cover their own repressive tracks. This modicum of support was all the

---

[19] Howard LaFranchi, "Syria, Under Pressure, Drops Bid for UN Rights Council. Is That Progress?" *The Christian Science Monitor* (May 11, 2011), http://www.csmonitor.com/USA/Foreign-Policy/2011/0511/Syria-under-pressure-drops-bid-for-UN-rights-council.-Is-that-progress

[20] Richard Norton-Taylor, Simon Rogers and Nick Hopkins, "Arab States Play Limited Role in Battle against Muammar Gaddafi's Regime," *The Guardian* (May 22, 2011), http://www.guardian.co.uk/world/2011/may/22/arab-states-battle-against-gaddafi

[21] Jonathan Head, "Libya: Turkey's Troubles with NATO and No-Fly Zone," *BBC News* (March 25, 2011), http://www.bbc.co.uk/news/world-africa-12864742

[22] Cyrus Sanati, "Qatar's Western Grip," *CNN Money* (May 6, 2011), http://finance.fortune.cnn.com/2011/05/06/qatar%E2%80%99s-western-grip/

[23] David B. Ottaway, "The Arab Tomorrow," *The Wilson Quarterly* (Winter 2010), http://www.wilsonquarterly.com/article.cfm?AID=1565 and Sanati, *op. cit.*

Arab Street was likely to get from these unabashed reactionaries. Nor could it expect much more from Western powers like the US. The State Department's standard prescription for popular unrest was the kind of "reform-lite" that was quickly promised by the monarchs of Jordan, Oman, Morocco, and Saudi Arabia, as well as President Abdelaziz Bouteflika of Algeria.[24] In that same spirit, at the League's March 2010 meeting, Tunisia's soon-to-be-deposed President Ben Ali had proposed making 2010 the region's "year of youth." Within a year, he more than got his wish.

Forces of youthful resistance were reaching critical mass across the entire Arab world. With 60 percent of the region's population under 30, and 25 percent of those unemployed, the stage was set for an even more potent youth politics than America got from its baby boomers in the counterculture years.[25] Ben Ali was hardly alone in his dim comprehension of this new "Street." Even specialists on Arab politics were stunned by the seemingly spontaneous democratism that ignited early in 2011.[26] And, needless to say, American policy makers were stupefied. Most began the year thinking that their worst problem in the region was Islamic Jihad. Washington had placed nearly all its bets on incorrigible autocrats like Egypt's Mubarak and Yemen's Ali Abdullah Saleh, who promised full cooperation in the US "war on terrorism," but conveniently defined nearly all political opposition as terrorism.

Even Syria's Assad got tacit American approval, despite the fact that he had offered himself as a faithful ally of Tehran, the unflagging patron of Hezbollah and Hamas, and the proud sponsor of anti-American insurgency in Iraq.[27] His record of sustained repression over the country's 74 percent Sunni majority did not prevent Hillary Clinton from declaring him a "reformer," partly perhaps because of his "free market" tilt. It should be recalled that the most infamous Baathist of all, Saddam Hussein, had likewise been accepted by Washington until he categorically broke with the globalist world order by invading Kuwait. In short, the decision to eliminate

---

[24] Alexander Smoltczyk and Volkhard Windfuhr, "Autocrats Gain Ground in Middle East," *Spiegel Online* (May 18, 2011), http://www.spiegel.de/international/world/0,1518,druck-762861,00.html

[25] We owe this baby boomer analogy to Fareed Zakaria. See Joelle Koenig, "La 'Rue Arabe' sert-t-elle de modèle aux américains?" *Le Monde.fr*, (February 21, 2011), http://www.lemonde.fr/idees/chronique/ 2011/02/21/la_1482916_3232.html

[26] Bernard Haykel, "The Arab Drama," *Project Syndicate* (March 7, 2011), http://www.project-syndicate.org/commentary/haykel3/English

[27] "Violence against Protests in Syria: Why the Mild US Response?" *The Christian Science Monitor* (April 1, 2011), http://www.csmonitor.com/Commentary/the-monitors-view/2011/0401/Violence-against-protests-in-Syria-Why-the-mild-US-response

Saddam had almost nothing to do with his domestic brutality. Assad had learned this lesson well.

Washington's tepid response to Syria's mounting crackdown is emblematic of its whole Arab dilemma. It so fears the "instability" that could result from Assad's ouster that it fails to recognize the potential allies under the dictator's heel.[28] Thus the world's leading democracy ends up condoning the last repository (after Saddam's exit) of Nazi-inspired Baathism. If there is any logical explanation for this liberal apostasy, it must rest on the dual supposition that (a) social unrest of any kind will open the door for Jihad, and (b) there is no moral cost in courting Arab dictators, since democracy and human rights have no possible place in Arab politics.

Washington has now been proved wrong on both points, and is reeling from the vertigo of its failed assumptions. If part of that shock effect owes to the oxymoronic feel of the words "Arab democratization," an equal surprise is the largely secular nature of these risings, at least in their initial phases. This seems to validate Sami Zubaida's thesis in *Beyond Islam* (published just as the Arab Spring was starting to make headlines) that modernization in the Islamic culture sphere is driven by the same secular and largely economic forces that operate elsewhere. Far from seeing Islamism (political Islam) as the main engine of Arab reform, Zubaida regards it as a xenophobic reaction to global forces. For him "de-sacralization" is a virtual prerequisite of modernization, such that Islamism could only have a debilitating effect on democratic processes that require pluralism.[29] The good news for Zubaida is that Islamism appears to be on the wane.

That is also good news for Gilles Kepel, who long ago questioned the conventional wisdom that Islamism would continue to define MENA politics.[30] Doubtless he feels vindicated by current events, but perhaps not for long. Already there are signs of the resistance movement's re-Islamization, thanks to a dearth of oppositional solidarity on the secular side. The first question

---

[28] On this cult of stability, see David Schenker, "Step Assad," *The New Republic* (April 9, 2011), http://www.tnr.com/article/86465/syria-assad-bush-obama-pentagon

What makes Washington's support of Assad all the more baffling is the fact that his overthrow by Sunni protesters would be a major blow to Iran. The Obama administration does not seem to have considered either the ethics or the geopolitics of its position. See Michael Young, "Obama's Great Escape on Syria," *Now Lebanon* (July 8, 2011), http://www.nowlebanon.com/NewsArticleDetails.aspx?ID=289438

[29] Zubaida's view is clearly at odds with Ernest Gellner's conception of Muslim society as fundamentally homogeneous. See Sami Zubaida, *Beyond Islam: A New Understanding of the Middle East* (London: I. B. Tauris, 2011), Chapter 1.

[30] See, for example, Gilles Kepel, *Jihad: The Trail of Political Islam*, Trans. by Anthony F. Roberts (Cambridge, MA: Belknap Press, 2002), 4–5.

is how much control organizations like the Muslim Brotherhood will gain over the consolidation phase of the revolts. Secondly, how sincere are these groups in their recent show of tolerance toward democratic pluralism? Will they, once in power, follow the militant course of Iranian Islamism of the Carter years or Algerian Islamism of the 1990s?[31]

What Kepel and Zubaida neglect are the solid grounds for hope that an "Enlightenment" or at least a "Reformation" is taking place within the Brotherhood itself. Assuming this democratic shift is genuine, it could help inoculate the Arab Street against more theocratic strains of Islamism. In May 2011, for example, radical Salafis took advantage of post-Mubarak chaos to launch savage attacks on Christian Copts. Not surprisingly, one of this group's most admired heroes is late Osama bin Laden. Its core preachment—not unlike the sermons of Ayatollah Ali Khamenei in Iran, where a renewed theocratic turn makes even Mahmoud Ahmadinejad look progressive[32]—is the need for an Islamic state as the only viable defense against American and Israeli designs.[33]

Even in Europe a debate rages over whether a democratic Islam is possible. A test case is the question of just how "modern" a moderate Islamist like Tariq Ramadan really is. This otherwise reformed Islamist refuses, for example, to condemn the practice of stoning liberated Muslim women. Incredibly the British–Dutch culture critic Ian Buruma defends Ramadan's position on stoning by calling it "political" rather than personal, much as Sartre's defense of Stalin was said to be excusable insofar as it was merely "political."[34] This bizarre defense is an insult not only to modern Islam but to the moral potential of politics per se. If such a debate (Buruma versus Ayaan Hirsi Ali, say) could persist in Europe, it obviously will be hard to overcome doubts about reformed Islamism in the Arab world itself.[35] Mubarak was so concerned about growing public trust in the Brotherhood

---

[31] See "The Uprisings: Islam and the Arab Revolutions," *The Economist* (March 31, 2011), http://www.economist.com/node/18486005/print

[32] Suzanne Maloney and Ray Takeyh, "Ahmadinejad's Fall, America's Loss," *The New York Times* (June 15, 2011) http://www.nytimes.com/2011/06/16/opinion/16Takeyh-Maloney.html

[33] Khalil Hamra, "Egypt Violence Heightens Concern about Growing Salafi Role," *The Christian Science Monitor* (May 10, 2011), http://www.csmonitor.com/World/Middle-East/2011/0510/Egypt-violence-heightens-concern-about-growing-Salafi-role

[34] Paul Berman, *The Flight of the Intellectuals* (New York: Melville House, 2010), 219.

[35] Walid Phares, "Muslim Brotherhood Riding the Crest of Arab Spring," *Newsmax* (June 3, 2011), http://www.newsmax.com/WalidPhares/muslimbrotherhood-arabspring-gadhafi/2011/06/03/id/398700 and David Ignatius, "What Happens When the Arab Spring Turns to Summer?" *Foreign Policy* (April 22, 2011), http://www.foreignpolicy.com/articles/2011/04/22/what_happens_when_the_arab_spring _turns _to_summer

that he cultivated radical Salafi groups as a counterbalance.[36] He knew full well that Jihadic Islamism boosted his legitimacy.

We have long argued that the best cultural investment the West could make in the Islamic world would be the establishment of close working relations with civil Islam. As the "Arab Spring" enters its long cold winter, and the euphoria of its youthful "Twitter" phase gives way to hard realities, Islamism will join the fray and could take command of the opposition. Vigilance is called for, but this Islamist turn could be less onerous than critics suggest, and might even be beneficial.

It is promising that except for Pakistanis, who were vexed about the invasive nature of bin Laden's assassination, few Muslims showed much concern about his death. The irony is that the whole bin Laden saga, from his US-funded Mujahideen debut to his White House-ordered demise, was largely a product of Western geopolitics. Even the Taliban was once supported by Washington as a mechanism of pipeline control. As late as 1997 Unocal (the Union Oil Company of California) was using the Taliban as its private Pinkerton police. Unocal executives had to know that the theocrats they were entertaining in Texas were at that moment putting most of the country's female population under virtual house arrest,[37] enforced by a literal reign of terror.[38] The lesson of those pre-9/11 years—when America opposed the progressive Islamist Ahmed Shan Massoud while funding the Taliban—was the need for a radical policy shift on Islamism. It boils down to a choice between civil and uncivil Islam, rather than secularism versus Islamism.

Theocrats have made bad puppets, so wherever possible Washington has favored secular dictators who vowed to keep Jihadism at bay. Unfortunately they did an even better job of keeping democracy and human rights at bay. That was of little or no concern to Washington, whose one abiding interest

---

[36] Yasmine El Rashidi, "Egypt: Why are the Churches Burning?" *The New York Review of Books* (May 17, 2011), http://www.nybooks.com/blogs/nyrblog/2011/may/17/egypt-why-are-churches-burning/

[37] William H. Thornton, *New World Empire: Civil Islam, Terrorism, and the Making of Neoglobalism* (Lanham, MD: Rowman & Littlefield, 2005), 121.

[38] Many of the same terror tactics are common in today's Pakistan. In addition to the usual "honor killings" and horrific acid attacks, victims of sexual assault risk gang rape by the police themselves if they dare to report an attack. This explains why the 3,000 reported rapes and 791 related murders in 2010 grossly understate the crisis of daily life faced by 49 percent of the Pakistani population. The US gives Pakistan more than $3 billion per year in economic and military aid, yet remains oddly mute on this subject. See Walter Rodgers, "US Should Cut Aid to Pakistan for its 'War on Terror' on Women," *Christian Science Monitor* (July 13, 2011), http://www.csmonitor.com/Commentary/Walter-Rodgers/2011/0713/US-should-cut-aid-to-Pakistan-for-its-War-of-Terror-on-women

was hegemony. That is why Saddam Hussein was targeted more forcefully than bin Laden himself. Though Saddam had been a major impediment to Al Qaeda, he came to be seen as a rogue secularist who had to be eliminated. Likewise, today's Arab Spring is all the more disconcerting to Washington because a democratic Arab world might be harder to control. At the very least, Arab autonomy could adversely affect the price of oil.[39]

This angst cuts both ways. Though Arab youth is drawn to Western culture and the freedoms associated with the very word America, all Arabs abhor control by Western powers. The new Arab rebels need outside help, as became obvious in Libya,[40] but what is manifestly not wanted or needed is the barbed gift of US planning and oversight. As Steven Metz points out, to recognize the autonomy of Arab political reform is to reverse the Bush/ Cheney conceit that Arab political culture is so atavistic that only Western coercion could prime it for democratic change.[41] The Orientalist notion that Arabs are incapable of reform in their own right was a prime factor in the invasion of Iraq. So too it allowed the US military "surge" of 2005 to take full credit for the turn of Iraqi Sunnis against Al Qaeda. What turned this tide, in fact, was local Islamist revulsion at Al Qaeda terror tactics such as decapitation.[42]

It is possible to reject neocon Orientalism without endorsing the jaded Left equation of all liberal intervention with Bush/Cheney imperialism. Charges fly that NATO intervened in Libya simply to coopt the Arab Revolt and corner the market on Libyan oil. Tariq Ali leads this chorus with his contention that NATO bombing was purely "an attempt by the West to regain the 'democratic' initiative after its dictators were toppled elsewhere." Granted, like most effective propaganda, this charge contains a grain of truth. What it manages to ignore, however, is the reluctance of America

---

[39] Nothing, of course, is quite that simple. It is worth noting that the New York Stock Exchange shot up by 5 percent as soon as the UN no-fly zone over Libya was imposed. Doubtless that initial glee would be negated, however, by all the cancelled arms sales to Arab autocrats, including Gaddafi. See Benjamin Bidder and Clemens Höges, "Democracy or Dollars? Weapons Sales to the Arab World Under Scrutiny," *Der Spiegel* (April 1, 2011), http://www.spiegel.de/international/world/0,1518,754224,00.html

[40] Charles Levinson, "NATO Ramps Up Libya Flights," *The Wall Street Journal* (April 6, 2011), http://online.wsj.com/article/SB1000142405274870410160457624633338 5350732.html

[41] Steven Metz, "An Obama Doctrine?" *The New Republic* (March 28, 2011), http://www. tnr.com/print/ article/world/85918/obama-doctrine

[42] Monitor Editorial Board, "Obama Speech on Afghanistan War: The Missing Moral Victory," *The Christian Science Monitor* (June 22, 2011), http://www.csmonitor. com/Commentary/the-monitors-view/2011/0622/Obama-speech-on-Afghanistan-war-the-missing-moral-victory

and many NATO members to enter the Libyan conflict in any significant way. Worse still, it ignores the grim fate that awaited thousands of Libyan freedom fighters if Benghazi and other rebel-held cities had been overrun.[43] A more morally apt criticism is why the West took action in Libya but not in Darfur or Syria.

TIM HETHERINGTON VERSUS
BARACK OBAMA

By revitalizing the case for democracy and universal human rights, the Arab Revolt reminds the West of what it has forfeited by allowing globalist economism to smother other policy concerns. So too it exposes the moral vacuity of the new isolationist case against any and all intervention, including action to prevent genocide. Such specious idealism would save Libyans from Western interference while leaving Gaddafi's mercenaries free to target civilian neighborhoods with missiles and cluster bombs. It should be obvious that absolute non-interventionism is a principle no moral strategist can countenance.

That is the tragic lesson of the war photographer Tim Hetherington, who died in Libya under a mortar barrage in late May, 2011. His last Twitter message read, "In besieged Libyan city of Misurata. Indiscriminate shelling by Qaddafi forces. No sign of NATO." Tim had repeatedly testified that in Sierra Leone and Liberia—two of the wars he had covered—peace was achieved only after Western military intervention quelled the conflict.[44] It followed from the "Hetherington Doctrine" that unqualified antiwar rhetoric is more the problem than the solution to 21st century conflicts like the Libyan civil war.

To be sure, the converse also holds: There is no place in 21st century geopolitics for the amoralism of pure "realism." As *The Economist* put it, one paramount lesson of the Arab Spring is that *realpolitik* can no longer claim a monopoly on "the world as it truly is." This time the idealists have usurped reality itself.[45] Kissingeresque realism could never process the call for "dignity" which lies at the heart of the present Arab revolts. While

---

[43] Tariq Ali, "Who will Reshape the Arab World: its People, or the US?" *The Guardian* (April 29, 2011), http://www.guardian. co.uk/commentisfree/2011/apr/29/arab-politics-democracy-intervention

[44] Sebastian Junger, "Hetherington Doctrine," *Vanity Fair* (June 3, 2011), http://www.vanityfair.com/politics/features/2011/06/sebastian-junger-tim-hetherington-201106

[45] "Gaddafi, and his Ilk: Blood and Oil," *The Economist* (February 24, 2011), http://www.economist.com/node/18231320

that demand is Islamic to the core, it readily interfaces with liberal values in the West, providing a solvent for civilizational clash. It is time to take a very close look at the vested interests that dictate US foreign policy, ranging from AIPAC (American Israel Public Affairs Committee) lobbyists to Saudi counterrevolutionaries. These strange bedfellows have jointly locked Washington into an anti-Islamist bias that is every bit as vile as the anti-Semitism that once suffused American politics. Paradoxically, the successful Western effort to eradicate anti-Semitism has paved the way for equally noxious anti-Islamism.

This double standard encourages the very policies that Al Qaeda has tried to conjure by terrorist actions like 9/11. It is time to give the last rites to the second of these twin abominations. We must jettison the zero/sum reflex that measures our respect for Israel by our hostility toward Islamism. One effect of this culture clash mentality has been a blanket distrust of the Arab Street, such that a good Arab government was thought to be one, such as those in Egypt, Yemen, Bahrain, or Syria, that could be depended upon to suppress grassroots Islamism.

The only thing that was considered worse than a rogue dictator like Saddam Hussein (after his globalist excommunication) or Muammar Gaddafi (prior to his globalist rehabilitation) was the Islamism they both opposed. This could only mean, from an Israeli or neocon perspective, the reign of Sharia law and Jihad. That is why Israel has curiously opposed the ouster of Syria's Assad, even knowing that he was the friend of Israel's most avowed enemies.[46] So long as it was assumed that he alone kept the Arab Street in line, his domestic oppression had to be excused. Likewise there was reluctance on Washington's part to expel Gaddafi, the Libyan equivalent of Assad. Obama therefore dithered while Libyan forces closed in for the "alley by alley" massacre that Gaddafi promised.[47] The president finally joined the NATO operation, but laid so much stress on the limits of US involvement that he effectively encouraged Gaddafi's renewed offensive.

Western air support forced Gaddafi to shift the brunt of his attacks from Benghazi to other cities. With its whole population under siege, Misrata would soon become the Guernica of the Libyan civil war, much as Daraa and Hama would become the twin Guernicas of the Syrian onslaught. In 1982, when Bashar Assad's father Hafez massacred 20,000 in Hama,

---

[46] Malise Ruthven, "Storm Over Syria," *The New York Review of Books* (June 9, 2011), http://www.nybooks.com/articles/archives/2011/jun/09/storm-over-syria/

[47] On the deeper structure of this violence, which the opposition is not entirely innocent of, see Scott Peterson, "The Deep Roots of Gaddafi's Psychology of Violence," *The Christian Science Monitor* (April 7, 2011), http://www.csmonitor.com/World/Middle-East/2011/0407/The-deep-roots-of-Libya-s-psychology-of-violence

the West had an easy excuse for inaction: It took weeks for word of the assault to get out. This time the silence of the West will not be so easily forgiven.

That indifference extends to the whole Arab Spring and borders on complicity in crimes against humanity. True to form, Obama refrained from using his substantial influence over the Egyptian military to push the Egyptian Spring beyond mere regime change. Although the new military overlords finally yielded to public demands to arrest and investigate Mubarak and his sons,[48] they had already made clear their attitude toward democratic reform. Legions of protesters returned to Tahrir Square on April 8, and again on July 8. Their call was for real reform, not just a new dictatorship under the command of Field Marshal Mohamed Hussein Tantawi. That April they were met with the kind of brutality that the military had surprisingly not used when the protest target was Mubarak. One woman carried a sign asking Tantawi, "are you with us or against us?"[49]

The answer came the next day with a violent crackdown on an estimated 100,000 peaceful protesters in the Square.[50] Meanwhile an Egyptian blogger was arrested and sentenced for the familiar crime of criticizing the government. None of this should be surprising, since the "new" government was mostly comprised of Mubarak's Old Guard. By July only one policeman had been prosecuted for the murder of hundreds of peaceful protesters earlier in the year. The final straw was the suspended trial of former Interior Minister Habib el-Adly, who was accused of ordering the shootings. In response, a new wave of protests erupted all across Egypt, and this time they had the official support of the Muslim Brotherhood.[51]

---

[48] Mubarak denied having anything to do with the killing of 900 protesters between January 25 and February 11. His defense was that his staff kept him completely in the dark about the protests. When asked why he did nothing to halt the atrocities once he definitely knew about them, he stated that no one paid any attention to his orders. See "Printemps Arabe: Moubarak Dément Avoir Donné l'ordre de Tirer sur la Foule," *Tribune de Genève* (July 14, 2011), http://www.tdg.ch/printemps-arabe-moubarak-dement-donner-ordre-tirer-foule-2011-07-14

[49] Kristen Chick, "Egypt's Army, Once the Darling of Protesters, Is Now the Subject of Criticism," *The Christian Science Monitor* (April 8, 2011), http://www.csmonitor.com/World/Middle-East/2011/0408/Egypt-s-Army-once-the-darling-of-protesters-is-now-the-subject-of-criticism

[50] Andria Cheng, "Anger Simmers in Egypt: Mideast Tensions Continue," *Egyptian Uprising* (April 9, 2011), http://www.egyptuprising.info/2011/04/09/anger-simmers-in-egypt-mideast-tensions-continue/

[51] Alastair Beach, "Return to Tahrir Square: Egypt Erupts in Protest," *The Independent* (July 9, 2011), http://www.independent.co.uk/news/world/africa/return-to-tahrir-square-egypt-erupts-in-protest-2309512.html

By then there was no doubt that the generals had used the original protests to camouflage their own coup against Mubarak. The patent fact, here and elsewhere in the region, is that outside pressure will be needed to carry reform beyond in-house rebellion. Much depends on Europe's intercession, given President Obama's record of inertia.[52] Even Jimmy Carter, who has often been tagged as the archetype of failed leadership, was dynamic by comparison. For the first two years of Obama's administration, observers of all political stripes tried in vain to discern his global strategy. Finally it began to dawn on them that he simply did not have one, and least of all in the Middle East.[53]

The presidential victory of a minority candidate and putative liberal had raised hopes throughout the world that US foreign policy might finally be brought into alignment with America's professed ideals. Unquestionably Obama's Cairo speech of June 4, 2009 gave impetus to the reform movement that came to fruition in 2011. On closer examination, however, that speech was so weak on substance that its real message, as Gilles Kepel noted at once, was a reaffirmation of the old double standards. Obama's ploy was to win over the Arab Street by showering respect on Islam. There was no mention of the fact that many of the Street's worst oppressors were US-funded. The reason for all that stress on Islam, Kepel suggests, was to divert attention from Obama's own democratic deficit.[54]

The real nature of his policies was revealed when he stood firmly by Bahrain's Sunni king, Al Khalifa, against the country's 70 percent Shiite majority. Even after the government made a predawn raid on Pearl Roundabout, leaving at least seven peaceful protesters dead, the White House refused to budge. Likewise it ignored the burgeoning protests in Yemen. Only after it was obvious that President Saleh was about to be toppled did the White House ever so politely suggest that he speed up his already promised departure. Syria's Assad was treated even more cordially. By late in the summer the administration still could not bring itself to say, as it had of Gaddafi on March 3, that Assad had "lost the legitimacy to lead."[55]

---

[52] Ana Palacio, "The Arab Spring and Europe's Turn," *Project Syndicate* (June 1, 2011), http://www. project-syndicate.org/commentary/palacio1/English

[53] See Michael Young, "Obama's America Prefers to Ignore the Middle East," *The National Conversation* (June 30, 2011), http://www.thenational.ae/thenationalconversation/comment/obamas-america-prefers-to-ignore-the-middle-east

[54] Gilles Kepel, "Barack Obama a fait de l'islam une religion américaine," *Le Monde.fr* (June 5, 2009), http://www.lemonde.fr/imprimer/article/2009/06/05/1202661.html

[55] P. J. Crowley, "Obama Must Tell Assad to Go," *The Washington Post* (June 201, 2011), http://www.washingtonpost.com/opinions/obama-tell-syrias-assad-he-has-to-go/2011/06/17/AGlZB 3bH_story.html

In sum, Washington continued to support some of the worst political oppression on earth. This was not just an allergic reaction to radical Islamism, for the same anti-democratic impulse has defined Obama's Asian policy. Two of its prime victims have been the president's fellow Nobel Peace Prize laureates Aung San Suu Kyi and the Dalai Lama. Obama ostracized both in response to Chinese pressure, and did the same to other religious rights advocates such as the Uighur Muslim leader Rebiya Kadeer and the Catholic Cardinal Joseph Zen.[56] In July 2011, when a host of ranking Tibetan Buddhists came to Washington for a World Peace Kalachakra, Obama and Hillary Clinton did their best to completely ignore it.[57] Bipartisan support for the Dalai Lama finally forced them to acknowledge the event, but it was clear by then that this administration answered first and foremost to the CCP.

It is fair to ask how this could happen when Obama's brand of globalism was supposed to be the vanguard of democratization and human rights as well as economic growth. Twenty years ago a new generation of globalists raised hopes for a different kind of world order. They seemed ready to depart from the Cold War amoralism that went by the name of realism. In practice, however, they let material interests trump their democratic values. As before, support was lavished on regimes that opposed almost everything Americans claimed to hold dear. In the name of "engagement" it was posited, with no deliberate irony, that the best way to promote reform was to abort reformism. This was more than a moral forfeiture, since there was also a price to be paid in terms of power politics. Washington was fast losing the soft power that accrues from being on the right side of history.

Stripped of its pro-democratic mission, a morally truncated globalism could recycle realist policies with a clear conscience. This ushered hard-core realists like Henry Kissinger and Zbigniew Brzezinski into the neoliberal fold. No capitalist power structure, be it the Chinese CCP or the Arab oil aristocracies, has been too undemocratic for these "neo-neoliberals" to befriend. For them the most pressing issue was not what to do about the state terrorism pouring out of Russia, China, Libya, or Syria, but how to discredit old-school liberals who balked at unqualified "engagement."

What made the Arab world special was that here engagement theory was considered redundant. Political reform had never been put on Washington's Arab wish list. It was assumed that "stability" (largely defined

---

[56] Will Inboden, "Another Cold Welcome for the Dalai Lama," *Foreign Policy* (July 8, 2011), http://shadow.foreignpolicy.com/posts/2011/07/08/another_cold_welcome_for_the_dalai_lama

[57] Saransh Sehgal, "Tibetan Prelates in US," *Asia Sentinel* (July 14, 20110), http://www.asiasentinel.com/index.php?option=com_content&task=view&id=3319&Itemid=189

by Israeli security interests) in this blighted culture sphere required perpetual authoritarian rule. Set against that dismal backdrop, Obama's overtures to the Arab world had seemed refreshing. His May 2011 "Arab Spring"
address seemed to open a space for meaningful adjustment in US-MENA
relations. To his credit, he did not allow himself to be the perfect dupe of
either Prime Minister Netanyahu or the ruling elites of the League.

However, as Sami Abu Zuhri of Hamas noted, nothing much was
inserted into this dialogic space. Shadi Hamid, Director of the Brookings
Doha Center, rather generously traces the problem to Obama's attempt
to please everyone. This of course would make him a disappointment to
almost everyone, and most of all to those in the Arab Street who had looked
to the president for more than happy talk. In retrospect it is obvious that
Obama's promise "to support reform across the region" was a clever ploy
to keep the Street in line. Clearly the president did not equate the word
"reform" with substantive democracy.[58] At most he and Hillary Clinton
were asking Arab rulers to boost their legitimacy and their anti-Islamist
potency by being a little nicer to their oppressed subjects.

DEMOCRACY FOR HIRE: GADDAFI'S LSE GLOBALISM

Oil production in the Arab world has required heavy political oversight
that was effectively outsourced to Arab dictators. These, however, needed
to be solidly embedded in the globalist world order. Toward that end a
whole legion of Arab academics was credentialed by globalist institutions
like the London School of Economics (LSE) and Harvard (via its links
to the Monitor Group).[59] Pumped up by Big Oil and a rising chorus of

---

[58] See Shadi Hamid, "In Middle East Speech: Where was Obama's Passion, Purpose,
Plan?," *Brookings* (May 24, 2011), http://www.brookings.edu/opinions/2011/0519_
obama_middle_east_hamid.aspx and Robert Fisk, "Reactions: Obama's 'Arab
Spring Address,'" *Al Jazeera.Net* (May 19, 2011), http://english.aljazeera.net/news/
americas/2011/05/2011519164415837225.html

[59] Wikileaks has unmasked a deal struck with Libya's National Economic Development
Board (NEDB) to send hundreds of Libyan students to Western universities. 400 were
slated to go to the LSE alone, with others sent to French and American schools. See
Jeevan Vasagar and Rajeev Syal, "LSE Head Quits over Gaddafi Scandal," *The Guardian*
(March 4, 2011), http://www.guardian.co.uk/education/2011/mar/03/lse-director-resigns-
gaddafi-scandal

Regarding Gaddafi's Harvard connections, via the Monitor Group, see "Lessons from
Libya," *Harvard Magazine* (July–August 2011), http://harvardmagazine.com/2011/04/
lessons-from-libya

so-called "cosmopolitans," Arab autocrats were rendered almost immune to reform from below. The new international attitude toward Gaddafi became so sycophantic that one LSE functionary, Alia Brahimi (who grew up in Algeria, Bahrain, and Cyprus, not Libya), introduced this dictator for life as her own "Brother Leader" (full disclosure: her LSE fellowship was funded by Libya).[60]

The point man for the new Arab globalism was Libya's heir apparent, Saif al-Islam Gaddafi, the son of Brother Leader. In 2008 Saif quite literally purchased an LSE PhD. in global studies. For four years his academic director would be David Held, the virtual pontiff of "Third Way" globalism. Ignoring the warnings of his colleague, the late Fred Halliday, Held took Libya's blood money and proclaimed that "I've come to know Saif as someone who looks to democracy, civil society and deep liberal values for the core of his inspiration."[61] Sir Howard Davies (the LSE director until his resignation in the midst of the 2011 Libya scandal) seconded that motion. Like Held and Lord Meghnad Desai (one of Saif's thesis examiners, and the founder of the school's Global Governance Unit, which just happened to receive £1.5 million from Saif's personal charity), Davies looked the other way as his student-patron openly bought the core ingredients of his thesis research from the Monitor Group, a Harvard-connected consulting firm that was under contract with Libya for Public Relations services.

Not surprisingly the resulting dissertation—with the glittering title, "The Role of Civil Society in the Democratization of Global Governance Institutions"—is now barraged with plagiarism charges. Saif's real attitude toward civil society and democratization was amply demonstrated at the outset of the Libyan uprising. Dismissing the opposition as "drunkards and thugs,"[62] this professed spokesman for global civil rights was caught on mobile phone video wielding a semi-automatic rifle and exhorting the regime's mercenaries to drown peaceful protesters in a "river of blood."

---

[60] Geoffrey Levy, "London School of Useful Idiots: How a Cadre of Blair Cronies, Ex-M16 Chiefs and Top Dons at a Top University Supported Gaddafi for His Millions," *Mail Online* (March 2, 2011), http://www.dailymail.co.uk/news/article-1362029/Gaddafi-supported-Blairs-cronies-ex-MI6-chiefs-LSE-millions.html

[61] Jamie Doward, "Saif al-Islam Gaddafi: The New Face of Libyan Defiance," *The Guardian* (February 26, 2011), http://www.guardian.co.uk/world/2011/feb/27/gaddafi-son-saif-al-islam-profile

[62] Amelia Hill, "Gaddafi's Son 'Will Be in Turmoil' Says LSE Professor Who Acted as Adviser," *The Guardian* (February 21, 2011), http://www.guardian.co.uk/world/2011/feb/21/saif-al-islam-gaddafi-turmoil and D. D. Guttenplan, "A London University Wrestles with a Gaddafi Gift," *The New York Times* (March 1, 2011), http://www.nytimes.com/2011/03/02/world/europe/02degree.html

As he deftly summed it up, "We have the means, the equipment, the weapons. We're fine."[63]

That of course was precisely his father's outlook, which somehow took the globalist community by surprise. In private interviews Colonel Gaddafi claimed to have converted to Western globalism, but that born-again persona was flatly contradicted by the regime's unabated oppression. Libya's Law 71 forbade any criticism of the regime, and although some cosmetic changes were made to the injustice system in 2005, including the closing of the infamous People's Prisons, political prisoners were simply moved to other locations in the Gulag. Meanwhile Freedom House continued to list Libya as one of the worst five nations in the world in terms of freedom of information.[64]

Ranking globalists nonetheless flocked to Libya to soak up the dictator's "Green Book" wisdom. The lucky ones—such as Tony Blair and his Third Way mentor at the LSE, Anthony Giddens—were granted personal rap sessions with Brother Leader himself. Their articles and speeches praised Gaddafi so effusively that it seemed only natural when in 2010 he was invited to serve on the UN's Human Rights Council. After all, he had established his credentials in the field by launching the Al-Gaddafi International Prize for Human Rights. Some of its winners, such as Fidel Castro, Hugo Chavez, and Recep Tayyip Erdogan, remained his loyal supporters after the rest of the world was ready to send in the NATO jets.

Gaddafi's former Western supporters feigned dismay when his regime dropped its globalist veil in the opening weeks of 2011. To avoid being taken for useful idiots (Stalin's term for his gullible Western admirers), some of these latter-day Gaddafites insist that they did not do it for the consulting fees but only for the good of ordinary Libyans. Dani Rodrik applies this "dirty hands" defense on behalf of friends who served Gaddafi, as he had served other dictators. By this account they all hated the job but felt dutybound to take it so as to coax Brother Leader to be more humane. Rodrik notes that Western academics and notables provide similar services for Chinese authoritarians with scarcely a word of criticism.[65]

---

[63] Kate Loveys, "London School of Economics Takes £1.5m from Gaddafi's Son as Chief Admits Embarrassment at Relationship with Regime," *The Daily Mail* (March 1, 2011), http://www.dailymail.co.uk/news/article-1361358/Gaddafis-son-1-5m-London-School-Economics-embarrasses-chief-Howard-Davies.html

[64] Amitai Etzioni, an excerpt from his *Security First: For a Muscular, Moral Foreign Policy*, Part II, *Huffpost Politics* (July 25, 2007), http://www.huffingtonpost.com/amitai-etzioni/an-excerpt-from-security-_1_b_57738.html

[65] See Dani Rodrik, "Saif Qaddafi and Me," *Project Syndicate* (April 12, 2011), http://www.project-syndicate.org/commentary/rodrik55/English

That is a very good point, though not in support of Rodrik's conclusion. The real question is not why Gaddafi's consultants are being vilified, but why Hu Jintao's Western advisors are not meeting the same condemnation. Until 2011 LSE/Monitor globalism was doing for the MENA sphere exactly what Kissinger Associates does for Beijing. Giddens was the LSE director in 2002 when Saif Gaddafi was recruited as a student and de facto liaison with the Libyan regime. After visiting Colonel Gaddafi in Tripoli in 2006, Giddens wrote reports that all but crowned this known terrorist as the region's globalist-in-chief. That adulation reached its apex with an article by Kristian Ulrichsen, published just before the Libyan rising. With almost comic mistiming, Ulrichsen declared Libya the most democratic nation in the region and the least likely to have a revolution.[66]

Some globalist stalwarts have tried to save face after the Arab Spring by explaining the region's unrest as a simple reaction to the world food crisis, as if the human rights violations that globalists failed to register could not have been a major factor. However, similar food riots had broken out in Egypt in 2008 without seeding regime change, much less a pan-Arab revolt. One missing ingredient in 2008 was a sense that fundamental political reform was possible in the Arab world. Tunisia's successful rising provided that requisite spark of confidence for Egyptian dissidents, who in turn passed it to the whole region.

None of this could have transpired if Arab progressives had not laid a solid foundation for resistance long before. Liberal criticism had been taking shape in Morocco for more than a decade,[67] while the Arab equivalent of People Power had been on the march in Egypt for years.[68] Mohamed ElBaradei, the former Director General of the International Atomic Energy Agency, had emerged as the Middle East's most vociferous democratic voice. In bold defiance of Egypt's ban on unapproved public gatherings, he attracted large crowds wherever he went, rebuking the West's support for authoritarian regimes and calling on Egyptians to join his National Front for Change. That Giddens and Ulrichsen looked to Gaddafi, of all people, as a fount of democratic reform says much about the assumptions they shared with the paragons of unrevised Cold War realism. Both groups felt at home dealing with puppet dictators, and paid scant attention to opposition currents that could not afford their consulting fees.

Why was Washington, with all its intelligence resources, equally oblivious to rumblings in the Arab Street? Obama blamed the intelligence

---

[66] Levy, *op. cit.*

[67] Miniter, *op. cit.*

[68] Rannie Amiri, "A New Wind Blows in Egypt," *The Tehran Times International Daily* (April 11, 2010), http://www.tehrantimes.com/PDF/10842/10842-15.pdf

community for his slow and loutish response to the Arab Spring, as if the mistake had been nothing more than a CIA (Central Intelligence Agency) oversight. The core problem had less to do with any informational shortage than with a mammoth moral and philosophical defect, of which the president was as guilty as anyone. Conventional wisdom held that the cardinal tenets of political liberalism were so indelibly "Western" that democracy and human rights were appropriate goals only for Western nations and a few developing countries that had adopted Western ways and means. These means were considered inappropriate for countries with pre-modern socio-religious structures. On this point the mostly Right-wing exponents of "civilizational clash" joined hands with Left-leaning multiculturalists in dismissing liberal political objectives for the Arab world and much of the Third World.

Multiculturalists often press their postmodern defense of "difference" so far as to charge their liberal opponents with "human rights imperialism." Meanwhile the Right leans increasingly toward a similar isolationism. Consensus has it that democracy promotion is especially futile in the Arab world. The US invasion of Iraq supposedly proved that democracy and the Middle East do not mix. Then came the uprisings in Tunisia and Egypt, which instantly demolished the notion that Arabs have a less rightful claim to human rights than the residents of Des Moines, Iowa. This was bad news for all opponents of liberal intervention. By February it was obvious that Washington had a bigger geostrategic problem on its hands than Islamic terrorism had ever been. The world's prototypic democracy now confronted the specter of radically unmanaged democratization: freedom without borders.

Bewildered, America and the West had nothing better to offer the Third World's democratic activists than calls for negotiation with their oppressors. Failing that, globalist power brokers like Hillary Clinton shifted to a call for an "orderly" transition. That sounded innocuous enough, but given the neocolonial associations of the words "order" and "stability," this response was not far removed from Glenn Beck's anti-Arab diatribes. The bottom line is that neither Clinton nor the EU Foreign Secretary Catherine Ashton were ready to accept the disorder they expected from grassroots Arab democracy.

DIGNITY BEFORE BREAD

One common question in the first weeks of 2011 was whether the burgeoning Arab Spring would end up as a colossal failure like the European revolts of 1848, or as something closer to 1989 (with reference to the Berlin Wall, not Tiananmen).[69] Either way, Washington faced a dilemma it could not have imagined just a few weeks before. Though Al Qaeda was a constant aggravation, its operations had never seriously challenged existing power structures or production capacities. From the vantage of the standard "stability" fetish, Al Qaeda's asymmetric tactics even had the salutary effect of pushing autocratic regimes farther into the American orbit, and vice versa. Suddenly this reactionary bond was broken by the Arab risings of 2011. In terms of geostrategic shock effect, this was another 9/11, for America's 17 intelligence agencies had utterly failed to predict it. One pundit on the Left wryly noted that Leon Panetta, director of the CIA, would have been better off watching Al Jazeera than reading his agency's classified reports.[70]

Part of the problem was the failure of the West to remember the revolutionary motives of its own distant past. One of the most superficial interpretations of the Egyptian rising came from Western commentators who tried to reduce it all to a by-product of Western technology—the Internet, Twitter, Facebook, etc.—as if poverty and repression had little to do with sending hundreds of thousands of demonstrators into the streets. Again this was a refusal to accept the Arab Street as a causal force in its own right. Casting it as a puppet on Western technological strings, part of an all-embracing Facebook teleology, was one way of recapturing the global center stage.

Likewise globalists sought to hold center stage by installing neoliberalism as the one true development path, in both economics and politics. The absence of the right neoliberal conditions would by definition preclude Arab democratization. The Arab Spring must therefore be a hoax: ersatz reformism that is bound to revert to Jihadic Islamism. Or, as in the case of Lebanon's 2005 Cedar Revolution, it can only lead to chaos and entropy. This neoliberal worldview made it impossible for the West to notice the signs of a pending Arab revolution.

One of the few Westerners to predict the revolution was Emmanuel Todd, who has also been credited with predicting the Soviet fall years in advance. The problem was that Todd, like Kepel, discounted the centrality of Islamism in future Arab politics. Rather, his causal focus was on the double-barreled impact of rising literacy and demographic factors such as sharply falling birth rates and the decline of endogamy (marriage between cousins). The end

---

[69] See Mary Elise Sarotte, "Is It 1989 All Over Again?" *The New Republic* (February 4, 2011), http://www.tnr.com/article/world/82815/protest-egypt-revolution-1989-europe

[70] Tom Engelhardt, "With an $80 Billion Budget, How did Our Intel Agencies Fail to See the Revolution that Exploded in Egypt?" *Alter Net* (February 15, 2011), http://www.alternet.org/story/149935/

result of all these demographic twists and turns, according to Todd, is the spread of individualism and the conversion of "subjects into citizens."[71]

Undoubtedly that analysis is an improvement over the reductive economism of most globalist accounts, as well as the crude technologism that attributes the whole Arab rising to Western products like Twitter. Nevertheless Todd remains mired in an Orientalism that measures regional progress by how fast Arabs adopt familiar modes of Western modernization. These patterns include not just political secularization but also the kind of cultural secularization that requires de-Islamization in the broadest sense. In short, Todd's model of democratization is packed with anti-Islamism and other Orientalist baggage.

While it is true that Islamist organizations like the Muslim Brotherhood played only a minor role in the initial phase of the present Arab Revolt, that does not mean they will not, as Walid Phares warns,[72] play an expanding role in the consolidation phase of the revolution. This was already happening by summer 2011. Moreover, Islamic values were integral to the pro-democratic uprisings at all stages. The literacy factor that Todd stresses is hardly a necessary and sufficient determinant of the revolts. A far greater level of literacy is found in authoritarian China,[73] which is hardly a prime candidate for a "Jasmine revolution."

In the absence of any ideological framework for resistance, such as the social justice motif of civil Islam, growth can be depended upon to buy political complacence. Todd's idea that the Arab revolts were primarily triggered by material progress is only true because potentially subversive Islamist values were already in place. The irony is that civil Islam has become one of the world's last effective agents of "Western" political liberalism. Even former Salafi hardliners such as Egypt's Kamal Habib have reinvented themselves as civil Islamists. Those who refuse to take this parliamentary turn can find themselves expelled from the Muslim Brotherhood.[74]

Nor is this liberal turn limited to Egypt or the MENA region. Civil Islam is equally on the march in Malaysia, where a viable opposition is once more taking shape under the liberal pluralistic banner of Anwar Ibrahim's

---

[71] Todd, *op. cit.*

[72] Walid Phares, "Muslim Brotherhood Riding the Crest of the Arab Spring," *Newsmax.com* (June 3, 2011), http://www.newsmax.com/WalidPhares/muslimbrotherhood-arabspring-gadhafi/2011/06/03/id/398700

[73] China's adult literacy rate is almost 95 percent, with secondary school enrollment at around 80 percent. See Stephen S. Roach, "Ten Reasons Why China is Different," *Project Syndicate* (May 27, 2011), http://www.project-syndicate.org/commentary/roach5/English

[74] Bobby Ghosh, "The Rise of Moderate Islam," *Time* (July 14, 2011), http://www.time.com/time/world/article/0,8599,2082964,00.html

"Bersih" (clean) Coalition.[75] Here again, the demand for social justice pervades the political street, giving rise to one of the most dynamic democratic movements in Asia. It is a gross error, then, to suggest that Islamism is an antiquated ideology that must be overcome to achieve political modernization. What the Arab world sorely needs is not radical secularization but a more definitive transition to civil Islam.

This is where President Obama, with his highly advertised respect for Islam, could have taken the lead in encouraging a broad Islamist reformation. Instead, with hundreds of thousands of protesters on the march in Cairo and other Egyptian cities, the president poured out his usual platitudes. He could not flatly denounce the risings, but neither could he muster the courage to break with the American habit of courting Arab dictators. Like Hillary Clinton, he could not bring himself to say a disparaging word about counterrevolutionary forces such as Saudi "riyalpolitik."[76]

Not surprisingly polls show that Obama now has a serious image problem throughout the Arab world. This has made for equally dismal ratings for the US in general. Indeed, these ratings fell even lower under Obama than they had been in Bush's last year in office.[77] In May 2011, realizing that a "reset" was needed, Obama promised that his upcoming Middle East speech would include "sweeping" policy revisions. That false advertising made the actual speech seem all the more inane. Though there were some critical words for the repression in Bahrain, no policy changes were specified. Nor was there any admission of past American mistakes. Even Bush had declared in November 2003 that "sixty years of Western nations excusing and accommodating the lack of freedom in the Middle East" must end.[78]

---

[75] "Malaysia Police Detain Hundreds at Rally," *The Guardian* (July 9, 2011), http://www. guardian.co.uk/world/2011/jul/09/malaysia-opposition-protests-elections

[76] For example, the Saudis have given the Al-Khalifa royal family in Bahrain billions in emergency aid. See Steven A. Cook, "After the Arab Spring," *The Atlantic* (March 28, 2011), http://www.theatlantic.com/international/archive/2011/03/after-the-arab-spring/73086/ And for a trenchant example of Washington equivocation, raised to the level of art form, see Hillary Clinton's interview in Jeffrey Goldberg, "Hillary Clinton: Chinese System is Doomed, Leaders on a 'Fool's Errand." *The Atlantic* (May 2011), http://www.theatlantic. com/international/archive/2011/05/hillary-clinton-chinese-system-is-doomed-leaders-on-a-fools-errand/238591/

[77] When Obama gave his now-infamous Cairo Speech in 2009, meretriciously titled "A New Beginning," US popularity in Egypt stood at 30 percent, but by 2011 it was at 5 percent. See Elliott Abrams, "0 for 2: Obama's Failed Middle East Policy," *The Weekly Standard* (July 13, 2011), http://www.weeklystandard.com/blogs/0-2_576820.html

[78] Shadi Hamid, "In Middle East Speech: Where was Obama's Passion, Purpose, Plan?" *Brookings Institute* (May 19, 2011), http://www.brookings.edu/opinions/2011/0519_obama_middle_east_hamid.aspx

For Arabs, the real message of the speech was Obama's smug and dispassionate tone.[79] Clearly this presumptive leader of the free world was unable to grasp the motive forces behind the Arab revolution. The Tunisian slogan that set the whole thing off, "dignity before bread,"[80] was incomprehensible to globalists like Obama. In that respect the Washington Consensus has much in common with the Beijing Consensus. Whatever their theoretical differences, in practice they both reduce "development" to GDP growth. One lesson of the Arab Spring is that today's crisis of democratic development is not an East–West issue. Huntington's "civilizational clash" thesis only obfuscates the real problem, which is the raw economism that goes by the name of globalization.

The current UN Human Development Report offers a partial corrective, but does not escape the modernist assumption that political reform will follow naturally from gains in areas such as health and education. By this reckoning the 2010 Report counted Arab countries, including Libya, as exemplary success stories. Some neo-modernists, such as Mwangi Kimenyi at Brookings, infer from this that today's Arab Revolt is the almost inevitable result of material development that renders Arab authoritarianism unsustainable. The region's democratic deficit thus constitutes an "Arab paradox" that must be resolved. For Kimenyi the only surprise is that the Arab Spring took so long in coming.[81]

What this neo-Lipsetian argument ignores is the remarkable success of Second World powers such as China in exploding the modernist formula for economically determined political development. The Arab Spring can neither be explained as a product of health and education nor of raw GDP growth. Kepel, Zubaida, Todd, Kimenyi, et al. miss the political intangibles, such as justice and dignity, that civil Islam adds to the developmental mix. Trying to understand the Arab Spring without reference to these core Islamic values would be like trying to understand America's pre-Civil War emancipation movement without reference to Christian values. "Dignity before bread" is the Arab world's signal contribution to our emerging post-globalist discourse.

---

[79] Ibid.

[80] Trita Parsi and Reza Marashi, "Arab Spring Seen from Tehran," *The Cairo Review of Global Affairs*, http://www.aucegypt.edu/gapp/cairoreview/Pages/articleDetails.aspx?aid=62

[81] Mwangi S. Kimenyi, "The Arab Democracy Paradox," *Brookings* (March 4, 2011), http://www.brookings.edu/opinions/2011/0304_arab_democracy_kimenyi.aspx

CONCLUSION

The Search for a Post-Globalist
Third Way

THE CONTEST OF RIVAL CAPITALISMS

For thirty years neoliberalism has lorded over American economic thought, promoting "reform" that amounts to regulatory anarchy. Recognizing no boundaries, this mode of globalization has reached out with missionary zeal to every corner of the earth, pumping billions of largely speculative capital into developing countries that draw no effective line between politics and commerce. This is the sphere of crony capitalism, and for those on its receiving end it has worked wonders. Some of the most reactionary regimes in the world have been enriched, enabling them to fortify themselves against domestic reform and to drive a wedge between economic and political development.[1]

Globalization on such terms has consistently betrayed developing countries that looked to Washington for democratic support. It is hard to say, however, which has been hurt most by neoliberalism, the Third World or the First. As of 2008 it seemed that recession would be the major US export for years to come. Some of America's most productive economic sectors have already been gutted and outsourced, but the worst damage has

---

[1] For more on this balanced or "concurrent" development model, see Songok Han Thornton and William H. Thornton, *Development Without Freedom: The Politics of Asian Globalization* (Aldershot, UK: Ashgate, 2008), *passim*.

probably been to the very idea of what modern liberalism entails. Under the "neo" prefix, liberalism's egalitarian essence has been expunged. Financial safeguards put in place during the 1930s, such as the Glass–Steagall Act of 1933, were jettisoned by the late 1990s, leaving Americans at the mercy of market forces beyond even Wall Street's control. The idea that this system, cut loose from government oversight, could somehow regulate itself requires a leap of faith bordering on religious conviction. From the days of Richard Cobden's battle against the Corn Laws in the 1840s to the present fight for "free trade" globalism, "liberal" economics has shrouded itself in faith-based assumptions that could never be refuted by mere empirical argument.[2]

This sacred house of cards came tumbling down in 2008. Neoliberal institutions will survive the Great Recession, but their legitimacy is mortally wounded. Thus the current financial crisis marks the real end of the 20th century, ideologically speaking. Not despite the ongoing recession, but because of it, US corporate politics is emerging stronger than ever, no longer needing the liberal prop it has leaned on since the Great Depression. More than ever, Wall Street is "coming out:" openly applying the kind of political extortion that used to be a covert operation. The corporate mantra of "too big to fail" pays no heed to moral hazard and turns neoliberal preachment on its head by fusing American government and business more tightly than ever.

The result is not just another capitalist contradiction, but the greatest democratic setback since the McCarthy years. Whereas 20th century progressivism set government against monopolistic gigantism, present bailouts have put taxpayers so conspicuously in the service of mega-capital that government is reduced to a Wall Street entitlement. Thus the countervailing powers of John Kenneth Galbraith's triad—the optimal balance of government, business, and labor—have been replaced by a streamlined corporate state. It is hard to imagine how, in a democratic country, the corporate welfare packages of recent years could have met so little resistance at a time when vital social programs were being gutted. In this respect the 21st century seems to be reverting to 19th century political mores, closer to the world of Marx and Engels than to that of Keynes and Galbraith.

Where is the democratic brake that 20th century liberalism applied to unrestrained capitalism? If the task of modern liberalism has been to reduce (or at least camouflage) the inequality and surplus repression of capitalism, it clearly has forfeited its mission. The question is whether

---

[2] John Ralston Saul, *The Collapse of Globalism and the Reinvention of the World* (Woodstock and New York: The Overlook Press, 2005), 40.

capitalism and democracy can coexist without this liberal buffer. Whereas Marx and even revisionists like Eduard Bernstein sought to transcend the contradictions of capitalism through socialism, liberalism after Franklin D. Roosevelt took the path of palliative reform, aimed mainly at saving capitalism from itself.

Nonetheless many paleo-liberals were deeply concerned about inequality. Keynes, for example, acknowledged in his *General Theory* that Western economic society had failed to provide anything like a fair distribution of wealth and income. Apropos of our present crisis, he advocated the complete dissolution of the rentier sector. Nothing less than that deserves the name "Keynesianism." Today that same rentier establishment, having won the "too big to fail" sweepstakes, is turning the focus of Western capitalism from production to finance. Worse still, it is financing chosen politicians in an effort to shut down the regulatory functions of government.

At this point something must give. The explosive incongruity of finance capitalism and broad-spectrum democracy cannot remain on public display without radical consequences, be they progressive or reactionary. After the Great Depression the system's liberal buffer had to vastly expand, with enough real concessions thrown in to keep the voting public mollified. By the 1960s this liberal construct was wearing out, and by the 1970s it was utterly dysfunctional. A major overhaul was going to be necessary. Given the political decline of labor, there would be no New Deal on offer this time. Instead the myth was propagated that capitalism, stripped of its regulatory incubus, could be rendered so productive that nearly everyone would benefit through the miracle of "trickle down" economics. By this logic no sane person could begrudge the inequality that the system presumably required.

The general public took the bait, democratically opting for its own economic and political subordination. This retreat from liberal egalitarianism is every bit as baffling as the refusal of the German proletariat to dodge the draft in World War I, not to mention its gleeful surrender to Nazism in the 1930s. How is it possible, in the throes of the worst economic crisis since the Depression, for America's working classes to vote en masse against their own manifest interests? To understand this curious lemming effect, we would be well advised to revisit Erich Fromm's *Escape From Freedom*, aptly updated by Carl Bogg's *The End of Politics* and John Kampfner's *Freedom for Sale*.[3]

---

[3] Carl Boggs, *The End of Politics: Corporate Power and the Decline of the Public Sphere* (New York: The Guilford Press, 2000); John Kampfner, *Freedom for Sale: How We Made Money and Lost Our Liberty* (New York: Simon & Schuster, 2009).

What we are witnessing is the final chapter of a depoliticizing process that began in the 1970s when market fundamentalism made its full political debut, moving quickly from the status of a rearguard economic theory to that of an almost unquestioned bipartisan ideology: "TINA," to borrow Thatcher's jargon. More was involved here than an oil crisis and a protracted recession. There was a broad feeling, in the aftermath of Vietnam, Watergate, and chronic stagflation, that America and the West in general was in steep decline and that liberalism was largely to blame.[4]

In the name of tossing out liberal elitism, this supposedly grassroots "conservatism" implanted Wall Street in the heart of American politics, where it has held sway ever since. It accomplished this feat not so much by arguing its case objectively as by closing off discussion of all alternatives.[5] TINAism holds that market fundamentalism is the only trustworthy agent of progress. The very word "liberalism" was stigmatized in the 1980s, just as "socialism" had been in the 1950s. By gradations the working classes were disempowered, albeit by democratic means.[6] Meanwhile, being a universal faith, neoliberalism cast off the national focus of Keynesianism. Neoliberalism and globalism would become almost interchangeable terms for an ideology that has no borders and allows no exceptions.

By its own anti-nationalistic and anti-geopolitical criteria, globalism was a fraud from the first, but it was only after 9/11 that this hoax became so glaringly obvious that a major ideological adjustment was necessary. Even inner circle globalists then pushed for military solutions to the disorder that globalization itself had wrought.[7] Thus in the early Bush years there was a melding of neoliberal economism and neoconservative militarism—Bill Clinton and Dick Cheney, so to speak. This post-9/11 synthesis, which we have elsewhere termed neoglobalism,[8] now stands tête-à-tête with other armed globalisms—most notably those of China and Russia—in a competition that comes down to a contest of rival capitalisms.

---

[4] Part of this liberal self-doubt and defensiveness may be explained by the natural tendency of liberalism toward ideological entropy and a failure of morale. Modern liberalism's inherent pessimism was diagnosed as early as 1947 in a classic study that contrasted it with the aggressive self-confidence of communism and fascism. See Fredrich M. Watkins, "Proudhon and the Theory of Modern Liberalism," *Canadian Journal of Economics and Political Science* 13 (August 1947): 429 (429–35).

[5] Likewise, as John Ralston Saul points out, globalism enforces the petrification of debate. See Saul, *op. cit.*, 8.

[6] David Harvey, *A Brief History of Neoliberalism* (Oxford: Oxford University Press, 2005), 39.

[7] Saul, *op. cit.*

[8] William H. Thornton, *New World Empire: Civil Islam, Terrorism, and the Making of Neoglobalism* (Lanham, MD: Rowman and Littlefield, 2005), 48.

After three devastating decades, neoliberal globalization has worse than failed. In the process of failing it has played midwife to an authoritarian network that will be even harder to contain than the economically enervated order that the West confronted during the Cold War. The new authoritarianism combines the political repression of the erstwhile Second World with the most dynamic processes of global capitalism. This formidable hybrid could prove to be the real "new world order," eclipsing the neoliberal version that declared itself "the end of history" and for two decades has passed itself off as "globalization" per se.

Already the revitalized Second World, led by China, is leaving First World globalization in the dust. One of its main selling points is the odious record of the Washington Consensus—the devil the Third World knows too well. Its "TINA" doctrine is read by the developing world as a declaration of cold indifference. This gives the new Second World a dark horse advantage over the justly vilified competition. By the time the Third World awakens to what Second World hegemony will mean, the new power structure will be deeply entrenched.

Meanwhile globalist discourse allows the Third World just two developmental options: the neoliberal first way or the neoauthoritarian second way. The search for a global "third way" must go beyond the call for a wider distribution of globalization's spoils, in the manner of the G20. To provide a real developmental alternative it must redefine development in liberatory terms that have no place in standard globalist discourse. From this vantage the current contest of rival capitalisms is more like a mafia turf war than a clash of civilizational values.

THE CHINA MODEL COMES OF AGE

It is little wonder that on a broad range of issues Washington and Beijing have worked in tandem, forging a functional symbiosis that has lead many in the West to imagine that global harmony is right around the corner. On that happy assumption, and in hot pursuit of exponential profits, neoliberals have made every effort to facilitate the Second World's economic growth, often to the detriment of Third World development.[9] Without this unprecedented capital injection the China model could not have survived even its gestation period. Had that capital been injected into other Asia Pacific nations, they would have fared much better in the aftermath of the 1997–98

---

[9] Keith Bradsher, "Recession Elsewhere, but it's Booming in China," *The New York Times* (December 10, 2009), http://www.nytimes.com/2009/12/10/business/economy/10consume.html

Asian crisis, and by the same token the whole Third World has been bled by China's developmental dominance.

Lately there has been a distinct role reversal, as China has assisted a flagging US economy by investing heavily in American debt instruments. By September 2009 the PRC held nearly 800 billion in US treasury securities, making it America's largest creditor. Significantly it increased these holdings by over 8 percent in that year of world recession, despite woefully low interest and a sharply falling dollar.[10] It may seem contradictory that a politically contrarian China would do anything to rescue its foremost geopolitical competitor, but the mystery is solved once it is recognized that global finance in the 21st century is a weapon of war, and there is huge strategic advantage in having the world's major superpower in your pocket. The Chinese understand that their $2.27 trillion in foreign exchange reserves (FERs) is geopolitical currency, whereas Americans tend to believe that economic interdependence, even in the form of stupendous debt, precludes serious conflict.

This naïveté traces in part to a classic American delusion about China's capitalistic transformation. It is still widely believed that Deng Xiaoping effectively joined the Western world system when he jettisoned Maoism and installed a market economy in China. There are several things wrong with this conventional telling of the tale. First, Deng and his supporters did not, as legend has it, wheel in a capitalist reform program when Deng came to power at the Third Plenum of the Eighth Party Congress. Reform of that kind was not on the Party agenda, and was not even discussed. Agricultural reforms that were credited to Deng had already begun in the countryside, and would simply be condoned by the Party,[11] more out of weakness than by willful design.

Deng's celebrated gradualism is often praised in contrast to Gorbachev's feckless impatience, but this feature of Dengism can best be explained by a lack of enthusiasm for changes that had to be accepted. Nonetheless Deng was prescient in recognizing fairly fast that some of these accidental reforms could buttress his party's power. He saw capitalism's rescue potential early enough to revivify the most repressive political machine of them all: the CPP, which makes even Singapore's PAP look progressive. While Singapore does at least give its policies a rule-of-law varnish, and has managed to get

---

[10] This brought China's percentage of US treasuries to its foreign exchange reserves to over 35 percent. See David Hunkar, "China Remains the Largest Foreign Holder of U.S. Treasuries," *Seeking Alpha* (November 23, 2009), http://seekingalpha.com/article/174817-china-remains-the-largest-foreign-holder-of-u-s-treasuries

[11] Paul R. Gregory and Kate Zhou, "How China Won and Russia Lost," *Policy Review* (December 2009–January 2010), http://www.hoover.org/publications/policyreview/72997307.html

a "partly free" rating from Freedom House, China does not bother with such liberal formalities.

That did not matter in the least to neoliberal globalists in their prime. Their development credo all but guaranteed that China and other capitalist police states would eventually liberalize their politics along with their economies. The question is how the world will respond to China's intensified repression after the Olympics. Will there be a reassessment of the bargain that was struck with post-Tiananmen China, on the assumption that capitalism and despotism were like oil and water? Under cover of this colossal neoliberal fallacy, the Beijing Consensus (as it was fondly labeled by Joshua Cooper Ramo, who in 2005 became the managing director of the flagrantly pro-China Kissinger Associates)[12] was able to integrate some of the worst elements of First and Second World governance.

That reactionary hybrid dwarfs the performance of democratic capitalism in sheer growth terms. Like Putinist Russia, but with much less bombast, China has been converting its economic capital into military and geopolitical might. Increasingly it is dropping its soft-power guise and rekindling the kind of nationalist fervor that was supposed to wither away through globalization. Robert Kagan sums it up in the first line of *The Return of History and the End of Dreams*: "The world has become normal again."[13]

In this "normalized" world the spread of democracy and human rights can no longer be taken for granted. Rein Müllerson is right to see these intangibles as a matter of history, not destiny.[14] More to our point, they are a matter of agency. Michael Bérubé, in *The Left at War*,[15] holds that active and sometimes invasive strategies will be necessary when the alternative is genocide, ethnocide, or world-scale ecocide. The problem is that progressive action, no matter how just and pressing the cause, runs against the current political grain on both sides of the Atlantic. America's occupation of Iraq has not only given a bad name to forceful liberal intervention, but even to hard diplomatic pressure for the democratic cause. At the worst possible time the Bush administration tarnished the image of democratic social justice by endorsing a neoconservative version of democracy promotion. The foreign policy disaster that followed will be even more difficult to repair than that other Bush legacy, a crippled economy.

---

[12] See Joshua Cooper Ramo, *The Beijing Consensus* (London: Foreign Policy Centre, 2004).

[13] Robert Kagan, *The Return of History and the End of Dreams* (New York: Alfred A. Knopf, 2008), 3.

[14] Rein Müllerson, "Democracy: History not Destiny," *Open Democracy* (November 27, 2008), http://www.opendemocracy.net/node/46836/print

[15] Michael Bérubé, *The Left at War* (New York: New York University Press, 2009).

If the twin goals of human rights and democratic reform are to recover from their global retreat (witness Freedom House's very understated 2007 report that one-fifth of the world's countries have experienced a deterioration in basic freedoms, and its 2008 report confirming a third straight year of this trend),[16] we must get beyond neoliberalism's democratic credulity. That artifact of the Washington Consensus ends up on the side of the power elite in nearly every country it touches. The needed corrective, however, is not a magic wand to eradicate all the world's ills. Its effectiveness rests with a recognition of stark practical limits. Like James Traub's democratic realism,[17] the moral realism we posit involves a pragmatic reform agenda.[18] This affords an ethical compass for foreign affairs yet avoids the kind of quixotic idealism that would keep America permanently at war, and mostly on the losing side.

The lesson of eight years under a swaggering George W. Bush was that geopolitical success in the 21st century has more to do with earning legitimacy than with "shock and awe" military might. The Princeton Project on National Security, conceived as an "X article" for our times, grounds global security in the spread of liberal democracy as opposed to mere order, which was the leitmotif of Cold War realism. Positively stated, the idea is to help developing countries come up to "PAR:" Popular, Accountable, Rights-based governance.[19] Negatively stated — or at least negatively implied — this project mandates the rejection of amoral, Kissingeresque realism as well as the nominally democratic but equally odious neoconservatism that the

---

[16] This understatement owes to Freedom House's criteria for its rating of "free," which allows a country to get a top freedom ranking simply for holding "free" elections, despite rampant corruption, media control, and general anti-democratic conditions. These defects are overcome by the massive Human Rights Watch *World Reports 2010*, which treats rights issues more inclusively and paints an even darker picture of the global crackdown on freedom. It documents, for example, the secret "black jails" that China uses to incarcerate those who petition the government concerning public problems such as corruption and police torture. See "Rights-Respecting Governments Should Speak Up to Protect defenders," *Human Rights Watch* (January 20, 2010), http://www.hrw.org/en/world-report-2010/news-release and on the limitations of Freedom House studies see Ronald Inglehart and Christian Welzel, "How Development Leads to Democracy: What We Know about Modernization," *Foreign Affairs* 88, no. 2 (March/April 2009): 44 (33–47).

[17] See James Traub, *The Freedom Agenda: Why America Must Spread Democracy (Just Not the Way George Bush Did)* (New York: Farrar, Straus and Giroux, 2008).

[18] See William H. Thornton, *Fire on the Rim: The Cultural Dynamics of East/West Power Politics* (Lanham, M.D: Rowman & Littlefield, 2002), Chapter 8.

[19] G. John Ikenberry and Anne-Marie Slaughter, "Forging A World of Liberty Under Law: U.S. National Security in the 21st Century," Final Report of the Princeton Project on National Security, *The Princeton Project Papers* (September 27, 2006), 6–7 (1–91).

Bush administration embraced. What made Bushism so injurious to the cause of social democratization was its appropriation of progressive language without substance. Words like freedom and democracy were cheapened, while American credibility was pulverized.

For all its good intentions, however, the Princeton Project ends up doing damage of a similar kind. By spreading its invitational net too widely, it loses the oppositional edge that social democratization requires. It is no accident that both of the project's coeditors have been soft on China, the world's most successfully anti-democratic regime. China poses the double hazard of being not only a renascent Asian empire but also a global archetype for development without freedom. Even United Russia, Putin's party, has increasingly looked toward the CCP as its model for one-party rule within the globalist system.[20] Putin's recent call for trans-party unity in the face of national crisis is understood by his opponents as an attempt to recharge his flagging political base by re-Sovieting Russian politics.[21] His actual goal is to "CCPize" Russia by ridding it of opposition parties and putting crony capitalism in its proper place: his own Kremlin pockets.

Oddly, neoliberal institutionalists like Anne-Marie Slaughter tend to take Russia's anti-democratic turn more seriously than China's. To her credit, she holds that the Russian invasion of Georgia warranted a more potent response than the EU was ready to muster, yet she does not press the issue. It says a great deal about today's "liberal" policy discourse that the flaccid measures Slaughter recommends earn her the reputation of being "tough on Russia."[22] We are not giving up on her, however. After her tour with the Obama administration, she did in fact take a tough stand on the need for more forceful support of Libya's freedom fighters.

It says much about the real priorities of today's globalism that Gaddafi could, with no visible change on his part, be adopted as the pet dictator of globalists on both sides of the Atlantic. Like the Georgia crisis, the Libyan

---

[20] Clifford J. Levy, "Russia's Leaders See China as Template for Ruling," *The New York Times* (October 18, 2009), http://www.nytimes.com/2009/10/18/world/europe/18russia. html

[21] "What's Behind Putin's Drive for a 'United Civil Front' in Russia," *The Christian Science Monitor* (May 10, 2011), http://www.csmonitor.com/layout/set/print/content/view/print/382944

[22] Due to this "tough" image, Slaughter was paired against Dmitri V. Trenin in a debate over the proper response to Russian aggression in Georgia. Her position was so bland, however, that she ended up agreeing with Trenin on most points. Her alleged toughness consisted mainly of saying that *something* should be done to let Moscow know that its actions will have consequences, but when it came to the question of what exactly must be done, she deferred to Europe, knowing full well that Europe would do nothing. See *The Economist* debate on "Assertive Russia" (September and October 2008).

civil war could be a blessing of sorts if it alerted Western leaders to the futility of most engagement policies and to the utter incommensurability of liberal and authoritarian capitalisms. Likewise we should thank Putin for helping us see the new Second World for what it is. By no means is his brand of Kremlin capitalism the most nefarious player in this new "great game." China's geopolitical agenda is all the more dangerous for being less overt. That is what makes the new Cold War—the contest of rival capitalisms—so perilous. To most Westerners it is still invisible.

THE COLD PEACE

One reason for that invisibility is the idea that the old Cold War was mainly about capitalism versus socialism, rather than democracy versus authoritarianism. To most, a Cold War between capitalisms is simply inconceivable. Since capitalism now has no enemies among the major powers, the Cold War concept has been laid to rest. Peaceful coexistence between world powers is taken for granted, with universal democracy waiting just over the horizon. This neoliberal augury hits a snag, however, for the corporate world that sponsors it has a dark secret: democratization has not only stalled in much of the world,[23] but is not even on the wish list of most TNCs.

It is no accident that global investors have shown a strong preference for engagement with dictatorial China rather than democratic India. This is despite the fact that India offers far better opportunities in terms of normal investment criteria. A recent study put the average price-to-earnings ratio of Chinese companies at 40.7, whereas India registered a vastly superior 14.6. The China bias makes no business sense, unless dictatorial fiat is registered as a positive variable. Investors claim to be leary of India's supposed lack of "stability" relative to a very "orderly" and hence "well-governed" China. However, a Legatum Institute study ranked China's governance at a lowly 93, as compared to India's 41, and also rated India above China in terms of general prosperity, which foregrounds human welfare rather than raw economic growth.[24] "Order" in the rule-of-law sense is not the issue here, for Chinese courts answer more to CCP dictates than to law.

---

[23] Joshua Kurlantzick, "The Great Democracy Meltdown," *The New Republic* (May 19, 2011), http://www.tnr.com/article/world/magazine/88632/failing-democracy-venezuela-arab-spring

[24] Tim Hanson, "The Price of Democracy," *The Motley Fool* (November 16, 2009), http://www.fool.com/investing/international/2009/11/16/the-price-of-democracy.aspx and Will Inboden, "India and the West: The Future Geopolitical Landscape," *Legatum Perspectives* (January 6, 2010).

What, then, lures foreign investors in droves to authoritarian China? The standard answer—cheap labor—does not suffice, for India also provides that. Two of the main draws are China's dearth of human rights, including labor rights, and its astonishing environmental laxity. However, since India also has a dismal environmental record, the deciding factors are clearly China's lack of democracy and human rights. Global capitalism claims to favor both, but if that were true, harmonious relations between Chinese authoritarianism and American neoliberalism would be impossible.

Neoliberals cling to the faith-based notion that China will eventually yield to friendly liberal persuasion—the kind that President Obama lamely applied on his November 2009 China trip and the subsequent Copenhagen fiasco. The idea was to convert China into a responsible stakeholder in a dependably neoliberal world order. For this Obama put human rights on hold, shoved the Dalai Lama aside, and courted China as a full partner in "G-2" globalization.[25] His China visit marked the farthest reach of globalism's halcyonic vision. Within two months the tide had begun to turn. However reluctantly, the White House issued a statement supporting Google's decision to refuse further Chinese censorship of its internet operations.[26] An arms sale to Taiwan and a belated presidential meeting with the Dalai Lama left no doubt that a more realistic agenda was in the making. For Washington this was a tacit admission that the Asian "partner" it had done most to promote for two decades was no ally.

As America loses its economic supremacy, it will increasingly be forced to retrieve its one remaining comparative advantage: its tattered but still reparable image as the world's indispensable democratic nation. At that point Washington will have no choice but to invoke the values-based geopolitics that we call moral realism. The point is to meet the security threats of our times without the sacrifice of democratic and humanitarian commitments. This moral injection into world affairs is not as radically new as it may seem. It has its roots in many of the same principles that inspired the formation of the UN and the original Bretton Woods institutions. These values were largely aborted as the Cold War intensified, but that was exactly when America most needed to be on the moral side of history.

In terms of his career, the architect of Cold War containment, George Kennan, was on the losing side of that policy shift. More dove than hawk, Kennan was in fact a moral realist. That made him an endangered species in policy circles. Having opposed the H-bomb and then the war in Vietnam,

---

[25] See Roger Cohen, "The Dragon's Swagger," *The New York Times* (January 12, 2010), http://www.nytimes.com/2010/01/12/opinion/12iht-edcohen.html

[26] Geoff Dyer, "Shadow Cast over hopes for US-China 'G2'," *Financial Times* (January 14, 2010), http:www.ft.com/cms/s/0/b09172ac-0135-11df-8c54-00144feabdc0.html

he increasingly found it necessary to withdraw from strategic affairs that were molded by hawks like his friend Paul Nitze. Needless to say he contested the even more heinous strategies of amoral realists like Henry Kissinger.[27] His alienation within the strategic community provides a window on what went wrong with American foreign policy in the shadow of the Truman Doctrine.

Logically it might have been expected that the end of the Cold War would have brought Kennan's style of realism in from the cold, affording a "peace dividend" and a moral upgrade in foreign affairs. That logic did not prevail. Indeed, as far as the developing world is concerned, the new era could better be termed the Cold Peace. The end of Cold War bipolarity retired the realist mandate for (highly selective) development assistance and relegated issues like social justice and human rights to the whims of the market. Neoliberal globalism, cut free from pressing geopolitical imperatives, went even beyond classical economics in its reduction of all spheres of life to raw commercialism.[28]

Riding this wave, the US Treasury and Commerce Departments gained an unprecedented voice in foreign affairs. This meant that relations with the global South would more than ever be decided by corporate needs. Where profit was not an issue, the underdeveloped world would be ignored. Too late it was realized that abandoning the South encouraged both its turn toward the resurgent Second World and toward clandestine income sources such as drug dealing, money laundering, illegal arms peddling, and a host of local enterprises such as "blood diamonds." This anarchic climate would also prove an ideal incubator for terrorism. Prior to September 11, 2001, however, any thought of a concerted response to this danger was bound to collide with the presumed lesson of Clinton's foray into Somalia: the exorbitant cost of any corrective action. The even higher cost of blanket inaction took years to process.[29]

---

[27] On Kennan and Nitze, see Nicholas Thompson, *The Hawk and the Dove: Paul Nitze, George Kennan, and the History of the Cold War* (New York: Henry Holt, 2009).

[28] Saul, *op. cit.*, 17–18.

[29] A recent Oxford study estimated the global cost of civil wars and other domestic strife at a conservative $270 billion a year. The startling postscript is that 80 percent of that price is born by the neighbors of failed states. Kenya, for example, is currently saddled with 300,000 Somali refugees, and the whole region must contend with Somalian piracy and terrorism. In 1998 the US embassies in Kenya and Tanzania were blown up by a Somalia-based cell of Al Qaeda, but by then the earlier "lesson of Somalia" was so deeply ingrained that the counter-lesson of 1998 was hardly registered until 2001. To the extent that the Somalia crisis was confronted at all, the goal was containment rather than correction, for the country had no oil or other commercial enticements. It marked a significant departure, therefore, when Secretary of State Hillary Clinton,

By the mid-1990s, when security mavens were just starting to sense the danger of the world's "coming anarchy,"[30] the question of how to deal with global recalcitrants came down to a stark carrot and stick choice: one either had to reconnect with the underdeveloped world by way of material commitments or to wield a much bigger stick. This amounted to a contest between preventive assistance and preemptive action. Since much of the world would interpret the latter as rank imperialism,[31] it should have been obvious that assistance was the far better option. 9/11 buried that option, along with any hope of a post-Cold War "peace dividend."

Like a wounded animal, Washington struck at a series of largely superfluous targets that had just one thing in common with the 9/11 assailants: they all happened to be Muslim. The Islamic world could not fail to notice the cultural prejudice this reflected. Thus the "war on terrorism" accomplished exactly what Al Qaeda hoped it would. Nearly a fourth of the world's population would now be prone to distrust or even despise the already overstretched superpower. That did not deter the Bush administration, which projected a militance unseen since the early Cold War. To put it mildly, these were not the country's best and brightest strategists. They were oblivious to the fact that America had neither the economic nor the soft-power means to afford such unilateral adventures.

It still has not dawned on most Americans that the current economic crisis is matched by an even greater geopolitical recession. Already America's loss has been China's gain. Despite its talk of a "peaceful rise," Beijing is going far beyond commercial motives in the anti-Western tilt of its foreign affairs. Clearly it makes the support of authoritarian regimes an end in itself, as does Moscow in its "Near Abroad." Suffice it to say that Muslim terrorism is not the foremost security threat of our times. That honor goes to the capitalist authoritarianism of the reemerging Second World.

If liberal-minded globalists do not flinch at these developments, it is because they are confident that powers like China and Russia will gradually be converted to liberal–democratic ways. While corporate-oriented neoliberals seek to pacify authoritarian regimes by enmeshing them in global trade, their liberal institutional cousins would do the same by embedding

---

on her infamously undiplomatic safari to Africa, saw fit to bestow a large amount of money, training, and equipment on Somalia's President Sheik Sharif Sheik Ahmed. See Jason McLure, "Black Hawk's Shadow: Why We Don't Care about Somalia Anymore," *Newsweek* (September 16, 2009), http://www.newsweek.com/id/215489/output/print and Barrett Sheridan, "Somalia Illustrates the High Cost of Failed States," *Newsweek* (August 20, 2009), http://blog.newsweek.com/blog/wealthofnations/archive/2009/08/20/somalia-illustrates-the-high-cost-of-failed-states.aspx

[30] This term was first used in Robert Kaplan, "The Coming Anarchy," *The Atlantic* (February 1994), http://www.theatlantic.com/doc/print/199402/anarchy

[31] Thornton, *New World Empire, op. cit.,* 25.

them in international organizations. Both strategies assume that global capitalism contains a moral dynamic that reduces the need for geopolitical vigilance.

It is only necessary to look at the maritime geopolitics of the South China Sea to realize how badly needed that vigilance is. What should be avoided is a return to pure power politics. Our moral realism has one thing in common with neoconservatism: it takes geopolitics out of retirement. It differs, however, in both its means and ends. So far as possible it favors soft power, and power that is directed toward global welfare, not just national interests. But in this age of globalization, national interests are so deeply enmeshed in global welfare that a highly exploitative or even isolationist foreign policy would be self-defeating.

Moral realism does its best to reconcile security needs with humanitarian objectives. In that sense it shares much with liberal institutionalism. Both prefer non-military solutions to world conflict. Moral realism, however, is better equipped to deal with an incorrigibly illiberal world. Its hope, as in the détente years of the Cold War, is a relatively peaceful coexistence within a geopolitical standoff. Giving equal attention to Kantian and Hobbesian imperatives, moral realism confronts the hard facts of "Cold War II" without recourse to the catastrophic excesses of Cold War I. The bad news is that authoritarian capitalism cannot be pacified by way of commercial engagement, as neoliberals imagine. The good news is that it is not always necessary to fight fire with fire. We need not resort to the nefarious tactics associated with the names Kissinger and Cheney. Indeed, as Andrew Bacevich suggests, we might even rediscover our better selves in the troubled times ahead.

The essence of moral realism is the application of realist means toward liberal and egalitarian ends. This will not get us out of history, but it could help to bridge the growing chasm between global haves and have-nots. America's greatest strategic blunder of Cold War I was to give up on goals like social justice and equitable economic distribution, thereby yielding the moral high ground of development to the "communist" Second World. The new Cold War ushers in a power politics that requires not just military might but soft-power legitimacy. That gives moral realism the geopolitical edge, putting it not only on the right side of history, but potentially on the winning side as well.

WHY INDIA MATTERS

Being on the winning side of history in a multipolar world means connecting with democratic forces emanating from the Third World. The case of

India, the most solidly democratic country in Asia, is especially germane since it points the way toward a very different set of "Asian values" from the ones we associate with authoritarian states like Singapore and China. The problem is that too many Indian leaders and intellectuals have shelved these endemic values in favor of imported ones that they see as essential for rapid growth. That complicity in the present globalist horror story fuels the world's most virulent anti-globalism: Maoist Naxalism and its more diplomatic affiliates, such as the Chasi Mulia Adivasi Sangh (CMAS).[32]

Delhi's brutal response to this call for social justice has thrown many parts of rural India into virtual civil war. At first glance it would seem that both sides bear responsibility for militarizing the conflict. In the name of peoples' democracy, Naxalism rejects all existing democratic processes and resorts to violence almost as a matter of principle. Closer analysis, however, leaves no doubt that the prime mover in this vicious cycle of terror is the government, which consistently takes the side of propertied elites against the rural poor. The worst victims by far are the tribal Adivasis, who are the poorest of India's poor. Even the storied untouchables, the Dalits, fare better than this rural underclass.

The Adivasis are largely illiterate and severely discriminated against in the modern labor market. The only things standing between them and literal starvation are their ancestral resources—jal, jangal, and jameen (water, forest, and land)—which are being ripped away from them with little or no compensation by local landlords and corporations, both Indian and multinational. Their attempts to hold or take back their land through legal means almost invariably fail, at which point they feel compelled to join the Naxalites in armed resistance.[33]

India's new elites have adopted the neoliberal faith in economic "shock therapy," an especially baneful version of Schumpeter's creative destruction. Though the World Bank has dropped India from its list of low-income countries,[34] the failure of this imported growth formula should be obvious to anyone who looks past the inner circle of Bangalore (India's Silicon Valley, and the capital of Karnataka) and Hyderabad (aka "Cyberabad") to the indescribable suffering of the country's most underprivileged members. The inevitable rebound effect has taken two main forms, Hindutva (Hindu fascism) and Naxalism, both of which are prone to extreme violence.

---

[32] Sudha Ramachandran, "India Drives Tribals into Maoist Arms," *Asia Times* (January 16, 2010), http://www.atimes.com/atimes/South_Asia/LA16Df03.html

[33] *Ibid.*

[34] The World Bank, "Data & Statistics: Country Groups", http://web.worldbank.org/WBSITE/EXTERNAL/DATASTATISTICS/0,,contentMDK:20421402~pagePK:6413

The BJP has mastered the trick of diverting social outrage away from its economic source by fanning the flames of Hindutva wrath against religious and ethnic minorities. Bangalore itself has had a rash of brutal attacks on Christians. In just one week in August 2008 there were 20 church destructions in Karnataka, which not incidentally came under BJP rule early in 2008. At least Naxalism strikes at real social injustice. If its violence could be reined in, and its implicit environmental message expanded, Naxal social dynamics might offer third-way possibilities. The question is whether it can reconcile itself with India's extant democracy, hopefully with better results than Nepal's Naxalites have had in their recent democratic rapprochement.

Unfortunately India's rural masses are starting to lose their faith in democratic solutions. Their dejection will make for an increasingly violent recoil, either by way of Hindutva, as propounded by Lal Krishna Advani and Narendra Modi, or of the equally heinous tactics of Naxalites like Charu Mazumdar. So long as there is no "third" option available, the grotesque failure of current globalist developmentalism will work against democracy. Throughout the developing world the economic prescriptions of Friedrich Hayek, Milton Friedman, Lawrence Summers, *et al.* have had their day in court, or rather their several decades. Now, even the World Bank reports that India, despite its rise in average incomes during its globalist period, has seen a pronounced decline in actual poverty reduction.[35]

Such statistics hardly convey the trauma that spills from the country's rising class gap. The one silver lining on this social crisis is that it encourages a search for radically different alternatives. This is the message of Pankaj Mishra's *An End to Suffering: The Buddha in the World*,[36] which notes that Buddha's home base, Bihar, is now India's poorest state. A friend once told Mishra that Buddha was a luxury "India could not afford," but he reverses that verdict: what India cannot afford is its present neoliberal maldevelopment. An economy that pillages its environment and casts over 450 million citizens into hopeless destitution is a factory for civil unrest at home and rank opportunism abroad.

This is the India that Arundhati Roy vilifies in her new book, *Broken Republic*,[37] which gives no quarter to India's democratic claims. For her India is a moral failure, whereas for Parag Khanna it is a geoeconomic

[35] Raghav Gaiha, "Poverty of Statistics," *Outlook India* (September 15, 2008), http://www.outlookindia. com/fullprint.asp?choice=1&fodname=20080915&fname=Column+Raghav+%28F%29&sid=1

[36] Pankaj Mishra, *An End to Suffering: The Buddha in the World* (New York: Farrar, Straus and Giroux, 2004).

[37] Arundhati Roy, *Broken Republic: Three Essays* (London: Hamish Hamilton, 2011).

sideshow: "big but not yet important."[38] That is to say that India is not in a league with China. Khanna's judgment says a great deal more about his development criteria than about either India or China. Not only is India the geopolitical epicenter of South Asia, but on a global scale it is the major testing ground for what Amartya Sen calls "development as freedom."[39] To call it unimportant is to downgrade political development relative to pure GNPism. Both Khanna and Fareed Zakaria fall into this economistic trap, very much as modernist development theory did during the Cold War and globalist theory has ever since. The world we now have—under the throes of environmental decay, financial collapse, and mounting geopolitical strife—bears ample testimony to the cost of these warped priorities.

For Khanna India's problems are exacerbated by its democracy. Sadly this lets the real culprit off the hook. It is not democracy that is breeding India's social disorder, but rather the rapacious capitalism that India has imported in the name of globalization. Like Russia's before, India's neoliberal revolution is generating so much social trauma that it is fast approaching a tipping point. If this disaster is not averted, nothing short of authoritarian rule, or at least a highly "controlled democracy," will be able to keep the system running. India will then become a political "Chindia," while Indo-globalization mimics Sino-globalization.

A graphic mark of these priorities is India's warming toward authoritarian regimes. Having once thrown its weight behind Burma's ousted president Aung San Suu Kyi, Delhi now supports her persecutors. There are of course practical reasons for this political apostasy. For India and China alike, Burma is not only a crucial resource hub but also a gateway into Southeast Asia. The fear is that a pro-democratic policy on India's part would make China all the more attractive to the Burmese junta. But is this concern worth the surrender of everything that distinguishes Indo-globalization from Sino-globalization? India can be a role model for 21st century development, or it can be a camp follower in thrall to the Beijing Consensus.

That question hangs over India's relations with other neighbors like Bangladesh, Nepal and Sri Lanka. Morgan Stanley's China strategist, Jerry Lou, notes that China is not just a major player on this regional stage, but a literal "game-changer."[40] Delhi has revised its domestic as well as foreign

---

[38] Parag Khanna, *The Second World: Empires and Influence in the New Global Order* (New York: Random House, 2008), 276.

[39] Amartya Sen, *Development as Freedom* (New York: Alfred A. Knopf, 1999).

[40] India's trade with war-torn Sri Lanka was roughly equal to China's up through the 1990s, but is now falling behind, owing in large part to Beijing's no-questions-asked development support. Already China is thought to be involved in a total of about

policy to fit this China model. The result is so much rural misery that the mystery is why the Naxal rebellions have not been even more extensive and explosive.

Khanna is right, then, about India's developmental plight, but he wrongly lays the blame on the country's democratic priorities. In his view China "has order and may one day have democracy," whereas "India has democracy, but … is chaotic."[41] In fact, China has more than its share of chaos, with estimates of local protests reaching 230,000 in 2009.[42] China simply manages its bad news better. Even in purely economic terms, without considering the intrinsic value of democracy, India holds the better cards. Right now it is not playing its hand very well, but that could change as the defects of prevailing globalist models become more glaring.

Zakaria (who in many respects could pass as Khanna's ideological twin) gets closer to the heart of the matter when he writes that the "Indian state is often maligned, but on one front it has been a roaring success. India's democracy … makes for populism, pandering, and delays. But it also makes for long-term stability."[43] We certainly agree, but with the caveat that stability is not the central issue. Rather, it is the paramount concern of corporate interests that view substantive democracy as a source of commercial risk. India offers living proof that economic and political development can be equal partners, and from our vantage—which we term the "concurrency model"[44]—economic growth without concurrent political reform is not development at all.

Nonetheless India remains a great developmental question mark. Global as well as Asian democratization is on trial here as nowhere else in the world. Though Western leaders and commentators are still in denial, the global demand for their ideological wares is plunging. The ongoing "Asian miracle," with Beijing as its new "lead goose," offers an alluring alternative to Western development teleologies such as Huntington's "third wave,"

$6 billion in projects here, and its port development at Hambantota will make Sri Lanka one of the most strategic points in the "string of pearls" that Beijing is counting on to encircle India both geopolitically and geoeconomically. See Vikas Bajaj, "India Worries as China Builds Ports in South Asia," *The New York Times* (February 16, 2010), http://www.nytimes.com/2010/02/16/business/global/16port.html

[41] Khanna, *op. cit.*, 277.

[42] Perry Link, "Waiting for WikiLeaks: Beijing's Seven Secrets," *The New York Review of Books* (August 19, 2010), http://www.nybooks.com/blogs/nyrblog/2010/aug/19/waiting-wikileaks-beijings-seven-secrets/

[43] Fareed Zakaria, *The Post-American World* (New York: W. W. Norton & Company, 2008), 140.

[44] Thornton and Thornton, *Development Without Freedom, op. cit., passim.*

Fukuyama's "end of history," and the democratic gradualism that Thomas Carothers has dubbed the "transition paradigm."[45]

BURMA'S FALSE DAWN

One of the most critical fault lines in this contest of rival globalisms is today's Burma. There is no place on earth where ethics and power politics merge more decisively than here. This volatile mix harbingers a coming contest over the very idea of development in the 21st century. Under the throes of ecological meltdown and resource depletion, development can no longer mean simple economic growth. A long list of intangibles comes into play, along with a host of hard political factors. But for the victims of Burma's September 2007 crackdown, and the largely unrecognized victims of the junta's long minority wars,[46] these complex issues boil down to the simple question of where one stands with regard to the Burmese dictatorship.

For now, despite the progressive posturing of its new charter, ASEAN stands solidly with the junta, while the U.N. stands for nothing at all. In April 2006, hopes for U.N. action had been raised when the Security Council reaffirmed the responsibility of the international community to protect innocent civilians from genocide, ethnic cleansing, and crimes against humanity. This put Burma front and center, because Bishop Desmond Tutu and former Czech President Vaclav Havel had recently commissioned a report documenting Burma's crimes against humanity.[47] Help, it seemed, was on the way. But in the September 27, 2007 meeting of the Security Council, one day after the Burmese crackdown, China and Russia stonewalled any possible UN action by declaring the whole Burma crisis an internal affair.[48]

As of mid-November 2007, the UN envoys Ibrahim Gambari and Paulo Sergio Pinheiro had nothing to offer Burma but another plea for dialogue.

---

[45] Thomas Carothers, "The End of the Transition Paradigm," *Journal of Democracy* 13, no. 1 (January 2002): 5–21.

[46] Like the Saffron demonstrators, the Shan resistance has a strong Buddhistic component. Nearly all Shan boys will serve as monks at some point in their lives, and many of the grassroots democratic impulses that surfaced in the September marches are prominent features in the revolutionary Shan state. See Antonio Graceffo, "In Shanland: Behind Enemy Lines in Burma," *Indymedia* (December 20, 2007), http://www.indybay. org/newsitems/2007/12/20/18468187.php?printable=true

[47] "Drum Beats Louder for UN Action on Burma," *The Nation* from Thailand (May 10, 2006), http://nationmultimedia.com/option/print.php?newsid=30003658

[48] "Destructive Engagement," *The Economist* (September 27, 2007), http://www. economist.com/PrinterFriendly.cfm?story-id=9868034

Even as Pinheiro noted that torture is routine in Burmese prisons,[49] praise was lavished on the junta for allowing a few interviews with political prisoners.[50] A writer in the Burmese opposition journal, *The New Era*, pointed out that by allowing China and Russia to block action on Burma, the UN threw itself into the same position of irrelevance that the League of Nations once occupied under the shadow of rising fascism. When Germany, Italy and Japan betrayed the League, Britain did nothing. Now, likewise, America chose to do nothing about the authoritarian globalism of China and Russia.[51]

Notwithstanding their pro-junta reversal at the November 2007 Singapore Summit, ASEAN members were hedging their bets, waiting to see if America would eventually wake up from its post-Vietnam stupor. Could it marshal the will to stand its ground in Southeast Asia against anything more threatful than a few ragtag Al Qaeda cells? Washington's so-called "second front" in its vaunted "war on terrorism" was not, to put it mildly, a cutting-edge geopolitical issue. Burma was that and more. To let it go the way of Tibet would be a grievous geopolitical blunder as well as a moral atrocity.

In the name of engagement, the First World is giving up on Burma, and the timing of this abandonment is perplexing. Under pressure from the Arab Spring, the EU is just starting to give belated attention to democracy and human rights in its dealings with neighboring countries, both Arab and East European.[52] Hopefully this will conduce to a return to the spirit of the 1995 Barcelona Process, which underwrote a broader development agenda than the narrow security concerns that have held sway since that time.[53] The present trend is toward sanctions and tougher aid criteria for oppressive regimes. Why then would the EU choose this of all times to relax sanctions on the Burmese junta?[54]

---

[49] "UN Rights Envoy Says Torture Routine in Burma," *ABC News* (November 17, 2007), http://abc.net.au/news/stories/2007/11/17/2093811.htm?section=world

[50] "Myanmar Sends Mixed Messages on Reform," *The New York Times* (November 18, 2007), http://www.nytimes.com/aponline/world/AP-Myanmar.html

[51] Kanbawza Win, "Will Sergio Paulo Pinheiro be another Ibrahim Gambari?" *The New Era Journal* (January 6, 2008), http://www.khitpyaing.org/english_page/november07/kanbawzawin_12-11-07.php

[52] "EU Plans Extra €1.2bn for Fledgling Arab Democracies," *The National* (May 26, 2011), http://www.thenational.ae/news/worldwide/middle-east/eu-plans-extra-1-2bn-for-fledgling-arab-democracies

[53] Ana Palacio, "The Arab Spring and Europe's Turn," *Project Syndicate* (June 1, 2011), http://www.project-syndicate.org/commentary/palacio1/English

[54] As of April 2011, sanctions had been partially suspended for one year, with a full review of the issue scheduled by the end of the year. See Sean Hamilton, "Burma

The standard excuse is that sanctions never worked. Beijing could be depended upon to make sure of that, and no pressure was ever put on China to do otherwise. Meanwhile ASEAN and India are playing their own version of the China card, further eroding any hope for effective sanctions. Nor has the West expended any political capital to alter these lucrative "engagement" schemes. In sum, the sanctions amounted to little more than "feel good" exercises that nobody ever expected to impact junta policies. As of this writing ASEAN is planning to make Burma its chair in 2014, contingent upon what it calls the junta's "steady progress and political developments."[55]

Except for a mock election and the very guarded release of Aung San Suu Ky (while over 2000 other political prisoners rot in Burma's gulags)[56] it is hard to imagine what "progress and political development" ASEAN has in mind. The junta's oppression of minorities continues unabated. 70,000 more Kayin (formerly Karen) state residents were rendered homeless last year, as the military demolished 113 more villages. India, which fears spillover from Burma's ethnic insurgency into its own war-torn Northeast, is deeply concerned about the collapse in June 2011 of a 17-year ceasefire between the ethnic Kachin Independence Army (KIA) and the junta. Other ethnic armies are likewise aborting their ceasefire agreements of recent years.[57] The supreme irony is that this could be happening while ASEAN is heaping praise on the new "civilian" junta for its social and political progress. NGOs working with Burma's refugees across the Thai border fear that the new international accommodation, fed by Burma's ersatz reform, could lead to the forced repatriation of thousands of hapless outcasts.[58] This could precipitate a slaughter comparable to Rwanda's, but with even more "free world" culpability.

Sanctions Debated After Change in Government," *Censorship in America* (April 19, 2011), http://censorshipinamerica.com/2011/04/19/burma-sanctions-debated-after-change-in-government/

[55] "Myanmar's Refugees: Bordering on Despair," *The Economist* (May 19, 2011), http://www.economist.com/node/18713618/print

[56] Most of these prisoners suffer from horrendous health problems, such as TB, with little or no medical attention. The new "civilian" regime is not only perpetuating these injustices, but expanding arrests under the Elections Act that targets communications media such as email. One outlawed word or phrase in one's computer can result in arrest, torture, and death by inhumane health conditions. See the Assistance Association for Political Prisoners (Burma), http://www.aappb.org

[57] Nicholas Farrelly, "Kachin State: The War Between China and India," *The Interpreter* (July 20, 2011), http://www.lowyinterpreter.org/post/2011/07/20/Kachin-state-The-war-between-China-and-India.aspx

[58] *Ibid.*

If Burmese dissidents are at risk, so is the West's claim to being on the democratic side of history. After years in the neoliberal wasteland, the concept of development that Washington pitches is a moral as well as geopolitical disaster. Neoconservatism was hardly the answer. By pasting democratic platitudes over the crudest power politics, the neocons discredited liberal responsibility, not to mention liberal intervention. This all but buried the dream of a new world order that would incorporate the Third World as a full member rather than an economic or strategic appendage. What the "free world" sorely needed, after the Iraq and Afghanistan quagmires, was a geo-humanitarian issue that was worthy of full support.

Burma's democratic movement could have provided that missing link. In that sense, and in geopolitical terms as well, America and its democratic allies needed Burma as much as it needed them. However, apart from a few toothless sanctions, which are now being lifted, the West has never given much support to Burma's democratic movement. The purely vocal encouragement it did give was highly deceptive, leading dissidents to believe that the international community was on their side. This was the same disastrous misconception the Tiananmen demonstrators got in 1989, with equally dire consequences.

HOPE FROM THE ARAB STREET

The big question is whether the Arab Spring will shock the West out of its geo-ethical hibernation, putting issues like Burmese democracy and Tibetan autonomy back on the geopolitical map. During the Cold War, support was lavished on friendly authoritarians in the name of fighting communism. Later the same was done in the name of fighting terrorism. There is no longer any excuse for playing these anti-democratic games. Al Qaeda's popularity was already receding in the Arab Street when the Arab Spring voided it entirely.[59] In Europe, too, the revolts stunned anti-Islamists into silence. Their basic tenet—the complete incongruity of Islamism and democratic values—had been pulverized.[60]

Globalism was struck just as hard, and with more pivotal consequences, since it was at the helm of world affairs. In the entire Arab world and much of the Third World, globalists had put all their bets on anti-democratic powers.

---

[59] Daniel Byman, "Al Qaeda's Terrible Spring," *Foreign Affairs* (May 24, 2011), http://www.foreignaffairs.com/articles/67864/daniel-byman/al-qaedas-terrible-spring

[60] Benjamin Dürr, "Farewell to a World of Blank and White," *The European Magazine* (March 1, 2011), http://www.theeuropean-magazine.com/219-duerr-benjamin/218-arab-revolutions-and-european-populism

They labeled this "engagement," and tacitly concluded that reform in Arab countries would have to be the top-down variety. The Arab Spring shredded that assumption in a few short weeks, leaving globalists like Anthony Giddens and his LSE colleagues with the task of explaining how they had let themselves become paid advisers to figures like Gaddafi. It would be an understatement to say they had mud on their faces. More to the point, they had blood on their hands.

Few globalists are willing to admit the scope of their authoritarian complicity. One of those few, who can at least be credited with candor, is William Ratliff of Stanford's Hoover Institute. As a staunch defender of old-school economism, he resists the political restoration that the Arab Spring mandates within development discourse. This is not to say that hardcore globalists like Ratliff oppose political development as such, but simply that they believe such wonders as democracy and the rule of law flow primarily from economic development, not vice-versa.

It is telling that Ratliff builds his entire development model around (in our view) ghastly examples of the Asian Tigers. This model not only embraces some of the most illiberal "Asian values," but promotes their export to the whole developing world. Ratliff flatly states that South Korea and Taiwan benefited enormously from the developmental advantage of "wise authoritarian leadership."[61] The tragedy of the Arab Spring, then, is that it forfeits the sage guidance of dictators.

We can at least appreciate Ratliff's candor, in contrast to those who court authoritarians through the back door of "engagement." The difference is more in the globalist package than its content. Either way, globalism has been so radically "economized" that democracy and human rights are rendered superfluous. Indeed, they are often treated as developmental obstacles. That helps to explain the shameless Western adulation for Chinese development, even in the midst of the most relentless crackdown since 1989. Some will argue that the CCP's seemingly phobic response to the Arab revolts belies the solidity of its power structure. However, it is precisely that solidity which allows the Party to behave this way, making no attempt to cover its draconian tracks.

It is the First World, rather, that has been shaken most by the Arab Spring. Some Western progressives think Arab demands for freedom and democracy will remind the West of the ideals it has jettisoned, and we certainly

---

[61] William Ratliff, "Cultural Values, Not Dictators like Libya's Gaddafi, are Chief Obstacle to Arab Progress," *The Christian Science Monitor* (March 18, 2011), http://www.csmonitor.com/Commentary/Opinion/2011/0318/Cultural-values-not-dictators-like-Libya-s-Qaddafi-are-chief-obstacle-to-Arab-progress

hope they are right. It may not be wise, however, for liberal reformists to put all their bets on an Arab Spring that could easily turn to winter. Not surprisingly Henry Kissinger describes these risings as "populist" in nature rather than democratic.[62] Little as we want to agree with this war criminal on anything, he could be right on this point. The Arabs have amply proved their ability to deconstruct authoritarian regimes, but their reconstructive ability remains to be shown. Only time will tell.

Meanwhile it is more prudent to build a post-Western development model on the foundation of a time-tested democracy. Six decades after its independence, India is uniquely positioned to tip the global balance in favor of social democratization, if only Delhi can rediscover its liberal heritage. That tradition is all but lost in the globalized agendas of the Congress Party and BJP, but is still a powerful force on the political periphery—for example, in Kerala's Left Democratic Front (LDF) and Uttar Pradesh's lower-caste-oriented Bahujan Samaj Party (BSP). However, if there is to be an Indian Spring, it will probably require the egalitarian auspices of Naxalism, assuming the movement can somehow be reconciled with mainstream politics.

Once India's political life was thought to come at the price of global insularity and a "Hindu" rate of growth. Now a globalized, "shining" India has shattered that myth. Much depends on the kind of globalization that India adopts in coming years. Books like Amy Chua's *World on Fire: How Exporting Free Market Democracy Breeds Ethnic Hatred and Global Instability* and Humphrey Hawksley's *Democracy Kills: What's So Good about the Vote?* warn of the destabilizing social impact of democratization in the Third World.[63] We would reverse those admonitions by charging that the main culprit behind today's social meltdown, in India as surely as in Russia, has been the anti-democratic effect of globalist development. Democracy may often look like the villain, but on closer inspection this usually turns out to be a co-opted democracy that answers to an elite and socially effete power structure.

Globalization works through these elites and in turn buttresses their power, rendering them immune to democratic resistance. Any remedy will have to include a radical regeneration of People Power, which is the real gift of the Arab Spring. Instead of a controlled democracy, such as Russia's

---

[62] Bret Stephens, "Henry Kissinger on China. Or not.," *The Wall Street Journal* (May 21, 2011), http://online.wsj.com/article/SB10001424052748703730804576321393783531506.html

[63] Amy Chua, *World on Fire: How Exporting Free Market Democracy Breeds Ethnic Hatred and Global Instability* (New York: Doubleday, 2003) and Humphrey Hawksley, *Democracy Kills: What's So Good about the Vote?* (London: Macmillion, 2009).

or Singapore's, what is needed is a humanely regulated globalization. It boils down to a choice between development for capital or for people. The underlying lesson of the Arab Spring is that development without People Power is a house of cards. Similarly, Minxin Pei's searing thesis in *China's Trapped Transition* is that Chinese economic development, in the absence of political development, is a transitory mirage.[64]

For us, the cardinal question is whether the Chinese, and especially the burgeoning Chinese middle classes, are really so politically inert as they seem to be. Does the yearning for human rights and social justice that motivates the Arab Spring not apply to the Chinese in their moment of economic triumph? Relative to Tunisians, Egyptians, Libyans, and other Arab recalcitrants, most Chinese appear to be political robots. The grand exceptions, such as the courageous signers of Charter 08, would appear to be such a small and insignificant minority that CCPism, contra Pei, must be taken as a secure and highly successful power structure. This solid Beijing Consensus, which amounts to 21st century fascism, differs from Singapore's Asian values in that it makes no democratic claims whatsoever. It is disturbing to see the Third World looking to this reactionary system as an alluring development model. That could spell the end of the liberal democratic era that came to fruition with the American Revolution and reached its pentacle at the end of the Cold War.

Nothing challenges that democratic ethos so much as Sino-globalization. The question is whether CCPism is a stable authoritarian system or a fleeting aberration. At the November 2009 APEC (Asia-Pacific Economic Cooperation) Summit, when a caustic comment was made about China's lack of democracy, Singapore's minister mentor Lee Kuan Yew fired back that the Chinese people are not worried about such paltry issues. What they want, he insisted, is the lifestyle of Singaporeans. Perhaps he is right, but if he is so sure that the Chinese want nothing more than this pig heaven, why should he worry about giving them the chance to say so for themselves? Why would he deny them even the *pro forma* democracy that Singapore grants its subjects? Lee counters that China has a better system for choosing its leaders: "It's not a random choice depending on the whims of the electorate. It's careful scrutiny by what they call the Central Organization for Discipline. It's an impressive system."[65]

---

[64] Minxin Pei, *China's Trapped Transition: The Limits of Developmental Autocracy* (Cambridge, MA: Harvard University Press, 2006).

[65] Jeremy Au Yong, "Chinese want better lives, not votes: MM," *The Straits Times* (November 14, 2009), http://www.straitstimes.com/STI/STIMEDIA/sp/apec2009/14112009_chinese_want_better_lives_not_votes.html

What makes this disciplinary ant farm so "impressive" to Lee and his ideological kin is its economic growth, which in turn has depended upon an astonishing degree of Western indifference to Chinese repression. The First World has done its very best not to notice human rights violations that it would never dream of tolerating at home. Presently the Third World also participates in this blackout, but that could change as there is more exposure to China and the new Second World.[66] First World globalism has already had so much overexposure that the very word "globalization" is embedded in a colonial narrative reaching back to the Conquistadors.

This would be a fair and accurate assessment, except that the West has no monopoly on globalist exploitation. The neocolonial torch has long since passed to China and the Second World. Eventually Sino-globalization will face the kind of opprobrium that the First World has justly earned. In fact this is already happening at friction points like Burma and some parts of Africa, but only in the court of public opinion. That scarcely matters so long as China meets approval from like-minded authoritarians who are only too pleased to join China's recolonization project. What most Africans think is irrelevant.

Likewise, the majority of the world's population has not been asked its opinion on what it wants in the name of development. If the Arab Spring is any indication, most underprivileged people want basic dignity and human rights as well as a fair slice of GDP growth. Real development requires, therefore, much more than economic progress. Nor is this postmaterial imperative an exclusively Western product. A new direction is already suggested by Buddhist economics, with its stress on well-being rather than GDPism. And now Muslim reformism, as reflected in the Arab Spring, demands fairness as well as mere growth. These intangibles are emerging as the brick and mortar of 21st century development. The day we cast off the incubus of both First and Second World economism will be the first day of the post-globalist era.

---

[66] Regretfully we must largely agree with Joshua Kurlantzick that democracy, despite the Arab Spring, is currently in a state of global meltdown. Where we perhaps differ with him is in the degree of hope we have that exposure to the Second World will have a self-corrective effect on authoritarianism's Third World attraction. Our greatest fear is that by the time this painful lesson is learned, the cultural and ecological damage will be beyond repair. It took almost half a century for the so-called "free world" to win the first Cold War. In ecological terms alone, we do not have the luxury of taking all those decades to win the emerging Cold War with the new capitalist Second World. Regarding today's democratic erosion, see Joshua Kurlantzick, *op. cit.*

INDEX

ABOUT THE AUTHORS

William H. Thornton is a professor of cultural studies and globalization at National Cheng Kung University in Taiwan. His previous books include *Development Without Freedom: The Politics of Asian Globalization* (co-authored with Songok Thornton, 2008), *New World Empire: Civil Islam, Terrorism, and the Making of Neoglobalism* (2005), *Fire on the Rim: The Cultural Dynamics of East/West Power Politics* (2002), and *Cultural Prosaics: The Second Postmodern Turn* (1998). He is the Editor for Asia at *The Journal of Developing Societies*.

Songok Han Thornton is an adjunct assistant professor teaching global studies at the Language Center of National Cheng Kung University in Taiwan. Her research specialties are International Relations and globalization/International Political Economy. She is the co-author of *Development Without Freedom: The Politics of Asian Globalization* (2008). Her other publications include articles in journals such as the *Journal of Third World Studies*, *The Journal of Developing Societies* (three times), *World Affairs* (twice), *New Political Science* (twice), *Development and Society* (twice), *Znet*, *Dissident Voice*, *CTheory*, *American Studies*, and *Mosaic*. She is on the editorial boards of *The Journal of Developing Societies* and *Asia Journal of Global Studies*.